UNTANGLING
THE WEB

Also by Ori Z. Soltes

Fixing the World
Jewish American Painters in the Twentieth Century

Our Sacred Signs
How Jewish, Christian and Muslim Art Draw from the Same Source

The Ashen Rainbow
Essays on the Arts and the Holocaust

The Problem of Plato's Cratylus
The Relation of Language to Truth in the History of Philosophy

Mysticism in Judaism, Christianity and Islam
Searching for Oneness

UNTANGLING THE WEB

A THINKING PERSON'S GUIDE TO WHY THE MIDDLE EAST IS A MESS AND ALWAYS HAS BEEN

Ori Z. Soltes

Bartleby Press
Washington • Baltimore

*In loving memory
of my mother-in-law, Judith,
who never stopped inquiring
into this web,
among so many others.*

ISBN 978-0-910155-84-7
Library of Congress Control Number: 2010939492

Published and distributed by:

Bartleby Press

8600 Foundry Street
Mill Box 2043
Savage, Maryland 20763
800-953-9929
www.BartlebythePublisher.com

Contents

Preface

A ll too often the difficulties of the Middle East is considered from too narrow a viewpoint. Plentiful are the
experts and authorities who understand the ins and outs of Arab
culture or of Islam or of the Israelis or the Iraqis or the Egyptians. Rarely does one encounter a discussion that encompasses
the extraordinary array of complications that interweave each
other to yield an answer to the question: why is this region
such a difficult region (in the sense of ongoing, never-ending
and diversely-directed strife and also in the sense of the ability
of outsiders to fathom it) of the world? The intention of this
volume is simple: to make accessible to an intelligent reader
that array of complications.

In so doing its goal is primarily to make its readers wary of
any "authority"—academic, journalistic or political—who glibly
asserts that the problem is simply this or the solution simply
that. Thus its intention is to function as a primer: each of the

areas encompassed can be studied in much greater detail in other works mentioned in the footnotes and bibliography.[1] Its goal is not to propose a given solution, (although I *do* offer some suggestions for thought along "solution" lines at the end of my narrative), in fact, but to follow the lead offered in Athens more than twenty-four centuries ago by Plato's Socrates. In dialogue after dialogue he asserted that, if the truth on any given matter were not easily attainable, the only hope for even coming close to it would be through *elenchos*—cross-examination. Socratic-Platonic *elenchos* is a close and continuous multiply-layered dialogue engaged in by determined intellectual explorers. What follows is also an *elenchos* of sorts.

Moreover, I must stress that the focus of this volume is to explore a very complex *past* history that is full of paradoxes and contradictions—as opposed to emphasizing the present and the future. While I do bring the discussion up to the "present" day and even offer a few ideas for dealing with some of the issues in the region that look toward the future, (such as a *three*-state Israel-Palestine solution), the reader and I must recognize two absolutes in the discussion that follows. The first is that my primary goal is to approach the present-future with a solid grounding in the layers and intertwining that define the past, so much of which is typically ignored as the politicians and academic prognosticators hold forth.

The second is that the region is so extraordinarily volatile that changes can and do occur—and certainly have occurred—with breathtaking speed. A situation that I might discuss in these pages as part of the present may well have been superseded by the time this volume hits the light of day and ends up in the reader's hands. Thus the concluding parts of my discussion are intended to be understood as tentative and temporary, even as the verities of the past encompassed in most of my chapters are so painfully enduring.

To this I must add that the vast majority of this narrative was written in 2004, when Ariel Sharon was still physically

healthy and serving as the Prime Minister of Israel and Yassir Arafat was alive and in charge of the Palestinian Authority. A good deal of water has passed under the myriad bridges of this discussion since then, from the eclipse of these two figures and the concomitant changes—multiple changes—in the leadership structures of those they once led, to the Israel-Gaza explosion. The number of real and imagined, potential and actual flash-points remains expansive, from Afghanistan and Iran to Iraq and Turkey to Yemen and the Sudan.

I have continued to update in accordance with new developments, even as current events continue to corroborate the essential themes and issues that I discuss through the majority of the text. By the time these words are being read there will have been further events and changes which will shift current nuances and perhaps future consequences but will further validate the time spent trying to understand the layered and interwoven past that has fed into the layered and interwoven array of presents in which we find the region and ourselves.

Notes

[1] In addition to the works that I shall mention as my narrative moves forward, each of which focuses on a discreet aspect of the region and its issues, there is a number of significant texts, much longer than this one, that cover much of the wide sweep that I am seeking to cover, but in a manner different from mine. Let me mention five of these, although there are always more. One of them is *A Concise History of the Middle East*, by Arthur Goldschmidt, Jr., and Lawrence Davidson. It differs from my narrative in four ways. It is obviously much longer, thus presenting the reader with a more arduous journey to arrive at an understanding of the region. (It is worth the journey if one has the time and the energy.) It nowhere offers a straightforward summary account of where the complications reside (as I believe I do in my introduction); it requires the reader to infer that summary. It reduces what I believe is a crucial story with ramifications continuous until today—that of the Crusades—to a mere three pages, thus underemphasizing its importance. Finally, I find it skewed: the Jewish presence in the Middle East seems suddenly to emerge with colonial Europe in the late nineteenth century, and that presence is not treated in an even-handed manner (for example, on page 279, the British during the period of the mandate "tended to back Zionist aims because of Jewish *pressure* on London," [my italics], while at the same time they "favored the Arabs, often influenced by concern for Muslim *opinion...*" [my italics]. The consistent usage (this is only one example) of terminology that is subtly different in nuance cannot but leave the reader with a skewed perspective. Nonetheless, the book is, on the whole, an excellent and clear one, offering a majestic sweep of the region and its history.

William Ochsenwald's and Sydney Nettleton Fisher's monumental *The Middle East: A History* was first published in 1979 and has been reissued in a number of subsequent editions, and is even more sweeping and in some respects more comprehensive than the volume by Goldschmidt and Davidson. It seems to me to suffer from the same sort of flaws. Thus it lacks a summary account that will guide the reader before s/he plunges into nearly 750 pages of text; so, too, the Crusades are minimized and no connection between them and the vast coverage of Ottoman history is offered. Finally, I find the anti-Jewish bias even more obvious: the Jews are virtually invisible in the coverage of antiquity—or misconstrued. Thus page 11 offers a historically inaccurate reference to King David's "expanding Jewish state." It was an Israelite state, which is something different; the word "Jewish" did not yet exist, and would not for more than another 1000 years. That inaccuracy will have repercussions for the [mis]understanding of the religious relationship among Judaism, Christianity and Islam. The index suggests that the Jews in antiquity are discussed on pages 17 and 18, but they are not—they are mentioned, again with historical and theological inaccuracy, in half a line on page 17. More

distressing is the fact that the Jews appear out of nowhere in chapter 36, but on page 448 we read that "the earlier development both of Jewish Zionist national feeling and of Arab nationalism were discussed in Chapter 27" when in fact only Arab nationalism is discussed there, so nowhere does one gain a sense of the complexities and layers of Jewish nationalism to balance one's understanding of nationalism among the Arabs. Similarly, the brief account of the Arab refugee problem that resulted from the First Arab-Israeli War hardly seems to share the unhappy credit for the problem between the two sides. Once again, however, this is a very useful book, provided the reader is aware of these drawbacks.

Peter Mansfield's much shorter *A History of the Middle East*, revised and updated after his death by Nicolas Pelham, is rife with fundamental definitional and terminology errors (once more we read that King David founded a Jewish kingdom, an even more profoundly anachronistic turn of phrase than that which refers to the Hebrews, not the Israelites coming out of Egypt under Moses' leadership) and imbalances—in this case most apparent in the discussion of the period leading from the assassination of Rabin to the beginning of the Second *Intifada*. While the book acknowledges that the details of the collapse of Israeli-Palestinian peace negotiations "remain shrouded in recrimination," (on page 360) it clearly places the responsibility on Israeli shoulders—the subhead is entitled "Israel's Missed Opportunity for Peace"—treating Mr. Arafat as blameless; Mansfield refers without footnote to post-Oslo "pogroms against Palestinians in Jerusalem" (on page 356) with neither a source nor an explanation for just what that means, and nary a word about Palestinian suicide bombers. This easily read book is in fact disturbingly lacking not only in even-handedness—even its "further reading" section, when one arrives at the section on Israel, is profoundly skewed toward those *critical* of Zionism or of the state!—but also in footnotes: there are none.

Struggle and Survival in the Modern Middle East, edited by Edmund Burke, III and David N. Yaghoubian differs from my narrative, as the title suggests, in focusing mainly on the modern era. It does so, moreover, by offering a series of biographies of a range of different everyday inhabitants from the region, thus presenting social history in large part through the perceptions of those being studied. Once again, I cannot help but be disturbed by an obvious shortcoming in an otherwise fascinating and illuminating volume: the only Jew among the individuals depicted is a settler in the West Bank. Certainly June Leavitt and what she stands for must be understood if we wish to understand the Israel-Palestine part of the Middle East's problematic, but it hardly seems legitimate to offer only that perspective as the representative of the Jewish and Israeli side of the equation. Moreover, this American whose "unconventional blend of spirituality and nationalism" (page 387) is not that unconventional within the settler population, although its basis in "her own somewhat secular formulation of Judaism" is certainly not the

formulation that one encounters every day, is thereby less representative even of the "settler movement" than one might suppose. By comparison, the very sympathetic presentation of the Palestinian woman, "Ghada: Village Rebel of Political Protestor?" furthers a prejudicial picture of untainted sympathy for the Palestinians and unmitigated criticism of the Israelis.

Finally, William L. Cleveland's *A History of the Modern Middle East* is an extremely incisive work that effectively digs beneath the varied surfaces of the region's problematic. The reader will already have recognized from this lengthy footnote that I find prejuducial perspectives most obvious in writers' discussion of the Israel-Palestinian or Israel-Arab focus of various books—more often than not, prejudiced against the Jewish/Israeli side of the equation—as is the case with varied obviousness or subtlety in the four other works I am discussing here. Cleveland's discussion of that aspect of the region shows even-handed sympathy for the complications, successes and ideological or moral failures of both sides. His book differs from mine most obviously in the narrower chronological band of its focus and its therefore more limited discussion of all the threads that interweave themselves in the tangled web.

I have belabored my discussion of this handful of books—and there are others that will be found in the bibliography, even as no bibliography can keep pace with the expanding number of them (in fact, I wrote these comments in 2004, and by now, 2010, many more books could be discussed)—in order to underscore what I hope will be recognized as the validity of my *elenchos*. I hope that my narrative is both even-handed and uniquely, if concisely, comprehensive.

Acknowledgments

It is my pleasure to acknowledge several individuals who were essential to the writing of this narrative. My first explorations of this topic were limited to the Arab-Israeli Conflict, which was the name of a course I was given the opportunity to teach many times in the 1980s at Siegel College (then known as the Cleveland College of Jewish Studies), for which opportunity I am grateful to David S. Ariel, then-President of the College. My colleagues, Moshe Berger and Bernie Steinberg, and my students were invaluable in helping me to think more clearly and hone my ideas. It was in preparing that course for the first time that I realized that one could not understand the Arab-Israeli conflict without understanding the much larger arena of the Middle East in which such a range of conflicts were taking place—and had been taking place for centuries. I also began to realize that the vast array of materials on the topic always seemed to include parts of it and exclude other parts.

In the 1990s I was privileged to lecture on the broader aspects of the Middle East and its complexities under the umbrella of a number of organizations, particularly Hadassah, the Conference on Alternatives in Jewish Education, and Washington and Lee University's Summer Alumni College, which provided further opportunities to research and think about this subject. I thank their leaders (particularly Rob Fure of W&L) for such enriching opportunities.

Most significantly, my good friend Mark A. Smith, more forceful than others in the past had been, pushed me to write things down, and read and commented on the first draft of the manuscript. His encouragement and more importantly his astuteness were essentials for turning verbal observations into written ones. Another good friend, Allison Archambault read the next draft with her usual sensitivity to nuance of both style and content. I am extremely grateful to both of them: to Mark for pushing me to the starting line and to Allison for pulling me toward the finish line.

Finally, I am grateful to Jeremy Kay, both for his editorial acumen and for his decision to get me *to* the finish line by entering a very crowded arena with this publication.

Fall, 2010   Washington, DC

Introduction

It has become fashionable, particularly as the months after September 11, 2001 have evolved into years, to focus
on the Israeli-Palestinian issue as the key to a solution to the
problematic of the Middle East. There is no question that this
is a crux—perhaps the crux—issue. At the very least, within
the Arab and Muslim worlds, this issue has, particularly in the
last few years, been repeatedly referred to as the most pressing
one with respect both to the Middle East and with respect to
the relationship between the region and the United States.[2] And
the narrative that follows expends a disproportionately large
number of words on the Israeli-Palestinian issue.

But to imagine that, even were this problem to be solved, the
region would shift into a calm and forward-looking mood is not
to understand its history, its culture, its multiple-dimensioned
personality. The elimination of Saddam Hussein has not solved

the problem of terrorism, much less the larger problem of the Middle East, nor will it. The elimination of Ussama Bin Ladin will not solve it. A change in the nature of the Saudi regime won't. Each of these and a large group of other issues play roles, but no single one among them is by itself the key, and the same is true for Israel-Palestine. Indeed, *had Israel never come into existence* or were it to disappear utterly, the Middle East would still be a hotbed of complication. So while Israel-Palestine is a key, it is only part of the larger problematic.

One might liken the Middle East to a tangled web, in which threads of two sorts interweave each other: those which, running from center to periphery we might call "parallel", but are actually intermingled rather than separate; and those which, in concentric waves and parallel to the center and periphery, are similarly intermingled with each other. In turn these two sorts of threads, instead of running at more or less right angles to each other are also intermingled in a snarl that, in sum, appears nearly impossible to disentangle. The threads that run one way (we might mix our metaphor and call them warp threads of a tapestry) are religion, ethnicity, politics, culture, nationality and economics. Those that run counter to these (let us call them weft threads) are conflicting and confusing definitions, aspirations and interferences.

The pages which follow seek to unravel that tangled web— that is, to isolate and elucidate the many threads that make up the web, as opposed to re-organize them into a nice, neat tapestry. Neatness is hardly possible, as I hope the discussion will make clear. But clarity is possible, even in a relatively brief compass. On the other hand, clarity does not mean simplicity (if simplicity were possible, neatness would be possible and the tangled snarl would be easily intelligible as a tapestry with threads shaped into sharply delineated shapes and colors). The most we can hope for is a clear delineation of the threads.

With this in mind, I have indulged in what, while it re- mains merely the tip of the iceberg of detail is yet considerably

detailed, offering a good deal to absorb in so few pages. My purpose will become obvious as one reads on: all of the details and each of the little complications are important to some faction or factor within the Middle East in its geography and its history. To ignore any one of them is to ignore what to some group is important and therefore to miss one of the reasons that the region is a tangled web. To ignore the massive volume of historical detail is to forget how tangled the web is and to be deluded into imagining that it can be easily disentangled. And even at that what follows is only the tip of the iceberg of detail. A reader consulting even a mere handful of the books offered in the bibliography will recognize this instantly.

At the end of this volume I shall repeat the following mantra: *the key to understanding—and possibly to solving—the problematic of the Middle East is developing the capacity to remember all of its historical complications (not just to cherry-pick the ones that are convenient for one's own point of view) and at the same time to forget all of the region's history.* To move forward toward resolution and peace, if it is possible, will only be possible when the protagonists can both keep in mind other protagonists' histories—there are Jews who still retain the house keys taken by their ancestors when they were forced to leave Spain in 1492, and there are Palestinians who still retain the house keys taken by their grandparents or great-grandparents when they were forced to leave what was becoming Israel in 1948, and there are Kurds who never achieved statehood and were massacred by Sadam Hussein's chemical warfare and there are Darfurians who were and are still being slaughtered by Arab and non-Arab Sudanese—and abandon the pain of their own; when they can clear the slate without erasing it and ask: where do we go from *here*?

Notes

[2] See the discussion of this in Shibley Telhami, *The Stakes: America and the Middle East*, 98-100.

Chapter 1

Definitions: Semites and Arabs

Consider the matter of definition. Terms are often used either inaccurately or in a falsely interchangeable manner when the Middle East is discussed.[3] Important terms in that discussion include "Semite," "Arab," "Muslim," "Jew," "Israeli," "Palestinian." The term "Semite" grows out of the changing academic landscape of nineteenth-century Europe. In that landscape, as the Bible was increasingly subject to secularized analysis and discussion, and as, at the same time, the colonial urge brought with it an increasing interest in how to understand and categorize the world in its entirety, the term "Semite" grew out of a web spun out of the book of Genesis. There, Noah's three sons include "Shem." As the discipline of anthropology evolved, the human race came to be understood as falling into three categories derived—actually or symbolically—from those three sons. Those descended from Shem were labeled Shemites, or Semites. In turn, the emerging field of comparative historical linguistics appropriated the term sometime

1

between the 1780s and the 1830s to refer to a group of languages spoken by Semites. Thus Hebrew and Arabic, for example, came to be called Semitic languages, whereas English, say, or Turkish or Farsi are not.

There is a paradox and an irony in the shaping of this biblically-based racial and linguistic category. The biblical Shem is represented in Genesis 9:23-27 as the wisest and most responsible of Noah's sons, and both Jewish and Christian medieval biblical commentators had already interpreted the statement that he would have dominion over his brothers as a divinely-ordained authority accorded to the descendants of Shem over the other races on the planet. But by the late nineteenth century the twisting of the linguistic term back toward racial category gave it a reversed, pejorative connotation. Thus when Wilhelm Marr, seeking election to the Prussian Reichstag in 1879 used the term "Semite," he applied it specifically to the Jews. His intention was to marginalize them as a group. By presenting the Jews to Prussian voters as a racial category, and by implication a group apart from the non-Semitic Europeans, he could assert the legitimacy and the importance of his vow to protect his fellow-Prussians from such dangerous outsider-interlopers.

The racialization of Jews by Marr and others, utilizing terminology that had been disconnected from its language-associative roots, was intended to suggest a direct connection between all Jews and the Near East, regardless of the fact that, historically, such a direct connection could neither be so clear and direct nor in any case expressible in pure racial terms.[4] It also ignored others who—assuming that the term "Semite" might refer to various groups inhabiting the Near East and speaking certain languages—should have been included in its purview. Among these other groups certainly the Arabic-speakers—i.e., Arabs—should be included. But that term, "Arab," itself refers not to speakers of Arabic (although most or all Arabs may be Arabic-speakers) but to those whose ancestry is traceable back to a geographic location. The 'arav is the western, central part of the peninsula that bears the same name (the Arabian peninsula). All those who are called Arabs in theory trace their

ancestry to that part of the peninsula in that corner of our planet, even as, based on the language category into which they all fit, they might also be labeled "Semites."

But understanding the roots and evolution of the term is not that simple. "*'Arav*" is cognate with the linguistically Semitic Hebrew term "*'aravah*," referring to steppe-like wilderness. The connotation of the Arabic term is of an association with nomadism—that is, Bedouin, as opposed to town-dwellers. A form of the term appears early in the history of the region at large, on an 853 BCE Assyrian inscription (Assyrian being another member of the family of Semitic languages) of Shalmaneser III in which, in boasting of his defeat of a series of princelings he includes in the list of those he conquered one Gindibu Arabi, together with his army of 1,000 camels. Both Assyrian and Babylonian inscriptions of the next two hundred years refer variously to *Aribi*, *Arabu* and *Urbi*; by about 530 BCE Achaemenid Persian documents begin to refer to *Arabaya*.

Not long thereafter the Greek playwright, Aeschylus, in his play, "The Persians" mentions a *Magos Arabos* as one of the commanders in Xerxes' army; perhaps he was an Arab. In "Prometheus," Aeschylus refers to Arabia as a distant place from which come warriors with sharp-pointed spears. Other Greek writers, like Herodotus, and subsequently, Roman writers, extend the use of terms such as "Arab" and "Arabia" to include the entire peninsula between the Red Sea and the Indian Ocean and its inhabitants. It is in such literature as well that the term "Saracen" first appears. While the word appears originally to have referred to a particular desert tribe in the Sinai region, it continued in use into the medieval period to refer to Nomads generally. Indeed, in the era of the Crusades that began at the end of the eleventh century, Christian writers began using the term "Arab" to offer a nomadic, Bedouin, piratical connotation, while using the term "Saracen" to refer to the Muslim population at large.

The first *Arab* use of some version of the term "Arab" is in south Arabian inscriptions where the term seems to refer once again to Bedouins or raiders—i.e., nomadic tribes that are differ-

ent from (and pose a threat to) sedentary groups. Such tribes are distinguished from dwellers in key centers such as Makka and Madina, yet the term "Arabic" comfortably refers to the language used by both the Bedouin and the dwellers in those centers, and ultimately "Arabic" will refer to the language in which the Qur'an will be written. In other words, a term with pejorative connotations in one context reverses its connotation to be emphatically positive (the Qur'an, after all, is no less than God's word, dictated through the Prophet Muhammad, thus that it would have been dictated in Arabic offers a powerful statement of the positive quality associated with the language called by that name). For that matter, Muhammad himself is an Arab in the following specific sense contemporary with his early life: while ostensibly from Makka, he was orphaned early and, impoverished, was raised most likely by his grandfather away from the city. Thus he would have been called an "Arab" in the non-sedentary, away-from-the-city-and-its-culture sense. This would also help account for the illiteracy ascribed to him by most scholars.

But Muhammad would grow up to bring out of the desert a form of faith which would sweep half the world. Within the context of terms that we have been reviewing, Islam, a religion, swept out of the 'arav, carried by Semitic Arabs, in the seventh century. It is important for this discussion that we keep in mind that Islam *is* a religion—a Muslim is someone who defines him/herself by the religious principles of Islam—and specifically one of the three faiths which, like Judaism and Christianity, see their point of spiritual origin in the figure of Abraham. It is a truism of the Abrahamic religions (as with most forms of faith) that they begin with revelation: the constituents of Judaism or Christianity or Islam or any of the other forms of faith that may be seen as offshoots of these, all believe that their founders were prophets to whom and through whom God spoke directly. So, too, all of these faiths continue forward in history by means of two modes of interpretation. The first generations after the founding prophets are gone argue as to whether (t)he(y) said *this* or *that* (i.e., *what* was said). Subsequent generations devote most of their energy—for the obvious reason:

God's word is at issue—to clarifying what the prophet(s) *meant* by the words finally agreed upon and written down.

So Jews vary as to whether they believe that Moses brought down a mere ten commandments from Sinai or the entirety of the Torah's 613; whether he wrote all of the Torah or whether it was written down over time and whether Ezra merely fine-tuned the text into its definitive form or substantially edited constituent parts written down at different times and places and then woven together by him. And Jewish history is gloriously rampant with argument over every word in the Torah, whether in the fanciful discussions over whether God created the heavens or the earth first or over what, precisely "thou shall not seethe a kid in its mother's milk" (in Exodus 23:19, among other places) means. How that phrase ends up meaning that a traditional Jew may not consume a cheeseburger is overrun with interpretive discussion.

Mainstream Christianity begins with no less than four variants on the theme of Jesus' life, times and words, none of it written down earlier than forty years after the Crucifixion. The patristic and scholastic students of those words, from Augustine to Aquinas,

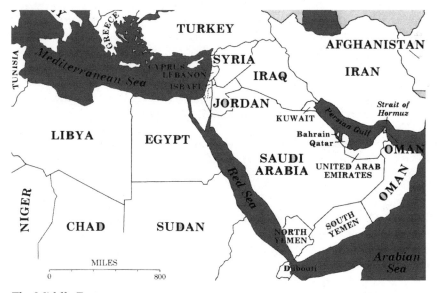

The Middle East

pour rivers of ink into the question of how ultimately to understand what lies beneath them. And Islam is no different from Judaism and Christianity in this respect: if it begins with Muhammad, viewed as the final prophet whose words are the ultimate expression of God's wishes for how we should be, its history is fraught with disagreement and argumentation as to how to *understand* the prophet's words—or rather, God's words spoken *through* the Prophet. Those words are recorded in non-chronological sequence in the Qur'an, a text written down a good generation after Muhammad's death, to which a second text—with words not universally accepted as coming from him and sometimes merely speaking *about* him—is, as it were, appended, as we shall see. In the lengthy section of this narrative that follows, I shall devote a good deal of space to the discussion of Islam because I assume that the majority of my readers will be Christian and Jewish Americans who will have less familiarity with Islam than with their own forms of faith.

Notes

[3] One might note that even the question of whether to use the phrase "Near East" as opposed to "Middle East" offers a double definitional issue. We have inherited our terminology from the British colonial era, in which context the area under discussion was referred to as the Near East, and between that region and the Far East lay the Middle East—India and its environs. More recently, though, and since for current political and related purposes India (but not, most recently, Afghanistan!) is a separate matter from the region under discussion, it is fairly common for an "updated" perspective to refer to the region formerly called the "Near East" as the "Middle East." The latter phrase, strictly speaking, seems to have first been suggested—coined—as far back as 1902 by the American naval theorist, Alfred Mahan. One could, as I am wont to do, use the first phrase to refer to the area that extends from Egypt to Iraq and the second to refer to Iran and its nearest neighbors (thus perhaps including Afghanistan but stopping short of Pakistan and India—or at least India). One might also note that in French, the phraseology was and remains "Middle East" (*Moyen Orient*). Conversely, in German, it is Near East (*Naeher Oste*). Of course all three languages also use versions of "the Levant," as well, (meaning "rising,"—as in where the sun rises, in the east, and therefore "eastward"). Then again, some use that term only to refer to the area between the Mediterranean and Mesopotamia i.e., what is now geopolitically defined as Israel, Palestine, Jordan, Lebanon and Syria.

The entire discussion of the previous paragraph, it should be noted, reflects changing details in what is in any case a Euro-American perspective. To India or China, the region that is our subject could surely be called the Near West! One could almost call it Western Asia, or Southwestern Asia, except that this would leave Egypt and the other North African countries from Sudan to Morocco, which can sometimes (Egypt always) be considered part of the region, outside of it. Simply put, terminology dogs the process of understanding this arena of history and geography from beginning to end.

[4] Simply put, not all Jews are necessarily traceable to the Middle East, period, much less to its "Semitic" parts. Aside from the general matter of occasional conversion or more frequent rape as dual methods of creating Jews from non-Jewish "stock" throughout the past fifteen centuries or so, there is the story of the Khazars. From the area just northeast of the Black Sea, they were a Turkic people said to have converted to Judaism en masse (or at least the upper classes did) in the late eighth century. With the destruction of their empire by the early eleventh century and subsequent putative migration north, up into Slavic lands, one could argue that a compelling percentage of Eastern European Jews are their descendants. Not all scholars, it must be noted, agree on this version of Khazar/Jewish history.

Chapter 2

Definitions: Muhammad and the Birth of Islam

Muhammad was born in 570 (or 571) CE in Makka, a city in the central-western Arabian peninsula—an area called the *hijaz*.[5] Makka was an important trading center because it was both coastal and central. It could mediate between traders from East and North Africa and those of the Persian Gulf, and between those coming from the southern tip of the peninsula and those coming from the north: Egypt on the one hand and Syro-Palestine (and beyond it, both Anatolia and Mesopotamia) on the other. A central point between very different economic trade worlds, Makka was a cosmopolitan city and also a largely pagan city.

We have fairly good evidence of the spirituality of the Makkans. They seem to have centered their cults in a shrine the central element of which was a black stone that had fallen from the sky—perhaps a meteorite. That shrine was called the

Ka'ba and was, together with the images around it, associated with gods of nature. Ritual defined the sacred area around the *Ka'ba*. Makkans consecrated other spaces as well. They made an annual spring pilgrimage—a *hajj*—to a site two miles east of the city, where three mounds of stone (*jamras*) were piled. There they left cuttings of hair and made animal sacrifices. These elements formed part of the rich religious tradition of the Makka of Muhammad's youth. Other parts probably included Christianity and certainly Judaism. The Judaism of Muhammad's time had developed in various directions and was an archipelago of spiritual and cultural islands within seas of other faiths, which themselves were not monolithic, but diverse in their sensibilities and spiritualities—and Makka was one of the places in which an island of Jews could be found.

The Prophet had a proclivity for wandering outside the city in the surrounding hills. At the age of forty, in the year 610 (according to the preponderant tradition) he experienced the first of a series of visions (which would continue for the rest of his life) in a cave on Mount Hira outside Makka. He was inspired by the angel Gabriel who spoke the words of God—the Arabic language word for which is "Allah"—directly to him.[6] According to Muslim tradition, Gabriel had communicated God's word to Abraham, Moses, the prophets of the Hebrew Bible, and to John the Baptist and Jesus, among 28 major and scores of lesser prophetic figures. All, including Jesus, are understood to be prophets, then, forerunners of Muhammad.

After his vision, Muhammad returned into Makka preaching repentance and an Armageddon accompanied by judgment to be meted out against those who do not repent. Those who did repent would form a group who submitted to the will of God. Thus the faith which Muhammad was beginning to articulate is called in Arabic, *Islam*, commonly translated as meaning "submission" (some mis-render it as "commitment" or "commission"): submission to the will of God. Its followers are called *Muslims*—those who submit themselves to God's will.[7]

Muhammad preached in Makka for about a dozen years, gathering a small group of followers. Ultimately the authorities came to perceive his preaching as a threat; by the year 620 he began to plan a strategy that included a departure from the city of his birth. In 622 he and his followers went to—were invited to—an oasis town some 280 miles (401 kilometers) to the north, called Yathrib. The tribal conflicts within Yathrib and Muhammad's reputation as an adjudicator and peace-maker combined to make him welcome there. The year of the migration—the *Hijra*, as it is called in Arabic—marks the beginning of the Muslim calendar. Yathrib would later be known as *al'Madina* (more commonly rendered simply as Madina)—"the City"—because of the importance that it would assume in the life of the Prophet.[8]

Madina/Yathrib, at the time of Muhammad's arrival, was inhabited not only by pagans but also by Christians and Jews—to be specific, three Christian and five Jewish tribes are known by name to have resided there. Some have argued that the Jews actually dominated the town numerically.[9] These Jewish tribes were distant from the Jewish mainstream, but were apparently familiar with the rabbinic traditions of commentary on the Torah and adjudication of everyday issues and problems by means of referring to the Torah and other parts of the Hebrew Bible, known as *Midrash* (Torah commentary) and *Talmud* (adjudication of issues). In the course of Muhammad's years in Madina, as he developed both a political organization and a more systematic spiritual foundation for Islam he seems to have had a good deal of contact with the Jews as well as with their Christian counterparts.

If Muhammad arrived as a peacemaker, he seems to have unified the divergent groups in Yathrib by about 627/8—which was also the time when a powerful force of Makkans, outnumbering the Prophet's followers nearly five-to-one, attacked and nearly destroyed the small Muslim community of Yathrib. But after nearly three years of conflict marked by three signal and unexpected, zeal-and-inspiration-driven victories, Muhammad not

only defeated them, he entered Makka in triumph. Contrary to the expected norm, he did not destroy his conquered enemies, but embraced them as they embraced his faith. He did destroy the idols that are said to have festooned the *Ka'ba*—but not the central stone. In other words he didn't completely sever the connection between the Makkans and their ancestors. He adopted and adapted the cult centered in the *Ka'ba*, suggesting that the rock from heaven symbolized 'Allah's abiding interest in and relationship with us—and moreover associating it with Abraham and Ishmael (as related in *Sura*—Chapter—2 of the Qur'an,[10] where we read that Abraham and Ishmael established the *Ka'ba* together, making it the first shrine in the Abrahamic tradition).

The spiritual and the secular, the religious and the political, intermingled as Muhammad's form of faith completed its beginnings. With the political power signified by control of both Madina and Makka, the consolidation of Islam's internal world began, and the term *'umma* (cognate with the Hebrew word *'am*, and meaning "people/nation" defined by a spiritual bloodline connection) came into use for his Muslim constituents. The tribal-based, ethnically-driven self-definition of the two cities was superseded by the faith-based spiritually-driven reality that Muhammad's revolution had brought about.

Muhammad articulated to his followers the marriage between the practical—political organization—and the spiritual: divine election and support. He in effect said that "the Yathribians asked me to come; but it was divine agency that caused them to seek me out. And my consolidation of Madina was a function not of conquest as much as acquiescence: acquiescence to 'Allah on my part meant acquiescence to me on their part, all of which reflects divine agency and not just human action." (See *Suwar* 3 and 21; this is my paraphrase).[11] For Muhammad's followers his understanding of his role in history is unequivocal; it is important to note that, over the centuries, ongoing interpretation can sometimes yield directly opposite views even of the Prophet's self-conception. I know at least one contemporary

Muslim scholar who maintains that Muhammad misunderstood the *means* according to which he was to take Makka: the word, rather than the sword was 'Allah's intended instrument, which is why the prophet died only a year or two later—analogous to Moses' death before the final crossing of the Jordan, which has been construed by the rabbinic tradition as punishment for his moments of doubt and anger through the course of his 40 years of leading the Israelites through the wilderness.[12]

When he died in 632 CE, Muhammad left behind a legacy of principles set forth in ongoing discourses and sermons. These were based on the revelations to Muhammad from 'Allah, and they were recorded—probably written down in its definitive form within about twenty years of the prophet's death—in the Qur'an. That these are oral teachings is underscored by the meaning of the word Qur'an: "recitation."[13] Most scholars assume that the prophet was illiterate—but even if he wasn't, he spoke rather than wrote the thoughts that divinely inspired him. It was some of the companions, fearful that the ideas would be lost with his death, who are said to have written down whatever they could on whatever was available, including camel bone and saddle leather.

The Qur'an is not a chronologically systematic and linear narrative as the Torah is and as each of the Gospels is.[14] It is not the story of Muhammad's life and that of his companions, as the Gospels and Acts of the Apostles tell the story of Jesus' life and of those around him and as much of the Hebrew Bible is the story of dozens of lives from Adam and Eve to the last king of Judah. The Qur'an is an assemblage of speeches and discourses from Muhammad to his followers in which he is the mouthpiece through which God speaks, analogous to those parts of the Torah where Moses sermonizes, or to the words of Isaiah and the other Hebrew biblical prophets, or to those parts of the Gospels in which Jesus offers sermons and declaratory statements—it is filled with parables and narrative fragments.

The Qur'an's 6200 verses are organized into 114 chapters

(*sura* in the singular; *suwar* in the plural), ordered (with the exception of the first, which is an affirmation of faith, and a few others) from longest to shortest. In other words the organization is strictly aesthetic, with absolutely no story line connecting one *sura* to the next—and no way of knowing for certain which sermons came earlier and which later. Thus if one seeks to chart the development of Muhammad's thinking, one will need significant powers of interpretation. This also means that ideas that appear to contradict each other (an inevitable facet of every religious tradition and its literature) will require extensive discussion. And given the fact that we cannot even know if it was all written down before or after Muhammad's death, and what may have been added, subtracted or interpolated, we are confronted with analogous questions to those we face in seeking an explanation for the different names of God used in different parts of the Torah or for the variant versions of Jesus' life and death (and its immediate aftermath) found in the different Gospels.

The difficulty of apprehending the absolute truth manifests itself soon after the Prophet's death—specifically with regard to the choice of a successor. For Muhammad designated nobody (unlike Moses—who, after all, is said to have known the hour of his death in advance, and who designated Joshua the son of Nun as his successor). His key companions were divided. A minority thought that it should be 'Ali, nephew and son-in-law of Muhammad, and therefore, they agreed, most privy of them all to the prophet's innermost thoughts and ideas. The majority—for reasons unknown to us—preferred to follow Abu Bakr, longest-held and closest friend of Muhammad.

The first group's belief system, as expounded by 'Ali, was called the *Shi'a*, (meaning "sect"), and that minority group within the schismatic Muslim world continues to be called *Shi'i* to the present day. The majority called (and still call) themselves *Sunnis*. The term *Sunna* might be translated as "custom" by which is meant that Abu Bakr and his followers agreed that Muhammad

preached an acceptance of many customs and traditions from among those whom Islam would come to embrace, adopting and adapting new customs and traditions in accordance with the needs of the people and thus maintaining a certain degree of flexibility for the Faith. He had exemplified this himself in his transformation of the focus on the *Ka'ba*, as we have noted: rather than destroying it, he re-angled the understanding of its significance.

By the 640s, in any case, the Muslims had swept up out of the *hijaz* and beyond the *'arav* (in effect, the Arabian peninsula) into the Near East. Islam swallowed the Sassanian Empire to the East and Egypt and North Africa to the West. By the year 718 the new Faith extended westward as far as the Pyrenees and eastward as far as India. Needless to say, whereas the initial Muslim conquerors were Arabs—from the *'arav*—the chain reaction of expansion, the further it got from its geographic source, was less and less an *Arab* expansion. A handful of Arab chieftains, for instance, led Berber armies into Spain between 711 and 718. Indeed when, five and seven centuries later, Turkic (not remotely Arab) peoples, Seljuks and then Ottomans, swept from south central Asia westward into the world of the Middle East, they embraced the Islam of those they *conquered* (about which more follows below).

Thus, when the Christian Byzantine Empire finally fell, its capital at Constantinople sacked in 1453, the Ottoman conquerors were Muslim conquerors but by no means *Arab* conquerors. On the contrary, political and even cultural nationalism would evolve in the Arab world later on, in the nineteenth century, initially as a desire to throw off their Turkish masters—the Arabic word for "throwing off" is *intifada*—as we shall also discuss in more detail below.

The Pillars and Edifice of Islam

The Qur'an is the foundational text of Islam: God's words

to humanity through the conduit of Muhammad, seal of the prophets and messengers of God. It teaches that there is one God—omnipotent, omniscient, the creator of all that exists, beneficent and merciful but stern in Its judgments. Man's primary duty is to submit to the will of God; those who rebel against 'Allah and His prophets will be punished both in this world and in the next. The Qur'an teaches that after death there is a Heaven and a Hell. Submitters to God's will—*muslims*—will experience Paradise (its terms are very physical and male-oriented: delightful food, drink and beautiful maidens); rebels against it will experience Hell (a decidedly unhappy fate, although the concept of Hell is not elaborated with nearly the complex vehemence that one gradual finds in Christian thought.) At the end of time there will be a resurrection of the dead and a final judgment, an eternal disposition of soul and body. The Qur'an also teaches that there is predetermination toward good and evil within the world, even as we are ultimately judged and thus are assumed to have free will in the matter of our behavioral patterns. Thus an important issue throughout Islamic history has been whether or not we can change anything if everything is predetermined (the same issue assails Christianity and Judaism).[15] Recognizing this tension is important not only for grasping Islam but for understanding some of the socio-economic fabric of the Near Eastern world dominated by Islam.

The Qur'an is viewed as the last in a *series* of revelations; it follows the Torah (understood as revealed to Moses), the Psalms (understood as revealed to David), and the Gospels (understood as revealed to Jesus). Islam thus understands the Gospels not as texts written about Jesus by others but as revelations by God to Jesus—it is not clear, then, how clear Muhammad's understanding of Judaism and Christianity was, or to what extent he believed their own understandings of their own texts to be in error. He developed *his* understanding, presumably, during the time he spent in Madina conversing with spiritual leaders within the Jewish and Christian communities, listening to their

sermons, and perhaps deriving a kind of "midrashic" sense of both Judaism and Christianity.

Within the vast seas of beliefs that surrounded him, Muhammad swam with an auditory, not a written life preserver—supplemented, of course, by what 'Allah Itself revealed directly to him. But this last point cannot be overemphasized and perhaps needs to be restated, eliminating the term "supplemented" that might or might not be embraced by Jews and Christians. For the Jews and Christians might altogether discount the direct "word of God" as a supplement; whereas from a Muslim viewpoint, the many contact points between passages in the Qur'an and those within the Jewish or Christian literary and oral traditions is solely a function of *God's* relationship to all three bodies of literature, and not at all a function of Muhammad's relationship to the *people* around him.

As the Qur'an is the last of the revealed texts, Muhammad is the last prophet: the *Seal of the Prophets*. But the Qur'an is supplemented, as Islam moves forward beyond the prophet's life and death, by *Hadith*. These are sayings and narrative sequences which were not universally embraced by Muslims and in any case are not recognized as divine in origin—and are therefore not worthy of inclusion in the Qur'an. They offer both words ascribed to Muhammad (the words of the Prophet, as opposed to the words of God *through* the Prophet) and accounts of him—and have in many cases acquired a stature near, but by no means equal, to that of the Qur'an. If the Torah and the Gospels are the heart of the Hebrew Bible and New Testament, respectively, and the Qur'an is the equivalent of the Torah and Gospels, the *Hadith* are not quite the equivalent of the other parts of the Hebrew Bible or New Testament but far more important than, say, the rabbinic or patristic literatures are.[16]

Together, the Qur'an and the *Hadith* comprise the beginning of "the way" in Islam. The Arabic word summarizing this is *shari'a*—"highway"—the conceptual analogue of the Hebrew word *halakhah* (the "way to go"). *Shari'a* may also be

understood as based on the Qur'an on the one hand and on the *sunna* (tradition) arrived at through the careful study and eventual consensus (*'ijma*) of the *ulama* (the leading legalistic minds) within a given sect of Islam.

Shari'a more specifically means a path to water. Since water is essential to survival—the more so in a desert environment such as that in which Islam was born—then one may recognize how essential commitment to *shari'a* is for traditional Islam, for survival in both the here and now and the hereafter. Moreover, the term also puns on the Arabic word *shar*, meaning water source, for the *shari'a*, the legal system that guides the life of a Muslim is as much the spiritual, emotional, psychological and intellectual source of life as water is its physical source.

*   *   *   *   *

The building blocks of Islam are two: *din* ("law") and *iman* ("belief").[17] What belief? That there is no God but 'Allah and that Muhammad is the Seal of the Prophets; that there are 28 other important prophets: eighteen Hebrew biblical ones, three figures from the Gospels and seven from other sources, including diverse historical and legendary figures such as Alexander the Great; belief in angels and *shaitanin* (evil spirits); belief in the divine inspiration of the scriptures; belief in a last day, the day of judgment; and belief in the predetermination of good and evil in this world.

Belief together with law *are* Islam. There are five pillars that have been erected on these two foundation stones. First, a testimony of faith (as expounded in the previous paragraph), the *shahada*, is similar in the intention of its opening words ("there is no God but God") to the *sh'ma* in the Jewish tradition: "Hear (*sh'ma*) O Israel, the Lord is our God the Lord is One"—and also to the Nicene creed for Christianity (in form if not substance), which expresses belief in the co-substantiality of the Father, Son and Holy Spirit. The second pillar is prayer.

Formal prayer, *salat*, takes place five times daily, (sunrise, noon, mid-afternoon, sunset and evening) although informal prayer—*du'a*— can take place anytime.

During the *salat* Muslims face Makka and engage in a seven-part process that involves the entire body: going down on the knees, placing the forehead on the ground twice, coming back up, going down again, and then rising again—reciting passages from the Qur'an at each stage. To pray, the individual must be ritually pure: the hands, feet, eyes, ears and neck must be washed. And one must perform the *salat* in a ritually clean *place*. The praying space must be separated from the surrounding, profane space; this might be accomplished by using a prayer rug but also simply by laying down newspapers or paper towels on the ground. Further, praying together as a community once a week at the mosque—Friday at noon—though not absolutely obligatory, is regarded as desirable.

The third pillar is *zakat*, charity for pious purposes. The term *sadakah*—free-will offerings is also used (a Jewish reader might recognize the cognate in word as well as concept with Hebrew *tzedakah*). The terms seem more or less interchangeable, referring to helping those in need, although *sadakah* also refers to gifts offered as acts of expiation, so it might be directed at, say, a relative whom I've offended, whereas *zakat* is the term more strictly in use with regard to charitable acts toward those such as the poor. Perhaps the highest form of *zakat* would be to enable someone without the necessary resources to make the *hajj* (see below).

The fourth pillar is fasting—*sawm*—during Ramadan, the ninth month of the Muslim year. Devout Muslims (unless they are ill) fast from sunrise to sunset each day of this month. Those who cannot fast either due to illness or because of other conditions, such as travel, are obligated to "make-up" those days as soon as they are able. As the Islamic calendar is a 355-day purely lunar calendar and doesn't adjust to the solar calendar,

Ramadan shifts each year 10 to 11 days back vis-à-vis the Gre-gorian calendar used in the west.[18]

The fifth pillar is pilgrimage—*hajj*. Pagan Makkans of Mu-hammad's day had used the word *hajj* to refer to a two-mile periodic visit to a sacred site outside Makka. Muhammad may have absorbed this concept into the development of his faith, just as he may have been aware of the pilgrimage traditions in Judaism and Christianity. After his death *hajj* came to refer to a journey to Makka and Madina, the locations central to the prophet's life. If possible, every devout Muslim makes an an-nual *hajj*—or at least once in his/her lifetime—to Makka, from there to Madina and back to Makka, repeating the route that Muhammad followed from the time of the *hijra*. The central focus of this is of course the *Ka'ba*, around which the pilgrim walks seven times, but includes other sacred sites in and around the Muslim capital.

There is a sixth element, not a pillar of Islam, yet a term more familiar than perhaps any other to non-Muslims: *jihad*. The word means "struggle" and contrary to the understand-ing of it by many Muslims as well as most non-Muslims, *jihad* need have no military connotation whatsoever. The first level of struggle is within one's self, to render one's self as purely and fully a Muslim—a submitter and committer to God's will—as possible. The second level is the struggle within the *dar al'Islam* (the realm of Islam)—the *'umma*—to render it as purely *muslim* (submitted to God's will) as possible. This is most obviously expressed in the centuries' long struggle between *shi'i* (the more common anglicization of this word is *"shi'ite"*)and *sunni*: what originated as a difference regarding leaders (*Khalifat*) evolved as a series of doctrinal differences over which many words and ultimately a good deal of blood have often been spilt.[19]

It is fair to say that the *shi'a* tends to take the narrower, strictly textual view and the *sunna* the broader view—that includes orally transmitted customs—of a given religious issue.[20] There are specific later echoes of the original basis for the schism, as

well. Thus there are those who believe in the future coming of the *mahdi*, a quasi-messianic figure (the "rightly guided one," who will effect the final victory of Islam by means of a divine catastrophe). Shi'is argue that he will be a descendant of the house of 'Ali, but Sunnis dispute that assertion. The majority of Shi'is, in fact, called "Twelvers," believe that he will be the twelfth spiritual leader in succession from 'Ali, which leader disappeared and is being held in abeyance by God until the proper moment arrives for his return.

The understanding of *jihad* shared by most non-Muslims is only its tertiary focus: to make those outside the *dar al'Islam*—in the *dar al'Harb*—recognize the ultimate truth from God that was preached by Muhammad. While that certainly can be and has been understood by any number of Muslims throughout much of history to mean a Holy War in the military sense of that phrase, even this aspect of *jihad* can be construed otherwise: that the struggle must be with the word and not the sword. It is with this idea in mind that Muhammad himself is said by some interpreters to have erred in the manner in which he conquered Makka.[21]

Moreover the Qur'an can be and is very specific—most famously in *Sura* 2:256, which reads "There is no compulsion in religion"—that God disfavors violent attempts to force Muslim faith on those whose faith is otherwise. There are more than a dozen other passages, as well as half a dozen *hadith*s that distinctly militate against violent behavior toward non-Muslims in general.[22] The few passages in the Qur'an that might, in isolation, be seen to embrace violent *jihad* against non-Muslims (specifically, 8.12, 9.5 and 47.4) may be seen rather readily not to offer that embrace when read in their historical (8:12 and 47:4) and literary/textual (9:5) contexts.

*   *   *   *   *

As there are pillars of Islamic belief, there are gradations of

practical observance. The first category includes *obligatory* actions, such as praying five times daily. Second are *desirable* and *recommended* actions, such as the *hajj* (one genuinely without the resources to make the pilgrimage will not be deprived of his place in paradise as a consequence of that omission—but woe unto the one who could have and did not). The third category is religiously *neutral*—such as the gray area of how to relate to non-Muslims. This is by definition the category most open to discussion and differences of interpretation.

The fourth category includes actions that are *objectionable* but not forbidden. Certain foods, for example, are thusly regarded (donkey's milk or meat, for instance). Similarly, for a man to take more than one wife, unless he has the economic means to insure the prosperity of the entire household—and can also insure the overall happiness of more than one wife—is objectionable, but not forbidden. The fifth category includes that which is absolutely *forbidden*, such as the consumption of pork or alcohol.

Moreover, as Islam developed over the centuries, a series of different schools of interpretation emerged. Three variations of Sunni orthodoxy might be called primary. The *Hanafi* school, founded by Abu Hanifa (who died in 767 CE) is based on patterns of belief that developed in Mesopotamia. The *Malaki* school, which developed in Madina, is associated with the name of Malik Ibn Anas (who died in 795). A third school, the *Al Shafi'i* school, based on the teachings of a ninth-century disciple of Malik Ibn Anas, combined Malik's and Hanifa's teachings. I mention these without the space to expand on their thought patterns; I merely wish to underscore the diverse, non-monolithic quality of Islam over time and across space.[23] Indeed many additional schools beyond these three developed between the ninth and eleventh centuries, in both the Sunni and the Shi'i communities.

Thus an ongoing body of discourse has continued to evolve—the analogue of the rabbinic and patristic-scholastic traditions. As Judaism doesn't end with the Torah, nor with the *mishnah* or the *gemara*—discourse within Judaism continues to the

present day—Islam moves from the Qur'an and *Hadith* and their synthesis with *sunna* (varied customs and traditions), to commentaries and discussions of specific issues adjudicated by *Muftis*—"expounders," the analogues of the *rabbanim* of medieval and post-medieval Judaism and of commentators like St. Anselm, Peter Abelard and St. Thomas Aquinas in the medieval Christian tradition. The *Muftis* have, over the centuries, recorded their opinions as *fatwas*—pronouncements ("expositions") on legal issues—like Jewish *responsa* literature and papal bulls. Entire collections of *fatwas* have been produced over time, focusing on how to live a life according to *shari'a*.

Islam, Judaism and Christianity: Theories and Practices

I have expended so much ink on a discussion of Islam within the discussion of definitions, to repeat, because I assume that the majority of my readers will be Christian and Jewish Americans who will have less familiarity with Islam than with their own forms of faith. Islam is a complex religion, beginning with a mixture of political and spiritual elements recorded in mixed oral and written traditions, which in turn bred a series of divergent sects, extending over a long history and a vast geography—from the Pyrenees to Southeast Asia. In each of the different parts of the Islamic world, and in different eras—Syria, Iraq, Spain, North Africa, Turkey, India, Indonesia—there arose different political structures and dynasties, which often exercised differing interpretations of religious principles. While one can reduce the foundations of Islam to five pillars as a matter of convenience, the conceptual and historical edifice is really far more complicated.

The complication is two-fold. First: how to understand the foundations in their context—the political and spiritual interweave in which Muhammad himself managed to engage is distinctly different from that in which Jesus is said to have noted that one should separate what one renders unto Caesar

from what one renders unto God, and that the sword should be put away, for "those who live by the sword die by the sword." It extends beyond even where Moses stood when, with arms upheld, he encouraged the Israelites in their bloody struggle with the Amalekites (Exodus 7:8-16). Second: how to continually reshape aspects of those foundations without undermining them in changing contexts across time and space.

For Jews and Christians, a particularly interesting facet of this issue is the degree to which Muslim customs, practices and beliefs are rooted in aspects of the two older Abrahamic faiths. Prophecy as an idea, of course, goes back to the Bible, whereas angels and *shaitanin* are far more a part of Christian than Jewish theology.[24] In certain respects, the prayer structure of Islam may be seen to have derived from that of Judaism, but Muhammad enlarged on Jewish practices. Rather than merely three times a day, he came to prescribe prayer five times and included the very body language of obeisance to 'Allah that Judaism eschews. (Not always: interestingly, Abraham Maimuni, son of Maimonides and his successor as *Nagid*—spiritual and political leader—of Egyptian Jewry, sought to introduce prostration into the synagogue service in the early thirteenth century, inspired to do so, in fact, by the Muslim custom). Originally Muslims prayed toward Jerusalem, as Jews (and Christians) do, but after his break with the Jewish tribes of Yathrib who had initially supported him—possibly even before Makka became his capital, with the *Ka'ba* as the central shrine of Islam (for some scholars argue that his break with Yathrib's Jews came as early as 624 CE)—the Prophet redirected Muslims to pray toward Makka.

Muslims initially fasted on the tenth day of Ramadan (the fast was called *'Ashura*, cognate with Hebrew *'esser*, meaning "ten"). According to a *Hadith*, when it was pointed out to Muhammad that the Jews fasted on the tenth day of their month Tishri, he changed the Muslim fast to the ninth day; the eleventh was preferred by some; the idea was expanded to encompass the first ten days of the month until finally the entire month,

from sunrise to sunset, was prescribed. The Jewish-Muslim interaction is further evidenced by the fact that, whereas Jewish tradition came to connect Yom Kippur with the giving of the second set of the Decalogue to Moses, Muslim tradition speaks of the *tanzil*—the sending down of the Qur'an from Heaven through Gabriel to Muhammad—as having taken place during the *'Ashura* fast.

So, too, *kashrut*, absorbed from Judaism, while in part eventually rejected by Muhammad, was retained to the extent that pork, blood and carcasses are forbidden foods; and ritual slaughter—*halal*—was decreed by the prophet for all animals intended for human consumption. Just as Judaism and Christianity diverged radically with respect to what the Second Temple period concept of *mashiah* means, the Muslim concept of the *mahdi* can be traced back to the same source but represents another variant on that theme. Where for Christianity the *mashiah* arrived specifically in the person of Jesus and it is Jesus who will return at the end of time as we know it, for Judaism a vaguer concept prevails. This is in part because, according to the Jewish view the messianic arrival has not yet taken place and thus whom—or for that matter, what—precisely Jews are awaiting is unclear (certainly the end of time as we know it is traditionally anticipated).

The Islamic concept is specific, in that the *mahdi* will come from a particular family, to complete the work of perfecting the world begun by Muhammad—but there is disagreement, as we have observed, as to which family, and not all Muslims accept the idea at all. As in the history of Judaism there has been a number of self-proclaimed messianic figures, so within Islam there has been a number of *mahdis* proclaimed by diverse groups of followers.[25]

The five Jewish tribes of Yathrib with whom Muhammad was initially allied did not unite against Muhammad as he was both growing stronger and turning against them—because they were involved in struggles with each other. They apparently

failed to notice that Muhammad was becoming a dangerous enemy. In the end, he defeated them one by one.[26] Toward the end of the 620s, just prior to his final assault on Makka, he attacked the Oasis of Khaybar, which had become the refuge of one of the Jewish tribes that he had ousted from Yathrib/ Madina. Upon defeating them after a siege of 45 days, he is said to have come to an agreement—a *dhimma*, or "pact"—which included a series of injunctions (such as the requirement that Jews cede half their produce to Muslims, and decreeing Muhammad's right to break the agreement and expel the Jews at will) which reduced the Jews but at the same time extended a certain amount of protection to them and the right to practice their faith more or less freely.

The official version of the *dhimma* was eventually called the *Pact of Umar*—but it is not clear whether the Umar who may be called the author of the definitive written version was the Ummayad *Khalif* Umar of the mid-seventh century, or the Abbasid *Khalif* Umar of the mid-eighth century. We possess no version from Muhammad's own time (and therefore no documentary proof that the *dhimma* as we have it stemmed in the *form* in which we have it from the Prophet himself). The Jews came to be called *dhimmi*—"people of the pact." That term over time came to refer also to Christians, Zoroastrians, Samaritans and Sabaeans—peoples with a text at the center of their faiths. It was Muhammad, indeed, who coined the phrase "People of the Book" in referring to the Jews. Peoples of the Pact were entitled to better treatment than pagans and other non-Muslims without books as the basis of their faith, in part because the Prophet recognized Judaism and Christianity as older sibling forerunners, albeit misguided forerunners, of Islam.

In retrospect it is clear, indeed, that as with Jesus, so Muhammad initially saw himself as a reformer, not as the originator of a new faith. But whereas the vocabulary of Jesus was specifically Judaean-Jewish, and his followers would eventually see him as an incarnation of God Itself, Muhammad's terms were

more generally those of Islam (by which I mean that Abraham and Moses, for example, were viewed as *muslims* in that they submitted to the will of God)—and his followers never view him as any more than the ultimate Messenger of God's word to those who seek to submit themselves to God.

To summarize: each of the edifices of Judaism, Christianity and Islam stands on four "foundation stones." They share a common belief in an all-powerful, all-knowing, all-good, all-merciful God that has historically been interested and involved in human history. They share a belief in the notion of a people that is unique in its commitment and devotion to and relationship with that God, and belief in a key text (or texts) that offer(s) an umbilical connection between God and that people. They share a sense that there are particular places on the planet that stand out in being extraordinarily conducive to carrying out that relationship. They differ from each other with respect to how each of these four elements is interpreted: Jews and Muslims maintain the certainty that God never assumes physical form; for Christians a physical God in the person of Jesus is central to their faith. For Jews the Hebrew Bible, with the Torah as its ultimate core is the central umbilical text; for Christians, the Hebrew Bible is called the Old Testament and is viewed as a prelude to the more central New Testament, of which the ultimate core is the Gospels.[27] For Muslims, all of these texts, divinely-given, have become corrupted by error, over time; the Qur'an offers the definitive Divine word in which all issues are correctly presented.

While all three Abrahamic denominations consider Jerusalem of great importance, for Christians there are other equally important sites (such as Nazareth and Bethlehem) which, like Jerusalem itself, are primarily significant for their connections to the life of Jesus and his circle, rather than for Hebrew Biblical connections. Similarly, for Muslims, Jerusalem is less significant than Makka and Madina and its primary importance derives from the *Hadith* that speaks of the Rock in Jerusalem that marks

a particular connecting point between heaven and earth: it is the place from which the Prophet ascended to heaven and to which he returned thence during his miraculous night ride (the 'isra, culminating with his ascent, mir'aj, to the throne of God)—rather than due to its Hebrew Biblical or New Testament connotations. For Jews the centrality of Jerusalem derives from the conviction that Abraham offered up his son Isaac to God on the hill (described in Genesis 22)[28] where, a millennium later, Solomon would build the Israelite Temple (described in I Kings 6). Ultimately it is primarily because Jerusalem offers the site of the Temple that it is important to Jews.

Finally, the messianic idea which takes full and specific form in Christianity as God-become-human remains unspecified and vague in Judaism and in Islam the concept is variously held—but with the exception of the followers of al'Hakim (whom most Muslims consider heretical) that concept as mahdi never includes the assertion of God as assuming human form.

Notes

[5] Until about 30 years ago, for reasons I cannot certainly explain—probably because they followed the pronunciational lead of the Ottoman Turks and their successors, who "Turkified" the Arabic words that Turkish absorbed into its vocabulary over the centuries—it was the norm for Anglo-American scholars to make no effort to render Arabic sounds as effectively as possible in English. The Arabic vowel system is based on a-i-u; "o" and "e" don't exist. Therefore the correct transliterations are Muslim, Muhammad, Qur'an, Makka, Madina, *hijaz*, Hashimite, Nasir, etc.

[6] The Arabic-language name, '*Allah*, is a crasis of *al'Illah*—and cognate with Hebrew *El*. Too often, Islamists will say "Allah" when speaking to a general audience, which tends to obscure the fact that the term simply means "God"—in other words, Muslims use the same term as do Jews and Christians, but in prayer and Qur'anic recitation, they are likely to use the Arabic term, as Jews will the Hebrew and many Christians the Greek or Latin, (among others), rather than the vernacular.

[7] Note the impropriety of calling Muslims "Muhammadans" or Islam itself "Muhammadanism." Christianity derives its name from *christos* (Greek for Hebrew *mashiah*; the two words are anglicized as "christ" and "messiah" respectively), which word came to express the belief that Jesus as the Messiah was God in human form. But Muhammad is never regarded as more than a prophet, albeit the *ultimate* prophet.

[8] It is symptomatic of how every detail within this narrative finds itself subject to definitional debate that, while the standard Muslim understanding of why Yathrib became al-Madina is as I have stated it—more precisely, that its full name was *Madinat al-Nabi* ("the city of the Prophet")—many Western scholars assert that the Jewish agriculturalists who first settled Yathrib (long before the Prophet arrived on the *hijra*) first gave to the expanding oasis the name al'Madina. See, for example, Norman A. Stillman, *The Jews of Arab Lands*, 9.

[9] See *Ibid*, 9: "They [the Jews] formed the majority of the population and were organized into tribes. The three most important were the Banu 'I-Nadir, the Banu Qurayza, and the Banu Qaynuqa'... Medina [sic] was also inhabited by two large confederations of pagan Arabs—the Banu Aws and the Banu Khazraj... A long struggle for dominance ensued in which the Nadir and Qurayza sided with the Aws, while Qaynuqa' allied itself with the Khazraj."

[10] See below, fn 28.

[11] The plural of *sura* is *suwar*.

[12] Others would disagree, even as to the precise timing of things: they would say that the conquest of Makka took place by 628, largely through choking the city by blocking her trade routes—and that Muhammad therefore

lived another 4 years, so that the argument that he was punished by 'Allah is specious.

¹³ The word is cognate with the Hebrew *miqra'*, with which term Jews often refer to the Torah.

¹⁴ Certainly Genesis, the first twenty or so chapters of Exodus, significant passages in Leviticus and Numbers and all of Deuteronomy represent fairly coherent narratives; between these narrative parts are sandwiched the extensive legislative elements of the Torah.

¹⁵ But this seems a particularly strong issue in at least parts of Islamic time and space. One might recall the account in T.E. Lawrence's *Seven Pillars of Wisdom* of how great an effort was required to gain active assistance for various actions from Muslim Arab associates who were more likely to consider events to be unchangeably "written" by God. To be more precise, the two primary theological perspectives in Sunni Islam disagree on the matter of free will and therefore disagree regarding the degree to which God exercises an absolutely predetermining will: the Mu'tazalites contend that humans have free will and that God chooses not to interfere in ways that would abrogate that attribute; Ash'arites on the other hand contend that we essentially have no free will, since everything is predetermined by God. There is far more that might be said about this issue, but a larger discussion falls outside the scope of this narrative.

¹⁶ With the incredibly rapid spread of Islam in the seventh and eighth centuries, it soon became apparent that some so-called *hadiths* were not legitimate, but creations of individuals with their own political motives for representing them as telling about or ascribed to Muhammad. The work of examining and compiling legitimate, reliable collections included, among early efforts, that of Muslim (ca 821-75). He gathered some 9,000 *hadiths* into a compilation so revered that it is known as *Sahih Muslim*: "[the] authentic Muslim [collection]." Ultimately Hadiths fall into different categories with regard to how "reliable" they are—how strongly or weakly the linkage is considered to be between a statement or story and the Prophet himself or those in his immediate circle.

¹⁷ The Arabic word *din* is the analogue of the Hebrew word *din*, but does not quite mean "judgement," as the latter does. It is more like the Hebrew word *dat*, which is usually translated as "religion" but which includes the connotations of "judgement" and "law." *Iman* is cognate with Hebrew *emunah*.

¹⁸ The Jewish calendar is lunar-solar; it also shifts about ten or eleven days every year vis-à-vis the Gregorian calendar but is adjusted by the interpolation of an entire leap month (*Adar* II) every fourth year, to send it back to where it began.

¹⁹ The spilling of blood in the context of doctrinal differences is, of course,

not unique to Islam. In Christian history, for example, both the centuries following the East-West schism of 1054—and even more so the Reformation/Counter-Reformation period in the West, from the 1520s to the early eighteenth century—were marked by considerable bloodshed.

[20] Because word of mouth is unreliable, the *shi'is* assert, how do the *sunnis* know that they are not interpolating customs not sanctioned by the prophet? They, the *shi'is* know what Muhammad did and did not sanction since he spoke specifically to Ali, who transmitted the legitimate orthodox traditions (the *sunnis* consider themselves orthodox and call the *shi'is* heterodox) from Muhammad through a line of divinely inspired *imams*. The Ayatollah Khomeini was to his followers such an infallible, divinely-inspired *imam*. He represented the largest of the *shi'i* sects, the *imami*—one of three major *shi'i* groups. Today, about 86% of Muslims are Sunni, and about 14% are Shi'i.

[21] See below, 121-22, for further discussion of *jihad*.

[22] Thus, for example, 16:82, 6:07 21:07-109, 88:21-22, 64:12, 60:8, among others.

[23] However, one might understand the Hanafis (found over time mostly in India, Central Asia and Turkey as the "Rationalists"; the Malikis (found mostly in North and West Africa) as the "Traditionalists"; the Sha'ifis, (found mostly in Egypt, East Africa and Indonesia) who developed as a kind of compromise between the Hanafis and Malikis in the 10th century, as "Rationalist-Traditionalists." A fourth group of Sunnis, the Hanbalis (found in Saudi Arabia) might be labeled "Fundamentalists."

[24] By the time of Muhammad, Judaism had already absorbed into itself the Christian tradition of angels and demons—which still prevails folkloristically in Jewish literature, although it is neither originally nor logically Jewish.

[25] The most historically significant of these is probably the Fatimid Shi'i ruler Al'Hakim, See below, 42 and fnn 33, 34. As a separate but related or at least interesting issue, one might wonder: if Muhammad had claimed descent from the House of David, and that therefore he was the *mashiah*, might he have been accepted in the long run by the Jewish tribes of Yathrib? But he claimed to be the last prophet, (and to even suggest otherwise is to speak as a non-believer rather than a believer: for believers, Muhammad claimed to be a prophet because that is what he *was*) and that was surely anathema to them—since prophecy was assumed to have disappeared by (or shortly after) the time of Ezra, not to return again *until* the time of the *mashiah*. It is perhaps even more complicated than this: the Jews of Yathrib apparently initially perceived him as asserting a role as *mashiah* (which I don't believe he did) but, since he was not descended (didn't claim to be descended) from the House of David he could not be the *mashiah*. So ultimately he and they

parted spiritual and political ways (to use an overly gentle turn of phrase; the parting was not overly friendly).

[26] The standard Muslim understanding of the collapse of good relations between Muhammad and the Yathribian Jews is that it was a function of the Jews' decision to turn against the Prophet and ally themselves with his enemies. Even this little detail has implications for the development and history of Islam and for the evolution of the relationship between Muslims and Jews. At issue is a pair of divergent interpretations of events for which there is no absolute and concrete record of how they played out.

[27] One can, of course further subdivide. What Catholics and Orthodox Christians call Intertestamental or Deuterocanonical texts (Susannah, Judith, Maccabees I and II, Tobit, The Wisdom of Solomon, Ecclesiasticus, et al) Protestants term apocrypha; like Jews, Protestants view these as other than God's word.

[28] Both Jews and Christians embrace this idea, although the two groups interpret the significance of Abraham's offering of Isaac differently from each other. Muslim scholars debated for centuries both the question of whether it was Isaac or Ishmael whom Abraham offered and whether it took place on that hill in what later became Jerusalem, or elsewhere, on a hill outside Makka. The vast majority of Muslims today understand the son offered by Abraham to have been Ishmael.

Chapter 3

Definitions: Arab, Muslim and Jew; Israeli and Palestinian

W hile Islam was founded in the *'arav*, and its first adherents were therefore Semitic Arabs, as a religion its rapid sweep not only up into the Near East and East Mediterranean but west as far as Spain by the early eighth century, and east as far as India by that time—and eventually as far as Indonesia—encompassed increasing numbers of non-Arab, non-Semitic peoples. Most of the Muslims who invaded Spain in 711-718 were non-Arab, non-Semitic Berbers from northwest Africa, for example. The Iranians are neither Arabs nor Semites; the language they speak (Farsi; a direct descendant of Old Persian) is much closer to English than to Arabic (even if it so happens that, for reasons beyond this discussion, Farsi uses Arabic *writing* to express itself non-verbally, just as both English and French use Latin letters). Not a single native Filipino or Indonesian who practices Islam is an Arab or a Semite.

To make matters more complicated, both the terminology

and historical infrastructure of Islam itself carry the term "Islam" beyond the simply *faith*-bound category into which one might place it. The term *'umma*, used to refer to members of the Muslim community, has a broader connotation than "faith." It suggests a comprehensive realm in which faith interacts with education, economics, commerce and culture, affecting aspects of life style that extend from gastronomy to symbols in art. At the same time, Islam, like Christianity and Judaism, has been schismatic almost from the outset, as we have observed above. Thus Sunni-Shi'i antagonism (and within each of these two groups, often hostility among varied sects and/or schools of thought) has been nearly as much of a factor in preventing cohesion in the Middle East as have Muslim-Christian, Muslim-Jewish or Jewish-Christian (as well as Christian-Christian and Jewish-Jewish) antagonisms.

Nor is this small array of definitional complications simplified when one turns to the word "Jew" and its cognates. Between the destruction of the Second Temple in the year 70 CE and the time of Wilhelm Marr's 1879 coinage, "Semite," to refer to Jews, the term most prominently carried a religious connotation. To the extent that Jews actively associated themselves in their minds or were associated by others in *their* minds with Jerusalem, the site of the Temple, and its surrounding real estate, the term might be understood to have also had a nationalist connotation. For Judaism—albeit in a far-flung diasporatic manner, rather than across a far-flung contiguous area, as is the case for Islam—the self-defining Hebrew term, *'am*, is cognate with the Arabic term *'umma*. The Jewish use of the term *'am*, even during those eighteen centuries of dispersion, intended a comprehensive reference to the same sort of elements as those which define the Muslim *'umma*. But Marr's designation of Jews as Semites, to repeat, was intended to recategorize them as a *race*—a race apart from the "Caucasian" Christian "race" of Europeans to whom he wanted to present Jews as dangerous interlopers.

A century and a quarter after the era of Wilhelm Marr's racialization of Jews, the question of how to define a Jew, Jewishness or Judaism is nowhere close to having found an answer. In the United States, Judaism is perceived by most Jews and non-Jews alike as a religion. In most of Europe, Judaism is perceived as a nationality. In the former Soviet Union this was explicit: one's internal passport indicated one's nationality as Russian or Azeri or Ukrainian or Georgian or Jewish—among others. But even in the West, in Germany, for example, when Jewish-Christian dialogue in the aftermath of the Holocaust is a discussion point, the phraseology that one encounters more often than not is "Germans and Jews"—not "German Christians and Jews."

Beyond this distinction, between Judaism as a religion and Judaism as a nationality, is the fact that there are many Jews (particularly in the United States) who don't believe in God, and who do not practice the religion of Judaism at all, but who understand themselves to be culturally Jewish—or in some cases, ethnically Jewish, but in any case *historically* connected to their Jewish forebears. Add to this the notion first articulated in the early 1930s by Mordecai M. Kaplan, that Judaism is best understood not as a religion or as a culture, not as a nationality or race, not as a body of customs and traditions, but as a civilization, and one begins to understand how this simple term and its cognates refuse a simple definition.

To the extent that a given Jew can trace his lineage to the Semitic-speaking parts of the Middle East, and to the extent that Hebrew as the primary language of the Jews is classifiable as Semitic, Jews might be labeled Semites. For that matter, by the time Muhammad was born in the *'arav*, Jews had been resident there for at least half a millennium, which means that, like Muhammad and those who embraced the form of faith that he was shaping, the Jews with whom he had such intense contact and eventually conflict, were also *Arabs*. That is, if the term is used in the historical sense that I have noted earlier to

refer to those who trace their ancestry to the *'arav*, there are certainly Arab Jews.

On the other hand, if we re-use the term "Arab" to refer to a political, rather than ethno-linguistic group, and therefore use it as in the phrase "The Arab World," then we broaden it to refer to peoples from Morocco to the border of Iran—and Jews would be excluded by definition, regardless of whether or not any of them originated in the *'arav*. The same might be said, of course, of Christians. In fact the Christian role in Pan-Arab Nationalism in general and in Palestinian Arab identity in particular, as we shall shortly see, is significant.

We shall also observe, in considering Jewish Nationalism, that the matter of how to define a Jew would be rendered exponentially more complicated by the advent of Jewish Nationalism in general and also the particular sense of Jewish nationalism that came to be articulated in Zionism by the late nineteenth century.[29] Both for the non-Jewish European world (incidentally, wrestling with how far to identify itself as *Christian* and how far as *secular*) and for the Jews themselves, the question arose: are Jews most properly and purely understood as adherents to a religion, and/or does the advent of Zionism, in recasting Jews as a nation with a homeland (and with it a language, literature, music, art and all the other concomitants of Romantic Nationalism) separate them from a religion-based definition? This question and the varied responses to it would have practical consequences both for shaping the Zionist movement and for shaping the State of Israel over the decades following its independence.

*   *   *   *   *

What *of* Israelis? And what of Israelis and Palestinians? Definitional complications apply here, as well. Israel is so often simply referred to as "The Jewish State" that one might assume that all Israelis are Jews. Indeed the government and its

infrastructure—from the make-up of the Israeli parliament (the Knesset) to regulations governing public transportation on the Sabbath—has from the outset been a wrestling match between the will to be governed by Jewish law and that to be a secular democracy. Israel is both a Jewish theocracy and a secular democracy and as such, its citizenship is comprised not only of Jews but of Christians, Muslims and other religious groups. While it is true that the majority of Israelis are Jews—many of whom define themselves as Jews by culture and history and not by their religious beliefs—a substantial minority are not. An Israeli is a citizen of the polity, Israel.

Some of those citizens might also be called Arabs and most of the latter might also be called Palestinians. Anyone who lives in Palestine, or who traces an ancestry to inhabitants of Palestine would be called a Palestinian. But where *is* Palestine? It is where Israel, Jordan and the parts between and around them, otherwise known as Gaza and the West Bank (otherwise known as Judaea and Samaria—and one's choice of terminology will depend largely upon one's political and/or religious point of view),[30] are currently located. Much of that area was called Judaea two millennia ago. Even then, though, the inhabitants of the polity Judaea distinguished it in the larger geo-political sense, from Judaea in the narrower sense, as separate from Samaria and the Galilee.[31]

In the wake of the failed but, from the Roman point of view, frustrating (because it took three years to suppress) Bar Kokhba revolt of 132-35, the Roman Emperor Hadrian astutely deduced that, if he could undercut the religion of the Jews he might be able to undercut the Jewish nationalist aspirations which had led to three major uprisings against Roman rule in 70 years. As another part of his program to suppress Jewish nationalism he renamed Judaea *"Palestina"*—apparently appropriating and adapting the Semitic designation, *Philistia*, formerly applied to that corner of Judaea that we now call "Gaza." The name *Palestina* remained in use in the Western vocabulary (but not

the Hebrew-language Jewish vocabulary) for the next nineteen centuries.

So a Palestinian would be anyone living in Palestine during those centuries—be that individual Muslim, Christian, Jewish or an adherent to any other sort of faith system, for that matter. That would be simple enough were it not for the history of the past hundred years or so. For reasons that I shall shortly consider, the British and the French carved up the Near East in the aftermath of World War I, and the area designated as Palestine fell under a British colonial administration, so that one reads and speaks of Britain's Palestinian Mandate. From that Mandate three entities would be further carved out over the following thirty years. The Hashemite Kingdom of Jordan would be supplied that part of Palestine east of the Jordan River (which would also supply it with its name) in 1946. Part of the area west of the Jordan would become the State of Israel in 1948. The part of western Palestine that did not become Israel—Gaza and the "West Bank"—continued to be called Palestine. Thus if one's understanding of that term is informed by a post-World War II perspective, rather than a post-Bar Kokhba/Hadrianic perspective, the term "Palestinian" refers only to someone dwelling in one of these two last-mentioned areas as opposed to those inhabiting either of those areas *or* Israel or Jordan.

Those who assert that there already exists a Palestinian state, east of the Jordan, are right. But those who insist that, over the decades since 1946-48, the continued separation between communities east and west of the Jordan has reshaped those to the east as functionally Jordanians, so that those to the west remain the only true Palestinians and their desire for political identity and statehood is legitimate, are *also* right. Those Israelis who, descendants of generations of dwellers in this area assert that they are Palestinians are also right, although few individuals in common parlance would be likely to recognize the cogency of that historical datum. And the non-Jewish—i.e., Muslim and Christian Arab—population that inhabits Israel? They are

certainly Israeli and also, to repeat, Arab, but particularly in the post-Oslo world since 1993 or so, many of them have re-identified themselves as Palestinians. Many, but not all.

Or perhaps better put: since 1993—the year of the Oslo Accords arrived at between Israelis and Palestinians—there exists a new layer to the tensions felt by Israeli Arabs for which the tightness increased exponentially after the advent of the most recent *Intifada* that began in 2000, regarding how to identify themselves, as Israelis or as Palestinians. As with every self-definitional choice available to a given group, its constituent members vary as to which one they select. This issue can be seen to apply along various religious and ethnic lines in varying degrees throughout the Middle East, and not only in the context of Israel-Jordan-Palestine, as we shall see in more detail in subsequent chapters of this narrative.

Notes

[29] See below, 66-7 and 69-73.

[30] I mean by this parenthetical comment to be more than parenthetical: even the small matter of terminology with respect to the West Bank/Judaea and Samaria is fraught with definitional challenges that are rooted in both religious and political issues.

[31] "Judaea" in the narrow sense was more or less the geopolitical area that was a lineal descendant of what had survived the Assyrian destruction of the Israelite north (722-21 BCE), and that subsequently resisted but was ultimately defeated by the Babylonians (586 BCE), and to which territory those who returned from the Babylonian exile came back with the Medo-Persian defeat of the Babylonians (538 BCE). That area eventually achieved independence under the Hasmonaeans (ca 140 BCE), and was in turn swallowed up by Herod the Idumaean (37 BCE). By the time of Jesus' birth a "Greater Judaea" encompassing Samaria and Galilee as well as additional territory had been achieved through military and diplomatic successes first by the Hasmonaeans and then by Herod, the latter as an important client and ally of Rome. For an excellent and detailed discussion of this, see Solomon Zeitlin, *The Rise and Fall of the Judaean State* (especially volume I and the first 100 pages of volume II.

Chapter 4

Interactions and Interferences: The Era of the Crusades

The issues of carving up Palestine and the conflict between forms of self-definition are part of a larger matter: conflicting and often confusing aspirations throughout the region during the past two hundred years. Further, the reference in the previous chapter to the British and the French and their role in redefining "Palestine" in the first half of the twentieth century reminds us that the third weft thread in this tangled web, *together* with definition and aspiration, is *interference*.

For chronological reasons we turn toward the issue of interference before furthering the discussion of definition and before turning in earnest to the matter of conflicting aspirations. Interference arrives into the complications of the Middle East in two related but different forms before we arrive into the modern era. The first interference by outside forces is that from the European Christian world, specifically in the form of the Crusades that dominate Christian-Muslim relations between

the end of the eleventh century and the middle of the fifteenth. The second form of interference will come from the opposite spiritual and geographic direction, taking the shape of a succession of Turkic and Mongol conquerors whose faith is animist. The most significant of these, for this discussion, are the Seljuk and Ottoman Turks.[32]

The two forms of interference interact on several levels. In the first place, it is the arrival of the Seljuks that most directly gave the impetus to the first Crusade. The Seljuk victory over the Byzantine—Eastern Christian—army at the Battle of Manzikert in 1071 and the subsequent Seljuk obstruction of the Christian pilgrims' route to Jerusalem was the most immediate reason for the call for a Crusade by Pope Urban II, in 1095, to liberate those routes. Of course there was an array of other issues as well. Christians would later look back and retrofit onto the call for Crusade as its first cause the burning of the Church of the Holy Sepulchre by the crazed Fatimid Shi'i Egyptian overseer of Jerusalem, al'Hakim (985/996-1021?), in 1009.[33] Nobody is quite certain why he did it, but al'Hakim himself disappeared into the desert a few years later, (in 1019, 1020 or 1021), never to be heard from again, and his successor promptly rebuilt this most important of Christian structures.[34] Nonetheless the burning of the Church would later be referred to as the first cause for the Crusade.

More significant surely were intra-Christian issues. These ranged from the great schism that separated the Eastern and the Western Churches in 1054 to the great conflict between Pope Gregory VII and the young German King Henry IV that culminated with Henry's arrival to Canossa, a mountain stronghold in northern Italy, in 1077, where he stood in the snow barefoot for several days before gaining the audience with the Pope in which he begged forgiveness for his audacious opposition to the Holy Father. Intra-Christian issues included the emergence of Cluniac reforms that revitalized the troubled monastic orders in Western Christendom and with the reforms a renewed zeal

for pilgrimages by the second half of the eleventh century. They included the fact that Urban, successor and disciple of Gregory, was himself a Cluniac and was already engaged in a struggle against secular feudal Christian lords who opposed his leadership of Western Christendom. This last issue would both inspire the Pope to think beyond the bounds of Christendom with regard to spiritual hegemony and offer a channel for the energy of such feudal lords, redirecting it away from—and rather reshaping it to function on behalf of—the Papacy. In other words, the promotion of a Crusade to the Holy Land against the Muslims would serve a range of papal needs.

On the other hand, the formerly "barbarian," pagan Normans and Magyars had recently come into the fold of "civilized" Christianity, which offered both an encouraging sense of how violent enemies could be made to enter the fold in peace and an instrument to be directed toward the *Dar al'Islam* as the ultimate enemy. Moreover, in Spain the Umayyad dynasty with its great capital at Cordoba had collapsed by 1031, reducing Islamic Spain to a series of petty kingdoms, called in Arabic *ta'ifas*. This development enabled the *reconquista*—the Christian reconquest of Spain—to move forward for the first time since the Muslim take-over of the early eighth century. Half of formerly Muslim Spain fell into Christian hands over the next half-century, culminating with the conquest of Toledo in 1085. Similarly, in the central Mediterranean, Norman Christians wrested Mahdia (Tunisia) from the Muslims in 1087 and by 1091 had established a new, Christian kingdom in Sicily.

Add to this array of issues the fact that in 1055 the Seljuk Tughrul Bey forced the Abbasid Caliph to make him Sultan and we understand that an astute observer of the Muslim world would have recognized that the dismantling of traditional infrastructures that had been in place within it for three centuries meant that the time to strike had arrived. Urban called together a Council at Piacenza, Italy in early 1095 and another at Clermont later in the year. Ostensibly he sought to restore

unity to the church; to heal the rift of 1054 by responding to the request of the Byzantine Emperor Alexius I for recruits for an army that could reclaim what had been lost in the Battle of Manzikert. In the end, though, the Pope instead sent his own army, under his own knightly leadership. Raymond IV, Count of Toulouse, accompanied by the Bishop of Le Puy, led volunteers from Southern France. Those from Northern France were led by Robert II, Duke of Normandy; Robert II, Count of Flanders; and Godfrey of Bouillon, Duke of Lower Lorraine—among others. And from Apuleia, in Southern Italy, came an essentially Norman contingent led by Bohemond, son of Robert Guiscard.

This disparate array of crusaders—"Franks" as they were called by the Muslim world—all converged on Constantinople between July, 1096 and July, 1097. It was an undisciplined horde, including pilgrims and clergy as well as a range of less spiritually-directed participants, rather than a well-organized group of recruits. Negotiations immediately began with Emperor Alexius: Bohemand demanded that he be granted the office of the Grand Domestic of the East in the presumed-to-be-inevitable event of a victory, which would have made him the Imperial Viceroy for the conquered lands. Alexius in turn asked that any of his territories which were conquered by the Franks be returned to his jurisdiction. By late 1097 the group had taken Nicea (in what is now Turkey, not all that far from Constantinople). There Alexius soon installed a contingent of Byzantine soldiers to limit the looting being accomplished by the Franks, which gesture naturally raised the level of hostility between the two groups of Christian fighters.

Between October, 1097 and June, 1098 the Crusaders besieged and finally took Antioch (in what is now Syria); had there been less disunity among them, the process would probably have been much quicker. Alexius began, rather late in the siege, to send reinforcements, but he got word that the Seljuk *atabeg* (regent) Kerbogha of Mosul was advancing with a large relieving force and he turned back in fear. Indeed the *atabeg* did arrive

at Antioch with his army shortly after the Crusaders took the city on June 3: the besiegers now found themselves besieged, but on June 28 Bohemand took on and defeated Kerbogha in a pitched battle before the city. Almost immediately, arguments ensued between Bohemand and Raymond as to who should be put in charge of the city.

The argument remained unresolved when the two set out with their combined forces toward Jerusalem in November. En route, just before Christmas, Bohemand turned back and took control of Antioch on his own. Raymond and his forces arrived at the walls of the Sacred City in June, 1099, where he encountered much stiffer resistance than he might have anticipated, given the very light opposition he had encountered along the way. But the Shi'i Fatimids, who had taken control of the city from Sunni Seljuks the previous year, understood both the symbolic and the strategic significance of Jerusalem as a key to the region.

Nonetheless, the Franks took Jerusalem on July 15. A massacre ensued; one Christian writer, reporting to the Pope, described the Crusaders as wading in blood up to the thighs of their horses. When the smoke cleared, and Godfrey of Bouillon had been appointed *advocatus*—defender—of the Church of the Holy Sepulchre (underscoring the retrofitting of the destruction of that edifice 85 years earlier as the cause for the Crusade in the first place), four Latin Crusader kingdoms had been put into place. As such, Jerusalem would remain a state between 1099 and 1243. Up the coast toward the Lebanon, Tripoli would take three years of further campaigning to be solidly in Crusader hands, and the Kingdom of that name would last from 1102 to 1289. Antioch, having been put under the charge of Bohemand, survived as a Crusader kingdom until 1268. Edessa, further north and east, and also having been taken in 1098, would last as a Crusader kingdom only until 1144.

The attempt at an Islamic counter-conquest—followed by the counter-counter-conquest of the Second Crusade—would not be that far in coming. In the first place, Zanji, the latest

atabeg of Mosul, seized Aleppo in 1128, and from there offered a clear threat to the Burdis in control of Damascus. The latter maintained positive commercial and cultural relations with the Crusader states, but didn't receive the assistance they should have from those states in the face of that common threat. In 1144, Zanji took the northernmost of the Crusader states, Edessa, but he died two years later. His son, Nurredin, declared a *jihad* against the three remaining Crusader states. But even had he not done so, the fall of Edessa shocked the Europeans and set quickly in motion the decision of Pope Eugenius III to declare a second Crusade. Among the respondents to that call were the French king Louis VII and the German king Conrad III—the latter inspired, in part, by Bernard of Clairvaux, the monastic reformer known otherwise for his destruction of the Christian scholar, Peter Abelard.

Disaster met the two monarchs every step of the way. Conrad was defeated at Dorylaeum on October 25, 1147 by the Turks and Louis was defeated by them at Laodicea in January, 1148. The siege of Damascus that they undertook with their remaining forces in late June proved disastrous and the prestige of the Franks as warriors, so high after the first Crusade, imposing fear on the Muslim inhabitants of the Middle East, was severely damaged. Shortly thereafter, Nurredin defeated Raymond of Antioch at Inab, in 1149. He sent his lieutenant, the Kurd, Shirquh, to Egypt where, in spite of his being a Sunni, he was accepted as a vizier to the Fatimid Caliph. Upon Shirquh's death his nephew Salah ad-Din Yusuf Ibn Ayub—better known to the West as Salah ad-Din, or Saladin—assumed that position as vizier, but by 1171, nominally still as lieutenant to Nurredin, he declared that Egypt now would answer to the Abbasid caliphate, effectively ending the Fatimid control of that region.[35] Saladin's military and political success had resulted, by 1183, in his control not only of Egypt but of the larger region that encompassed Antioch and Tripoli; Jerusalem fell to his sword on October 2, 1187. It is worthy of note that *no bloodbath followed*

that conquest, and that, on the contrary, *Christians, Jews and others were permitted to continue to live their lives without much interference from their Muslim overlords in the years of Saladin's control.*

Nonetheless, the new dominance of the Muslims provoked a new response on the part of new Popes: Gregory VIII and Clement III declared a third Crusade in 1189. The key respondents this time were the English king Richard Coeur-de-lion and the Holy Roman Emperor, Frederick Barbarossa. The most serious tangible result of the campaigns of Richard were the reclamation of the coastal cities south of Acre that gave to the truncated Kingdom of Jerusalem the wherewithal to survive for another century; so, too, by 1192 Richard gained the right by treaty for Christian pilgrims to visit the Church of the Holy Sepulchre. One might note, as a reminder of how confusingly divided both the Christian and Muslim worlds remained within themselves and not only with regard to each other, that on his way home Richard was waylaid and held for ransom by the Viennese, who demanded and received a substantial supply of silver from the English in exchange for his release.

On a similar note, the fourth Crusade began shortly after, in 1199, instigated by Thibaut III, Count of Champagne, with the blessing of Pope Innocent III and with the assistance of the Venetians under Doge Enrico Dandolo. This Crusade yielded as *its* most tangible consequence the enriching of Western Christendom and Venice in particular (to whom the French and other Crusaders owed a good deal of money) through the plundering of Eastern Christendom. Indeed the Crusaders never got further east and south than Constantinople, which they sacked in 1204, and from which they sent or brought back an extraordinary range and volume of precious materiel. Thus to the massacre of Muslims in Jerusalem and elsewhere during this era, and the massacres and expulsions of Jews both there and back in the Rhineland on the way to the Holy Land, may be added the massacre of their Christian brethren by these champions of the God of Love.

They established a new Latin dynasty in Constantinople which, although it lasted only until 1261, would assure that Byzantium would never become the sort of power it had once been. In retrospect one might argue that this helped make the Empire vulnerable to the Ottomans when they arrived on the scene. Indeed when Constantinople itself was under siege in the mid-fifteenth century, the memory of the cruelty of their Western brethren was profound enough that the Greek Orthodox citizens of the city preferred conquest by the Turks to submission to the Papacy as the price for its assistance.

Innocent III and his successor to the Papal tiara, Honorius III, pushed for the fifth Crusade that finally arrived in 1218. Honorius was the same Pope who, in part in response to the unresolved problems of corrupted monasticism and heresy within Christendom—and to the challenge to Papal authority afforded by far-flung and materially successful monastic orders such as the Cluniac order had become—sanctioned two new monastic orders. The Franciscans and Dominicans were distinguished from their monastic predecessors in being mendicant orders that, it could be expected, would never set down the kind of land-based permanent roots that might lead to material power and with it, anti-papal behavior. Moreover, the Dominicans in particular would evolve as servants of the Papacy who in the course of the century became famous for their rooting out of heretics. They developed Boards of Inquiry—known in the vernacular as the Inquisition—into the faith of believing Christians, first in northern Italy and southern France and eventually in southern Italy and Sicily; and finally, by the fifteenth century, in Spain.

As for the Crusade sponsored by Honorius, its direct spiritual leader, the Papal legate Cardinal Pelagius of Albano, wrested defeat from the jaws of victory by his stubborn refusal to accept rather favorable terms offered to him by his Muslim counterpart. Pelagius might have regained full control of Jerusalem. The sacred city had remained in Muslim hands since the time of Saladin, even if the "Kingdom" continued to have nominal

Christian "rulers" (essentially limited to the Church of the Holy Sepulchre and its immediate environs). But through his hunger to conquer all of Egypt, Pelagius lost the chance to regain full control. And so Frederick II, who had taken the cross in 1215 but never sailed off, and was crowned by Pope Honorius III as Holy Roman Emperor in 1220, responded to the call for a sixth Crusade by Pope Gregory IX in 1227.

Frederick turned back shortly after setting sail in September, on the grounds of being seasick. The turn-around earned him excommunication, but in the summer of 1228 he set forth once more and with more diplomacy than warfare concluded a treaty with the Egyptian Sultan al-Kamil that gained Jerusalem and other sites within its ambit and a promise of peace for ten years. But the Pope condemned his having negotiated with, rather than warring with, Muslim infidels, and declared a "crusade" against Frederick's own lands in Italy. In the decades that followed, the Franks were more involved in fights with each other than against Muslim foes, except when they fought as allies with one Muslim force against another. It was in the course of such interchange that Jerusalem was captured by an army of Khwarizmian Turks in July, 1244 working as mercenaries for the Egyptians.[36]

In December of that year, the French king Louis IX took the cross, and by 1248 he had set off on the seventh Crusade. The aftermath of six years of that debacle—the most significant moment of which was the capture of Louis himself in 1250; and the most interesting fact that in the aftermath of Louis' ransom his hopes for re-enforcements from the Papacy were disappointed because Innocent IV was too busy with a "crusade" against Conrad IV, son of Frederick II—was a return home by the French king with the growing conviction on his part and those of others that God is simply indifferent to crusades! But meanwhile, in the very year of Louis' capture, the Mamluks of Cairo, war-loving slave troops in the service of the Seljuks, asserted their own rule in Egypt.

Other developments shaped the following decade. In 1258, Hulagu the Mongol sacked Baghdad, ending the Abbasid rule of that city and an Empire which had lasted, at least nominally, since 750. Two years later the Mongols took Aleppo and Damascus. In the same year, the Nestorian Christian general of the Mongols, Kitbugha, was defeated and killed at 'Ayn Jalut, near Nazareth, by the Mamluk Sultan Qutuz of Egypt and his general, Baybars. The primary significance of that moment was that the pagan Mongols embraced Islam, convinced that it was a stronger faith than that of Christianity. This would have repercussions into the next century, when the successors to the Mongols, the Ottomans, arrived onto the scene.

In any case, the continued depredations of the waning Latin kingdoms by Baybars, who soon became Sultan himself, brought a response from Europe in the form of an eighth Crusade, in which once again Louis IX took up the sword. He began his new enterprise in 1267. Within three years, though, Louis was diverted to Tunisia through his brother, Charles of Anjou, King of Sicily, since the latter did not want a Crusade to distract Western Christendom from the war he was contemplating against the Byzantine Christians—and besides, he was on good terms with Baybars. With Louis' death in Tunisia that same year, (apparently of dysentery), Baybars was able to take the last of the inland Crusader fortresses. One might say, in the formal historiographic sense, that the Crusades were at an end, leaving behind a legacy of increased intolerance in Christian Europe, whether against the Muslim world or against non-Western Christians or against Jews or against heretics: the thirteenth century saw, among other God-inspired events, the virtual extermination of the heretical Albigensians, (also known as the Cathars), burned in their hill towns in the south of France by the Dominican inquisitors.

On the other hand, the increased and intensified intercourse between Europe and the Middle East brought new commercial interests and directions back into Europe, together with new

tastes in food and new thinking with regard to long-distance commerce effected by the abstraction of a banking system that used *checks* (from the Arabic word, *sak*). The development of a money economy and with it of a rising merchant class affected nobles and serfs alike. So, too, the Crusaders brought back to Europe an interest in and understanding of massive stone masonry construction; it is no accident that the thirteenth century marks a precipitous increase in the size of churches, cathedrals and castles. The development of heraldic emblems, of chivalric codes, and of heroic narratives, are also part of that legacy.

Nor did the Crusades really end when they ended. Chivalric orders continued a presence in and around the region. Thus the Templars held out on the small island of Arwad, two miles off Tortosa, until 1303. Their brother knights, the Hospitaliers would make their way to the island of Rhodes, whence they would be forcibly finally removed in 1522 by a massive Ottoman effort; they would re-establish themselves on Malta, before slowly fading toward the backstage of history by the Napoleonic era. But with the arrival of the Ottoman (Osmanli) Turks into Anatolia by about 1350, and ultimately with their taking of Constantinople in 1453—bringing to an end Byzantine history that had played out for a thousand years after the collapse of the Western Roman Empire—the zeal to Crusade, while nominally pointed toward the Holy Land, more often directed itself toward some other site that served more generally as a symbol of Christian-Muslim hostility.

Interactions and Interferences: the Ottoman Era

Historically, one of the more interesting interactions between religion and politics is when the Ottoman Turks, as conquerors of a substantial portion of the Muslim world, embraced that faith rather than imposing the Turks' own form of animist paganism upon those they conquered. Unusual, but not entirely surprising, if one considers the inherent logic in seeking a faith dominated

by a single God for a group that evolved from a nomadic sweep of tribes to a dominating sedentary empire governed by one all-powerful leader. That said, in retrospect the choice of Islam rather than Christianity may ultimately be traced to the choice made by the Ottomans' predecessors in the wake of that previously mentioned critical moment: the defeat of the Christian-led Mongols by the Muslims in 1260 at 'Ayn Jalut.

In any case it was against the Ottomans that efforts were mounted in the fourteenth and subsequent centuries, from an attack on Smyrna on the western coast of Turkey in 1344 to the crusade called by Pope Pius II which remained still-born in 1464: the Pope waited in vain that summer on the eastern coast of Italy for the ships promised from various quarters to arrive and set sail. In the end they never arrived and he contracted dysentery and died on the way back to Rome. But the interaction between the Ottomans—as the ongoing representative of Islam—and Christendom continued along a handful of significant paths as the decades and then centuries moved forward. A generation after the death of Pius II, in 1492, the Jews were expelled from a newly unified Christian Spain—and from Portugal in 1496-7—and one of the places where many of them took refuge was the Ottoman Empire. Sultan Beyezit II is said by some traditions not merely to have invited them but to have sent ships to transport them from the coastal cities of Barcelona and Malaga.

Beyezit was not merely being gracious or simply Judaeophilic. The Sephardic (Spanish and Portuguese) Jews brought with them something of an international trade network and considerable experience at intermediating commercially and culturally between the Muslim and Christian worlds. They also brought with them knowledge of movable type. (The first books printed in the Muslim world, in Istanbul, as Constantinople was now called, were—ironically enough, given subsequent history—Hebrew books). Most of all the Jews brought with them from Christendom knowledge of the technology of gunpowder and cannonry,

which new knowledge would transform the Ottoman Empire into a spectacular military machine. In the following century, a Jew known as Joseph HaNassi (Joseph the Prince) would rise to the position of vizier to Beyezit's successor's successor, Suleiman the Magnificent. HaNassi would be honored with a Dukedom—he became the Duke of the Greek territory of Naxos—and granted permission to establish a semi-autonomous Jewish community in the northern Palestine area of Safed and Tiberias. This would mark the first activated non-messianic attempt on the part of Jews to return to the Holy Land since the fourth century.

Suleiman the Magnificent would extend the Ottoman presence into the heart of Europe and offer a weight equal in historical significance to that offered at the other end of the Mediterranean by Charles I of Spain (otherwise known as Charles V the Hapsburg Emperor) and Francis I of France, as well as Henry VIII of distant England. In retrospect, the unanticipated defeat of the Ottoman navy of Suleiman's successor, Selim, by a combined Christian force at the 1571 Battle of Lepanto marked the beginning of a long swoon that would finally bring the Empire to its end only three and a half centuries later, during World War I. Much, though, would transpire in the course of those centuries, including the near-taking of Vienna in 1683—the second time an Ottoman army had stood beneath the walls of that city (Suleiman had unsuccessfully besieged it more than 150 years earlier).

It was the fortuitous coincidence of three factors that saved the city and with it, central Europe: the arrival of a relieving army under the Polish leader John Sobieski; the arrogance of the Ottoman generals in being so entirely focused on the siege that they ignored what was happening at their rear, assuming that either no relieving army would come or that it would pose no threat; and dysentery that ran rampantly through the Ottoman army at virtually the same time, helping to necessitate the withdrawal of the Turkish forces.

Within the century that followed the last Ottoman siege of Vienna, Europe's industrial, technological, scientific and secular

intellectual revolutions were beginning to surge. In the period between about 1760 and World War I, the Christian world made spectacular progress on the first three of these fronts while the Ottoman and Muslim world did not. By the nineteenth century, as Ottoman power was shrinking back toward the Middle East, European colonial ambition and imperial rapaciousness were beginning to encircle the globe and, in the Mediterranean world, to swallow piece after piece of Ottoman-held North Africa.

The culmination of that process for the purposes of this discussion was the entrance of the Prussians into the Near East at the behest of the last somewhat significant Ottoman Sultan, Abdul Hamid II, who arrived onto the imperial throne in 1876. The invitation to Kaiser Wilhelm was extended with the hope that the Prussians would replenish Abdul Hamid's empty coffers and build railroads connecting Istanbul to the Persian Gulf on the one hand (the more efficiently to move troops back and forth between the Ottoman capital and the gulf) and from Damascus to the *hijaz* on the other, all the way to Makka.[37] This was not only in order to be able to move troops back and forth, but to add more weight to the Sultan's claim to be the Caliph of Islam as the protector of its primary holy sites. Most significantly, Abdul Hamid wanted the Prussians to modernize his army by shaping new officers' training schools.

This last issue would have important consequences with respect to the final dismantling of the Ottoman Empire. It would also have important consequences for the evolution of nationalism among the Arabs. For one thing, some of their leadership would be developed—and gain new military and general organizational skills—in those training academies. For another, the dismantling of the Empire from within, due to an uprising of modernist Turkish officers against the Sultan (in 1908),[38] would turn its back on the modernist Arab officers who participated in the uprising. This would leave that well-trained Arab leadership frustrated and eager to find a different outlet for national self-expression, as we shall see in the discussion that follows.

Notes

[32] "Animist," in brief, means that they worshipped many different gods embodied in the forces of nature.

[33] To further complicate the historical picture, it should be noted that al'Hakim's mother was Christian. Having chosen his father's faith, his antagonism to Judaism and Christianity and attempts to force-convert Jews and Christians raises interesting psychological questions beyond the scope of this study.

[34] Al'Hakim's disappearance led his followers to develop a cult around his memory the adherents to which asserted that he would return at some indeterminate future date. Those followers, who diverged from, while remaining rooted in Islam, became the Druze. Mostly dwelling in northern Israel, Lebanon and Syria, they are another population whose cultural, spiritual and political concerns offer a challenge to defining who is who even within that subregion of the region at large. Of course, this leads to yet another definitional matter: who and what really *are* the Druze? In brief, they are the descendants of followers—Arab followers—of al'Hakim. More properly called *Muwahiddun* ("monotheists"; they call themselves *Ahl al-Tawhid*, which in Arabic means "People of the One"), the group is popularly known as Druze after the eleventh-century preacher Darazi who, together with the mystic, Hamza ibn Ali ibn Ahmad, was one of the first to proclaim al'Hakim to be the Incarnation of God. (The notion that the *mahdi*—whoever he might be according to whichever Muslim group—is divine, constitutes an absolute heresy for Islam; Darazi was ultimately excommunicated and executed for his distortions of the message). Strictly speaking it was al'Hakim's associate, Baha al'Din who led the group after al'Hakim's disappearance. The *Muwahiddin* consider themselves bearers of the core of the Muslim message, but Muslims don't regard them as Muslim, since they do not maintain the Five Pillars as a guide to spiritual and/or everyday life and because of their notion of a divine *mahdi*. Politically speaking, having been granted autonomy by the League of Nations in 1921 they were shortly thereafter swallowed up by the French Mandatory power and never again regained autonomy. Today they total somewhere between 350,000 and 600,000, (depending upon whose count), dwelling mostly in Lebanon in the vicinity of Mount Hermon; there are also communities in Syria and Northern Israel and also about 75,000 living in Jordan.

[35] Saladin is arguably the most famous Kurd in history. The Kurds are yet another group whose definition and aspirations must be included in an understanding of the tangled web of the Middle East. For a brief discussion of them, see below, 112 and fnn 188, 189.

[36] In fact, the sack of Jerusalem by the Khwarizmian nomads was fol-

lowed by one of the most disastrous of battles for Christian Crusaders in the course of all of the Crusades: the Battle of Formie, near Gaza, in which Templars, Hospitaliers and Teutonic Knights and their Syrian and Bedouin allies were cut to ribbons by the Mamluk Sultan Baybar's forces of Egyptians supplemented by Khwarizmians.

[37] To an already extant railway line from Istanbul to Damascus Abdul Hamid added a section connecting Damascus to Madina—which is as far as the project got by the time World War I intervened to force its discontinuance.

[38] The insurgents came to be known as the "Young Turks."

Chapter 5

Aspirations: Nationalism Among the Arabs

That the range of confusing and conflicting definitions cuts across complicated, confusing and conflicting religious and political lines should be clear at this point. But the complexities cut across the issues of ethnicity and nationalism as well, particularly as we turn our focus from the category of definitions and interferences to that of aspirations. This last word, as it applies to the history of the region in the last two and a half centuries or so, refers primarily to nationalist aspirations, on the part of various groups among the Arab and non-Arab Muslim and Arab Christian peoples as well as among the (primarily but not exclusively non-Arab) Jews. The first effort toward fulfilling what might be called Arab Nationalist aspirations came in the early nineteenth century, but drew on a religious issue for some of its early strength and ultimately foundered in large part on an ethnic issue.

I am referring to the efforts of Mehmet and Ibrahim Ali to

create a pan-Arab state between about 1805 and 1848. Mehmet was an Albanian Ottoman of putative Arab descent—albeit who spoke no Arabic—and who served under the Ottomans as an army officer against Napoleon. It was Napoleon, we may recall, who effected the final demise of the Hospitalier Knights and in 1798 mounted the first European invasion of the Middle East since the Crusades.

The reported success of Napoleon's invasion re-enforced the growing European Christian notion that had gradually evolved from the time of the Battle of Lepanto in 1571 through the failed Ottoman siege of Vienna in 1683 and the subsequent erosion of Ottoman power in Hungary and central Europe, that the Muslim foe was not nearly as fierce as had once been the case. In retrospect it set the stage not only for an expansion of archaeological interest in the Near East (one recalls that it was Napoleon's expedition that yielded the Rosetta Stone which led to the decipherment of Egyptian Hieroglyphs by 1820) but for the effort to colonize it.

Conversely, the reshaped forces that would eventually oppose such colonization also began their development in the context of Napoleon's invasion. When Napoleon eventually departed, Mehmet decided that, rather than continuing to answer to a weak administration in far-away Istanbul, he might establish himself as an independent ruler. He sought to break up the old feudal structure not only in Egypt but in Syria and to unify that entire region under his command as an Arab state. That state would not only be separate from the shrinking Ottoman Turkish state, but use the extensive cultivation of cotton in Egypt to develop closer economic ties with Christian Europe, in particular England (Napoleon's implacable foe).

In spite of the rather profound disability of speaking virtually no Arabic (although he referred to himself as an Arab by way of his parentage), Mehmet[39] managed to initiate the unifying process, which was continued with still greater success by his son, Ibrahim—who at least spoke the language of those he was

seeking to unify. One of the keys to Mehmet's success was his astute turn south toward the *hijaz*, where he gave support to the spiritual revolution then in progress led by followers of the Hanbali scholar, Muhammad Ibn 'Abd al-Wahhab. Ibn 'Abd al-Wahhab had made a pact in 1744 with Muhammad Ibn Sa'ud, prince of the market town oasis, Dar'iya, to enforce purer Islamic doctrines than had prevailed during the previous centuries.

Specifically, the doctrines preferred by the Wahhabi movement were those that had been articulated in the early fourteenth century by Taqi al-Din Ibn Tayamiya of Damascus (d.1328), which were anti-innovational in general and opposed, in particular, to the veneration of saints (Taqi has been called the "Martin Luther of Islam") and even to excessive veneration of the Prophet Muhammad. Taqi, and Ibn 'Abd al-Wahhab in turn, were not afraid to say that *'ijma*—consensus—is not always right, or even emphatically to declare it wrong: in other words, the Wahhabi movement, as a purist movement, may be understood as a descendant not only of Taqi's teachings, but ultimately, conceptually, of the Kharajite branch of Shi'i Islam. Mehmet Ali threw his support to the Wahhabis, who in turn supported him and helped position him as a champion of independent Arab Islam after centuries of subjugation to Turkish and other rulers.

When the situation had stabilized under his control, Mehmet turned his back on the Wahhabis, ignoring their religious hopes and aspirations and indeed crushing them as a force in 1818. The same (hostile, not friendly) stance toward Wahhabism remained in place under the rule of his son, who successfully expanded this new Arab state from Egypt to the edge of the Tigris-Euphrates valley. Mehmet's motives and accomplishments were not merely political; they were cultural as well. He founded new schools and training colleges and made use of a battery of new printing presses that he imported into his state to publish some 243 books in Turkish and Arabic between 1822 and 1843.

But ultimately the state collapsed because neither Mehmet nor Ibrahim was able, in the long run, to engender a sufficiency

of enthusiasm for a unified Arab identity to compete with the familial and tribal loyalties that continued to define that part of the world so vehemently. Islam, at least at the outset of its own history, was able to offer itself in place of such loyalties, but within two generations of its birth was already being torn apart in part by tribal strife, and the echo of that issue on a more purely political front came twelve centuries later with the first failure of a politically pan-Arab movement.[40]

By the time of the demise of that movement, another means of shaping pan-Arab identity was beginning to emerge from an unexpected source. American Protestant and French Catholic missionaries arrived into Syro-Palestine and its environs by the 1830s and, through the end of the 1860s established a series of schools throughout the region.[41] Their intention was simple: if they could educate Arab Muslim children from an early age along the Christian path that such schools offered, they could in the end convert them to Christianity. Not only schools but printing presses were established.[42] The consequence of this process was twofold. First of all the number of Christian Arabs was significantly multiplied (to supplement the earlier Christian Arab communities, such as the Maronites in Lebanon.) Second of all, however, in introducing young Arabs among other things to their own language as a writing instrument and vehicle for literature, (and their own rich literary tradition), the mission schools not only created a literate community, but a yearning to further Arabic writing and literature. This in turn produced not only a revival and extension of such literature but, more broadly, an Arab cultural nationalism.

By 1860 there were 33 schools in operation—with a pupil population that included among its constituents about 20% girls—and by 1866 the Syrian Protestant College in Beirut was fully operative. By the end of the 1860s specific developments regarding specific Arab leaders were manifesting themselves. Thus Nasif Yazagi, (1800-1871), a Christian Lebanese, for instance, became a key literary figure, producing books on Arabic

grammar as well as on rhetoric and logic. His writing inspired both Christian and Muslim Arabs to think in expanding terms of Arabic language and literature. Similarly, Butrus Bustani (1819-1883), also a Christian from Lebanon, spent ten years translating the Bible into Arabic and created the first modern dictionary of the Arabic language in 1870 as well as an Arab Encyclopedia (of which he had completed six volumes by the time of his death).

Bustani also produced what may be construed as the first political journal in Syria, the *Clarion of Syria*, which, in the aftermath of the massacre of 5,000 Christian Arabs in Damascus in 1860, had as a goal to douse the flames of religious hatred that prevailed, arguing for a primacy of Arab sensibility over Muslim or Christian religious sensibility, and also preaching that knowledge is the key to ending discord among diverse religions within the Arab ambit. Bustani founded a "National School" to promote Arab thought, ideas and ideals in 1863, in which Yazagi was the principal teacher of Arabic language. Seven years later he (Bustani) began publishing another journal, *Al-Jenan*, a political and literary review which, like its predecessor journal, had as a goal to fight against religious fanaticism and to preach Arab unity and a broad-based concern for Arab national welfare.

Earlier in their careers, both Yazagi and Bustani had established a *Society of Arts and Sciences* in Beirut, together with Eli Smith and other missionaries. There were no Muslim or Druze members in the original group of about 50 members, but this was the first society in the Arab world of its kind; the first organized collective effort not based on traditional ethnic, tribal or religious considerations. Three years later, no doubt inspired by this largely Protestant effort, the *Oriental Society* was founded by the Jesuits. Both organizations disbanded around 1852, but many of the principals in both entities reorganized themselves as the *Syrian Scientific Society* five years later, with about 150 members, including Muslim and Druze as well as

Christian Arabs. By 1868 the *Syrian Scientific Society* had been officially recognized by the Ottoman authorities and extended membership to those outside Syro-Palestine, as far afield as Istanbul and Cairo.

It was in the context of the *Syrian Scientific Society* and its symbolic presence as the first outward manifestation of a collective Arab national consciousness that Ibrahim Yazagi—the son of Nasif—was inspired to write a patriotic poem speaking of an Arab resurgence and calling for an Arab insurgence against the Ottoman rulers. The poem spread by word of mouth. One might see this as the first act of purely indigenous political (as opposed to merely cultural) nationalism among Arabs.[43] The era of the poem coincided with the penultimate phase of the petering out of Ottoman leadership: Abdul Aziz (Sultan, 1861-76) was erratic and extravagant and draining the Ottoman coffers of their already-shrunken funds. His nephew, Murad V succeeded him but lasted only three months on the throne. He was in turn succeeded on 31 August 1876 by Abdul Hamid II.

Cultural nationalism had bred political nationalism in the course of the middle decades of the century. The notion of an *intifada*—a movement of "throwing off" the Turkish presence from the Arab world—was in part inspired, ironically enough, by that aspect of European nationalism become colonialism that saw the French eliminating the Turkish presence in Algeria by 1830 and in Tunisia by 1881, and the British effecting the same result in Egypt in 1882. The consequent unrest was sufficient so that shortly after his accession to the throne, Sultan Abdul Hamid II offered a new Constitution on 23 December 1876 for the inhabitants of his now-truncated realms. The Constitution included full rights for the Arab peoples under his governance with respect to cultural autonomy. The following year, the Ottomans found themselves buried in a war with Russia that ended in 1878 with the Treaty of Berlin, which complication gave Abdul Hamid II the excuse to eliminate the constitution that he had trumpeted two years earlier.

Notes

[39] "Mehmet" is, incidentally, a Turkish version of the Arabic-language name, Muhammad.

[40] If one considers the matter of "oriental" carpets, so diverse in style, with each style derived from a particular tribal group, and then one further understands that each of those tribal groups possesses fierce familial loyalties and cultural, social and political identities that distinguish them emphatically from other tribes, one begins to understand how profound the issue of tribal, as opposed to national or broadly ethnic political thinking is.

[41] To be precise, the first American Protestant missionaries, ahead of the main chronological curve, were Levi Parsons and Pliny Fisk, dispatched from Boston in 1819 by the American Board of Commissioners for Foreign Missions. Parsons arrived and stayed briefly in Jerusalem in 1821, primarily distributing Bibles, but died the following year on a journey to Alexandria, Egypt—at not yet 30 years of Age. Fisk focused more on language studies, so that he could preach, and began to do so in 1825—but died on October 23rd of that year, on a trip to Beirut, at age 33.

[42] For example, the printing press set up by the American Eli Smith as early as 1827.

[43] One recalls that Mehmet Ali was an Albanian, and thus not indigenous to the region, although his ancestry was presumably from the 'arav.

Chapter 6

Aspirations: Jewish Nationalism

In the aftermath of Abdul Hamid II's new Constitution—which, since he never put it into force, failed to fulfill its promises of cultural and linguistic respect for the Arabs, among other things—the Arab leadership inevitably became more politicized. Meanwhile, the Jews were in the midst of shaping their own nationalist aspirations. Indeed Jewish hopes were, in retrospect, moving on a course that made collision with at least part of Arab aspirations almost inevitable.

In the aftermath of the very industrial and political revolutions that would so radically reshape western and central Europe between the 1750s and the end of the eighteenth century (and which would thrust Christendom ahead of the *Dar al-Islam* in technological, political and cultural development over the following two hundred years) and in part following the era of intra-Christian (Protestant Reformation) crisis and questioning of the sixteenth century, and the secularizing movements as-

sociated with Descartes, Spinoza, Leibnitz, Bacon and others in the seventeenth, the western and central European world began to open up for the Jews. From the "Jew Bill" in England in 1753;[44] to the decrees of Hapsburg Emperor Joseph II in 1764 granting a range of socio-economic rights to "the Jewish nation" and subsequent decrees permitting Jewish participation in the Hapsburg armies and in medicine and law throughout the Hapsburg domains in the 1780s; to the decree of the new French government on September 28, 1791 that recognized Jews as fully French; to the granting of a new range of socio-economic rights to the Jews of Prussia in 1812—over the course of four decades, Emancipation began to shift Jews from the periphery toward the center of European cultural, social, economic and eventually even political life.[45]

Concomitant with and following this era was the double development of European Romanticism—which saw a powerful, even mysterious, certainly emotion-governed, identity relationship between individuals and the land in which they (and their ancestors) were born, lived and died, the language that they spoke, the literature and folk songs of which that language is the key instrument, the visual art and dances that are endemic to the land and its inhabitants—and European Nationalism. The latter supplemented the former not only in articulating the relationship between a people and its land in political terms, but in inspiring a desire to expand into and/or reclaim more land, often thought of as having been wrested from one's ancestors at some distant or more recent time in the past. That movement, taking shape between about 1780 and 1850, would yield the fragmentation of the Hapsburg Empire, the urge to spread out on the part of the Prussians and the conviction on the part of the English that a world-encircling British Empire was divinely ordained and part of their morally superior "White Man's Burden."

Among the many groups inspired along Nationalist lines were the Italians, whose land had, virtually since the late fifth

century and the collapse of the Western Roman Empire, been a crazy quilt of city-states and kingdoms in constant conflict and kaleidoscopically shifting alliances or dis-alliances with each other. The articulator of the notion that Italy could and should become re-united and that ultimately it could re-claim the imperial glory that belonged to Rome in antiquity was Giuseppe Mazzini. He and his discussion of the *risorgimento* in turn inspired a German Jewish writer, Moses Hess, to pen the work *Rome and Jerusalem* in 1862. With that treatise, Hess might be said to have given birth to Jewish nationalism in the modern European sense just described.

Meanwhile, European attitudes toward Jews were moving steadily backwards from where they had been by the end of the previous century—away from acceptance toward new bases for intolerance. Wilhelm Marr was quickly creating the terminology of modern political anti-Semitism referred to above (2, 34) and with it, the marginalizing racialization of Jews, in 1879. Other politicians and journalists were picking up that idea. An anti-Semitic professor at Berlin University—Eugen Duehring—published a book in 1881 entitled *The Jewish Question as a Racial, Moral and Cultural Question*, inspired by and extending Marr's political ideas.[46]

In France—regarded since 1791 as the paragon of tolerance and secular modernity in Europe where Jews were concerned—the journalist Edouard Drumont, publisher of a feuilleton, *La Libre Parole* ("Free Speech") authored a book that appeared in 1886, called *La France Juive* (*Jewish France*). In it he warned his fellow Frenchmen of the powerful threat to their country: its take-over by Jews and Jewish influences. The world in general and Jews in particular were shocked not only by the appearance of the book but by its embrace by the French readership.

Between the time of Marr's coinage and Drumont's publication and in the aftermath of the pogroms of Russian Jews sponsored by the Tsarist regime after the assassination of Alexander II in 1881, two developments of particular interest for this

discussion are observable. First, literary leaders like Mendele Mocher Seforim and after him, Y.L. Peretz and then Shalom Aleichem—the European Jewish equivalent of Nasif Yazagi and Butrus Bustani—were engaged in reviving the Hebrew language as a functional profane literary instrument (as opposed to one limited to prayer and sacred scholarship) that would ultimately yield Hebrew as an everyday spoken street instrument. The culmination of this process in pure linguistic terms would be the work accomplished by Eliezer Ben-Yehudah to organize a modern Hebrew language dictionary—and the effort he and his wife made to bring up their children as the first native speakers of Hebrew since mid-antiquity.

Second, a Jewish physician by the name of Leo Pinsker led what was a growing discussion of the problem of anti-Semitism in his 1882 work *Auto-Emanzipation (Self-Emancipation)*. Pinsker was the first among several thinkers to refer to anti-Semitism as an incurable disease process. The spreading ugliness of that disease seemed confirmed in the next decade, when in so-called-liberal France a Jewish army captain was framed by his commanding officers and charged with having engaged more than twenty years earlier in espionage. The French army, still smarting a generation after its defeat by the Prussians in the Franco-Prussian War of 1870-71, and unwilling to admit that its armaments had been archaic and those of the Prussians mod-ern, still seeking a scapegoat to account for its defeat, found it in the Jew, Alfred Dreyfus, who was accused of having passed secrets to the enemy at that time.

More significant, perhaps, than the framing of Dreyfus by the conservative army or than the fanning of flames of anti-Semitism by the Catholic Church and by members of the French Press, such as Drumont—so that not Dreyfus, but "Dreyfus the Jew," was excoriated—was the vociferous embrace of this propaganda by the French masses. The Dreyfus trial became *l'Affaire Dreyfus*, and precisely a century after Emancipation, French Jews found

themselves subject to the intense heat of unprecedented hostility from their Catholic neighbors.

Among those dispatched from other lands to report on the trial, who were struck by this turn of events, was a Jewish reporter for the *Neue Freie Press* in Vienna by the name of Theodore Herzl. Herzl was an upper middleclass, highly assimilated Jew who grew up thinking of himself as an Austrian who happened, by descent and cultural continuity, to be Jewish—rather than as a Jew living in Austro-Hungary or, for that matter, a Hungarian in Austro-Hungary. In 1882 he read with shock Eugen Duehring's anti-Semitic volume.[47] That shock marked the beginning of a turning point in his life and his thinking that completed its first twist the following year. Herzl was a member of an exclusive student fencing fraternity, *Albia*, which helped sponsor festivities on March 5, 1883 honoring Richard Wagner's memory, several weeks after the composer's death. But when those festivities became an extended anti-Semitic outburst (Wagner himself had been virulently anti-Semitic), and that outburst included among its protagonists vociferous members of *Albia*—close friends, or so Herzl had thought—he not only withdrew from the fraternity, but he became suddenly more conscious both of himself *as* a Jew and suddenly more intensely aware of "the Jewish Problem."

Within the following decade, Herzl wrote a popular play, *The New Ghetto* (1894), among other works. In the play he represented even assimilated Jews (like himself) as caged in an invisible ghetto both by their own mentality and by the mentality of their secular Christian neighbors. In that play the hero, a Jewish physician, plays what may easily be construed as the role of a secular messiah to his Jewish neighbors—and one recognizes in him Herzl's self-image.

Arriving into the City of Light in 1891 as the Paris correspondent of the *Neue Freie Press* Herzl became fairly quickly aware of the Drumont-led anti-Semitism rampant in the French capital. Thus when the playwright–journalist covered *l'Affaire Dreyfus* in 1894, all of these mental paths converged. The result

was a pamphlet that he wrote in a white heat, and which was actually published in 1896: *Der Judenstaat—The Jewish State.* In it, he offered his radical solution to the Jewish problem: the creation of an independent Jewish polity. Herzl's contention was that, given an opportunity to develop as an autonomous entity with its own economy, no longer as a minority of "guests" "hosted" by one Christian state or another, Jews would be able for the first time in nearly two millennia to stand on equal ground with their Christian neighbors.

They would be dealing government to government with those neighbors, be it economically or be it politically, militarily or otherwise. Moreover, the departure of Jews from Christian communities would eliminate Jews as competitors for slots in the socio-economic infrastructure, undercutting the antagonism toward Jews which, he argued, derived from that competition and its uneven playing surface. "There will be an inner migration of Christian citizens into the positions relinquished by Jews," he wrote. His plan was not limited to theoretical thinking; he suggested practical ways in which the plan that he conceived could be implemented. Thus the entire project would be placed in the hands of a corporation formed to fulfill this mission. A "Jewish Company" would define Jews in the legal sense, "to conduct economic activities," and a "Society of Jews" would "deal with all but property rights" and thus function on behalf of the Jews as a "moral person." "The Jewish Company will be the liquidating agent for the business interests of departing Jews, and will organize trade and commerce in the new country... The Society of Jews will treat with the present authorities in the land, under the sponsorship of the European powers, if they prove friendly to the plan."[48]

"We shall not dwell in mud huts; we shall build new, more beautiful and more modern houses, and possess them in safety. We shall not lose our acquired possessions; we shall realize them. We shall surrender our well-earned rights for better ones.[49] We shall relinquish none of our cherished customs; we shall find

them again... The very creation of the Jewish State would be beneficial to neighboring lands, since the cultivation of a strip of land increases the value of its surrounding districts."[50] Furthermore, "anti-Semitism will cease at once and everywhere... a wondrous breed of Jews will spring up from the earth... The world will be liberated by our freedom, enriched by our wealth, magnified by our greatness. And whatever we attempt there for our own benefit will redound mightily and beneficially to the good of all mankind."[51]

In the passages from which I have quoted there are at least four issues that might interest us. The first is his absolute conviction that the Christian states of Europe will applaud and assist with this plan; concomitantly, the second is that anti-Semitism will cease. It is interesting to note that there was Christian interest, particularly among the groups called the Restorationists, in America, in seeing Jewish "exiles" ingathered into the Holy Land. This group sent emissaries to Palestine in the 1840s through 1860s to teach indigenous and incoming Jews to farm.[52] This effort may be seen as somewhat parallel to the American religious interest in creating schools throughout the Middle East with the ultimate goal of converting Arab Muslims (as discussed in the previous chapter). For the conviction of the Restorationists was that, ultimately the ingathered Jews would see the light of Christianity and turn to it.

The third aspect of Herzl's plan of particular interest to our discussion—apropos of Arab Muslims—is his certainty that the new State will benefit its neighbors, who might be expected to embrace it as much as the Europeans will; indeed the whole world will benefit. The fourth issue has two elements. The first is that he seems to assume that the land which will be devoted to the new state will be previously uncultivated, concerning which none of the indigenous neighbors will have a prior claim; second, that in fact the two places he discusses as possibilities are Palestine and Argentina, although he prefers Palestine because it "is our unforgettable historic homeland,"

and while he suggests that "the holy places of Christendom could be placed under some sort of international extraterritoriality," Islam's concerns or those of the Arab world in general (to the extent that such a settlement specifically in Palestine was countenanced) are nowhere to be found in his narrative. This is hardly surprising: he is a child of his Victorian-Edwardian era and its Eurocentric prejudices.

Herzl's modestly bold proposal caught fire more quickly than his friends (most of whom thought that the idea was over the edge) expected: by August, 1897, the First Zionist Congress, as it was called, was taking place in Basel, Switzerland with 205 delegates from all over the world in attendance. Between that year and the year of Herzl's sudden death at the age of 44 in 1904, a succession of Zionist congresses met and with them a growing array of questions with regard to how to concretize the theoretical plan set forth by Herzl in business-report detail in his 1896 treatise and in more poetic form in his work, *Alt-Neu Land* (Old–New Land), of 1902.

Herzl became increasingly concerned about the future of Eastern European Jewry during this period. The unrelenting progress of pogroms in the Tsarist Russia of the Romanovs as the nineteenth century spilled into the twentieth and his personal visit to some of the communities in the East pushed him to emphasize the importance of the Zionist idea as offering salvation for a beleaguered people. Thus his vision focused on physical survival and sought a political means to effect that survival—he was willing to negotiate with almost any relevant power.[53]

By contrast, there emerged Zionist leaders like Ahad Ha'Am (the pen name—meaning "one of the people"—of Ukrainian-born Jewish writer Asher Ginzberg) who, coming out of the Eastern European pogrom-ridden milieu, argued that no threat of physical extermination had yet succeeded in destroying the Jews, and that what was needed was, on the contrary, a key to spiritual survival. For those like Ahad Ha'Am, the Zionist idea offered a means of spiritual rejuvenation, not physical salvation.

This meant focussing itself on Eretz Yisrael and no other place. While a concomitant of that was the continued goal of fulfilling specifically Eretz Yisrael-directed national aspirations, those aspirations did not necessarily require full political fulfillment. In other words, spiritually-based *nation*hood, perhaps under Ottoman governance, not politically-based independent *state*hood.

A subset of the spiritual side of Zionism was *cultural* Zionism. The most obvious concrete manifestation of this was the decision to establish an arts school in Jerusalem that opened under the directorship of Boris Schatz in 1906. Schatz had been court painter and sculptor to the Bulgarian King Ferdinand III at a time when, in the early 1890s, having established its independence from the Ottoman Empire, Bulgaria was seeking to define its identity along the lines of Romantic Nationalism that had been percolating all over Europe for the previous century. Schatz had been a key figure in synthesizing different visual ideas in order to create what could be recognized as a distinctive Bulgarian national art.

With the support of the Zionist leadership and important Jewish figures such as the philosopher and theologian Martin Buber, Schatz set out to create a Jewish National visual art at the Jerusalem academy and museum named for Bezalel, the ancient Israelite artisan whose efforts at devising the Tabernacle in the Sinai wilderness are described at the end of the Book of Exodus. Bezalel arts and crafts, as they evolved during the next twenty-five years, may be understood in both aesthetic and political terms.

The use of specific symbols was promoted. Thus, for example the image of the rising sun appears again and again to suggest renascent Jewish nationalism. The recently internationally-recognized six-pointed star—made international and specifically "Jewish" by its appearance in 1897 on the cover of Herzl's publication *Die Welt* (*The World*)—as a Star or Shield of *David* suggested a connection back to ancient Israel at the Davidic beginning of its Golden Age. The older and more familiar symbol found for

centuries in Jewish art, the seven-branched candelabrum, offered a doubly relevant implication. Not only does it symbolize the ancient Temple in Jerusalem. In its seven-ness, it offers connotations of that moment at the foot of Mount Sinai—between servitude and freedom, Egypt and the Promised Land—of the Covenant between God and the Israelites. That Covenant insisted, among the other commandments, that the Israelites must keep the *seventh* day holy.

So, too, the subject matter of Bezalel art. Individuals either from the heroic Hebrew-Israelite-Judaean past, such as Abraham, Moses, David or Judah the Maccabee; or heroic figures from the present, such as Theodore Herzl, were endemic to the vocabulary of Bezalel art. These might be synthesized, as when the image of Moses in a woodcut by Ephraim Lilien, one of the school's master-teachers, offered Herzl's familiar black-bearded face as the image of the leader of the Israelites out of slavery. Or landscapes, both the divinely-wrought hills, rocks, trees and wildernesses of Palestine or the man-made buildings, the familiar dome-on-cube architecture and its variants, became stereotypical in Bezalel imagery.

At this time in Europe various arts and crafts movements were elevating the importance of objects beside drawings, paintings and sculptures to status as art: an ashtray could be as invested with aesthetic significance as a canvas. Variously, the *art nouveau* and *jugendstil* movements of France, Belgium, Germany and Austria were championing the swirling curlicues and repeating geometric forms coupled with vegetal and floral elements found in Arabo-Islamic art—coining the term "arabesque," in fact, to describe this stylistic proclivity. Schatz and Bezalel pushed both in the arts and crafts direction and in the stylistic direction of the Arabo-Islamic world, to further underscore the Near Eastern origins of Jewish nationalist identity.

Even the substance of much of Bezalel art and craft was connected to The Land. Thus the objects produced in the school frequently were shaped with materials such as olive wood from

the hills of Galilee, stones and rocks from the Negev Desert, copper and silver metals associated with the mines of King Solomon in that heroic Israelite age of the distant past. The goal of Bezalel art and craft was to form a concomitant of the spiritual side of Zionism that insistently connected the Jewish present and revived future both to the land of Israel and to its pre-diasporatic past.

In contrast to the palestinocentrism that was endemic to spiritual and cultural Zionism, Herzl as a political pragmatist was prepared, in 1903, to accept an offer made by the British to reserve Uganda as a haven for the Jewish people, so desperate was he to find a place of refuge (the offer was in any case shortly withdrawn due to the protests against the idea on the part of the British public). For that very year was also marked by the most horrifying of the pogroms in Russian history, those at Kishinev. What marked these as particularly painful was that the pre-pogrom environment had been one of denouement between the Jewish and non-Jewish communities, based in part on the higher level of secular education and therefore capacity for intellectual interchange in Kishinev than had been true elsewhere. The pogroms in Kishinev cemented the sense that Herzl and others had that anti-Semitism was a disease with no hope of a cure anywhere in the Diaspora. But Ahad Ha'Am and others were horrified at the very idea of looking anywhere but *Eretz Yisrael* for a Jewish homeland.

The sense of the Diaspora as both hopeless with regard to a future and eminently forgettable because of fifteen centuries of past experiences would have implications for the terminology of the Zionist movement—so that once again we have returned to the realm of defining terms. Thus the Jewish State in the end would not be called *Juda* (in German, which in English would translate as something like "Jewland"), but rather *Israel*. This was a distinctively ideological, and not a casual or accidental decision: it marked the desire to leapfrog backward past the diasporatic centuries of exile toward that period when

the peoplehood of Judaism was in its golden age under Kings David and Solomon as the unified Kingdom of Israel.

Similarly, as the Zionist movement developed between the era of Herzl and statehood—and in the first decades after statehood—it thought of and sought to shape a "new man." Building on the notion of "muscular Judaism" that was taking shape in late nineteenth and early twentieth century Central Europe and subsequently borrowing, ironically enough, imagery spawned by the new Soviet State, Weimar Germany and Fascist Italy in the 1920s, right-wing Zionist leaders such as Ze'ev Jabotinsky spoke of "a new psychological race of Jew." There is irony here in the adoption—albeit adaptation—of an ethno-racial category for "Jew" that Wilhelm Marr had introduced into European discourse.[54] As a practical matter, the word "Jew" was eschewed by the Jabotinsky-ites as far as possible in favor the term "Hebrew." "Jew" was by definition being re-defined as an inwardly-focused, bent-over, easily bullied, pale, urbanized, long-suffering victim of the Diaspora; "Hebrew" was intended to refer to a proud, handsome, athletic, farm-comfortable, suntanned rural throwback and step-forward to pre- and post-diasporatic life.

There were also Jewish leaders who not only ignored the Zionist idea but who actively opposed it. It is fair to say that the biggest enemies of Zionism in its infancy were Jews. There were the Socialists and the Marxists who saw a Jewish nationalist movement as by definition antithetical to the universalist principles nuanced with regard to socio-economics espoused by the Socialist and Marxist movements in which so many Jews had become active. These Jews believed that the eradication of socio-economic divisions in the world was the key to ending anti-Semitism; that the liberation of all peoples would encompass the final Emancipation of the Jews. *Social* Zionism offered a response to that concern, which didn't mean that all those voicing that concern were satisfied with such a response.

Ultra-Orthodox rabbis saw the movement as a heresy—also perhaps fearing that it would undercut their authority as com-

munity leaders. Many regarded it as offering a secularizing af-
front to the truths of religious Judaism. More profoundly they
argued that it contravened the messianic idea as it had been
spelled out by God for Judaism; to attempt to lead the Jews out
of the Exile and back to the Holy Land before the advent of a
Divinely-ordained Messiah was construed as sacrilege. But there
also emerged Orthodox rabbis, like Abraham Isaac Kook, who
shaped *religious* Zionism. He argued that since the messianic
idea in Judaism is notoriously vague, there was no reason not
to embrace Zionism, for it could be God's plan that we be the
instruments of our own Redemption; that the messianic idea
was being fulfilled and not contradicted by Zionism.

On the other hand were those Reform Jewish leaders who
feared that Zionism would compromise the societal gains that
Emancipation had provided for Jews. One can certainly see
this in the German Jewish community which had given birth
to Reform Judaism back in 1810-11, but one sees it elsewhere
as well. In England, for example, one of the most interesting
instances of the Jewish Zionist-versus-anti-Zionist dynamic is
the debate between two Jewish ministers in the government,
Herbert Samuel (a Zionist) and his cousin Edwin Montagu (an
anti-Zionist).

The first, who became the first British High Commissioner in
Palestine, would be instrumental in furthering the sentiment that
would lead to the "Balfour Declaration" in 1917;[55] the second,
as Minister of Munitions and subsequently Secretary of State for
India, would fight against that sentiment. Montagu's words on
the subject (in a letter to Prime Minister David Lloyd-George)
are instructive of the concerns of many secular and Liberal
(Reform) Jews of that era:

> The country for which I have worked ever since I left the
> University—England—the country for which my family have
> fought tells me that my national home, if I desire to go there,
> therefore my natural home, is Palestine.

His concern as one who saw himself as a British Jew rather than a Jew residing in Britain was that the Zionist movement would encourage anti-Semites both to see Jews as not really British after all and to push for their emigration—in effect, their expulsion from Britain.

The hostility to Zionism on various Jewish fronts is nowhere more concretely apparent than in this: that Herzl had intended for the First Zionist Congress to take place in Munich in August 1897, but at the eleventh hour he needed to switch the location to Basel, Switzerland due to the intractable opposition of Germany's rabbis to the Zionist movement. There is particular irony, given subsequent history, both in Herzl's intention to center the nascent Zionist movement in Germany and in the steadfastness with which the German rabbinate articulated its opposition to that intention as something inconsistent with the sensibility that Jews ought "to serve the fatherland to which they belong with utmost devotion and to further its national interests with all their hearts and strength."[56]

Notes

[44] The proposed bill actually failed at that time; too many British Christians were not yet ready to accord equal civil status to their Jewish neighbors. But this first raising of the issue set the stage for later Emancipation success.

[45] Note that the Hapsburg decree refers to the Jews as a nation, whereas the French edict is based on an understanding of Judaism as a religion. As discussed above, that definitional problem has yet to be solved in our own time.

[46] Duehring was a German socialist whose book, *The Jewish Problem as a Problem of Race, Morals and Culture*, published the previous year, espoused a biological view of the world, in which the German/Nordic "type" was superior to all others, and the Jews—their depravity an innate function of their biology—capable of any and every sin and crime, represented a threat to the future of that race. He argued that Prussia must be purified of its Jews, by racial war, if necessary. At the very least and as a start, laws needed to be passed that would eliminate Jewish influence in education, the press, finance and business.

[47] Herzl was actually born in Budapest and only moved with his family to Vienna in 1883, when he was 18 years old. There he became a lawyer to satisfy his parents' concern (and perhaps his own) that he have a financially viable profession, but he identified as an Austrian not a Hungarian (and not per se, as a Jew, which, in the unassimilated corners of the Austro-Hungarian, Hapsburg world, would have been separate from either Austrian or Hungarian identities). He aspired to success as a playwright and journalist, rather than as a lawyer, writing in German, (again, rather than in Hungarian) since that language was the primary language of both the Austro-Hungarian Empire and most of Middle Europe.

[48] See Theodore Herzl, *The Jewish State*, of which there is any number of English-language editions. I am quoting from the translation by Sylvie D'Avigdor used in Arthur Hertzberg's *The Zionist Idea*.

[49] He is referring to the hard-fought gains of Emancipation, according to which, in most central and western European countries Jews had achieved a degree of theoretical socio-economic, cultural and political parity with their Christian neighbors by the late nineteenth century—although it must be remembered that it was the shock of the Dreyfus Affair and what it meant for the actual insufficiency of that achievement that prompted Herzl to write his pamphlet.

[50] This last statement is as close as Herzl gets to actually acknowledging the presence of Arabs and others in the area where he envisions his State. He is very much a European, a child of his time, who views any and

every imposition of Europeanism on any and all indigenous populations as drawback-resistant and positive. See my further comments below.

[51] I have not quoted all of these passages in the order in which Herzl offered them. His comment about "mud huts," etc., comes from chapter one and the references to the work of the Society and the Company as well as that regarding "benefits to neighboring lands" from chapter two of his pamphlet.

[52] A further aspect of this American Christian interest in shaping the Middle East is reflected in the number of Civil War veterans who went to Egypt in the late 1860s and 1870s to train soldiers. This training program soon became a program of teaching reading and in turn offering broader education that would include civic values and shape nationalism and patriotism—with obvious political implications for the Ottoman Empire's waning ability to control its Arab provinces. See Michael Oren's excellent book, *Power, Faith and Fantasy: America in the Middle East, 1776 to the Present*. On the other hand, American policy with regard to the Ottomans between about 1850 and World War I turns out to have been largely based on the briefings provided to our State Department by several key figures among the many, mainly Congregationalist, missionaries active throughout Ottoman territory during this period. Watch for the discussion of this in the not-yet-published Georgetown University Liberal Studies PhD dissertation by Elizabeth Worth Shelton, *Setting the Stage: Nineteenth-Century American Protestant Missionaries in Turkey and Their Influence on American Foreign Policy, 1840-90*.

[53] For a brief summary of this, see Howard Morley Sachar's *The Course of Modern Jewish History*, chapters 9, 10 and 13.

[54] See above, 2, 34

[55] See below, 88, regarding the "Balfour Declaration."

[56] This phrase is quoted from a letter of protest written by a handful of German rabbis at the announcement of the impending conference. The entire text may be found in the Central Zionist Archives, 4 Zalman Shazar St, Jerusalem.

Chapter 7

*Aspirations, Interferences and Conflicts
into the Twentieth Century*

Considering the same issue that exercised Montagu, Herzl arrived at the opposite sort of conclusion. He had reasoned that anti-Semites would ally themselves with the Zionist idea and help impel its success for the very reason that Montagu feared it. For Herzl saw getting Jews out of Europe both as undercutting the negative consequences of economic competition between Jews and their Christian neighbors and as assuring the latter that the Jews who remained behind were unequivocally French or German or British. Herzl was also willing to compromise with his plan of Palestine as the Zionist goal, as I have noted above. His turn toward Uganda was also in part fueled by his sense of how impossible it would be to reclaim part of Palestine for the Jews.

Ottoman history had moved miles from the era of Joseph HaNassi and Suleiman the Magnificent. Although there had been a continuous Jewish presence in Palestine since antiquity, it had

been a small one.[57] Herzl's audience with Sultan Abdul Hamid II to seek permission to establish a semi-autonomous Jewish polity within the still far-flung Ottoman Empire (as Joseph HaNassi had once done) had yielded little by way of a clear or concrete result.

This was the same Abdul Hamid II who (to repeat) had issued a new constitution to his constituents in 1876, offering his Arab citizens a degree of cultural and linguistic identity, but who failed in most ways to live up to that promise. This was the same Abdul Hamid II who had tried to use religion as a rallying point to convince his Arab subjects to embrace rather than reject him as the Caliph of Islam (rather than seeing him as the Ottoman Sultan); who substantiated his claim to the Caliphate by repairing and embellishing mosques in Makka, Madina and Jerusalem—and who even appointed a Syrian Arab, Izzat Pasha al'Abad as his Second Secretary.

This was the same Abdul Hamid II who established a good relationship with the Prussians and their Kaiser Wilhelm II, who among other things helped reform the Sultan's military academies. The new officers being trained in modern methods of warfare and strategy included a handful of Arabs along with a majority of Turks. But when that new officers' corps rose up and, in 1908, succeeded in deposing Abdul Hamid II—this was the "Young Turks" rebellion—the Turkish officers who dominated it quickly turned their backs on their Arab brethren.

Thus once again the aspiration for Arab political fulfillment or even significant participation was thwarted. The consequence of this was the meeting that took place five years later—in July, 1913, in Paris—of the First Arab National Congress. In other words, the Arab cultural-and-military-become-political leadership finally acted on its own to push the movement of Arab Political Nationalism forward. So, too, the culmination of this movement may be seen to have paralleled the Jewish National Movement in approximate time and in organizing itself *away* from the Middle East where it was nonetheless rooted.

Even more so than in the Jewish Nationalist movement, the

Arab Nationalist movement was fraught with questions of self-definition in three different ways. First because of the delicate (or indelicate) balance between the sense of the convening Arabs as Muslims and as Arabs; second because of long-standing ethnic issues dividing communities within communities (such as the long-standing hostility between the Qais and Yamani groups dating from the eighth century in the far-away 'arav which continued into the twentieth century in the Palestine to which both groups had migrated); and third because of political antagonisms that were already surfacing at that time (many of which survive to this day).

The interweave of Arabic with Islamic issues may be seen once again in the rebirth of the Wahhabi purist movement at around this time in the context of religious support rendered to 'Abd al-'Azaz Ibn Sa'ud in his efforts to expand his base of power by annexing Hasa in 1913. In the aftermath of World War I he would annex Jabal Shammar in 1921 and the *hijaz* in 1924-5, all of which actions reshaped the majority of the peninsula as a new kingdom, the Kingdom of Saudi Arabia, by 1932. The family of the Sharif Hussain, dispossessed of its power in that region sought a new seat of power elsewhere. The British provided that seat in the central portion of the zone that came under their control after World War I.[58]

One of the significant definitional distinctions that ought to be offered here is this: Jewish nationalism, as I have intimated, was modeled on various other forms of European nationalism, in the sense of possessing a certain focus. Italian nationalism, German nationalism, French nationalism, Bulgarian nationalism, Serbian nationalism share the property of focusing on a particular piece of territory and its concomitants of identity for the Italian, German, French, Bulgarian, and Serbian peoples, in spite of any number of disagreements by their respective constituents as to how most efficiently to effect that identity. The ideology of Jewish nationalism was similar to these other European forms, as it evolved in Europe in the last third of the nineteenth century.

By contrast, nationalism among the Arabs never coalesced in that sort of a focused manner. All Arabs might possess nationalist aspirations, but they were—at that time and continuing to this day—rarely focused on a vision of identity for "the Arab people" or "the Arab nation." Recognizing this may help us understand how the history of Arab nationalism—or, better stated, nationalism among Arabs—has been consistently undercut by the other religious, cultural, ethnic and political aspirations that are part of this discussion.

On the other hand, although Jewish nationalism was inspired by and conceptualized by a European mindset, it is significantly different in three obvious ways that are relevant to its perception by the Arabs. One, the nationalist sentiment that became Zionism and focused on *Eretz Yisrael*/Palestine came from no single place: the arrival of Jews from Europe cannot be simply compared to the arrival of the French or the British or Americans as missionaries or political colonialists. Those Jews who arrived, in arriving from diverse locations, were not seeking to *expand* the colonial *imperium* of their homeland as the French and British and other European nationalist expansionists were. They were seeking to *reconnect* to what they understood to be their historic homeland. Two, in an increasing number of cases, as time went on, there was no particular place, and often no place at all to which such Jews could *go* if they left Palestine, unlike the Europeans who, if they left, simply went back to their own countries. There was no "their own country" elsewhere for the Jews, per se. And three, even before the turn from the nineteenth to the twentieth century, a large number of those Jews came not from Europe but from areas of the Middle East and North Africa.[59] Thus the discussion by Palestinian Arabs and others, at various times, of an *intifada* of the Jews from Palestine modeled on that against the Turks or the British, fails as a historical model, as I shall repeat later on.[60]

But I run ahead of myself. The Jewish nationalist hopes and the Arab nationalist hopes—the one shaped by a European

consciousness and focused on an area of the Ottoman Empire between Syria and the 'arav, between the Mediterranean and the eastern reaches of Palestine; the other culminating its shape in Europe but framed by a Near Eastern Arab consciousness and focused on an area more or less from Egypt to Persia and from Turkey to the Yaman, but without clarity as to how that vast region would or should be reconfigured—might either have met and achieved some sort of rapprochement or they might have simply collided, left alone by outsiders. But outside interference was unavoidable.

And since the various involvements from without (i.e., the Prussians, the British, the French—for starters) had their own agendas, it was *inevitable* that the Arabs and Jews would collide *without* rapprochement. The collision interwove the collision of European interests that led up to and exploded into World War I. Put otherwise, a new round of the Crusades was beginning, albeit under a more overtly economic and political banner, with religion hidden beneath the surface, as opposed to the medieval expression which bears the imprint in its very name ("crusade" after all refers to taking up the Cross) of religious intention even as politics and economics were its covert engines.

To recapitulate a layered historical datum: Abdul Hamid II invited the Prussian presence into his realms to accomplish three tasks for him. One, the reforming of his military machine; two, the building of railroads between Istanbul and both the Persian Gulf and Makka. In other words, in order to assert that he was not only the Sultan of a polity called the Ottoman Empire, but the Caliph and thus key leader of the Arabo-Islamic world, it was important that he assert a more workable connection between his political capital and the spiritual capital of the Empire. And as a practical matter, a railroad system would also allow more efficient troop movement from the capital to the gulf on the one hand and to the *hijaz* on the other. The third aspect of the Prussian role was to jumpstart the failing Ottoman economy and replenish the dwindling contents of the imperial coffers.

We have seen that one of the most significant—if unintend-ed—consequences of the Ottoman military reform program was the overthrow of the Sultan who put those reforms in motion. As for the railroad system, it was never completed, and it is probably fair to say that the project of replenishing the coffers moved forward but not as far as perhaps it might have had other issues not intervened. The other issues were the British and the French who, we recall, had been swallowing up bits and pieces of the Empire since 1830—by 1882, Britain had taken effective control of Egypt, although not in an "official" manner.

More to the point: the British vision of a colonial empire that would stretch from India to South Africa—and perhaps of a triumphant return to the lands from which their Crusader ancestors had been ejected six centuries earlier—was obviously and significantly undercut by the Prussian presence now lodged in the very heart of that geographic vision. As if that were not enough, the matter of petroleum—oil—had by the late nineteenth century begun to assume enormous significance for any and all states expecting to be industrial, military and political powers in the twentieth century. What is referred to in the history of science and technology as the "Third Industrial Revolution" was taking shape in the context of the discovery of oil and its uses. If Britain, home to the first, coal-based Industrial Revolu-tion of the late eighteenth and early nineteenth centuries, were to remain in the forefront of industrial capability and not fall behind Prussia (progenitor of the Second Industrial Revolution in the middle third of the nineteenth century), then it could not stand idly by while the Prussians assumed control of a region rife with petroleum possibilities.

So the gradual British encroachment closer to the heartland of the Ottoman Empire was in part a response to the significant presence of the Prussians as honored "guests" in that heartland. While it is true that World War I had among its causes disputes regarding Belgium and the Hapsburg concerns (and concerns of various nationalist groups within and against the Hapsburg

domains) symbolized by the assassination of the Hapsburg archduke in Sarajevo, it seems clear that the most significant issue forcing the explosion of August, 1914 was the question of the future of the Near (Middle) East.

World War I and the Reshaping of the Near East

Within the first year of the War the British were already seeking Arab allies against the combined Prussian and Turkish enemy, using Arab nationalist aspirations and shaping the assertion that Arab assistance could remove the Turks from the scene and yield to the fulfillment of those aspirations as a wedge. In 1915-16 the British organized a revolt against the Ottomans in Syria. In exchange they promised an independent Arab state after the war. More precisely, "The Revolt in the Desert" was led by the Hashemite Sharif of Makka, Hussain Ibn'Ali and his sons, 'Ali, 'Abd'Allah and Faisal.[61] The rebels conquered Makka and Aqaba, surrounded Madina and sabotaged the Hijaz Railway (that portion of the Prussian-Ottoman railway project that had been completed).

By 1916 the British and their French allies were already meeting to consider in some detail how the Ottoman Empire might be carved up into their respective spheres of interest after the end of a war that they anticipated winning. The Sykes-Picot Agreement would leave the British in charge of the territory that extended from the northern edge of the Sinai to the southern border of Syria and from the Mediterranean shore to the Persian Gulf; the French would control the parallel territory north of the British region. They would retain their respective control or influence in the various areas in which they had already established themselves during the previous 85 years.

By 1917–18, the right wing of British General Allenby's armies—led by the Hashimites under Faisal—advanced into Palestine and Syria, entering Damascus. The British permitted

the raising of the Arab flag there.[62] Meanwhile the British also made a gesture to the Jews in 1917 with regard to Zionist aspirations. The letter from Lord Arthur James Balfour to Baron Nathan de Rothschild on November 2, 1917 included the text of a statement that had "been submitted to, and approved by, the Cabinet" of His Majesty's Government, asserting that "His Majesty's government looks with favor upon the establishment in Palestine of a national home for the Jewish people...." The letter with its statement came quickly to be referred to as "The Balfour Declaration" and interpreted by Zionists and their supporters as an edict calling for a Jewish state.[63]

So the promises to the Arabs in 1916 and to the Jews in 1917, each understood in its particular way by the two respective groups receiving the promises and by the groups offering the promises, might seem to offer a collision course. On the one hand, the geographic non-specificity of the promises to the Arabs could suggest that a collision was not inevitable, assuming that they (the Arabs) were to interpret those promises to refer to areas other than Palestine in its entirety. On the other hand, the notion of a collision would not necessarily have worried the British: their colonial method was often to introduce conflict between groups—to divide and conquer or, as the case may be, divide and maintain control. This was a method that they continued to use in India (which, we recall incidentally, British terminology referred to as the *Middle* East) virtually up to Indian independence, for example: antagonisms between Muslims and Hindus were exacerbated by colonial governors.

It may be of interest to note that meanwhile the United States had not gotten involved in all of this—only, in fact, became involved in World War I, on the side of the British and French, because of the 1917 sinking of the Lusitania, a distinctly non-military ocean liner, by the Prussians. Part of the reason, it turns out that, up to that point, President Wilson desisted from declaring war on Ottoman Turkey (which would have been the United States' natural enemy if Britain and France were consid-

ered allies), is the concern that American Christian missionaries and the small Middle Eastern outposts that they had established would be at risk if he were to do so—so religion played a role in a political decision, not for the first nor for the last time in this long history.[64] Wilson waited, preferring to remain neutral, until his hand was forced, and he then declared war on Prussia, but not on Ottoman Turkey—and of course the United States immediately withdrew from the scene after the Great War was over barely a year later.

Within two years of the end of World War I, as victors whose major ally, the United States, had stepped back into isolation, the British and French were indeed in a position to divide the region into spheres of interest, influence and control. The French Mandate established in 1920 encompassed the area that would eventually yield the states of Syria and Lebanon in 1943 and 1944 respectively. The British Mandate of the following year encompassed the realm of greater Palestine and the area between Palestine and the Gulf. The latter region, comprised of three *vilayets*—provinces—of the now-defunct Ottoman Empire would be cobbled together as the new geo-polity, Iraq, by 1932—just as a chunk of one of those *vilayets* would be reconfigured as an independent polity, Kuwait, by 1962 (by which time Iraq had gained its independence—in 1958).

The point imbedded in the previous long sentence is this: that in its desire to control the oil production from two different areas that, by the 1920s and 1930s were yielding more petroleum than any other sites in the Middle East, by putting them under one British-governed roof, the British colonial government created Iraq by putting together by fiat three regions with little in common, historically, politically, ethnically or even religiously: three different provinces made up of Kurds on the one hand and Arabs on the other; in the latter case, one Arab group of which was Sunni Muslim and the other Shi'i Muslim. And they disconnected from what had been a continuum for several centuries under the Ottomans that part of the continuum which came to be

called Kuwait, for the same oil-driven reasons. The repercussions of this double decision would be felt all the way into the end of the 1980s and the beginning of the 1990s when Iraq invaded Kuwait and the Americans took the lead in restoring the British-made status quo of sixty years earlier.[65] Indeed the repercussions are still being felt in the year 2004 (2009) in which I write in the aftermath of a more absolute American invasion of Iraq.[66]

The same might be said of the other part of the British Mandate. Eastern Palestine would ultimately be reconfigured ethno-politically with the creation of a new state, Jordan—named for the river that served as its western border—christened as a kingdom ruled not by a Palestinian leader but by the Hashemite family of the Sharif Hussain. This was the family that had been so essential to the British against the Ottomans in 1917-18 (as noted above) and which held sway in the Kingdom of the *Hijaz* until 'Abdal-'Aziz ibn Sa'ud, with Wahhabi spiritual support, had gradually increased his influence from the original annexation of Hasa in 1913 to Jamal Shammar in 1921 to the entire *hijaz* region in 1924-5. Sharif Hussain, having declared himself King in 1916, declared himself Caliph in 1924 but was shortly thereafter forced to abdicate and died in exile. His oldest son, 'Ali, sat on the throne for less than a year before Ibn Sa'ud drove him out; 'Ali died in exile in Baghdad.

By 1932 Ibn Sa'ud had created the new Kingdom of Saudi Arabia—and it was other members of the dispossessed Hashemite clan whom the British placed in power in eastern Palestine.[67] Decades later, September, 1970 would become known in the Palestinian Arab world as "Black September"—for during that month the King of Jordan killed more Palestinians than have been killed in over sixty years of struggling with Israel. We may understand that part of the reason was King Hussein's fear of a Palestinian *intifada* against his non-Palestinian rule.

As for Britain's rule of western Palestine, given the promises and counter-promises made to Jews and Arabs (and ignoring the definitional issue of Jewish Arabs, so that the latter term—

"Arabs"—may be treated as if it excludes Jews and refers primarily but not exclusively to Muslims, but also to Christians) it is no surprise that it would offer a more imposing challenge than placing the entirety of eastern Palestine in Hashemite hands or even the shaping of a new Iraqi state. The complicated 1916 Allies' plan for Palestine actually placed the Lebanon area, reaching as far south as Safed, under French control and created an independent Arab state east of the coastal area (i.e., Syria). The plan also created an Arab state, but under British protection, south of Hebron on the West Bank, encompassing all of the area from the southern Gaza area across to the Dead Sea and down to Aqaba; and leaving the area between that east-west line just south of Hebron north toward Safed as a "new area" to be under joint British, French and Russian protection, with the exception of the area around Haifa and Acre, both of which areas were to be under British rule.

In February, 1919 the Zionists offered a counter-proposal at the Paris Peace Conference, with their vision for a Jewish polity. They sought to have set aside for Jewish settlement the entire coastal area from Sidon in the Lebanon and down the Mediterranean seaboard as far as Rafa (just south of the "Gaza Strip") and inland south by southeast to Aqaba; and with an eastern border that led from Aqaba north by northeast on what, at Ma'an, becomes a parallel line to the *hijaz* railway line, about twenty-five miles *east* of the Dead Sea and Jordan River, just west of Amman and coming to within twenty miles or so of Damascus. This proposal was rejected by the allies. In April, 1936 the British appointed a royal commission to inquire into the effective working of the Mandate after a repeated series of Arab attacks against Jewish life and property. The result was the Peel Commission Partition Plan that in July, 1937 suggested dividing western Palestine into a pair of Jewish and Arab states with a British controlled corridor from Jaffa to Jerusalem.[68]

According to this plan the Jews would have been allotted the area along the coast from about thirty miles south of Tel

Aviv to about fifteen miles north of Acre; east by northeast to Metulla and down along the eastern coast of the Sea of Galilee, continuing about fifteen miles south, toward, but just short of Beit Sh'an and then turning west toward Afula; the western border of the Jewish polity from that point and south would have more or less paralleled the coast, about ten miles from the Mediterranean. The remainder of the area as far as Aqaba, following the Jordan River to the Dead Sea and following a line southwest from the southern tip of the Dead Sea down to Aqaba would have been an Arab state. At that juncture, the Jews reluctantly accepted the plan and the Arabs rejected it outright.

In the aftermath of the Peel Commission Report and partition proposal, the Jewish Agency once again put forth its own proposal. This one called for dividing the area west of the Jordan into six sections. Both Jewish sections were somewhat larger than what the British had proposed. Where the latter had seen a substantial Arab state and a small area to remain under British control, the Jewish Agency proposed three smaller areas as an Arab state with a much larger area to remain under a British Mandate. Jerusalem, rather than being encompassed by the British would be on the border between and divided between the British and Jewish areas of governance.

In turn the British undertook another study of the situation by a group headed by Sir John Woodhead—the Woodhead Commission—later in 1938, which offered a proposal that reduced the two Jewish State sections to less than the Peel Commission had, but validated areas of Jewish-owned land within the proposed Arab State. The latter was similar to what the Peel Commission proposed in overall scale, but also granted to the Arabs an enclave around Jaffa and on the other hand officially acknowledged the Jewish-held areas within the Arab State and also expanded the continued British Mandate beyond where the Peel commission had taken it—it would encompass Ramallah to the north of Jerusalem and include territory to the south beyond Bethlehem.

One can hopefully see by means of this last series of para-

graphs that merely the discussion of the definition and aspiration and interference conflicts with respect to western Palestine (Palestine-Israel) in the period between the two World Wars involves an astonishing level of complication. How much more tangled the picture when one considers the entire region over the sweep of its incredibly long history!

Notes

[57] At least four cities—Safed, Tiberias, Jerusalem and Hebron—had a continuous Jewish presence since antiquity; about another 25 had Jewish inhabitants again by and since the medieval period, including Gaza, Jaffa, Caesarea, Haifa among others. By 1880 there were about 24,000 Jews in Ottoman Palestine; by 1914, that number had grown to about 90,000. By contrast, the non-Jewish Arab population went from about 47,000 to 500,000 during that same 34-year period. How much of this was from influx and how much from birthrate has not been documented, to my knowledge.

[58] That is, the British created the state of Jordan as a kingdom for the Sharif, carving it out of the eastern portion of "Palestine."

[59] Yemenite Jews, for example, began to come in large numbers to *Eretz Yisrael* in 1881—impelled not by Zionist fervor but by messianic hopes. The passage in Song of Songs 7:8—"I will ascend to the date palm tree"—was interpreted by their spiritual leaders to refer to ascent of the anointed one to the Holy Land in the year of the palm. The latter was deduced by deconstructing the three consonants (*t-m-r*) that comprise the word "date palm" (*tamar*) as signifying the equivalent of the year 1880. (The Jewish year dates itself from the putative beginning of the world. In September, 2008 we entered the year 5769, which is where we will still be with the arrival of the Gregorian year 2009). The year 1880 would have been 5640 in Jewish accounting. Every letter in Hebrew has a numerical value, and thus the year 5640 is rendered with the Hebrew letters *t-r-m*, which equal 640, the "5" of five thousand being assumed. Another twist gave, instead, 1882, for "*in* the year of the date palm" would add the Hebrew "*b*", which means "in" and equals "2", therefore yielding the equivalent of 1882.

[60] See below, 182.

[61] The term "Hashimite" reflects the assertion that the family descended from the Quraish tribe and indeed Muhammad himself by way of his grandson, Hussain, (hence: "*Hashimite*") who was the son of Fatima (the Prophet's daughter) and 'Ali.

[62] Note the turn of phrase "the British permitted": even in raising an army to support British interests, the Arab nationalists were neither accorded full authority by the British nor were they in a position to assert it without British acquiescence.

[63] The full text of the letter with the full text of the British Cabinet statement may be found in Laqueur's *The Israel-Arab Reader: A Documentary History of the Middle East Conflict*.

[64] See Michael Oren, *op citum*.

[65] Regarding the Kurds, see below, 112 and fnn 188, 189.

[66] The vast majority of this narrative was written in 2004; the last parts were significantly re-written prior to publication in 2009. Obviously my statement regarding repercussions is not effected—except perhaps that it may be stated more emphatically in 2009 than in 2004.

[67] Once more let us consider some of the further complexities in this part of the larger picture. It was the second son of Sharif Hussain, 'Abd'Allah, who became his father's Foreign Minister and political adviser after the latter assumed the title of King of the *Hijaz* with British support in 1916. 'Abd'Allah's younger brother, Faisal, was proclaimed King of Syria, whence he was expelled by the French in 1920. 'Abd'Allah assembled troops for the purpose of marching to Damascus to restore his brother's throne but the British prevailed on him to go no further than Amman. Eventually the British made Faisal king of Iraq—from which throne his grandson, Faisal II was removed by assassination in the coup of 1958 in which Saddam Hussein was a participant, (although it would take Saddam twenty more years to assume full power in Iraq). 'Abd'Allah, the British-imposed Emir of Transjordan in 1921, took the title of King in 1946 and in turn became King of Jordan in 1949, changing the name of the country after his annexation of the West Bank. He was assassinated in the al-Aksa Mosque by a Palestinian follower of the Grand Mufti of Jerusalem (see below, 98, 100) on July 20, 1951. The recently-deceased King Hussein was 'Abd'Allah's grandson. Hussein's son and successor and Jordan's current ruler is 'Abd'Allah II.

[68] For the purposes of the discussion of statehood within western Palestine—and really, during the entire discussion of Arab nationalism—I am again using the word "Arab" in the common parlance sense to exclude Jews and encompass primarily but not exclusively Muslims, even though I have been at pains to demonstrate that, in the larger historical context, this is at least an oversimplification and at most an inaccuracy. The ease with which we necessarily slip into such small but not insignificant inaccuracies is discouraging.

Chapter 8

World War II, the Holocaust and the Problematic of Israel-Palestine

The next seven years would be the most trying in Jewish history and to a large extent in Western if not world history. By 1938 Hitler had been in power in Germany for five years and his regime had begun both to deprive a range of groups—most emphatically, the Jews—of all their legal rights and to begin swallowing up pieces of nearby central European territories. World War II would break out "officially" the following year and the Holocaust of six million European Jews, together with the destruction of more than that number of other European civilians would define the period that ended in mid-1945.

For the Jews as the group toward which Nazi animosity most fully, consistently and systematically directed itself, a question arose by the end of the 1930s with some urgency. Where might they go in order to survive? The Johnson-Reed Act of 1924 which finalized the quota system for immigration

into the United States, and similar systems in Canada and elsewhere, definitively capped the numbers who might escape across the northern Atlantic. Some countries in South America offered refuge up to a point. So did some European countries, but if and when they were overrun by the Nazis the safety net became a death trap. Given the developments of the previous four decades the obvious question was: what about Palestine?

By 1933, the year in which Hitler arrived into power, Arabs had begun working with his regime—specifically with Adoph Eichmann and the Waffen SS—toward military recruitment, sabotage and propaganda; funded by the Nazis, Palestinian Arabs staged riots and attacks on Jewish communities within Palestine that helped encourage the British to minimize Jewish immigration to Palestine over the next several years.[69] For the British preferred not to exacerbate their relationship with the Muslim and Christian Arab population which was not eager to absorb a large influx of Jews. The most famous pro-Nazi Palestinian Arab was the Grand Mufti of Jerusalem, Haj Amin al-Husseini, who met Hitler in Germany in 1941. Without grounds for his claim, the Grand Mufti would assert in a Radio Berlin broadcast two years later that the Jews planned to destroy the Al'Aqsa mosque.[70]

Winston Churchill would comment on this state of affairs in angry terms before the British House of Commons during this period:

> So far from being persecuted, the Arabs have crowded into the country and multiplied until their population has increased more than even all world Jewry could lift up the Jewish population.... We are now asked to submit, and this is what rankles most with me, to an agitation which is fed with foreign money and ceaselessly inflamed by Nazi and by Fascist propaganda.[71]

My intention is not to espouse or endorse Churchill's perspective, since I believe that he was quite capable of strong biases and over-generalization ("the only good German is a dead

German" is ascribed to him as a sentiment). It is to supplement the other issues I shall raise when I arrive at the discussion of selective and absolute memory and the implications of memory for moving forward toward solutions to the problems of the Middle East that I raise the issue of particular aspects of Arab behavior during the Holocaust and World War II.

By the time of the outbreak of the war no solution had yet been reached regarding a partition plan of Palestine into Arab and Jewish areas of political autonomy or semi-autonomy, much less statehood. And as the situation of European Jews grew more desperate the British, in large part due to the Arab pressure just reviewed and in part due to their own convictions that the Jewish Problem could find no solution in Palestine,[72] tightened restrictions both with respect to where Jews might continue to settle (so that the three main areas of Jewish settlement by that time, around Jerusalem and Beersheba and north of Acre became inaccessible to expansion) and with regard to how many Jews might enter Palestine anew: fifteen thousand per year between 1939 and 1944 was the maximum number of Jewish refugees allowed.

From the Jewish point of view a large number of Hitler's *potential* victims were being forced into *actualized* victimhood and those permitted to escape were being confined "to a small Pale of settlement similar to that which existed in Czarist Russia before the last war, and such as now exists only under Nazi rule."[73] From the Arab point of view, with the development of the Holocaust, permitting Jews to seek refuge in Palestine in whatever numbers was to import a European problem into the Middle East. Put otherwise, from the Arab Muslim perspective, the establishment of European Christian Crusader kingdoms was being echoed, albeit obliquely, by the establishment of small but growing European Jewish communities.[74]

From the Jewish point of view the Arab stance loses whatever legitimacy it might otherwise have when placed against the Arab complicity in the destruction of European Jews and

in the Nazi effort to defeat the British. In 1941, before either the Soviets or the U.S. had entered the war, and when it appeared that the British might lose the war, Arabs in general and Palestinian Arabs in particular, led by the Grand Mufti, were instrumental in fomenting a revolt in Iraq the success of which would have been decisive in crushing the British. The Empire would have been sliced down the middle and cut off from its primary source of oil. After the war, in 1947, the American Christian Palestine Committee would offer a report commenting on how "it was indeed a critical moment that the Iraqi [Syrian and Palestinian] rebels, prodded and aided by the ex-Mufti of Jerusalem, chose for their uprising. . . At the call of Haj Amin. . . subversive elements throughout the Middle East were touched off into activity."

The report would further observe, in part: that "now in 1947 we seem to be returning to the policy of appeasement in dealing with precisely those Arab leaders who did their utmost to aid the Axis powers. . . . It is not claimed that the facts stated in this document constitute a revelation. They do not appear to be in dispute in any reasonable quarter. There seems, however, to be a tendency to ignore them as no longer politically relevant. This (is) unfortunate, for the data herewith presented point to conclusions that are still valid with regard to the political reasoning prevalent among the Arab peoples."[75] Whether the actions of a half a century ago should then or can now be used by non-Arabs as a guide to "the political reasoning prevalent among the Arab peoples" may be debated by many, but it is beside the point to the extent that non-Arabs perceive an "Arab mentality"—or a "Muslim mentality"—that is different from and cannot be bridged to a "Western Mentality." In other words, there are those who assert that two worlds are engaged in as fiercely an implacable struggle as were the United States and the Soviet Union during the darkest years of the Cold War.[76]

In any case, as complexities interweave complexities, a moment that ties the Holocaust era to the decade that preceded

it and at the same time has implications for how Israeli leaders are today measured with regard to their dealings with the Arab world is this: Haj Amin al-Husseini had been banned by the British from the territory of the mandate in the 1920s, for fomenting pogroms and assassinating Arab moderates. Sir Herbert Samuel, the British Jew,[77] when he became High Commissioner, as an act of appeasement toward Arab extremists, pardoned al'Husseini, passed over the *three* winning candidates of a Muslim election and granted to al'Husseini the post of Mufti—and with it the power to lead his followers into the active Nazi collaboration just described that followed not long thereafter. The memory of Samuel's act and its consequences has haunted every discussion of the past half-century among Israeli leaders regarding negotiations with the Arabs in general and the Palestinians in particular.[78]

It should be noted, apropos of the question of Arab or Palestinian sympathies or assistance to the Nazi cause, that the *Yishuv* itself did not offer much help to European Jews seeking refuge during the Holocaust—perhaps because the *Yishuv* was itself too small and weak and struggling with both the Arabs and the British during that period, but afterwards there would even be some accusations of complicity between *Yishuv* members and the Nazis for personal or ideological reasons.[79] Those who argued that there had been Jewish traitors against the Jews asserted generally that the motivation *was* ideological: to give a final stamp to the notion that the only viable place for Jews to live real and secure lives was *Eretz Yisrael*.[80] Certainly many, including David Ben-Gurion, seem to have been less than overly sympathetic to the plight of European Jews, for either ideological or psychological reasons.[81] Others have seen significant evidence of feelings of guilt in *Yishuv* members in the aftermath of the Catastrophe precisely because they had been too helpless.[82]

A number of writers have taken up the question of how to evaluate the impact of the Holocaust on the founding of the

State of Israel. The discussion and the efforts to actualize the discussion toward a Jewish state were in process from the end of the first World War to the end of the second. But perhaps that discussion would have continued for a much longer period of time had not the Holocaust intervened to help impel something more active. Yet no further progress toward activation was made during or even in the immediate aftermath of the Holocaust; rather, a slow process continued to be fairly slow until 1947 and 1948. As Emil Fackenheim observes, "Historians see a causal connection between the Holocaust and the foundation of the State of Israel. The reasoning is as follows. Had it not been for the European Jewish catastrophe, all the centuries of religious longing for Zion, all the decades of secularist Zionist activity, together with all such external encouragement as was given by the Balfour Declaration, would have produced no more than a Palestinian ghetto... Only the Holocaust produced a desperate determination in the survivors and those identified with them, outside and especially within the *Yishuv*; ended vacillation in the Zionist leadership as to the wisdom of seeking political self-determination; and produced a moment of respite from political cynicism in the international community, long enough to give legal sanction to a Jewish State. Even so, 'the UN resolution of 1947 came at the last possible moment.'[83]

But Fackenheim continues: "This reasoning is plausible; no more so, however, than its exact opposite. Why were the survivors not desperate to stay away from Palestine rather than reach it—the one place on earth which would tie them inescapably to a Jewish destiny? (After what that destiny had been to them, the desire to hide or flee from their Jewishness would have been 'natural.') Why did the Zionist leadership rise from vacillation to resoluteness rather than simply disintegrate?. . . As for the world's respite from political cynicism, this was neither of long duration nor unambiguous while it lasted."[84] In any case, as the State of Israel was taking shape, and in the first two decades of its existence—until the eve of the June War of 1967—the

Holocaust was a largely ignored—an almost taboo—subject. This derived from a combination of the culminating sense of the need to separate Israel from diasporatic Jewish history and of thinking of that history as one of passive victimization in contrast to the strong and actively self-sustaining present symbolized by the State of Israel.[85]

Fackenheim's discussion is offered by him in the context of the theological question of whether or not God allowed the Holocaust to take place and if so why, and whether as a God-allowed event it was allowed in order for the State of Israel to come into existence. It does not address (or seek to address) the question of whether the Arab perspective is valid.

For that question one would need to approach it from a different angle of consideration from that of Fackenheim, who is looking at a piece of history with a theological issue in mind and with a largely Jewish audience in mind for his thinking about that issue. Rather than wondering about God's plans for the Jews, we need to consider the plans of humans, who both perpetrated the Holocaust and built the State of Israel. From the Arab perspective, the European Christians dumped the European Christian-Jewish Question into the non-European, predominantly non-Christian Middle East. One may well be able to argue this simply from a "statistical" perspective: if the fact of Jewish refugees and the problem of where to settle them due to immigration quotas in countries such as the United States meant that that problem needed solution elsewhere, then the already-in-process matter of relocating Jews to the Middle East either as a politically independent entity, or not, surely offered itself. And one could argue that pushing from "either or not" to "definitively" a politically independent entity grew out of guilt for what was done to Jews and not done to *save* Jews during the Holocaust.

But that there was already such a process in place, that the discussion of a Jewish homeland and/or an independent Jewish state was taking place for half a century or more before the

beginning of the Holocaust militates against limiting the answer to the question to such a perspective as often viewed by the Arabs. That discussion from within the Jewish world was accelerating, as we have seen, before World War I and long before World War II. With regard not to the numbers of European and American immigration quotas, but of who was present in the Middle East prior to 1948, we have also recognized two things with regard to the Jews: first, that there were never *not* Jews in the region and second, that the number of Jews continued to escalate during the entire course of the modern era. Between the thirteenth and the nineteenth century, indeed, the Jews constituted the primary population in some parts of Palestine, specifically the area from Safed to Tiberias where Joseph HaNassi attempted to establish a semi-autonomous state under Ottoman patronage in the sixteenth century.[86]

We can complicate matters still further by this numbers game: if by the time of the birth of the State of Israel the majority of its population came from Europe (or at least the Christian world as opposed to the Muslim world) thereby proving to some analysts that Israel is a European infix into the Middle East, in the period following the first Arab-Israel War, a far greater number of Jews emigrated *from* Arab and Muslim countries— thereby demonstrating to other analysts that the population of the State was indigenous to the region, and thus that the State should be understood to be indigenous.

In the aftermath of World War II and the Holocaust there was at any rate a continued or even a reinvigorated discussion within and outside the Jewish community regarding whether there might be a Jewish State and how it might be configured. While by April, 1946 an Anglo-American Committee of Inquiry had arrived at a plan for a single bi-national state under British control, with an immediate grant of 100,000 immigration certificates to Jews and an end to the land purchase restrictions of 1940, once again the Jewish Agency put forth a proposal for two separate states west of the Jordan. (This was

the same year in which the area east of the Jordan became the Hashemite Kingdom of Transjordan under British patronage). The Agency's plan would have created a Jewish state slightly larger than what was eventually obtained three years later (after the Israeli War for Independence) but would have created an independent Arab state on the West Bank and an independent Arab enclave around Jaffa; Jerusalem would have been put under international control.

The following year the United Nations—itself an offspring not only of World War II, but ultimately of two world wars and the failure to organize a concerted League of Nations between those wars—offered its own proposal. On November 29 the General Assembly voted to establish a Jewish State and an Arab State. This time the proposal called for three segments to comprise the Jewish State that touched each other but were barely contiguous. The Arab counterpart consisted of three sections (and the Jaffa enclave), similarly touching but barely contiguous, and Jerusalem and its environs were to remain an international zone. The plan also called for an Arab-Jewish Economic Union. As with the Peel Commission proposal of ten years earlier, the Jews reluctantly accepted it as a final validation of their statehood aspirations, and the Arabs rejected it. Over the following six months there was a virtually daily stream of small-scale attacks against Jews by Arabs and counter-attacks by Jews against Arabs, or less frequently attacks by Jews against Arabs and counter-attacks against Jews by Arabs.

The culmination of this process, which included the departure from Jewish-held areas of Palestine of nearly 120,000 Arabs by May 5, mostly encouraged to flee by their own leaders, (and in some cases, discouraged from doing so while in others strongly encouraged to do so or even pushed to do so by Jewish leaders) was the Declaration of Independence of the State of Israel on May 14, 1948 and the invasion of the nascent state by six Arab armies (those of Egypt, Syria, Transjordan, Lebanon, Saudi Arabia and Iraq) on the following day. Although a truce was

signed on June 11, it did not last long. Fighting ultimately continued until 1949. The final point of the war, brought to an end by way of a truce negotiated on the Island of Rhodes was, for the purposes of this discussion, threefold in its development. First, the Israeli forces enjoyed considerable success, so that, the longer the war raged, the more land was conquered, leading ultimately to a State of Israel after January, 1949 remarkably close in size and disposition to what the Jewish Agency had proposed in 1946 and much larger than what the United Nations had proposed in 1947.

Second, a massive movement of populations ensued. Some 591,000 Jews from across the Arab world immigrated to the State of Israel, either out of fear of hostile activity against them by their host countries or because such activity was taking place or because the Zionist leadership encouraged them to come and to believe that such activity was imminent. Conversely, some 663,000 Arabs left the Jewish-held areas of Palestine (now parts of the State of Israel). Of these some 256,000 were absorbed into Lebanon, Syria, Iraq, Transjordan or Egypt. About 190,000 of them went only as far as Gaza and another 280,000 as far as the non-Jewishly-held area of the West Bank—which, it was expected, would form the basis of an Arab State as the UN Partition Proposal had set forth. Somewhat over 160,000 Arabs remained in Israel or returned to their homes there during 1949.

Third, for those Arabs who neither remained nor returned to Israel nor settled in other already-established Arab polities—who anticipated shaping an Arab Palestinian State—disappointment rather than political fulfillment marked this period. Egypt occupied the Gaza Strip, which remained a kind of no man's land for the two decades that followed, its inhabitants limited as to their movement and as far as their ability to become part of the Egyptian world that was not only practically distant (its centers of life beyond the Sinai Peninsula) but culturally and politically very different. (Even Arabic language dialects distinguished the Egyptians from the Gaza Palestinians). On the

other hand, those Palestinians residing in the West Bank found their territory not merely occupied by Transjordan in 1948 but annexed to the Hashemite Kingdom in 1950. The annexation was opposed by the Arab League and recognized by only two members of the United Nations (Britain and Pakistan) and led to the formal renaming of the entire kingdom on both sides of the Jordan River as Jordan.

The condition of West Bank Palestinian refugees was economically somewhat better than that of their Gazan brothers and sisters (from which they were now separated by Israel's territory) but still horrendous. One of the prevailing debates regarding the shaping of both these populations regards the matter of why they left Israel in 1948 and 1949 and did not return while a window of opportunity presumably still existed (the peace treaties that Israel signed with her neighbors were variously negotiated between 24 January and 20 July 1949). It seems certain that, initially, the Arab leaders themselves encouraged emigration, promising a triumphant return which became increasingly unfeasible as the Israeli army continued to expand its realm of conquest. But it seems equally certain that, either initially or after a certain point, the Israelis both encouraged such emigration with words or in some cases physical violence—terrorism—that pushed whole villages to flee in fear.

Notes

[69] See the Report of the *American Christian Palestine Committee*, 1947, 8-12, 17-21.

[70] See ACPC, 17 and MG, 165

[71] MG, 155

[72] See Richard Rubenstein, *The Cunning of History: The Holocaust and the American Future*, 16-21 and in particular his quote (on 17) from Lord Moyne, British High Commissioner in Egypt in 1944, regarding the possibility of saving a million Jews through Adolf Eichmann's "blood for trucks" offer: "What shall I do with those million Jews? Where shall I put them?" Palestine as an answer to that question was less viable to the British government than mass extermination (providing the Germans did most of the dirty work).

[73] From a speech by David Ben-Gurion delivered on 28 February 1940. See the Central Zionist Archives, 4 Zalman Shazar St, Jerusalem.

[74] See below, 103, but see also 232.

[75] *ACPC*, 5

[76] I am referring, most obviously, to Samuel P. Huntington's strident thesis, expressed in his *Clash of Civilizations and the Remaking of the World Order* (which appeared in essay form in *Foreign Affairs*, Summer, 1993, 72(3), 22-49 and subsequently in book form); and to a less severe extent to the viewpoint expressed by Bernard Lewis in his *What Went Wrong? The Clash between Islam and Modernity in the Middle East*.

[77] See above, 77.

[78] As I shall point out shortly, that did not in the end deter Begin from signing a peace with Anwar Sadat or prevent Yitzhak Rabin from signing agreements with Yassir Arafat and King Hussein. See 127-8 and fnn 107, 126.

[79] "*Yishuv*" ("settlement") refers to the community of Jewish inhabitants of Palestine before 1948. The term came into common Jewish use in the late nineteenth century with the expansion of that population during the proto-Zionist and early Zionist period.

[80] The matter of Jewish leaders, particularly Zionist leaders, as complicit with the Nazis has a painful history within the pained history of the Holocaust. The most prominent moment in that narrative surrounds the name of Rudolf Kastner, formerly a leader of the Hungarian Jewish community, which community went with surprising silence into the Destruction Camps toward the end of the war. When by the mid-1950s Kastner was a member of Ben-Gurion's Mapai party, he was accused of having negotiated with Eichmann to allow a small group of Jews—his family and friends—to escape to Palestine

in exchange for spreading the necessary fictions regarding where Jews were all being sent by the Nazis in order to maintain calm acquiescence from the community at large. I don't believe that the absolute truth on this issue will be known in the near future.

[81] See Tom Segev, *Elvis in Jerusalem: Post–Zionism and the Americanization of Israel*, 100-101: "Over and over people asked survivors how they had survived. By implication they were asking not how but why, and the question contained an insinuation of guilt. Ben-Gurion said: 'Among the survivors... were people who would not have prevailed had they not been what they are—hard, bad, and egotistical. . .'" Also see Benny Morris, *Righteous Victims: A History of the Zionist-Arab Conflict, 1881-1999*, 162: "If I knew it was possible to save all [Jewish] children of Germany by their transfer to England and only half of them by transfer to *Eretz Yisrael*, I would choose the latter—because we are faced not only with the accounting of those children but also with the historical accounting of the Jewish people." See also the book-length focus of Tom Segev's *The Seventh Million: The Israelis and the Holocaust*.

[82] See Segev, *Elvis*, 100: "Many were ashamed of the Jews' weakness; some were ashamed of the Zionist movement's inability to save them. Some blamed themselves for not doing more."

[83] Fackenheim is quoting here from Walter Laqueur, *A History of Zionism*, 593.

[84] Emil Fackenheim "The Holocaust and the State of Israel: Their Relation," in Eva Fleischner, ed., *Auschwitz: Beginning of a New Era? Reflections on the Holocaust*, 209-210.

[85] See 75-6.

[86] See above, 53.

Chapter 9

The Varied Problematic of the Middle East Before and After 1948

Not only geo-political borders and their populations but the nature of the governments contained within them—which had been evolving variously since the middle of the First World War, in the soon-to-be post-Ottoman Middle East—continued to evolve beyond the period between the Second World War and 1948. This refers not only to the obvious reconfiguration of Israel. But, as with the Arab-Israel or Israel-Palestine issues, so with other states (and non-states) within the region one can observe the more recent difficulties emerging and evolving decades or even centuries earlier. If we point our lens back once again to the aftermath of World War I and then again to the era around 1948, there are at least three places where we might immediately examine things more closely to find change and perhaps confusion for the examiner.

The first of these is Turkey. In the aftermath of the defeat of the Ottoman Empire and its allies in World War I at least

three matters of particular relevance to our overall discussion come to the fore. The first is that, having succeeded for the most part in ridding themselves of non-Arab, albeit Sunni Muslim, rulers, the majority of the Arab world, both (Sunni *and* Shi'i) Muslim and Christian, found itself enthralled to new rulers. And although the Christian British and French made any number of promises, as we have earlier observed, regarding a more independent future for the Arab world, the fulfillment of such promises was both slow in coming and/or complicated by counter-promises to others (as, for example, the Jews with respect to western Palestine).

The second matter relevant to our discussion is that the ambition of the British and the French was not limited to the areas over which they assumed mandatory control. It included the entirety of the area north of their mandates—what was left of the former Ottoman Empire. But in that region Mustafa Kemal, who would later be known simply as Attatuerk, had taken control and managed to hold his own well enough against the British and the French that in the end they withdrew into more limited areas of domination and influence and thus, by 1923, the independent post-Ottoman state of Turkey was born. But among the inhabitants of that state would be a section of non-Turkish inhabitants, Kurds, who, concentrated in eastern Turkey, northern Syria and northwestern Iraq, were also promised some form of an independent polity by the allies during World War I but received nothing. Separated by re-drawn geopolitical lines and divided among themselves along various tribal lines, the Kurds add yet another ethnic and political complication to the tangle of the Middle East and to all three post-World War I states which they inhabit. Nowhere is this more obvious than in Turkey, even more than eighty years after Attatuerk founded the new state.[87]

The third matter of significance is that, in founding the new state of Turkey, Attatuerk created a secular republic in 1923. That is, he abandoned the notion that a predominantly Muslim

state must be an *Islamic State* in the modern world in which
he wished to see Turkey assume a role. Thus, for example, the
Haghia Sofia, that, in its transformation from Church to Mosque
after 1453 had become such a symbol of victorious Islam, was
transformed into a secular State Museum. Its architecture and
its internal art works, both Muslim and Christian (for its long-
hidden twelfth-century Christian mosaics were uncovered for
all to see) now became part of the *cultural* heritage of Turkey,
rather than the *spiritual* heritage of Sunni Islam and its caliphate. So, too, Attatuerk dramatically disconnected the modern
state from its predecessor by rejecting the Arabic writing system
(which with its consonantal emphases was never particularly
conducive to the vowel-emphasizing Turkish language) and
developing the modified Latin-letter system with which Turkish
has been written ever since.

These acts tied to secularization would not only have repercussions in the shaping of the state during and after the
time of Attatuerk—and, in retrospect, be emulated more than a
generation later by Syria, but with very different consequences
for the internal history of that state and for the relationship
between the two states and Israel (and each other)—they would
have peculiar consequences as recently as 2001. For in speaking before the video cameras in the aftermath of the September 11 attacks on the Twin Towers and Pentagon, Ussama Bin
Ladin would assert, among other things, that he was avenging
the insult to Islam and thus to God meted out in 1923. That
rather peculiar—and to most auditors and viewers completely
obscure—reference was to the sacrilege of Attatuerk.

The validation of an act of violence and brutality by reference
to an event nearly 80 years in the past which most would not
likely construe in any case as an attack on Islam or a sacrilege
against God recalls the thinking of the first Crusaders in 1095-
96 who claimed that they were righting the wrong committed
by al'Hakim in 1009 when he burned down the Church of the
Holy Sepulchre in Jerusalem. Both assertions are symptomatic of

a form of long-memoried religious extremism that has obvious implications not only for the region, but for the world.

Mention of Syria brings to the forefront a second instance of dramatic political reconfiguration, this time in the aftermath of the first Arab-Israeli war. After the signal failure to prevail against the nascent Jewish state, Colonel Hosni al Za'im seized control of Syria on March 20, 1949, one of the consequences of which was the setting up of a secular judicial system. Za'im replaced the Qur'anic legal system with one based on the Napoleonic code. This would mean (among other things) that in the interweave of religion and politics as part of the web of the Middle East, Syria would now follow Turkey in possessing a dual secular and Muslim identity, which could be (at least theoretically or potentially) consequential for its relations both with other Arab—Muslim—states and with Israel.

In turn, since the primary clients for Syria's tobacco and grain were Jordan and Iraq—royalist friends of the West—Za'im was pushed into putting Syria into an economic relationship with the United States, in spite of the negative view of America as Israel's primary sponsor.[88] Syria would sway back and forth over the next six or seven years in its relations with the Western powers and the Arab states. By the mid-1950s a new party was on the rise, the Ba'ath Party, which saw itself as the party of Arab renaissance. It had been created by a Christian Arab, Michael Aflaq, and his Muslim friend Salah al'Bitar, and in 1954 it won 16 of 142 seats in the Syrian House of Deputies. As an entity, however, it was not confined to Syria, for as a champion of Arab unity it was able to sprout branches in Jordan, Iraq and to a lesser extent, Lebanon.[89]

In the context of the 1956 Suez crisis, the USSR provided Syria with $140 million in technical aid, and relations with the United States soured—and in late 1957 the government sought political union with Egypt, so that a new United Arab Republic came into being on February 1, 1958, with Egypt's Abdul Gamal Nassir as its president. But on September 16, 1961 a new high

command had taken charge within Syria and the UAR collapsed. In February, 1962 a Ba'athist coup toppled the government of Iraq and the Syrian premier, Khalid al'Azm, sought a political merger; the new Iraqi government refused even to meet with the envoys from Damascus. On March 6, the army occupied Damascus, al'Azm was deposed and, with Michael Aflaq working behind the scenes, Salah al'Bitar established a new Ba'ath government. Two years later al'Bitar was deposed by the army and Dr. Yussuf Zayin was put in place as premier—the fifteenth Syrian government in nineteen years.

Zayin's rapid reforms were essentially Marxist in nature and, as such, he eventually sufficiently displeased the general who had installed him in power (General Amin al'Hafiz) that by December, 1965, the latter deposed Zayin and re-installed al'Bitar—who this time lasted all of two months before being taken into custody by another general, Salah Jadid (whom al'Bitar had sought to remove as Chief of Staff due to Jadid's excessively leftist leanings) who returned Zayin to the position of premier. Against this background, the disastrous June, 1967, war with Israel took place.[90] Three years later, a second military disaster unfolded as, during the Jordanian Civil War[91] the Syrian regime sent tanks to support Palestinian forces near the border but without air cover. The Jordanian air force easily demolished the Syrian tank column. The consequence was another coup, led this time by Chief of Staff, General Hafiz Assad, who established a new government devoid of Marxist content and laying claim to the championing of Arab nationhood. Assad was elected President (unopposed) by ninety-nine percent of the vote in a referendum held in March, 1971. He remained in power until his death a few years ago, when he was succeeded by his son, Bashir.

This brief excursus into Syrian history—one corner of the region during barely a generation—offers yet another instance (in addition to that briefly offered at the end of Chapter VII, regarding Israel-Palestine between the Wars) of what gives one

pause (or should) as one considers the possibilities for unraveling the tangled web of the region in its entirety in both time and space. As this discussion has arrived by different paths toward the middle third of the twentieth century, by which time there was a number of new polities within the region, we inevitably think toward the unresolved problem of the Israeli-Palestinian relationship as it moves through the second half of the century. But we ought not to be lured into the false assumption that the tangled web of the Middle East is limited in its confusions and complications to the problem of the Israelis and the Palestinians or even the Israelis and the Arabs, as complicated as those issues are—the brief look at Syria makes that emphatically clear. As the second half of the century rolls itself out there arises a range of issues involving both new polities artificially created by outside forces and old groups whose negative inter-involvements have never been cleared up.

And in considering some of the array of complications that grow out of the reconfiguration of the Middle East between the end of World War I and the 1950s, one might also briefly examine the case of Lebanon. The reason for this is two-fold: first, simply because Lebanon offers a microcosm of the tangled larger web which we are exploring; second, because in some senses Lebanon offers a parallel to part of the problematic of Israel, in its identity as a non-Islamic state within a mostly Islamic region. For Lebanon was, as an independent state, a polity whose leadership was largely Christian. Created by the French as an enclave carved out of their mandate, it was designed to offer to a largely Christian Arab community what Syria proper, newly reconfigured, offered to a predominantly Muslim Arab community. The irony is that the configuration devised by the French, in extending the province to the sea, actually brought in many Muslims, diluting the Christian identity that had prevailed under the Ottomans for this *sanjak*.[92]

Indeed, Lebanon is actually, over its brief independent history, surprisingly complicated. For one thing, it stands out among

Arab states in having established political stability with the help of the clergy, rather than by dismantling clerical power. For another, the complexity of its religious configuration is somewhat echoed in the manner in which that power has been delicately balanced through most of its modern history. Lebanon offers a Christian majority. Of this about seventy percent are Maronites (one of the many branches of "Eastern" Christianity) and the rest a mix of mainly Greek Orthodox, Syrian Orthodox, Syrian Catholic, Roman Catholic, Assyrian and Chaldaean denominations. There is, as well, a substantial Sunni Muslim minority as well as a substantial Druze minority. In the initial phase of its independent, post-French condition, these three factions were able to work out a fairly comfortable political arrangement that consisted of power-sharing signified by having a Christian President and a Sunni Muslim Prime Minister with a Druze Foreign Minister. The parliament was organized so that no sect could dominate and thus a union of Church and State would be impossible.

Several relevant observations might be made about this situation. One is that, with the French gone from the scene after 1946, the Syrian desire to exert control over Lebanon expanded dramatically. A second is that the condition of Lebanon as compared with that of Syria in the realm of terrorism vis-à-vis Israel underscores how fragile the arrangement of power-sharing was and how ultimately unstable and in certain fundamental ways impotent that state was: from Syria, for all of its animosity and verbal as well as occasionally physical bellicosity toward Israel, no terrorist incursions to speak of came over the decades; from Lebanon, without such animosity, frequent attacks arrived that were not fully solved even by the Israeli invasion of Lebanon in 1982.

A third observation is that, although some Middle Eastern specialists have observed that Lebanon does fine as long as there is no outside interference,[93] by paradox, the withdrawal of the French created the instability which only ended when, in the

aftermath of the first Persian Gulf War, Syria was rewarded for its role as an ally against Iraq by being permitted, for all intents and purposes, to swallow Lebanon up with no interference from the West. Thus while the country was stabilized, it came to be controlled by Syria and all but lost its independence.

That is: its stability derives from what most Lebanese would probably call outside interference, even as the Syrians would assert that, by definition, their involvement is from within, not without, since Lebanon was historically—i.e., pre-French Mandate—not a separate entity, but part of Syria. As we shall note later, this is the same logic that Sadam Hussein employed to justify his occupation of Kuwait, which led to the war that yielded control of Lebanon to the Syrians. Moreover, the issue of interference—both with respect to distinguishing "inside" from "outside" and with regard to helping create, as opposed to helping to solve, the tangled web of paradoxes and problems, as we shall also note later on, applies to other key areas in the Middle East and not only to Lebanon.[94]

Put another way—with potential implications for the Israeli-Palestinian and Israeli-Arab conflicts—since the aftermath of the first Gulf War, Lebanon has ceased to be an independent *dhimmi* or quasi-*dhimmi* state. The implications of that fact for the further discussion of the Israel-Arab and Israel-Palestine aspects of the Middle East web are profound. For it raises the religion-based (as opposed to culture-based, ethnicity-based, nationalism-based, or economy-based) question of the ability and willingness of the Muslim Arab world to accept the presence of an independent *dhimmi* state—which is what Israel is—within the heart of the *Dar al-Islam*.

To answer that question we must first return our thoughts briefly to the word *dhimmi* in the early and subsequent history of Islam.[95] If a Muslim believes that the earliest text of the *dhimma* as we have it derives from Muhammad's original agreement with the Jews of Khaybar, and if s/he believes that Muhammad's agreement was divinely dictated, then how can s/

he possibly countenance an independent *dhimmi* state within the *dar al'Islam*? But nowhere is the *dhimma* specifically referred to, much less described in the Qur'an. And indeed if one reviews what the Qur'an says about Jews—what it says about both Jews and Christians—one arrives at an ambiguous conclusion regarding the Prophet's view of them.

Thus we find instruction in Sura 9:29 to "Fight against those to whom the Scriptures were given, who believe not in God nor in the last day..." But this by no means refers to the *dhimmi* in general, but rather to those *dhimmi* "who do not believe in God nor in the Last Day"—and by the way, this assumes that some form of the *dhimmi* concept is what the text intends, although the term itself comes into actual usage outside and later than the Qur'an. More clearly and negatively we read in *Sura* 5:51 "Take not the Jews and the Christians as friends." But we also read in *Sura* 2:256 that "there is no compulsion in religion" and in the same *Sura* (2:67) we read: "Believers, Jews, Christians, and Sabaeans—whoever believes in God and the Last Day and does what is right—shall be rewarded by their Lord; they have nothing to fear or to regret." And so on.

So the answer to the question regarding the acceptability of a *dhimmi* state will depend upon how one reads the Qur'an, or which passages one selects as a guide for one's viewpoint. Whatever might further assist us that comes from the *Hadith*, is by definition not the word of God, but the word of the prophet or words about the prophet and, depending upon the nature of its transmission, of heavier or lighter weight in guiding our thinking.[96] If, finally, we examine the historical sweep from the seventh century to the twentieth century, we will encounter a range of conditions from Spain to the Holy Land to Persia and points yet further east with respect to the treatment of *dhimmi*.

This is not surprising, given the far-flung world of Islam, the range of schools of interpretation and of interpreters within those schools, and the manner in which politics and religion interweave across the human (and not only the Muslim) expe-

rience. That range includes conditions where *dhimmi* (primarily Jews) have been viziers to caliphs and sultans, and on the other hand serious oppression of *dhimmi*, with a variety of conditions falling between these two extremes. So history is no guide—and in any case, in no historical case do we see a fully independent *dhimmi* state within the *dar al'Islam* that could offer us a model situation. The closest we come, perhaps, is the brief and somewhat abortive attempt by Joseph HaNassi to create a semi-autonomous Jewish polity in the vicinity of Safed and Tiberias under Ottoman patronage, in the mid-sixteenth century.

Islam's record of tolerance of non-Muslims when it is in control is far better than that of Christianity's tolerance of non-Christians (at least until the twentieth century, or perhaps the nineteenth). But when not in control (as has been gradually the case since the late seventeenth century) the story is perhaps different. For many observant, devout Muslims who believe in the inviolability of a Muhammad-ordained *dhimma*, it may never be acceptable for a member of the *dhimmi* to be on a footing equal with, much less superior to, that of a Muslim. If Islamic fundamentalists come to dominate the *dar al'Islam*— and fundamentalism has surged in varying degrees in Jordan, Algeria, Tunisia, Egypt, even Turkey; and has been terribly feared by the Saudi leadership ever since the overthrow of the Shah of Iran—there is virtually no chance for permanent peace with Israel, since that would mean legitimizing a *dhimmi* state within the heart of the *dar al'Islam*. The Muslim opposition to Israel is not a simple case of anti-Semitism—to think of it in those terms is to import a Christian European vocabulary into a Middle Eastern situation dominated by Islam. It's not that the Jews must be exterminated or even driven out, but that an *independent Jewish state* is unacceptable.

But the idea that an independent *dhimmi* state will not be accepted in the Muslim world is affirmed from the viewpoint of many Israelis not only because of the fate of Lebanon but by their own history. Israeli historiography records the attack on the

nascent state by the armies of six Arab states. It does not—or at least did not until the beginning of the 1980s—remember the request from Syrian president Husni Za'im to meet with Ben-Gurion in 1949. Za'im had apparently intended to offer a peace agreement under which Syria would have absorbed between 300,000 and 350,000 Palestinian refugees as permanent residents in exchange (according to Ben-Gurion's diary) for "half of the Sea of Galilee."[97] Israel remembers the Suez crisis precipitated by Egypt's Nassir as the source for the Sinai war of 1956, in the aftermath of which the Israelis and their French and British allies withdrew under pressure from the United States, demanding in exchange negotiations that might lead to peace—a demand which was never met. It recalls the terrifying crisis of the months leading up to the extraordinary victory of 1967 and extending the hand of peace in the aftermath of that war and once again finding the hand slapped back.[98] It mourns the high number of Israeli dead occasioned by the attack on Israel on Yom Kippur, 1973, in which, instead of preemptively defending itself, the Jewish State waited for diplomacy to do the work that it (diplomacy) never did. Israelis cannot forget the incursions into the northern part of the state from terrorists lodged in Lebanon in the later 1970s and early 1980s.[99]

Cognate with the question of whether Muslim Arabs—and thus most particularly, the Palestinians (although not all of them are Muslim, of course)—can accept a *dhimmi* state is that of how, in this context, one might understand the tertiary meaning of *jihad*.[100] Thus with respect to struggling or striving with forces beyond one's internal self and outside the Muslim community, the Qur'an offers specific conditions under which one is obligated, or at least permitted, to fight. Among these the most relevant passage is that of *Sura* 22:39-40: "Permission [to fight] is given to those... who are driven out of their homes without a just cause." If the Palestinian view is that Muslim Palestinians have been driven from their land by Israelis or by Israel's existence, it is difficult to conceive how they would respond

as Muslims other than by continuous warfare until that land is reclaimed. Once again we are confronted with selective memory and historiography: how many Palestinian Arabs left for which reasons and how many were allowed to return after 1949 and did so? What was left behind and as such, how religiously valid would be an ongoing struggle to claim how much of it?[101] The interpretive answer to that question will affect the answer to the *jihad* question within the context of *Sura* 22.

There is also a more complicated twist to this last issue of *dhimma* and *jihad*. If Israel is an expression of secular Jewish *nationalism*, then what relevance does the matter of Jewish *religion* have to this entire issue? So we are impaled on the problem of definition once again. The PLO charter of 1968 denies legitimacy to the Jewish claim to any part of Palestine in part because "Judaism, being a religion, is not an independent nationality. Nor do Jews constitute a single nation with an identity of its own; they are citizens of the states to which they belong." This is the very issue with which Jews began to wrestle in the late eighteenth century and it is precisely the claim of Jewish nationalism that this sort of formulation is wrong.

This matter is more complicated by the fact that, on the one hand the PLO—as it moved toward peace negotiations and the new identity of its dominant *Fatah* wing, as the Palestinian Authority—began to renounce anti-Israel violence as a methodology by the end of the 1980s, and even to recognize Israel's existence as legitimate (which helped set the stage for the Madrid-Oslo developments of 1991–1993.[102] On the other hand, the *Muslim Brotherhood* in Palestine, part of an Islamic revival movement founded in Egypt in 1928, reemerged along radical lines to fill in the "gap" left by the PLO's turn from violence to diplomacy. Thus *Hamas* and *Islamic Jihad* were born. Aside from the uncomfortable physical fact that they absorbed suicide-bomber methodology from *Hizb'Allah* is the spiritual fact of how they identify themselves.

Whereas the PLO in general and *Fatah* in particular were

and are in effect secular organizations, so that the grounds for their relations with Israel are political-national, *Hamas* and *Islamic Jihad* shaped themselves as religious organizations. Thus where, for example, the PLO charter has asserted that Palestine is "an indivisible part of the Arab homeland," the *Hamas* charter refers to "the land of Palestine [as] an Islamic trust [*waqf* is the Arab word] upon all Muslim generations until the day of Resurrection." The PLO charter refers to the enemy as Zionist imperialists; the *Hamas* charter refers to "the unbelievers." The latter refers to a *Hadith* which speaks of the Day of Judgment as arriving only when "the Muslims fight against the Jews and the Muslims kill them..." This in turn returns the question of religious definition to the interior of Islam: if I accept this *Hadith* as valid there is not much hope for reconciliation, but I can both denounce a *Hadith* as not legitimate, or at least as not binding, since at *most* it is the word of Muhammad and not the word of God (as a passage from the Qur'an would be).[103]

Conversely, of course, Israelis argued for years that Palestinian nationalism is not legitimate. Thus Prime Minister Golda Meir commented in 1969: "There was no such thing as Palestinians. When was there an independent Palestinian people with a Palestinian state?" Such a conviction continued through the 1978 Peace Accords with Egypt and as far as the Peace Conference in Madrid of 1991. It was not until 1993 and Oslo that Israel began the shift toward recognizing Palestinians as a distinct entity—and that the Palestinian charter slipped sufficiently into dormancy to allow for recognition of a Jewish state. But both sides of this recognition-non-recognition equation remain fragile and clearly require reinforcement.

Notes

[87] I am ignoring as tangential to this particular discussion (but not to the problematic of human history or even to that of the Middle East considered broadly enough) the driving out, forced relocation and/or genocide of perhaps a million Christian Armenians by the Ottomans in 1916, in the midst of World War I, but that matter is not easily forgotten in Armenia, just as many Greeks have not yet forgotten their quarrels with the Turks that go back to the early nineteenth century and the Greek struggle for independence against the Ottoman Empire, which animosity still lives on actively on the island of Cyprus. There are also Greeks who refer to the expulsion of 1.5 million Hellenes by the Turks in 1923 (see the reference to this in the 2007 resolution of the International Association of Genocide Scholars) in a forced population exchange that also brought tens of thousands of ethnic Turks into Turkey proper from Greece. The fact of continued distrust or hostility on both of these fronts offers another potential complication for the larger Middle Eastern picture. But it is interesting that in a May 25, 2009 article in the *California Courier*, Harut Sassounian reports that the current Turkish Prime Minister, Rejeb Erdogan "admitted for the first time that the expulsion... was a 'fascist' act. Reuters reported... [that] Erdogan [also] made an indirect reference to the tragic fate of other groups, such as Armenians, in Turkey." As usual in the context of such a declaration, there are those who praise Erdogan's conciliatory remarks as historic, while others immediately jumped in to question the level of his sincerity and commitment to back up his words with "the restitution of rights to those who have been expelled, the return of confiscated properties, or compensation." Aside from the obvious fact that it is too soon to know what the long-term consequences are of the Prime Minister's remarks, we may also see parallels to the Israel-Palestinian situation, where similar sorts of actions are discussed regarding Palestinians displaced from what is now Israel.

[88] The relationship began in the form of granting a franchise to the United States-owned Trans-Arabian Pipeline Company for the shipment of Iraqi oil *through* Syria to the Mediterranean.

[89] Lebanon's large middle-class mercantile population tended to oppose the concept of overall Arab unity, preferring to push its own capitalist system into enriching contacts with the West, and so the Ba'ath party made narrower inroads—it was denied a place on the ballot by President Camille Chamoun when he came to power in 1952. For opposite reasons, Egypt offered an inhospitable environment: Nassir was already engaged in developing his own program of Arab unity and socialism.

[90] For a full and very excellent discussion—perhaps the finest in a single volume—see Michael Oren's *Six Days of War*.

[91] In which King Hussein was asserting his control and crushing Palestinian resistance—it culminated with Black September, 1970.

[92] This is the Turkish word for a sub-province; the term *vilayet* refers to an entire province.

[93] For example, John Voll, former Director of Georgetown University's *Center for Muslim-Christian Understanding*, in a lecture delivered at an Alumni College on the Middle East for Washington & Lee University in July, 2004.

[94] See 142, 213-8, 238-9.

[95] See above, 26.

[96] By "heavier or lighter" I mean with respect to the manner in which individual *Hadith*s are weighted, depending upon the nature and directness of transmission, back (or not) to attestations ascribable to the first group of companions of the Prophet or to the second generation of his followers, and so on.

[97] See Segev, *Elvis*, 129. Since Za'im was murdered shortly thereafter, the issue for the purposes of the present discussion is not as much that of a lost opportunity and what might have evolved toward an Israel-Arab peace as the principle of selective memory and how the Israelis and Arabs understand each other's behavioral history.

[98] Moshe Dayan, "hero" of the Six-Day War, announced to Israelis on the state radio station, "Soldiers of Israel, we have no aims of conquest." To the BBC he said, "The war is over; now we are waiting for a phone call from Hussein." That call never came.

[99] Ironically, a version of the phone call from Jordanian King Hussein referred to in the previous note came ten days before the Yom Kippur War, warning the Israelis that Egypt and Syria were likely to attack the Jewish State. The message was ignored, for the Israelis neither conceived of the Arabs being ready for war nor imagined that Sadat, in particular, would be willing to fight a war that the Arabs would lose militarily for *political* gain. The over-confident sense of difference between their own abilities and those of the Arabs which lulled the Israelis was shattered even with the actual eventual military victory of 1973. Paradoxically, the shattering of Israeli triumphalism and the concomitant rise in Arab self-esteem opened a door to peace through which Sadat walked a few years later.

[100] See above, 20-21.

[101] As we shall shortly see (below, fn 148) this is the other side of the view by those religious Jews who see a "Greater Israel"—from the Mediterranean Sea to Mesopotamia—as a God-originated mandate.

[102] The interesting manner in which the renunciation was initially made

was by declaring the PLO Charter *caduc*—not an Arabic term, but a French one meaning "lapsed." Those distrustful of Arafat argue(d) that this term falls short of a full-fledged renunciation of violence on the one hand and recognition of Israel on the other, analogous to the way in which *sulh* falls short of full-fledged peace (*salaam*).

[103] See above, 17, 21, fn 16 and also 180-81. This *Hadith* is said to be related by al'Bukhari and Muslim, neither of whom was a direct companion of the prophet. The *Hadith* (quoted in Chapter One, Article Seven of the *Hamas* Covenant) continues: ". . .and until the Jews hide themselves behind a stone or tree, and a stone or tree says: 'Muslim or Servant of God, there is a Jew behind me; come and kill him. . .'" The *Hamas* Covenant may be found in English translation, among other places, on the internet.

Chapter 10

Israel and the Palestinians

The *dhimma-jihad* sensibility militates against an easy willingness on the part of Israelis to believe that the Arabs will ever accept an independent Jewish State. This essential distrust of the Arabs—Muslim or Christian—is reinforced each time some anti-Israel statement is made or action takes place. Thus not only the declared wars of army against army but the declared or undeclared *intifadas* of civilians against civilians corroborates this distrust. Each such instance validates the sense of distrust cultivated by the memory of the post-World War I through post-World War II era and in particular the role of which Haj Amin al-Husseini is the symbol.[104]

There is, in addition, the following progression of reinforcements of a single issue: with whom do we Israelis negotiate? Thus from the death of King Abd'Allah in 1951 (assassinated by one of Haj Amin's followers in large part because of Abd'Allah's willingness to talk peace with the Israelis) until 1977 (and Sa-

dat's visit to Jerusalem) no Arab leader was willing to talk to the Israelis—for talking meant recognizing Israel's right to exist. Thereafter, as that situation began to change and became more fully focused on the Palestinians, for the next fifteen years the Israelis claimed, with some justification, that they could not determine with *whom* they should negotiate.

That is, not only were there Israelis who refused to recognize the Palestinians as a legitimate group with legitimate group aspirations, but of those who were more open-minded the question was: would we negotiate with the PLO, and then: *Al'Fatah* or the PFLP or the DFLP or the PFLP-GC or with *Saiqa* or with the ALF?[105] And if with one or more of these groups, what of those that are left out of the negotiations? Will some continue to attack us while we are speaking peace with others? As I shall repeat below, this situation would be made more complicated by Israel's own actions, specifically the 1982 Invasion of Lebanon that ended up producing *Hizb'Allah* as a force to contend with. By the time of the 1991 Madrid talks, and certainly by the time of the 1993 Oslo Accords, this question had been swept aside, at least for enough Israelis, and the PLO and its leader—Yassir Arafat had long since succeeded Ahmad Shukayri as its Chairman, as *al'Fatah* had long since become the dominant presence in the PLO—were acknowledged as the legitimate opposite party with which to negotiate, even with the more limited but very noteworthy interventions by *Hizb'Allah* and *Hamas* during the period that followed.[106] With the break-down in the peace process seven years later, the level of distrust of those across the negotiating terrain escalated again.

At the inception of the period between Oslo and the Second *Intifada*, Israel also wrestled with whether and how to negotiate with Hafiz Assad-led Syria toward a peace concerning which some feared that whatever concessions were made, including the return of the entire Golan Heights, still Assad could not be trusted. There may be an irony here, since, historically, whatever else may be said of Assad, he could be relied upon to stick to

the letter of his agreements (as opposed, say, to Saddam Hussein, who was consistently unpredictable and unreliable, to say the least). Nonetheless, the perception of him by many Israelis was an intensified microcosmic encapsulation of their broader fear and distrust. Yet negotiation proceeded—until the assassination of Yitzhak Rabin in 1995; they hovered again on the edge of possibility under Ehud Barak but fell apart definitively when the Israeli-Palestinian peace process collapsed in 2000.

But if we look to Israel's distrust of its Arab neighbors near and far as a significant issue militating against a simple solution to the Israeli-Palestinian and Israeli-Arab problematic, we cannot limit the discussion to that issue. For from the Israeli perspective—the Jewish Israeli perspective—there is also the larger picture of a Christian Euro-American world that cannot be trusted not to abandon Israel to destruction when push comes to shove. This second issue of fear and distrust is rarely articulated. But it is largely why Israel so consistently rejects the idea of international monitors to help supervise agreements, as for example when Secretary of State Colin Powell endorsed such an idea in June, 2001.

Three interlocking elements feed into this gut-level response to the world and the siege mentality that, even now—perhaps especially now—nearly six decades after Israel's independence and the development of one of the most powerful armies in the world, nags at the Israeli heart and soul. There is, to be sure, the powerful history of fifteen centuries of Jew-hatred taught ("the Teaching of Contempt") and practiced at political, economic, social as well as theological levels. That Jew-hatred did not disappear or even, apparently, dissipate with the secularizing tendencies in Western Christendom of the past two to three centuries, as we have seen; it merely metamorphosed into modern anti-Semitism.[107]

The culmination of such hatred arrived in the middle of the twentieth century in the form of the Holocaust. And the significant thing about the Holocaust for this part of the dis-

cussion is not Nazism, per se, with its acolytes not merely in Germany and Austria but elsewhere as well. It is not simply those whose ideology included an active interest in annihilating the Jews and Judaism and whose ideology perceived Jews insistently as racialized, so that someone who was already two generations beyond being or feeling Jewish was susceptible to destruction. It is rather those who aided and abetted the Nazi dream by refusing to act contrary to that dream, where the saving of Jews was concerned. In other words, the Lutheran and Catholic Churches in Germany that embraced Hitler and their concomitants across Europe. In other words, the British who closed the gates to Palestine and the Americans who refused to bomb the train tracks to Auschwitz. We may read stories of this Priest or that who risked his life to save Jews or of how the Danish King wore a yellow star in solidarity with his Jewish subjects. But as stunning as such stories are, they shrink in the selective memory to which all humans are subject against stories like that of the Slovakian Archbishop Kametko, approached by a former colleague and friend, a respected Slovakian rabbi, regarding the impending expulsion of the Jews.

> "The archbishop. . . decided to enlighten him regarding the true fate that was awaiting the Jews in Poland. These were his words: 'This is no mere expulsion. There—you will not die of hunger and pestilence; there—they will slaughter you all, old and young,women and children, in one day. This is your punishment for the death of our Redeemer'."

—or the comment of the Papal Nuncio regarding the same situation: "There is no innocent blood of Jewish children in the world. All Jewish blood is guilty. You have to die. This is the punishment that has been awaiting you because of that sin (meaning the death of Jesus)."[108]

This Holocaust-induced distrust is the second element that amplifies the first, in the matter of distrusting the Christian West. One might argue rationally—but humans, our minds and our

memories, our hearts and our guts are not rational—that the era of the Holocaust is long enough past that it should not cast a shadow over Israel's willingness to trust the Christian world monitoring and/or engaging the progress of its relations with the Arabs. But even were it possible for pure reason to eclipse emotion, many Israelis might find the record of Christian-Israel "relations" since the Holocaust troubling.

It is interesting to recall that, until 1967, a substantial percentage of American Jews were not particularly interested in or supportive of Israel. They feared that to do so would find them the object of an accusation of dual loyalty (and indeed such an accusation could be heard often in the 1950s, 1960s and 1970s). Or they worried that, given the extraordinary and unprecedented opportunities that the United States offered to Jews, it would be foolish to focus on an enterprise ten thousand miles away with little relevance to the reshaped Jewish reality *cum* American Dream. In the case of the Ultra-Orthodox, the conviction that Israel as an enterprise that had not been created by Divine act was a contravention of Divine Will and thus a sacrilege was still in place. These objections to Israel's existence echoed the layers of Jewish opposition to the Zionist idea at the turn between the nineteenth and twentieth centuries to which I earlier referred.[109]

The months leading up to the June War began to change that objectionist viewpoint in most places. As it appeared that Israel would be annihilated, and as the Western powers shrugged their political and diplomatic shoulders and acted as if there was nothing they could do about the situation, more and more Jews—particularly American Jews—smelled something all too familiar. With the Holocaust barely a generation behind them—and the memory of it even fresher in their minds than it might otherwise have been due to the capture and trial of Adolf Eichmann only six years before—there emerged a sense that once again push was coming to shove and the Christian world (calling itself secular, in the West, at least, but also in

substantial parts of the Soviet East) would turn its back on a substantial Jewish population that was about to be destroyed. If massive Jewish support for Israel was one consequence of this event-thought sequence, the other, in spite of the stunning Israeli victory, was the affirmation of distrust for the Christian world, which distrust might otherwise have dissipated within a generation or two after the Holocaust.

So this is the third link in the chain of fear—reinforcing the first two—that invests the Jewish Israeli soul (that if we don't take care of ourselves, nobody will, that we will be abandoned to the Arab wolves if we allow ourselves to be sheep). This link amounts to everything that feeds that fear based on history and on the Holocaust in the decades *since* June, 1967. Thus the sense of imminent destruction on the eve of the 1967 war and of a sense that the Christian world would do little to avert it was and is joined, even after the extraordinary success of the June War, to the inability of the Western Powers to push for a ceasefire in the first two weeks of the 1973 Yom Kippur War. That no ceasefire could be arranged when the Arab armies were advancing successfully and Israelis were dying in much larger numbers than had been true in the previous two wars (i.e., that of 1956 and that of 1967)—which inability was quickly transformed, once the Israelis had counter-attacked and encircled the Third Egyptian Army on the one hand and advanced to within a stone's throw of Damascus on the other—is interpreted by Jewish Israelis as another symptom of how the West cannot be trusted.

Israeli Jews—and many of their co-religionists in the Diaspora—find sources of ongoing distrust in what they perceive as a double standard of expectation for their behavior from a Western Christian world—including the United States—that exhibits none of the morality on the political and military fronts that it demands of Israel. They find it in specific issues, such as the ongoing refusal of the Vatican to recognize the State of Israel (which situation changed, however, in the 1990s—but

only in the aftermath of Oslo and the Vatican's recognition of the Palestinian Authority in an equivalent manner). Every time the media shows a Palestinian being injured by an Israeli soldier without showing the attack on the Israeli soldiers that precipitated a violent response or the United Nations excoriates Israel for destroying an Iraqi nuclear reactor or airplanes on the ground at Beirut Airport with no loss of human life but ignores the bombing of a bus filled with Israeli schoolchildren, it confirms the conviction that the West is still dominated by Jew-hatred merely reconfigured as anti-Israel sentiments.[110] When the French Ambassador to Britain refers to Israel as "that shitty little country" and accuses it of being responsible for the world's problems and he receives not even a scintilla of a rebuke from his government, much less recall, it furthers that conviction.[111]

Aside from the double distrust, of their Arab and Muslim neighbors near and far and of the Secular Christian Western world so focused on Middle Eastern oil and its concomitants, there has emerged in the last thirty-five years another component within Israel's other-then-easy-ability to commit itself wholeheartedly to peace discussions with the Palestinians: religious conviction. For one of the clear changes in Israeli demographics after 1967 was the upsurge in immigrants from the West—particularly the United States—with powerful religious convictions asserting the divinely-mandated legitimacy not only of an independent Jewish state, but one that extends from the Mediterranean Sea to the Jordan River or, in the minds of some, to Mesopotamia. This is a classic case of interpreting God's word so that the revelation accords not only with one's spiritual beliefs but with one's political position. There is obviously a double irony here: much of the Orthodox and certainly the ultra-Orthodox Jewish community by and large disavowed the legitimacy of an autonomous Jewish State between 1896 and 1967; and American Jews in general were remarkably unconcerned and unsupportive of the Zionist idea during that same period.[112]

This religion-based demographic is still more complicated,

it seems to me, by the fact that so many of the "settlers" *are* American. If establishing themselves in the heart of Hebron or the outskirts of Bethlehem—the Israeli frontier—is justified by their convictions regarding what God intended for this piece of real estate, deep in their guts is the sort of simple certainty famously expressed by the American actor John Wayne during the Vietnam era, when he observed that the United States should "just go in there and clean the enemy out" the way he so often did in his movies: walking into a bar and gunning down three or four bad guys at a pop. That cowboy imagery is wedded to the vision of settlers successfully protecting themselves from Native Americans (the "Indians") as they establish a growing number of beachheads for Euro-Americans across the continent. The very word "frontier" resonates with most Americans toward Wild West images.

It was the mid-nineteenth-century concept of "manifest destiny" that justified in the minds of thousands of Euro-Americans—well before there were movies to further romanticize their efforts—their God-given right and responsibility to push their presence all the way to the Pacific Ocean.[113] How many thousand upon thousands of Native Americans were dispossessed of their lands, livelihoods and even their lives as Europeans settled the America that became the United States?[114] What I am suggesting is, in a sense, two things. The first (to repeat) is that, psychologically, a majority of the Israeli settlers—numbering, depending upon who is counting, somewhere between 160,000 and 200,000 as of 2002—have established themselves in the Palestinian Territories not only out of conscious Jewish religious-national convictions but out of an unconscious American frontier-heroic-cowboy-John Wayne sensibility. (Note the terms "settlers" and "frontier" and their resonance for American history). The second is that, given this complicated psycho-spiritual condition, the possibility of simply removing them is nil (which means a different solution, if there is one, must be sought) and that whatever role the United States might play

in working toward an Israeli-Palestinian peace is more layered than one might otherwise suppose.

From a less religious and more historico-political perspective is the assertion that, just as the shape that the State of Israel took in 1949 was a consequence of a war fought because a more truncated version proposed at the United Nations in 1947 was rejected by the Arabs, so the expanded shape after 1967 reflected the rejection by the Arabs of the more limited version of Israel that had prevailed between 1949 and 1967. Therefore, just as the one became accepted by the international community, so ought the second—and besides, the times and places in world history where the changes in borders due to war have been reversed by concessions from the victor are few and far between. But the answer to that is simply that after 1967, part of the non-acceptance picture changed: a post-1949 Israel has been acknowledged as legitimate by Egypt since 1979 and by Jordan since 1994. Thus if territorial concessions to the Palestinians will complete a new picture, of *acceptance*, then it is worth breaking with historical precedent.

*   *   *   *   *

But there is still more to the issue of religious conviction: ignoring for the moment the problem stated in the previous paragraphs and what it implies, for example, regarding the "legitimacy" of Jewish settlements under Israeli governance in Gaza and the West Bank, there is a subtler and more profound issue to be considered. Supposing an Israel that returns to its pre-1967 borders, and an Arab population within that Israel similar in size and disposition to that which existed prior to 1967, how can that population function with a sense of its own identity and yet as Israeli—as opposed to experiencing a sense of alienation from either Israel or itself or both? *How*, given both the very different Palestinian Arab consciousness that has evolved for that population not only since 1967, but since 1982

and especially since the Madrid-Oslo period of the early 1990s and the Second *Intifada* that began in the aftermath of the 1999-2000 collapse of Israeli-Palestinian negotiations? Put otherwise: how can even a geo-politically smaller rather than greater Israel remain both a Jewish state and a Democracy?

The Israeli Declaration of Independence explicitly pledges that the new state will "foster the development of the country for the benefit of all its inhabitants; it will be based on freedom, justice and peace as envisaged by the prophets of Israel; it will ensure complete equality of social and political rights to all of its inhabitants irrespective of religion, race or gender; it will guarantee freedom of religion, conscience, language, education and culture. . ." This sort of declaration is reminiscent of the principles underlying the American Declaration of Independence and the U.S. Constitution. And like the United States, Israel has not managed to live entirely up to the ideals its founding fathers posed for it.

It is true, for example, that Arabs serve in the Knesset, and that an Arab judge served for a year—but only a year—on the Israeli Supreme Court. It is true that the first Muslim Arab member of the Knesset, Abdulmalik Dahamsha gave his inaugural speech, in 1996, in Arabic, and succeeded in having a mosque established in the Knesset building, and that the Christian Arab Azmi Bishara (also elected to the Knesset in 1996) even mounted a campaign for election as Prime Minister in 1998. It is also true that Israeli Arabs are freer and economically better off than their counterparts *anywhere in the Arab world*, and that some of the limitations they endure derive from not doing army service (which has been a key to success in Israel both because of the respect accorded to those who serve and due to the connections one makes, practically speaking, while in the army)—and their not serving in the army has, for most of Israel's history, been a mutually agreed-upon situation that recognizes potential conflicts of interest for Israeli Arabs.

But the Arab representation in the Knesset is still significantly

lower than the percentage of the Arab population of Israel, and Bishara was stripped of his parliamentary immunity in 2001 to face charges of supporting terrorist organizations after he gave two controversial speeches. In August, 2000 he had hailed the Israeli withdrawal from Lebanon as a victory for *Hizb'Allah* and the following year, in Syria, called upon Arabs to "enlarge the sphere of resistance."[115] I am not passing judgment on his treatment under the circumstances.[116] But by comparison, although the 1983 Israeli commission headed by its Supreme Court president, Yitzhak Kahan, found Ariel Sharon guilty of "indirect, but personal responsibility for having disregarded the danger of acts of vengeance and bloodshed by the Phalangists" in the 1982 massacres in the Sabra and Shatila refugee camps in Lebanon, and as a consequence, he was forced to resign as defense minister, he was permitted to remain in the government as a minister without portfolio. More to the point, it may have taken nearly two decades, but ultimately he could and did mount a successful campaign to become Prime Minister.[117] In spite of such a—murderous—history.

What one might glean from this handful of data is that if Israel has not managed to fulfill the letter or spirit of its own Declaration of Independence, part of the blame for that failure falls on the complicated conditions in which Israel has existed from its inception: the fears and distrust of Muslims and Christians for long-term historical reasons in general, and more to the point, of its own Arab population in particular, given shorter-term history. This does not mean that more strenuous efforts ought not to be made to bring reality and the ideal of full democracy closer together, it merely reminds us that that effort will require multi-lateral and not unilateral attention. And if, for the sake of argument, a comparison be made with the American historical relationship with First Americans and with African Americans, Israel does not fare so badly both with regard to failure to fulfill its own ideals and with regard to the conditions that militate for or against successful fulfillment.

Any number of different thinkers in Israel has addressed this issue from their respective perspectives. Thus for example, Ilan Pappe wrote (in a response to an article in *Ha'aretz* in 1994 on a related issue[118] in which Aharon Megged quoted from Pappe) that "I will continue to argue that we must resolve the serious contradiction between a Zionist and Jewish statehood and civil rights and democracy, not just as a way of repairing the injustices of the past, but mostly to make normal life in the future possible. A democratic and pluralistic Israel as part of the Mediterranean basin is also an Israel of varied historical narratives, of more than one truth. Such an Israel bears hope for a common future."[119]

When Minister of Education Yossi Sarid, leader of the left-wing Meretz Party, announced at the end of February 2000 that some poems by Mahmud Darwish—generally considered to be one of the greatest of the modern Arab language poets, but an Israeli Arab who in political exile became a PLO leader—would be placed in the Israeli school literature curriculum, Uzi Landau, of the right-wing Likud Party responded with horror: "When they say more Darwish there's less Bialek.[120] There is less Zionism and more post-Zionism and less Jewish history and more fabricated Palestinian history and fabricated Zionist and Jewish history." Ron Milo, of the Center Party, commented: "My fear is that they're not studying enough Israeli history, that they are not studying enough about the land of Israel, that they're not studying enough history of the Jewish people. That's my fear. If they have that, I'm not scared of Darwish." Re'uven Rivlin, of Likud, said "I understand that we are a nation that has to a large extent lost its need for symbols, for an ethos, for a tradition that has led us and brought us to this point, but still it is a matter of honor. . . There's no censorship. You can buy Darwish in every store. . . But to put him onto the school agenda—that makes a statement: that says there's no honor, you can do whatever you want with us, because we aren't worth anything."[121]

Ruth Gavison, a professor of Law and an expert on civil

rights has "likened the status of Israel's Arab citizens to the status of Jews in the United States... she does not believe that their [the Israeli Arabs'] sense of alienation justifies the assertion that Israel is not a democratic state" since they enjoy significant and equal political rights together with personal freedom and security. Should the Arab Israelis' *sense* of limitation or *actual* limitations "take precedence over the right of the Jewish people to a state in which it governs and in which it is the majority?"[122] Sami Smooha, an Arab professor of sociology at the University of Haifa has called for cultural autonomy for Israeli Arabs: governed by The Basic Law of Human Dignity and Liberty, Israeli Arabs would be guaranteed democratic rights. They would function officially as they mostly currently do unofficially: as a non-territorially separate entity—the equivalent of the condition of the Ultra-Orthodox Jewish community in Israel—in which a supreme Arab council, empowered by the Knesset following a referendum of all Israeli Arabs, and centered around an executive committee, would represent the Arabs to the authorities in all areas of public life. Israel would remain functionally Jewish but more effectively democratic with respect to its primary non-Jewish minority.[123]

More recently, in Daniel Gavron's brief January 12, 2009 article in *Newsweek*, the author argues that "Israel could break the stalemate [regarding Israeli voters' views of how to achieve peace with the Palestinians] by fully enfranchising its Arabs, who make up about 14 percent of voters."[124] Largely excluded from proximity "to the center of power," an invigorated Israeli Arab voting population might have given Tzipi Livni's more leftist, two-state-advocating party the Prime Minister's office over Binyamin Netanyahu's more rightist, two-state-questioning, -doubting (or even -opposing) party.

Writing prior to that election, Gavron observed that, "[f]or that to happen, the Israeli peace camp must declare in advance its willingness to ally with Arab parties. Such an Arab-Jewish coalition would also have a galvanizing effect on Israel's popu-

lation and help address years of discrimination. Israeli Arabs are feeling bitter about the Gaza attacks, but one of their own was the second victim of *Hamas* rocket fire in the first days of fighting, which should make it easier to emphasize that they are an integral part of Israeli society." Gavron's discussion seems almost too simple to me, as far as the bold title of the article is concerned, and more fundamentally, as far as turning the identity complications *felt by* Israeli Arabs into the political solution *derived from* Israeli Arabs. But even so, his articulation of the specifics of how the playing field might be made somewhat more level and the positive consequences of that leveling for both Jews and Arabs within Israel—and perhaps also for Palestinians—deserves serious consideration.

The discussion within Israel is almost endless on this issue. Israel is, in this respect, at the opposite end of where its founders were over a century ago—and perhaps even sixty years ago—when the question of where the non-Jewish indigenous Arab population might fit into the Zionist vision seems not to have crossed anybody's mind. Ironically enough, it seems to me that then the founders were being no better and no worse than humans everywhere, be they European, African or Asian, be they Western or Middle Eastern; and now indeed the Israelis engaged in this discussion are living up to the positive side of a double standard typically applied by the outside world that demands of them that they operate from a Jewish perspective that is based on the best, most ideal of Jewish senses of justice, carved out during centuries of diasporatic political, social, economic and cultural disenfranchisement. The vociferousness of the debate is to Israel's credit as a democracy.

If in the end, Israel remains a state that follows a Jewish calendar and is attached to all sorts of Jewish cultural and even religious ideas, then it could be legitimately viewed as no more than the single Jewish mirror of the myriad secular Christian and very few secular Muslim states in which Jewish minorities live in relative psychological comfort and yet with what must

be, at times, an intense sense of alienation. Whether we look at the United States—with a National Cathedral in Washington, DC that is nominally both non-denominational and omni-denominational but actually Episcopalian (when was the last time anyone suggested that the leadership of the Cathedral be passed over a multiple-year cycle, among leaders from various *Christian* denominations, much less Christian and *non*-Christian denominations?) and where Christmas breathes through every pore of the nation between Thanksgiving and New Year's Day—or we look at Catholic France or Italy or Muslim Turkey; we are looking at states that are theoretically secular but that actually, in varying degrees, pursue cultural and/or spiritual courses in which those who are not part of the majority can play only an uncomfortable or unreal part.

Can't Israel simply be—or can Israel simply *not* be—the mirror of such a condition, only with Judaism as the majority? In what way is this issue legitimate, and in what way might the very raising of it suggest a different standard to which Israel is being held than is held, say, by Americans for America? (And this ignores the present power-struggle within the United States between segments of the Christian Right—and their overt desire to assume the necessary political control that will "bring America back to its Christian roots"—and those whose vision of America, and whose understanding of the founders' vision of America is, of a secular state in which all denominations are free not only to follow their form of faith but to feel fully enfranchised as Americans).

*   *   *   *   *

So from the Israeli side—to return to this issue—the roadblock to peace includes, among other matters a significant volume of distrust and fear that is not merely directed to the Arabs but to the world beyond the Middle East.

All three groups that have been the primary elements in

this narrative—those with conflicting aspirations and those who add to these their own aspirations and interferences—are joined in a circle not only of confusion and conflict but of fear, perturbation and selective memory. This is in spite of certain rather significant progress in Arab-Israel relations that emerged during the 1970s. The most obvious was the unexpected decision of Egyptian Prime Minister Anwar Sadat to come to Jerusalem to address the Israeli Parliament—the Knesset—and ultimately to sign a peace accord with Israel in 1978.[125]

That stunning moment has at least two aspects that are important for this discussion. One is the context in which Sadat justified his offering the olive branch to Israel. He distanced himself from the Arabs, rhetorically questioning why Egypt, a "non-Arab state" had spent the previous three decades fighting wars with Israel "on behalf of the Arabs." In this rhetorical question we find the matter of definition with respect to the word "Arab" once more before us.

The other aspect is contained within the assassination of Sadat that followed several years after the peace with Israel. Muslim extremists—they were associated with the *Muslim Brotherhood*-derived group calling itself *Islamic Jihad*—gunned him down on October 6, 1981 as he presided over an anniversary celebration of Egypt's success against Israel in the Yom Kippur War and conversely, the Egyptian-Israeli peace treaty.[126] In their court trial they argued that Sadat had betrayed Islamic principles and thus the Islamic world by an entire series of actions. Of these, the peace with Israel was only one and not the first on the list that they read before the court. Modernization and improper attire and behavior permitted to women such as Sadat's own wife were considered as or more significant, as was the use of force during the previous month to suppress political dissidents. But Sadat's assassination might and did raise doubts among many Israelis regarding whether a larger peace with their neighbors would be possible, just as it would raise the bar of fear another notch for Arab leaders considering peace with Israel.

On the other hand, not only has the peace with Egypt held through the decades since Sadat's death and the ascent to power of his successor, Hosni Mubarrak—none of the conditions has been abrogated in the thirty years since Sadat and Begin signed it—even if it has not been a warm peace. Moreover, one of the leaders of the group that assassinated Sadat—Karam Zuhdi—stated in a July, 2003 interview that if he could go back in time "I would interfere to prevent it [the assassination]." He suggested that *Islamic Jihad* misinterpreted the *shari'a* in perceiving religious grounds to justify Sadat's assassination. The point of this assertion is that even apparently intractable religious perspectives can shift if there is a desire to think and rethink spiritual matters and not to remain embedded in a given viewpoint.

The fuel of Israeli fear is stoked when they hear from a leading Palestinian like Salah Ta'mari, an important associate and supporter of Yassir Arafat, that "I have not abandoned my dream of a democratic state in all of Palestine where Palestinians—Jews and non-Jews—will live together." For they interpret such a comment, for good historical reasons, as encoded: there will be no Israel, the Arabs will be in charge, and Jews may live here under a Palestinian umbrella as elsewhere across Arab Muslim-Jewish history and geography. Israelis hear *dhimma* in that comment and given the absence of a single democracy in the Arab world in the past or the present, fear the reality behind its generous-sounding words as uncomfortable, to say the least. When they hear Ta'mari comment, regarding Arafat, that "the minute he loses faith in this agreement [the Oslo-Wye Accords], Arafat does not lack the courage to say 'the agreement is finished, and we are no longer abiding by it.' He has great courage, both in war and in peace"—they hear duplicity, not courage, and a reinforcement of their conviction that they cannot trust Arafat or the Palestinians.[127]

In the years since Arafat's death, a good deal of further water has flowed under the bridge. In the first place Arafat's "successor"—at least as a theoretically interested partner with

Israel in arriving at some sort of lasting peace arrangement between the two parties—Mahmud Abbas, has shown himself to be minimally capable of delivering on peace-initiative sorts of agreements with the Israelis. More to the point, he and the *Fatah*-based Palestinian Authority that he leads found themselves unable to sustain a position of leadership, much less unity, within the Palestinian world at large. They were removed from power by the electorate of Gaza in 2006-7, leaving that side of the playing field entirely in the hands of the *Hamas* organization, which has fairly consistently denounced the Oslo Accords and any arrangement that provides for the ongoing existence of the State of Israel.[128]

More significantly from the Israeli point of view is the idea that the Israeli decision—under the leadership of Ariel Sharon, of all people—to unilaterally pull out of Gaza in 2004-5,[129] as a presumably preliminary act of a further process of land-for-peace negotiation, has led only to disaster, to date. Aside from the internal Israeli political and religious debate—a coalition of right-wing rabbis pronounced a curse on Sharon;[130] and his key competitor in his own political party, Binyamin Netanyahu, mounted an internal offensive against Sharon's continued leadership—there were many outside Israel who suspected his motives, based in part on an October 8, 2004 interview in the Israeli newspaper, *Haaretz*. There he asserted both that peace could only come when the Palestinians renounce terrorism against Israel, (fair enough), and that the withdrawal from Gaza would meanwhile freeze the peace process (meaning what exactly? But certainly a suspicious-sounding comment).

But the point is, that if, in the aftermath of the withdrawal there *had* been such a renunciation, then the net effect would not have been to freeze the process, but to further it. However, in the aftermath of the Israeli withdrawal, little positive seems to have been attempted on the part of the Gazan leadership, before or after *Hamas* took charge, to shape anything resembling an effective, forward-looking infrastructure, along cultural, social,

economic or political lines. On the contrary, everything seems to have moved in a negativist, retrograde direction.

We can see this on at least three fronts. One is that, while the Israelis had been present in Gaza, they had invested in a good deal of building besides houses and several synagogues—including, for example, an extensive array of greenhouses, using hydroponics to produce food and other flora in the fairly unforgiving natural environment of the Gazan area. Rather than continuing—even furthering—such projects, the Gazans simply destroyed them, exhibiting little but pointless rage the endpoint of which was to deprive themselves of resources that were theirs for the taking.

Two is that the rage and frustration with the *Fatah*-led Palestinian National Authority leadership's corruption and inability to provide leadership, services or hope—abetted by the Bush administration's forcing the issue of free elections and openly expressing its support of *Fatah*—led (to repeat) to an overwhelming victory by *Hamas* in the elections of 2006 and a change in Gaza's leadership, after a civil war between *Hamas* and the *Fatah*, by 2007. Aside from how one might abhor the intense violence enacted by members of *Hamas* against their defeated political opponents, one might also feel dismay that they in the end offered very little that improved the lives of Gazans.[131]

What they did do (and this is the third symptom of negativist, retrograde development) was to expand and extend a program of military activity against Israel, raining hundreds of rockets from Gaza into southern Israel. Those attacks waxed and waned over the course of the next few years—there was even a brief ceasefire, which, depending upon whose perspective one assumes, either means that *Hamas can* renounce violence under the right circumstances and come to the peace conference table; or that *Hamas'* renunciations are smoke screens behind which they consistently prepare greater violence. In any case, after two years of this, the Israelis finally responded with a merciless and blistering attack on Gaza in December, 2008-January, 2009, in

which not only members of *Hamas*, but hundreds of Palestinian innocents lost their lives.[132]

Thus from the increasingly majority Israeli perspective, pulling out of Gaza led only to endless harassment until the ugly day of reckoning finally arrived, for which most Israelis felt there was no choice. Moreover, in a pattern reminiscent of the circumstances in 2000 of failed Israeli-Palestinian negotiations that helped bring Ariel Sharon into the Prime Minster's office, certainly the catastrophic relationship with Gaza culminating with "Operation Cast Lead" helped return Bibi (Binyamin) Netanyahu to that office—and Netanyahu has, to date, not expressed enthusiasm for any sort of Palestinian state. On the contrary, he has presented the impression of someone willing and even eager to establish further Israeli settlements in the West Bank.

Israelis on the political left are struggling to provide an answer to the question of who on the Palestinian side should be their counterpart—and whether the government of Mahmud Abbas, still in power in the West Bank, and still nominally engaged in dialogue with the Israelis, can deliver a true peace treaty with or without the cooperation of the *Hamas*-led Gazans.

Notes

[104] See above, 98.

[105] These different organizations were very much still in play in the 1980s, between the time of the Israel-Egypt Peace Treaty and the developments leading to the Oslo Accords. PLO means "Palestine Liberation Organization;" it was officially established (at a conference in the Ambassador Hotel in Jordanian-controlled East Jerusalem). One might call the PLO's central core the group which Yassir Arafat had founded with a small circle of friends in Kuwait in 1959 when Arafat was working as an engineer in the emirate's public works; it is (or was) called *al'Fatah* ("the opening" or "conquest"). PFLP stands for "Popular Front for the Liberation of Palestine" and emerged as Fatah's primary rival within the PLO or apart from the PLO by late 1967. DFLP stands for "Democratic Front for the Liberation of Palestine" and split off from the PFLP in 1969; DFLP-GC means "Popular Front for the Liberation of Palestine—General Command" and it also split off from the PFLP, but in 1968. *Saiqa* ("the Thunderbolt") was a Palestinian branch of the Ba'ath Party created by the Syrians in October, 1968; and ALF stands for "Arab Liberation Front" and was created by Iraq in order to counter Syrian influence within the PLO but with a more pan-Arab than merely Palestinian make-up and agenda. Each of these splinters, in fact, has its own agenda. For details, see Aaron David Miller's excellent small book, *The PLO and the Politics of Survival*, especially 40-65. If by now most of the details are moot, the general issue of fragmented negotiating partners is not.

[106] The Americans pushed the Likud Party Israeli Prime Minister, Yitzhak Shamir to the Madrid Peace Conference in October, 1991, after which the infant peace process might have died a crib death, but when in 1992 Yitzhak Rabin and his Labor Party were elected, the process gained the momentum that brought it to Oslo the following year.

[107] See above, 2, 34.

[108] Both passages are quoted in Eliezer Berkovits, *Faith After the Holocaust*, 17. There are other similar quotes from similar individuals quoted by Berkovits, the sum of which would make one despair of any future for Jewish-Christian relations were there not antidote passages during the Holocaust and since. More recently, Steve Martin's documentary film, *Three Theologians and Hitler* tells the chilling story of how three prominent German Lutheran theologians used their engagement of the Bible and other Christian texts to validate Hitler and used the power of their position as religious leaders to garner support for him and his cause.

[109] See above, 76-8. Echoes of this are heard in-between these eras, as well, of course. Thus at the time of the birth of Israel, the Chief Rabbi of Iraq, Sassoon Kliadouri, denounced the creation of a Jewish state—he continued

to espouse that view as late as 1969 even when Iraq hanged several Jews, as well as some Muslims and Christians for "spying" for Israel. Whether in both cases this was due to religious conviction of the sort to which I have referred above or as an act of survival in a dicey political environment is difficult to say with certainty.

[110] See the discussion of this by the Catholic theologian, Eva Fleischner, in her 1974 paper that was part of a conference, "Auschwitz: The Beginning of a New Era?" held at the Church of St. John the Divine in New York City, and inspired by the events of the Yom Kippur War. Other papers by Christian theologians from that conference, notably those by Gregory Baum, Aarne Siirala and Johannes Christiaan Hoekendijk, are also of interest and were all gathered in the volume of that name edited by Fleischner. The letter to the conference from Gabriel Habib is also significant both for what it suggests regarding the relationship between the Holocaust and the Israeli-Palestinian conflict and for what Habib fails to understand with regard to the overall content of the conference. Most recently this issue of a double standard seemed to reveal itself in January, 2009, when the entire world seemed up in arms regarding the Israeli attack on Gaza but with nary a comment or a reference to the hundreds upon hundreds of rocket attacks from Gaza into southern Israel that provoked the Israeli attack, nor any reference either to the cynical use by *Hamas* of mosques, hospitals and, in general, civilians, as hideouts, arms-storage facilities and shields; of their massacres of their political opponent fellow-Palestinians; or of the lengths to which the Israelis went to warn civilians of impending attacks on buildings they understood to be containing *Hamas* fighters or arms caches. I am not debating the issue of how appropriate or inappropriately large the Israeli response was, but commenting on the general media failure to consider these other aspects of the situation. Interestingly, the most notable exception to this was the Arab leadership and its media, which reacted far less strongly to the Israeli attacks than one might have expected.

[111] Barbara Amiel reported that French Ambassador Daniel Bernard had made the comment at a party at her home. It was reported in the *London Daily Telegraph* and subsequently elsewhere. I first saw it cited in the *National Review* in a January 10, 2002 article by Tom Gross.

[112] See above, 76-7 and 131.

[113] The concept was first floated by the young New York City journalist, John L. O'Sullivan in 1839, although he first used the actual phrase in a pair of articles in 1845.

[114] This should, incidentally make those Americans who are critical of the settler movement less self-righteous about it: critical, yes, but not self-righteous, since our own American history—our secular Christian American history—did on an exponentially larger scale in North America what the

settlers are seeking to do in the West Bank. And on the other hand it should reinforce criticism of the settlers since the imagery of American injustice toward Native Americans stares us in the face as a sufficiently reasonable comparative experience to that evolving in Israel-Palestine.

[115] In the first case, he went on to refer to that "victory" as one producing "a spark of hope;" in the second case there is some debate as to what he actually meant in the larger context of his remarks.

[116] Did he *hail* the withdrawal or *adjudge* the withdrawal as a victory for *Hizb'Allah*? If the former, and depending upon what he meant by "enlarging the sphere of resistance," then what were the options facing the Israeli courts? (I am asking this straightforwardly and not rhetorically.) What would happen to a US congressman who made comparable statements? Except that there are no comparable statements simply imaginable, since the United States is not in a comparable position vis-à-vis its neighbors or with regard to internal disaffected groups to that of Israel.

[117] More subtly with respect to Arab participation in the Knesset is the fact that the Arab political parties are never invited to become part of the sort of party coalitions—are barred by tradition from joining coalition governments—that are always part of such a multi-party system. Those who are part of a coalition may often wield some negotiating power for issues dear to their party, even if they are a small party; those who don't participate are virtually powerless. In the January 12, 2009 *Newsweek* article by Daniel Gavron, the writer observes that "Arabs have served in the cabinet, but only if they were members of Zionist (Jewish) parties. On a few occasions, Arab parties have formed temporary blocking coalitions with Zionists, but the Arabs were never allowed close to the center of power." It should also be remembered, on the other hand, that the political voice of Israeli Arabs has become complicated by divisions within the Israeli Arab community both since Oslo and since the beginning of the Al 'Aqsa *intifada*; and that that voice not only dwarfs that of Jews in any and all of the Arab lands, but most of the of Arabs in most of the Arab countries. See also, below, fn 124.

[118] The issue was the "new historiography" of the "post-Zionist era" of the past fifteen years in which the historiography regarding the founding decades of the state has been under aggressive review.

[119] Ilan Pappe, "A Lesson in New History," *Ha'aretz*, 24 June 1994. He is quoted (on page 140) in the discussion offered in Segev, *Elvis*, 133-56.

[120] Haim Nahman Bialek is regarded as the ultimate modern Hebrew poet, and commonly referred to by Hebraists as the father of modern Hebrew poetry.

[121] I have selected only a handful from the assortment of quotes offered in Segev, *Elvis*, 146-50.

[122] Both quotes come from Segev, *Elvis*, 151.

[123] *Ibid*, 152-6. Not all Israeli Arabs agree with Smooha's proposals, mainly out of fear that, if implemented, they would cement a condition of inferior civil status—turning Israeli Arab Christians and Muslims, in effect, into *dhimmi*. Of those who agree in principle, not all agree on the details.

[124] Daniel Gavron, "Israel's Arabs Are the Answer," *Newsweek*, January 12, 2009, 33—and see above, fn 117.

[125] To be more precise, the Camp David Accords brokered by President Jimmy Carter were initiated in September, 1978 but, due to several crises, it was not until March, 1979 that the full peace treaty was signed. In spite of the relatively cold nature of the aftermath relations between Israel and Egypt, at least since Sadat's assassination in 1981, the treaty has never been abrogated by either side. Perhaps the best—certainly the most thorough—one-volume account of the diplomatic backdrop to the Egyptian-Israeli treaty is William Quandt's *Camp David: Peacemaking and Politics*.

[126] Both comments were made by Ta'mari in a 1998 interview with Anton La Guardia. See Anton La Guardia, *War Without End: Israelis, Palestinians, and the Struggle for a Promised Land*, 147.

[127] The group's name morphed several times before arriving at *"Islamic Jihad"* and would shortly thereafter become closely allied with Ussama Bin Ladin and al-Qaeda. Prior to the assassination of Sadat the group obtained a *fatwa*—a religious ruling—approving the act on theological grounds, from Umar Abdul-Rahman, the cleric later convicted in the United States for his role in the 1993 World Trade Center bombing.

[128] I say "fairly consistently" as opposed to "consistently" in order to split a hair. Since *Hamas* has desisted, at times, from the rocket attacks from Gaza into Israel, and did agree, briefly, to a ceasefire with the Israelis, one could say that even they are not absolutely unsusceptible to the possibility of a peace agreement. Critics of this thought would argue that the ceasefire was abrogated all too quickly, demonstrating complete unsusceptibility.

[129] The decision made in 2004 led to Israeli soldiers forcibly evicting 9,840 Jewish settlers from 21 settlements in Gaza (and from four West Bank settlements), between August 16th and 30th, 2005. Every settlement structure, with the exception of a few synagogues and an array of greenhouses, were bulldozed by the Israelis. The last Israeli soldier formally withdrew from Gaza on September 11, 2005 and the border fence at Kissufim was closed.

[130] Seriously. In accordance with an ancient tradition, the group of rabbis, led by Rabbi Yosef Dayan, pronounced the *Pulsa diNoura*—literally, "lashes of fire," in Aramaic—which calls upon the Angel of Death to smite him. The Torah—and with it, the mainstream rabbinic tradition—forbids the act of praying that disaster befall someone; rather, one is enjoined to pray

that the evil inclination within a given individual perish so that s/he becomes righteous. I have no doubt that there are many who believe that the stroke that reduced Sharon to a coma and a vegetative state in early January, 2006 was a result of the curse. One keeps encountering additional ways in which religion and politics interweave each other.

[131] Put another way: *Hamas'* record of creating and maintaining a range of social services in other contexts was hardly in evidence in the roughly two years between their take over in Gaza and the Israeli reprisal attacks.

[132] The story is still incomplete and being told of that attack, both in terms of actual numbers of injured and killed (the Western media almost inevitably accepts the Palestinian statistics which more often than not turn out to be exaggerated; the Israeli numbers may be under-exaggerated but are typically ignored) and the kind of efforts made (or not) by Israel to minimize the "collateral damage"—as well as the role of *Hamas* in maximizing that damage to public relations advantage.

Chapter 11

Palestinians and Israel

This array of issues leads to the question of how these terms apply on the other side of the fence: in focusing on the Palestinians first and then more broadly on the Arabs in general—before returning to the question of Islam still more broadly—what militates against denouement with Israel? Let us, for the moment, ignore—as all too often, most journalists, politicians, diplomats and publicists tend to—the period before 1967. We shall return to it before this discussion has run its course. After the June, 1967 war, the areas where Palestinians had been resident outside Israel but not assimilated into Arab countries—Gaza and the West Bank—fell under Israeli rule. In military terms, Israel became the occupying authority, thereby, by definition, echoing the British before them and the Ottoman Turks before the British as an outsider presence.

So from the perspective of the Palestinians the nearly forty years since have mostly been years of humiliation and frustra-

tion. Particularly in the last few years this has become intensified by the post-peace-talks collapse and with it the *Second Intifada* on the one hand and the Sharonist mood of Israel on the other. It is certainly true that suicide bombings which target children on school busses and teen-agers in discos or celebrants of Passover Seders fall outside (among other things) the lines of behavior that might fill Israelis with trust in the humanity of the Palestinians. But so are the events precipitated by an occupying authority become afraid that every flower contains an explosive within its pistil, thus undermining Israeli humanity as it *affects* Palestinians.[133] From crowded border checkpoints, to the construction of a security fence and sometime wall that slices and dices the West Bank, to the overwhelming attack on Gaza, many—perhaps most—Palestinians despair of the willingness of the Israelis to really live side-by-side in peace with them.

> What choice do the occupied have in this state? Most Israeli Jews think that because the Palestinians refused to accept the "generous offer" they wished to impose on them, they should have waited patiently and continued talking indefinitely. But since February, 2001, if not earlier, the Palestinians have not had anyone to talk to or anything to talk about, apart from cosmetic changes in the way they are being dominated or an agreement to turn the occupation state back from temporary to permanent. . . And the occupation continues, the violence continues, the dispossession continues. What choice do the Palestinians have?[134]

> I can imagine what it was like in Ram'Allah when an F-16 bombed the police station there. I am not talking about civilians who were killed there—cooks from Gaza, not troops. I am talking about bombing a densely populated city. I am talking about liquidating people on the main street, from a helicopter, with three passersby also killed. It's impossible today to say that this was "collateral damage," that we didn't intend to kill civilians, because when a plane bombs a populated city, you take into account that civilians could get killed. . . I read this

week what the head of the Civil Administration, Brigadier General Dov Tzadka, said about the authorizations he gives to demolish houses and groves, and how the army then goes hyperactive and levels the area he authorized twice...I am constantly dumb-founded at how these people get up every morning and go to work. . .[135]

The PA [Palestinian Authority, empowered with responsibility for civic affairs in the Territories after the Oslo Accords] was given responsibility for civic affairs, like sewage, education, and road-building, for three million Palestinians. . .

But. . . it was administrative control over people without authority over most of the area in which they lived, and without any room for development, a requirement for every government. . . Nearly every administrative function by the PA required approval by the Israeli authorities. . . Israel controlled—and continues to control—all external borders, the passages inside the West Bank and from it to Gaza and back, the water sources, the economy, the movement of population into the Territories, and the registration of the Palestinian population.[136]

The authors of all three passages just quoted are neither Palestinian nor Arab nor are they Europeans or Americans. They are Israelis who are part of the small but significant voice that persistently speaks out regarding how impossible conditions have been for thirty-five years (now forty) and have become more than ever in the last three years (eight years) for the Palestinians under the Israeli occupation (and regarding how deleterious the occupation also is to the Israeli soul). The point is: if patriotic Israelis feel this way, how must the Palestinians themselves feel? How can they be expected to trust Israel when, with the shift from one regime to another the mood of reconciliation seems to alter so dramatically? How can they overcome their distrust and distaste honed through decades of this experience and come back to the table of negotiation?

And if we do step back beyond 1967 to 1948, we may see this condition as exponentially multiplied: the Palestinian view is that of having largely been pushed from lands that then became Israel in (and around) that year, into land much of which was occupied by Israel in 1967. Rashid Khalidi puts it simply, that "most of the population of the Strip is not originally from there, but rather from a swath of villages in the southern regions of Israel, whose inhabitants were driven or fled there during the fighting of 1948-49, and were never allowed to return from their homes."[137] Put otherwise, the rocket attacks into southern Israel from a Gaza Strip become free of Israelis in 2005 are viewed—at least by some Palestinians—as attacks into territory from which they had been forcibly ejected in 1948 and therefore *still* as attacks against occupiers, not legitimate inhabitants.

The question then becomes: is there a solution to a problem in which fundamentally the two antagonists both feel legitimately entitled to the same piece of property—particularly when we have no way of gauging in some objective manner who was precisely where sixty years ago and who did or did not try to return to where when it was possible and how possible it was at that time? We might then further ask to what extent violence is justified if the one committing the violence feels fundamentally dispossessed and that there is no other way to reverse the dispossession? And we might ask how to weigh the levels of violence from the two sides of the conflict fence: is there a different weight to be given to the two sides, Israeli and Palestinian, given who dwells where and who possesses the more substantial military power?

Moreover, if we are to grasp the layers of this issue within the larger issues of the Middle East, it is important to keep in mind that during the thirty-five (forty) years since 1967 the complications of functioning as a people have not been limited to those imposed on the Palestinians by Israeli governance. The most obvious example is the massacre effected by the Jordanians under King Hussein between September, 1970 and July, 1971—

known in Palestinian historiography as Black September—in which more Palestinians died than in all of the combined confrontations with Israel between 1948 and 2000.[138] And when the Israelis invaded Lebanon in 1982, because that is where militant factions of Palestinians had established themselves in the aftermath of the Black September debacle, they (the Israelis) were initially hailed as liberators by the local population, which had been brutalized and oppressed by the Palestinian militants among them for several years.

Nonetheless, just as Israel both overstayed its welcome in Lebanon and facilitated actions against Muslim Palestinians by Christian Lebanese allies of the Israelis in the 1980s, so the mainstream population of Palestinians found themselves in increasingly straitened conditions as the Israeli occupation plowed on through the 1970s and 1980s and into the early 1990s.[139]

More fundamentally, Palestinians became increasingly aware that their future would not be guaranteed from without: the various Arab states that made noises or even supplied guns or money for their cause would, in the end, not be able to pressure Israel sufficiently to provoke consideration of a Palestinian State. With that in mind, the willingness to escalate antagonistic efforts toward an *intifada* of the Israelis grew. There is a further ironic twist in this. The Israeli incursion into and continued presence in Lebanon in and then beyond 1982 had, as one of its unanticipated consequences the creation of a new Palestinian organization. In the aftermath of the hornets' nest of inter-relationships that had been stirred up, there emerged *Hizb'Allah*—the "Party of God"—a radical Shi'i movement that had, in part, drawn its inspiration from the religious revolution in Iran that had replaced the Shah with the Ayatollah Khomeini in 1979. The tactic that they adopted—of suicide car bombings—which first manifested itself in the attack that left 241 U.S. Marines and 30 Israeli soldiers in Tyre dead in late 1983, would eventually redirect itself, after the Israelis finally pulled out of Lebanon, into Israel itself.[140]

By then a complication and a breakthrough for Palestinian life arrived at the center of the historical stage. The complication—and this will yield an entire further, important direction of discussion to be picked up in more detail below—was the eight-year-long war between Iraq and Iran in 1980-88 and in the aftermath of that war, the invasion of Kuwait by Iraq and the attack on Iraqi forces by an American-led coalition that defined the period 1990-92. What the complication meant for the Palestinians was (in a nutshell) twofold. First, hundreds of thousands of Palestinians making very good salaries in Kuwait, whose labors supported the economic infrastructure back home, were suddenly out of jobs and forced out of Kuwait and back to Palestine.

Second, Palestinian leader Yassir Arafat's ill-fated attempt to act as a go-between in the period leading up to the Iraqi invasion of Kuwait and from the invasion to the time of the American-led coalition's arrival on the scene, ironically enough, worsened the Palestinian leader's image (and the Palestinian position overall) in the West, and also among the Arab leadership that joined the coalition. For it was hard to distinguish Arafat as a go-between from Arafat as a supporter of Saddam, and coupled with the cheering by the Palestinians for the scud missiles that Iraq sent toward Israel, the image was created of Palestinians as supporters of Saddam Hussein—with all of the concomitants thereunto appertaining. All of this undercut the Palestinian cause by creating a perception throughout much of the world that they were not interested in peace.

By paradox, given the proximity in time of one moment and another—indicative of the unpredictability of events in the Middle East—the breakthrough came shortly after the complication of these events with the Madrid negotiations of late 1991 and Oslo Accords that suddenly seemed to open new possibilities in Israel-Palestine relations by 1993. The Israeli Lebanon venture had something to do with that, as well. For increasing numbers of Israelis were beginning to doubt the inviolable sanctity

of their army as a consequence of that debacle, and from that doubt to question where the occupation was leading them. The internal debate had sometimes extraordinary side-moments, as when Yael Dayan, a new member of Parliament (and daughter of Moshe Dayan, icon of the 1967 June War) met with Arafat in Tunis (to which his headquarters had been exiled after the dual removals by the Jordanians from Jordan in the early 1970s and by the Israelis from Lebanon in the early 1980s) and referred to him as a "symbol of peace and compromise" rather than the neo-Hitler that most Israelis saw in him up to that point.

If one follows forward through the decade after the culmination of the Oslo Accord moment of 1993, there is a number of points along the way that leap out at one. After the handshake on the White House lawn in September between Yitzhak Rabin and Yassir Arafat, there was a period of heady hopes on both sides of the Israel-Palestine fence. Those hopes were nurtured by three possibilities. The first of these was Rabin's capacity to think outside the box of historical fear that I have described above, to focus less on history and more on future possibility, and to convince a majority of Israelis to follow his lead. The second was the willingness on the other side for Arafat to believe in and convince Palestinians that the path on which they were now moving would ultimately lead—would finally lead—to the end of their frustrations and humiliations and to the realization of their dream of an independent state. The third was the skillful diplomacy of Bill Clinton in commanding the trust of both sides to intermediate between them and facilitate their coming closer together as negotiations moved forward.

In the aftermath of that moment on the White House lawn a concatenation of events pushed the peace process forward—and then backward. King Hussein of Jordan signed a peace agreement with Israel in 1994, at the same time renouncing any further interest in the West Bank territory that had been under his control between 1948 and 1967. This arrangement, together with Egypt's abandonment of Gaza, accomplished several ends

simultaneously. The peace between Israel and two of its most significant Arab neighbors, which had evolved between the end of the 1970s and the early 1990s, paired with the peace negotiations with the Palestinians, seemed to presage a broader and fuller peace in that corner of the region.

This, in spite of the unresolved relationship between Israel and Syria (but even that seemed to be moving forward, and in any case their common border had remained essentially quiet throughout this entire period). This, also in spite of the question of Lebanon, vis-à-vis Syria, the Palestinians, Israel and itself. At the same time, the precise answer to the question of how to shape a Palestinian future, placed simply into Israeli or Israeli and Palestinian hands, now presented itself as a potential time bomb, should certain things go awry. The question had arrived after more than twenty-five years not only of Israeli military occupation of Gaza and the West Bank, but of expanding settlements of Jews in both those territories.

Things did go awry in the unexpected form of the assassination of Rabin by a Jewish Israeli right-wing extremist. Encouraged by his rabbi both to believe that Rabin's movement toward denouement was leading to the giving up of lands divinely designated for the Jews (this is the opposite of the Ultra-Orthodox anti-Zionist perspective!) and to imagine that murdering the Prime Minister would be justified, indeed praised by God, Yigal Amir shot Rabin down at an enormous peace rally in Tel Aviv in the evening of November 4, 1995.[141] In retrospect, what the madman murdered was the hope for peace for both Israel and the Palestinians—at least until such time as another leader capable of thinking outside the box of fear arises. Initially this may not have seemed to be the consequence of Rabin's death; negotiations between Israelis and Palestinians continued and some progress continued to be made with regard to Israel's relinquishing authority to the Palestinians over some areas within the Territories, limitations with regard

to new settlements and a continued moratorium on terrorist attacks against Israelis by Palestinians.

As the Clinton administration slid deeper into its second term, discussions moved into the lush setting of the Wye Plantation outside Washington, DC, and complicated arrangements shifted forward. The Wye River Memorandum signed by Prime Minster Binyamin Netanyahu and Palestinian Authority Chairman Yassir Arafat and witnessed by President Clinton on October 23, 1998 provided an interim agreement in which "The Israeli side's implementation of the first and second Further Re-Deployment will consist of the transfer to the Palestinian side of 13% from Area C as follows: 1% to Area A and 12% to Area B. The Palestinian side has informed that it will allocate an area/areas amounting to 3% from Area B to be designated as Green Areas and/or Nature Reserves. The Israeli side will retain in these Green Areas/ Nature Reserves the overriding security responsibility for the purpose of protecting Israelis and confronting the threat of terrorism. . . ."

The memorandum put into place both more detailed redispositions of territory than had been articulated in the Oslo Accords and further delineations of cooperation not only between the Israelis and Palestinians but, under prescribed conditions, trilateral activity that involved the United Sates as well. It encompassed security issues and matters such as the opening of an International Airport in the Gaza Strip and broader cooperative economic issues. It laid out an intricate and precise timeline for events and meetings, to culminate with a meeting scheduled for May 4, 1999 by which time the matters encompassed were to have been dealt with and plans for the next phase of negotiations would take place.

By then, the Clinton era was moving toward its sunset. Those familiar with Israel's political scene and hopeful of progress toward a final peace with the Palestinians, that would ultimately include a viable independent Palestinian state and an agreeable handling of Jerusalem from both Israeli and Pal-

estinian perspectives, breathed a collective sigh of relief when Ehud Barak became Prime Minister in 1999. Whereas Netanyahu had been a reluctant partner, pushed hard by Clinton toward the negotiation table, Barak seemed very much to be cut in the Rabin image: a soldier with leftist sympathies who was eager to make peace. Discussions between the Israelis and the Palestinians, with American mediation, continued.

With optimism the last round of Clinton-mediated talks moved forward, reconvening at Camp David, the historic site where Jimmy Carter had successfully brokered a peace agreement between Israel and Egypt which marked the first crack in the seamless hopelessness of Arab-Israeli relations two decades earlier. There Prime Minister Barak offered to withdraw from between 86 and 91 per cent of the West Bank (the amount varies according to how one does the estimates). But suddenly everything collapsed.

Ostensibly, the reason for the collapse is that, although Chairman Arafat was presented with terms that eventually offered 97 per cent of what he sought, rather than either accepting or suggesting that he would need to consider and counter-propose, he argued that what he had been offered was not enough, that it would be suicidal of him to accept it—and he stormed out of the negotiations. There is very little question in most analysts' minds that Arafat was an important part of the problem; that he was ultimately much more comfortable as an embattled revolutionary than as a paper-pushing diplomat seeking to engender a stable state in peaceful co-existence with the erstwhile object of his revolution.[142] As one of his strong supporters, Salah Ta'mari, observed in 1998 "When it comes down to it, it's not so romantic dealing with sewage, taxation, salaries, and unemployment."[143]

A closer look at what he was offered helps explain his response—although responding with a counter-proposal would unquestionably have been more fruitful than merely storming out of the negotiations. (Thus I *am* suggesting that his ability

to think forward toward peace rather than backward toward revolution was decidedly limited). The precise structuring of territories—in which barrier settlements and roads that divide the territory were to stay in place—would have deprived a newly independent Palestine of most of what it needed to function. This includes, to give one salient example, control of water supplies through access to the aquafer *below the surface* of the area under discussion.[144] It may well have also made it very difficult for the Palestinians to believe that Israel would ever accept a genuine Palestinian state without Israeli barriers imbedded within it.

What the world saw was Arafat's tantrum, but what it failed to perceive was the precise nature of what he rejected. What it also heard little about was the continuation, in spite of the tantrum, of discussions between Israeli and Palestinian negotiators determined to arrive at a solution to their joint problem. After Camp David, these discussions took place back in the Middle East, in Taba, Egypt. It is there and then, in January, 2001 (the last days of the Clinton administration) that the next link in a disastrous chain was forged. As the Israeli elections approached and as Barak's apparent failure to assure a stable and solid peace was pushing the Israeli electorate toward the unabashedly hawk-like stance espoused by Ariel Sharon—who had led the brutal incursion into Lebanon in 1982, made a personal fortune as the Housing Minister for whom the idea of more settlements therefore offered possibilities of personal enrichment—Barak suddenly pulled his negotiating team out of the discussions that had been inching forward.[145]

Barak's motive was arguably two-fold. He presumably imagined that in so doing, and thus in presenting himself as more of a hardliner than his earlier Rabin-like stance had suggested, he might not lose the election. But more fundamentally, perhaps, when push came to shove he could not step outside the box of distrust and fear that would have moved the discussions forward instead of abandoning them—and abandoning

Israel and the Palestinians—to the violence that has ensued in the now-nine years since. It is certainly true that Arafat did nothing to help assuage the distrust and fear, but the fact of Barak's fear cannot be discounted when trying to understand what ultimately drove the situation toward failure.[146] Sharon was duly elected, the "Second *Intifada*" was duly begun, the brutal attempts to suppress it blossomed and the circle of fear, mistrust and vicious violence spun upward. (I don't mean to suggest that violence would ever be other than vicious; I mean to express by the deliberate use of hyperbole how high the level of ugliness has been during this period of time.)

If Barak and Arafat each in his own way contributed to the collapse, Sharon was doubly at its heart, although the collapse did not occur just because of Sharon. Not only did he cast his corpulent shadow across Barak's consciousness (but it was the demons of Barak's inability to escape his own view of the Palestinians that pushed him into the shadows). He personally blew on the very sort of embers that could and did become the flames of the *intifada*. I refer to his notorious visit to the Temple Mount/Haram al'Sharif area on September 28, 2000. It was certainly his right as a Jew, as an Israeli, as a human being—as a private individual—to make that visit. But to do so accompanied by a retinue of 1,000 policemen, as the head of the Likud party, both gave to the visit an official air (indeed Barak was apparently asked for and gave permission for the visit, so it was being made clearly in an other than private-citizen mode) and offered an obvious provocation to the Palestinians. In the context of still-delicate questions regarding the ultimate status of Jerusalem in a future two-state reality it smelled of a political statement, an assertion that Jerusalem would remain non-negotiable, all-Jewish property. Confrontation with Palestinian demonstrators followed; these led to the deaths of four Palestinians, the injuring of some 200 of them and the wounding of fourteen Israeli policemen.

While it is true that a subsequent investigation by an

American-led commission concluded that the visit by Sharon ultimately seemed to be "no more than an internal political act; neither were we provided with persuasive evidence that the Palestinian Authority planned the uprising," nonetheless the Palestinians would continue to see the event as provoked by Sharon and the Israelis would continue to see the demonstrations and subsequent rioting as part of an Arafat-initiated *intifada* designed to help scuttle the peace talks. Thus the beginning of the "Second *Intifada*"—also known as the *al'Aqsa Intifada*—actually preceded the collapse of the final-attempt talks at Taba, and no doubt added fuel to Barak's inability to think outside the box of fear and distrust.

* * * * *

Before moving forward to pick up the thread of what has transpired between the disaster of 2000-2001 and the present time, (2009), it is important to step back for a moment and to re-address the matter of selective memory and that of fear and distrust. It has become too common in the last few years to assert two things that make the solution to the Middle Eastern problematic nearly impossible to achieve. The first (as I keep underscoring) is to speak or write as if the sole complication for the region is the Israeli-Palestinian issue; that to solve *that* problem would be to lead us out of the overall regional morass. I will return to this shortly. The second is to speak or write as if the Israel-Palestine problem emerged in 1967 with the Israeli conquest of the West Bank, Sinai and the Golan Heights, and therefore that the root of the problem is Israel's intransigence regarding matters such as Palestinian statehood and the status of Jerusalem.

It is certainly true that, with a gradual crescendo, arriving at a *fortissimmo* level during the Sharon era, Israel has held most of the cards in this matter. It is true that a key, if not *the* key, to solving this particular subset problem of the larger problem

is the inability of a majority of Israelis and certainly their current leaders—particularly now that we have arrived full circle, so to speak, from "early" Sharon back to Netanyahu—to think outside the box of fear and distrust. That has led to unilateral actions such as the highly-charged decision to build a barrier to separate Israel and protect it from Palestinians, every one of whom seems to be assumed by Israel's leadership to be a potential or even likely suicide bomber. It must be noted that, on the one hand, this "security fence" has cut down the number of suicide bombings within Israel by more than 90%, which statistic makes it difficult for outsiders to criticize the existence of such a barrier. On the other hand, the decision of precisely where the barrier goes and what it encloses and excludes was not only arrived at unilaterally, but to some critics, at least, seems to maximize both the discomfort level of the Palestinians and the comfort level of particular Israelis, namely those inhabiting the "settlements."

More fundamentally, it is also true that, as occupiers, the Israelis have grown into the ugly role they too often now play, unfamiliar to them or to the principles that undergird Judaism but all too familiar to history at large. In other words they have not been able to escape becoming normal—a desideratum when it was articulated by Herzl over a century ago, and perhaps a desideratum where hamburgers and shiny cars are concerned, but not where oppressing and humiliating another people is concerned. This development can be seen in scores of unhappy incidents, small and large, involving Palestinians at the checkpoints and elsewhere.

It is also true—so that this becomes viciously circular—that the consequences of over forty years of Israeli occupation, culminating with a post-failed-peace-effort-era of unprecedented cruelty, has imbued the Palestinians with profound distaste for Israelis and more important, profound distrust of them. They are as certain that the Israelis will never yield to peaceful co-existence as the Israelis are that the Palestinians never will.

And just as every frustrated radical who becomes a suicide bomber is construed by Israel to be a component of a monolithic Palestinian bloodlust, every God-clinging Jewish radical who pitches a tent in the Territories and every Israeli soldier who is abusive in his interrogation of a Palestinian youth—or old man or pregnant woman—is construed by Palestinians as a component of a monolithic arrogant Israel, lusting for more territory. As every Jewish settler in Hebron thinks of every Arab in the city as a blood relative of those Arabs who massacred 60 Jews in the riots of 1929 (and don't even acknowledge that there were Arabs who hid whole Jewish families to protect them at that time), every Arab in Hebron believes that every settler is another Baruch Goldstein, who gunned down 29 worshippers in the Ibrahimi Mosque in February 25, 1994.[147] Fear and frustration feed frustration and fear from both ends of an endless line.[148]

But this is where, if we are to unravel the tangled web, we must not only step out of the box and disengage from the line (easier said than done) but must not forget that the box and the line were not created in 1967—and that even since 1967 there has been a number of hands in the mix churning it into a mess. We might step back as far as the period between World War I and 1948, during which no proposal, however modest as far as allotting territory to the Jews, was acceptable either to the Palestinians or to their Arab brethren. If we have seen that the British and the French certainly helped sow discord between the Jewish and Arab communities, nonetheless during those decades it appears at least that the Palestinians and their brethren were the intransigent ones.

We might jump from that era to the next, in which, between 1948 and 1967 the Palestinians who neither stayed nor returned to Israel after its independence (there was an admittedly small window of opportunity to return, and it is fair to say that Israel was not encouraging it, but then neither were Arab leaders at that time) found themselves in territories controlled by Jordan and Egypt. It was the Jordanians and the Egyptians who created

the refugee camps in which for two decades enormous frustration built up; that frustration was already firmly in place when
the camps and the territories where they were located fell into
Israeli hands after the Six-Day War. I might add that at that
time, Israel seems from most accounts not to have intended to
maintain control over those territories, but hoped to use them
as bargaining chips in the peace negotiations for which the
Jewish State was at that time so desperate, and in which the
Arabs, for their part, evinced no interest.[149]

Nor, it must be further added, did the Arabs as a whole
exhibit much concern for their Palestinian brothers and sisters.
Certainly not between 1948 and 1967 and not really after 1967
either. It was only in the aftermath of the 1973 Yom Kippur War,
when the military option regarding Israel's survival or destruction seemed clearly to have failed that the larger Arab world
began to use the Palestinians and its alleged concern for their
welfare as a chip with which to generate anti-Israel sentiment
on a world scale. Indeed if we continue forward back toward
the Oslo Accords and their aftermath in the 1990s—and one
ought to remember that between 1967 and 1992 the darkest
moment in Palestinian history had nothing to do with Israel,
but was, rather, to repeat, the massacre of Palestinians by the
Jordanian army known as Black September (1970-1)—and we
arrive at the moment of maximum post-Oslo hope, we find the
following situation.

That apart from the Israeli failure to be more aggressive with
regard to dismantling recent Jewish settlements in the Territories,
and in thinking forward toward the shaping of a Palestinian
state with a capital, possibly in Jerusalem, (and I by no means
intend to minimize the significance of this last matter by placing it in a dependent clause) there were other issues militating
against success. That neither the Arab nor the Western powers,
who promised funds to help develop a Palestinian infrastructure,
came forth with the volume of support that had been promised.
That of the funds that *were* poured into Palestine, there is good

evidence that a disproportionate amount ended up in Yassir Arafat's Swiss bank accounts. There seem, then, to have been failures on all sides, the repercussions of which were furthered exponentially by the assassination of Rabin.

All of which must be kept in mind, even as they are typically ignored when we narrow our lens to the past fifteen years (and in the long run it *must*, as I will argue again below, be ignored in a certain sense, if, having come to some understanding of the problem, we entertain any hopes whatsoever for a solution). During that time, to repeat, Israel has been largely in charge of the situation. Arafat had been placed by Israel under house arrest, at the time of the first iteration of this writing,[150] settlements continued to be built in the Territories, suicide bombings were rising and falling in number without a rational reason, both the Israelis and the Palestinians were in the grips of terror regarding each other, and the United States, under the Bush administration, rather than assuming a role of leadership and intermediation, had reduced itself to a blind supporter of Israeli policy and a source of both Palestinian and Arab distrust, not only because of its unqualified support of Israel but because the President refused even to speak with Arafat who, regardless of what one might think of him, was the duly appointed and elected leader and spokesperson of the Palestinians.[151]

As I write this paragraph several years after most of my previous words were written, two obvious changes in the matrix of these issues have come about which require further comment. The first is the change in the American Presidency and with that change, new possibilities with respect to the overall discussion of the Middle East morass and the specifics of the Israel-Palestine issue. I shall reserve my comments on this matter for the chapter that follows this. But the second matter within the matrix is that, in the aftermath of the 2005 Israeli pullout from Gaza and the arrival to political hegemony there by *Hamas*, (as previously noted), there followed a fairly continuous rain of small-scale rockets onto Israeli towns and villages within strik-

ing distance of the Gaza border. The eventual Israeli response was, as we have also noted, a massive assault on Gaza, which some have seen as justified and others as excessive.[152]

There are three angles from which to view that Israeli action. The Israeli perspective—that there was no choice—I considered toward the end of the previous chapter. The international perspective I shall consider in the chapter that follows this one. The broader Arab perspective, which was particularly interesting, all things considered, I shall also consider, as a subset of the international perspective. For the issues being addressed in this chapter, the Palestinian perspective is largely and simply that the Israelis are not to be trusted not to resort to extreme violence when conditions become uncomfortable: they see themselves as always looking at the Israelis from the receiving end of a gun barrel and never being quite sure when it will go off.

More than that, Rashid Khalidi refers to what he terms

the obstinate refusal of both the Bush administration and the Israeli government to accept the results of the 2006 Palestinian Legislative Council elections, and their international campaign to try to force the Palestinians to go back on their democratic choice, [which] is also crucially important in understanding why Palestinians were fighting over the ruins of their refugee camps in 2007. This campaign has included Israel's withholding of Palestinian taxes, and an American-led international financial and diplomatic boycott of the [Hamas-led] PA. ...it involves the Israeli refusal to ease its choking restrictions on movement and goods...and most ominously, the Palestinian slide into the abyss involves United States government arming, training, funding and encouragement of Fatah in order to bring it to attack its rivals.[153]

Khalidi writes this without attempting to minimize the responsibility of the Palestinian leadership in general or Hamas in particular in shaping the conditions to which the Gazans in particular were relegated by 2007.

Interestingly, he is writing before the major escalation toward

the incessant rocket attacks into Israel orchestrated by *Hamas* which in turn culminated with the 2009 Israeli attack into the Gaza Strip. But that time-blip matter underscores the issue of perspective: the Israelis feel provoked by the rockets; the Palestinians feel provoked to support *Hamas* whether or not most of them support the rockets. The desperation leading to that support is a function of conditions since 1967, but also since 1948—but perhaps that predate 1948 not only as far back as 1920 or 1517 but to who can say what chronological point at which the first chicken or the first egg appeared within this context?

Which brings me to one last issue with regard to how the coin of Israeli-Palestinian history, memory and perspective has two sides. For Jews in the second half of the twentieth century there are, as we have seen, two major events that have defined that century, the Holocaust and the establishment of the State of Israel. Jewish Israelis have come to commemorate the one event and celebrate the other in back-to-back proximity among the annual cycle of celebrations and commemorations that mark their calendar. Both of those events coincide as one event, as it were, on the Palestinian calendar. The process of establishing the Jewish state was a process that included among its details the destruction of more than 400 Arab villages during the exodus of their inhabitants. The moment is referred to in the historiography of those refugees as *al'Nakba*—"The Catastrophe."[154]

My intention here is not to weigh the comparative responsibility of Arab and Israeli leadership in provoking that exodus and its attendant destruction or in creating the refugee community, because each side will argue its case until it is blue in the face without convincing the other, and I have yet to read an outsider's account which failed to exhibit strong prejudice in one direction or the other. The issue is also not to argue the objective legitimacy of comparing the Palestinian *Nakba* of exile and destruction to the mass murder of Jews accomplished by the Nazis. If this were a matter of sheer numbers that would be absurd. And in any case, as Anton La Guardia observes, "the

extermination of the *Shoah* belongs to a different universe of evil to the dispossession of Palestinians in the *Nakba*."[155] This sort of equation discussion is reminiscent of the one that emerged after the creation of the United States Holocaust Memorial Museum among American Blacks and Jews, the former asserting that the process of bringing their ancestors into slavery from Africa constituted a Holocaust. Too often that discussion became (and too often remains) a competition for the "we-have-suffered-the-most" award.

Such a competition is pointless, just as it is pointless to engage in that sort of competition with regard to the Jews and the Palestinians. Nor does the ironic fact that, as Israel has remained the governing authority in the Territories for over four decades now—particularly during the last nine years, in the context of the Second *Intifada*—and the security methodology of occupation has increasingly assumed a form that to some historians seems to echo the method enacted toward Jews in Nazi Germany in 1933-39, justify the injudicious and angry labeling of the Israelis as Nazis. The Final Solution evolved by the Nazis for their Jewish victims has no counterpart at all in the Israeli treatment of the Palestinians.[156]

The point is that, if we are to begin to find a means of unraveling these tangled threads within the tangled web of the Middle East, one of the starting points on both sides of the Israeli-Palestinian fence is to acknowledge and respect both the suffering and the *sense* of suffering that each has endured. This is the counterpart to the demand each side makes of the *other* for that recognition of its *self*. A simple, graphic expression of this is that particularly Jews who still retain the house keys taken by their ancestors from Spain after the expulsion of 1492 must recognize the at-least equal legitimacy of emotion pertaining to Palestinians who retain the house keys taken by their grandparents or great-grandparents after fleeing the nascent state of Israel in 1948. Perhaps the Palestinians need to recognize both the differences between the conditions of those

two exoduses and the differences between the Jews who arrived from wherever and whenever they arrived into Palestine and have shaped a state and the Turks, British and French who arrived into the region with very different goals in generations and centuries past.

Notes

[133] There is considerable irony in the fact that the legal and political tradition to which much of the current political leadership in Israel belongs recognizes the legitimacy of violence—or at least some forms of it—as a means of *intifada* (to borrow a term from Arabic), since that tradition employed it against the British (and the Arabs) nearly sixty years ago.

[134] Adi Ophir, "A Time of Occupation," in Roane Carey and Jonathan Shainin, eds., *The Other Israel: Voices of Refusal and Dissent*, 61. As I shall shortly note, this is an Israeli writing, not a Palestinian.

[135] Yigal Shochat, "Red Line, Green Line, Black Flag", in Carey and Shainin, 128.

[136] Amira Hass, "Are the Occupied Protecting the Occupier?" in Carey and Shainin, 163-4.

[137] Rashid Khalidi, *The Iron Cage: The Story of the Palestinian Struggle for Statehood*, XII.

[138] It should be noted that the lead-up to that arduous event was that the PLO had lodged itself in Jordan by 1968, and aside from using Jordan as its base of terrorist attacks into the West Bank and pre-1967 Israel, had begun to function as an autonomous "state" within the state of Jordan. There was no central authority, minimal discipline, with various groups, increasingly splintered, functioning separately from each other but all ignoring or denouncing the legitimacy of the Hashimite government. Between mid-1968 and the end of 1969 there were no fewer than 500 violent clashes between Palestinian guerillas and Jordanian security forces, together with a good number of kidnappings of and violence against Jordanian citizens by armed PLO members. Armed Palestinians established their own systems of visa control, customs checks and checkpoints in Jordanian cities. King Hussein began a campaign against the PLO between February and June, 1970, during which about a thousand lives were lost. By September 15, after several failed attempts to assassinate the king, three plane highjackings by the PFLP and the declaration by the PLO of the Irbid area and its camp as a "liberated region," Hussein declared martial law. To make a long story somewhat shorter, the Jordanian army attacked PLO headquarters in Amman as well as camps in Irbid and five other areas, supported by Iraqi reserve forces that had been in Jordan since the 1967 war. While Arafat would later claim that the Jordanian army killed between 10,000 and 25,000 Palestinians, other estimates were as "low" as one to two thousand.

[139] The most notorious instance of Israeli assistance or acquiescence in the massacre of Palestinians by the Christian Lebanese Phalangist militias came two days after the assassination of President Bashir Gemayil, who came

into office with Israeli support and the promise of a peace treaty between Lebanon and Israel. The Phalangists, eager for revenge (for the assassination, but no doubt also driven by the anger that had built up through a decade of an oppressive PLO-led presence), who were supposed to be mopping up PLO fighters on behalf of the Israelis, massacred at least 500 civilians, including women and children in the Palestinian refugee camps of Sabra and Shatila. (These were post-1970 camps, not camps such as those in Gaza and the West Bank that came into being after 1948-9). The Israelis at least stood by without intervening to stop their allies; at worst they provided illumination for them as day became night (in more than one sense).

[140] The methodology of suicide bombings would be less evident in the *intifada* that began in 1987 and ended when the Oslo Accords were put into place than in the *intifada* that began when the negotiations that stemmed from those accords fell apart at the end of the 1990s.

[141] For those with a technical interest, the religious justification that Amir claimed for his act was *din rodef*—"law of the pursuer"—according to which someone in pursuit of someone else with the intent to kill that individual may/should himself be killed before he is able to do any harm. (Thus Amir's rabbi perceived Rabin as doing and able further to do a good deal of harm should he continue on his path, and thus viewed Amir's bullets as forestallers of such further harm). Of course even that "law" presumes that all other options for stopping the would-be killer have been exhausted.

[142] Among the ironies in this is that while he was running the infant Palestinian polity he was so obsessive about maintaining personal control over everything that his days, like his desk, were buried in slips of paper: he insisted on reviewing and signing off on every conceivable detail of administrative life—even requests for leave from middle-level administrators were addressed by his signature.

[143] Quoted in Anton La Guardia, *War Without End*, 147, from the interview La Guardia had in 1998 with Ta'mari.

[144] A good deal has been written in recent years regarding the division of water resources within the region at large and in particular within the area encompassed by Israel, Palestine, Jordan, Syria and Lebanon. While rainfall is beyond anyone's control and the attempts to direct and otherwise control the water that comes from above-ground rivers and lakes is an obvious way of altering the natural availability of that resource, less obvious is the management and/or manipulation of water found deep *beneath* the earth's surface. In part the ability to do so depends on technological capabilities, in part on political control. See Tony Allan, *The Middle East Water Question: Hydropolitics and the Global Economy*; Gary Hoch, "The Politics of Water in the Middle East;" Elisha Kally and Gideon Fishelson, *Water and Peace: Water Resources and the Arab-Israeli Peace Process*; Nurit Kliot, *Water Resources and Conflict in the Middle*

East; and Aaron T. Wolf, *Hydropolitics Along the Jordan River*; among other recent discussions of this issue. I have listed a few more in the bibliography.

[145] See Jeff Halper's discussion of this on pp 35-6 of his essay, "The Key to Peace: Dismantling the Matrix of Control," in *The Other Israel*. Most commentators seem unaware of Barak's last-minute pullout. Anton La Guardia, for example, credits him with negotiating "with the Palestinians virtually to the last day of his government," by contrast with Sharon. (Anton La Guardia, *War Without End*), 336. Given La Guardia's often imbalanced coverage of the two sides of the coin (he seems to me far more critical of the Israelis than of the Palestinians—but more on this below in footnote 155), his willingness to exonerate Barak of any responsibility for the breakdown in peace negotiations is significant. I would not for a moment wish to minimize the negative role played by both Arafat and Sharon in this horrific drama, but it is larger than they and others have contributed to its tragic quality, including Barak.

[146] As always, there is still more than meets the eye. According to La Guardia (*Ibid*, 363) "Arafat himself seemed to have a flash of realization in June, 2002. . . when he told an Israeli interviewer that he belatedly accepted the Clinton parameters set out 18 months earlier. . . But by the time he reached this belated conclusion, it was too late. Israelis had lost faith in him." If La Guardia is right—which is difficult to assess, because as usual he gives us no footnote to tell the reader where this information comes from, so we cannot attest to its accuracy, aside from how we might evaluate the interpretation— then Arafat himself remains the main flaw in the flawed process, and the tragedy of mis-timed realizations and recognitions achieves an unprecedented profundity given what was lost and where things have gotten since Taba.

[147] The 1929 massacre was the culmination of riots fomented by the Mufti of Jerusalem as part of his campaign to "defend" Muslim holy sites from what he asserted was the threat to them from militant Jews. The militant Jews, on the other hand, were mainly focused on gaining control of the Western Wall. The dispute over the wall became a series of Arab riots in Jerusalem by August in the course of which 133 Jews and 116 Arabs were killed. The denouement was the Hebron massacre, unique because the Jewish population of 600 was mostly non-Zionist, had lived there for centuries and believed that it would not be attacked by its long-term Arab neighbors. They were neither wrong nor right, since some Arabs rioted and attacked and others hid and protected. Goldstein's horrific act was the first instance in Israeli history in which a Jew carried out a massive and unprovoked attack on his Arab neighbors. The majority of settlers elevated him to virtual sainthood; the Israeli left and Rabin's government excoriated him.

[148] And to repeat and amplify: since 1967, the growth in Israel not only of the population of Jews with visions of a Greater Israel which they regard as divinely-driven, but also of secular messianic Jews who share similar visions

has further complicated the issue of how to configure two states. Not only has an expanded range of settlers de facto expanded the borders of pre-1967 Israel—and as such, been party to expansionist plans of successive governments from both sides of the Labor-Likud fence. Many of them have been a recalcitrant and dangerous force at such times as the Israeli government has sought to pull back from such expansionist plans, because, like their Muslim counterparts, who cannot accept an independent *dhimmi* state in the region, these groups cannot accept an independent Palestinian state which would deprive them of political and religious control of the entire area encompassed by a Greater Israel.

[149] See above, fn 98.

[150] At the time of this final editing, Arafat has died in Paris, so that his role in this drama has been altered from present and future to past. See above, the final pages of chapter ten and below, the last few pages of this chapter.

[151] I am for the moment ignoring the larger Middle Eastern arena in which President Bush earned Arab distrust and/or enmity toward the United States (most obviously, his bankrupt and blatantly imperialist Iraq policy and general disregard for the importance of international cooperation regarding terrorism), although obviously that is essential as we re-widen our focus away from Israel-Palestine to encompass the entire region.

[152] This last issue has at least two aspects to it. One deals generally with the volume of force. The other refers to the volume of "collateral damage" in the form of civilian Gazan, non-*Hamas* injuries and deaths. This second issue also has at least two different aspects. One pertains to whose numbers one believes: there is a long history of inconsistency with respect to injuries and body-counts between the two protagonists, (as even between the Palestinians and the Jordanians in the aftermath of Black September), and of irresponsibility on the part of the Western media with regard to reporting numbers without any attempt to verify them. The more profound issue is the question of whether and how and the degree to which the Israelis did or did not make every effort to avoid civilian casualties; and whether and how and the degree to which *Hamas* used civilian shields and covers in order to make it impossible for the Israelis to succeed at minimizing civilian casualties.

[153] *The Iron Cage*, XIII. I am neither endorsing nor criticizing Khalidi's perspective; I am merely pointing out how important it is to acknowledge and understand his perspective. And he does not deny problematic internal Palestinian issues, referring to the factionalized infighting of Palestinian leaders and their cohorts as offering "an almost criminal level of irresponsibility."

[154] The term was first used in 1920 in the context of the post-World War I carving up of the Near East into British and French areas of colonial

administration: the destruction of hopes for Arab unity and independence was referred to as *al'Nakba*.

[155] La Guardia, 155. La Guardia's book, by the way, offers a good case of my point regarding books and articles by outsiders who fail to be objective. He certainly *claims* to be objective and for the first two chapters appears to be, but I found myself less and less convinced of this as I read through the rest of its 400 pages. While ostensibly even-handed, virtually every comment he made about Israeli actions he presented in a negative manner; no matter how positive an Israeli effort, he sensed a negative nuance to it. I did not find the same negative attitude when he discussed Palestinian actions and efforts. Moreover while quite thorough in delineating negative Israeli actions (such as the demolishing of two small mosques in opening up the area around the Western Wall in 1967) he somehow missed far larger counterpart actions on the other side of the fence (such as the wholesale destruction of every synagogue in Jerusalem's Jewish quarter by the Jordanians between 1948 and 1967). I should add that a 400-page book with nary a footnote is troubling, in spite of its impressive bibliography: if one's purpose is to explain a difficult problem and to educate one's readers, then one ought to provide them with the instruments with which not only to look further but to examine and even challenge one's interpretations. In spite of these objections, La Guardia's narrative is an excellent one overall, extremely detailed and exhibiting an admirable grasp of both the history and the sensibility of both worlds.

[156] This does not necessarily mean that there are not mad and militant Jews in Israel who would be happy to pursue a Nazistic, exterminationist path toward the Palestinians, but fortunately they are relatively few and far between—and every group of people has its mad militants.

Chapter 12

The United States and Israel-Palestine

One might ask what it is that the three principal current forces—Israel, the Palestinians and the United States—might consider as a way out of this conundrum.[157] What follows in my discussion assumes a greater level of both reason and courage than is apparent in the current leadership of at least two of the three entities, (a year ago I would have said all three entities), so I recognize that we are not likely to find my "proposals" executed in the immediate future.[158] But I would hope that they would at least provoke thinking as serious as that necessary to grasp the complexities of the tangled web which I have been seeking to unravel up to this point.

The first shift is one that I would make, were I the Prime Minster of Israel and both brave and capable of thinking outside the box and outside the circle of ugliness. It would be not to dismantle Jewish settlements in the Territories, but to unilaterally withdraw the Israeli military forces from the Territories—or

minimally, to withdraw to encompass the three areas conceded by the Palestinians at Camp David in exchange for comparable territory from behind the "Green Line." Or to withdraw them into a series of security outposts.

There is an interesting aspect to what at first may strike some readers as overly simplistic. Among the institutions within Israel that were either born or received a new lease on life in the aftermath of the Six-Day War of 1967 as part of the upsurge in Jewish religious fervor that the six-day "miracle" yielded was *Merkaz ha-Rav* Yeshiva in Jerusalem. It was founded by the first Ashkenazi Chief Rabbi of Palestine, Avraham ha-Cohen Kook—to whom I earlier referred as the Orthodox rabbi who had embraced Zionism in the first part of the twentieth century and argued to his followers that Zionism's secular shapers might well be instruments in God's hands for bringing about messianic redemption.[159] When Rabbi Kook died in 1935, leadership of the yeshiva passed to his son, Rabbi Tzvi Yehudah ha-Cohen Kook, and in the course of the 1950s the ideology of rapprochement between Orthodox Judaism and the secular Zionist community—now become the State of Israel—tightened to the point that the *Merkaz* became a center of nationalist religious thought, asserting that the state and also its strong right arm—the army—are holy elements in God's plan.

It was the *Merkaz* and its leader, the younger Rabbi Kook, who in turn became the center of religious rightist assertions after the 1967 war regarding the God-given intention for a Greater Israel. If at first glance all we might note is the irony that so many ultra-Orthodox who opposed the Zionist idea now oppose anything less than its broadest geo-political interpretation, (together with Orthodox Jews whose spiritual antecedents accepted the idea)—and thus offer a solid stumbling block on the road to peace—a second glance offers hope. Religious passion impelled Rabbi Kook, on Israel Independence Day, 1967 to deliver a sermon in his yeshiva in which he rent his spiritual garments rather than celebrated: because parts of the land in-

tended by God for the Jews had been given into Arab hands after the 1948 war.[160] The same passion caused him to expound upon the events of a few weeks later as divinely-accomplished, and to teach thereafter that to give up any of the land of Greater Israel was a sin as serious as idolatry and murder.

Rabbi Kook viewed that State as part of the Divine Plan for Redemption and its leaders therefore as individuals who "should be honored as 'the judge that shall be in those days' (Deut. 17:9). What to do when the state failed to follow God's will to settle the land? The conundrum was resolved by according to the state a conditional holiness. *The state was the means of settling the land, as opposed to the traditional Zionist view of settling the land as a means of creating the state.*"[161] But in that case, my proposal should accord perfectly well with the needs of Orthodox settlers in the Territories: if the state pulls back to the Green Line, that does not eliminate their divinely-appointed work of settling the land. This would also be consistent, in fact, with Spiritual Zionism as it was espoused from the beginning by thinkers such as Ahad Ha'Am, for whom statehood was the wrong goal of a Zionist movement whose purpose was the spiritual rejuvenation of Judaism, not a physical refuge for Jews.[162] I am not being "cute" with this argument; I am addressing the religious right in it own terms.

If, in turn, a fence need be built to assure security against the madmen who will not immediately disappear, then build it, but along the "Green Line," rather than in and out of gerrymandered potential Palestinian areas of governance. I would certainly negotiate with the Palestinians to allow the Jewish settlers to stay—but I would let them (the settlers) know that they would now be inhabitants of the new state that I would be the first to recognize: the independent State of Palestine. And in withdrawing to the "Green Line" I would also be leaving behind not only sufficient landmass, but sufficient landmass of quality with respect to water and other resources to make a Palestinian state viable. More than that, I would be leading

Israelis to a perspectival change in attitude: leaving behind not only Palestinian territory but more significantly, surrendering control of Palestinian life.[163]

Were I the leader of the Palestinians I would reiterate to the Israelis and to the Palestinians how emphatic my intention is to arrive at a final peace with Israel. This would include doing what Arafat never did, discrediting and delegitimizing terror—not merely *renouncing* its use, as Arafat did do in September, 1993, but emphatically *condemning* its use. I would make every effort to root out the extremist madmen and express with warmth my hope and expectation that Jewish settlers who choose to live within our borders would be accepted, safe and indeed welcome. I would make it clear that I do recognize how limited is the paradigm that inspired *al'Fatah* in the early 1960s: that, as the French could be evicted from Algeria through armed struggle, the Jews could be evicted from Israel by similar means. The Jews are not France and the Palestinians are not the Algerians.

The counterpart of the change in Israeli attitude toward Palestinian Arabs would be the change in Palestinian attitude that I would promote: that we are not merely and always *victims*. That sensibility, shaped into a strategy and not merely a condition by Arafat, has led to a sense of not being accountable and of not being required to compromise. "This tendency to avoid accountability has become an aspect of the political culture of the Middle East [and not only the Palestinian world]. In part, it is explained by a pervasive narrative of victimization. . . . This sentiment is held by governments in the region as well as members of the public."[164] In abandoning that strategy I would be leading the Palestinians forward toward an ability to negotiate successfully with the Israelis and offering the Israelis reasons to believe that negotiations could succeed.[165]

These measures on both sides might help push us all out of the box and beyond the circle of fear and distrust, eventually. It would make feasible the negotiation of another matter: Jerusalem. And I would, were I leader of the one side or leader

of the other, express my willingness to share the city as a dual capital. To a certain extent it has functioned that way since 1967, in that the Muslim Holy Places have been administered not by the Israelis but by Palestinian authorities. So to extend that principal to the point where one authority is not subsidiary to the other, but both stand on equal ground and join together to maintain the city, is far-fetched more for psychological than for logistical reasons. And in fact negotiators on both sides had arrived virtually to that point of agreement before the entire situation collapsed in 2000.

Part of the oddly interesting reason that they had virtually arrived at that point of agreement is that Bill Clinton posed to both sides a question designed to help them think about the earthbound Jerusalem instead of being so intensely focused on its heavenly counterpart and confusing the two. The two groups of negotiators were enjoined to come up with—and did so with a remarkable degree of ease and consensus—a list of 60 municipal needs that the two sides could share. They laid out a tentative "plan" to deal with everyday details—from garbage disposal to water and electricity service to the delivery of mail. To co-administer the mundane aspects of the city and leave the sacred sites to the various religious authorities may not please everyone, but surely the majority of reasonable individuals on both sides who hope for peace rather than more violence could embrace such a notion.

There are, I believe, compelling arguments that could convince my fellow Israelis and my fellow Palestinians to follow my lead. I would argue to both sides that the only hope for our children and our grandchildren to grow up in an environment that might be construed as normal is one in which "basic training" refers to sports and not war; that if we wish for long, prosperous lives for our descendants then we can only wish for a framework of peace in order to accomplish that. I would argue to my Israeli constituents that no wall, however high, and no fence, however strong, will guarantee this as effectively as

a determination to live side-by-side in peace. I would remind my Israeli constituents that, if we remain in control of the Territories, we will be a minority within our own country by the year 2010—or 2012, or 2015, but sooner or later—and that accordingly, either the nature of Israel as a Jewish state or as a democracy will by definition be lost.

I would argue to my Palestinian constituents that no number of suicide bombers will drive the Israelis out or destroy the State of Israel—that the Israelis are not the Turks or the British, regardless of where the Zionist ideology and its initial primary population derived from geographically or ethnically (and I would remind my Palestinian constituents that an enormous percentage of the Israeli population derives from the Middle East and Africa). Their parents, grandparents and ancestors for many generations have suffered too much for too long for them to give up and go home—and there is no other home for them to go to.

I would remind my Israeli constituents that the Oslo Accords did set in motion a series of significant forward movements with regard to Arab-Israeli relations even if the specifics of Israeli-Palestinian relations showed less forward movement than most would have wished. Thus not only did Jordan move rapidly to conclude a peace agreement with Israel, but Morocco, Tunisia, Qatar and Oman began to develop economic relations with the Jewish State. Moreover, acts of terror precipitously dropped year-by-year between 1993 and 2000, from Oslo to Camp David, one of the consequences of which was that Israel's economy boomed as it was able to focus on more than its military.

I would argue most strenuously that refusing to think toward a Palestinian shaping of what Jews had demanded be shaped for them a century earlier—an independent, autonomous state—cuts deeply into the very Jewishness that, in its best, most-justice-obsessed sense, defines Israel at its best. It is indeed embodied in Israel's own Declaration of Independence; the difficulties of living up to the democratic ideal posited in

that document are rendered exponentially more difficult by the Occupation.[166] The moral Jewishness of the Jewish State is being sacrificed to—highjacked by—the inevitable inhumanity of being an oppressor.[167] Far from having merited the right to oppress others as long-term victims in history, the Jews—of all people—are obligated to learn from history and seek to eradicate oppression wherever they can, nowhere more emphatically than in the heart of a Jewish state. This is contained in that most essential of rabbinic phrases, *tikkun olam*.[168] I would plead with my Israeli constituents not to forget the history of the Jews as it led up to and culminated in its most unhappy aspects with the Holocaust; that to oppress another people is virulently antithetical both to Jewish teachings and to what, as humans in the best (as opposed to the worst) sense Jews should have learned from our own experience.

Ultimately I would argue to them that they have no choice, for, as long as the current status quo remains in place, as occupiers of a territory whose inhabitants are dispossessed and disenfranchised in their own lands, humiliated daily and frustrated constantly in their attempt to live lives of dignity for themselves and their parents and hope for themselves and their children—that as long as that situation obtains, violence will breed itself and Israel will have no choice but to humiliate, frustrate and suppress the Palestinians. The cycle of viciousness will continue to circle around itself. So the only solution to that problem is to change the status quo.

And the only means of changing the status quo, to change the conditions that are deleterious both to the Palestinians *and* to the Israelis, *both* physically *and* spiritually, is to pull back from "the Territories" as well as from an attitude of control and both to recognize a Palestinian State and to leave that state sufficient space with sufficient resources to shape itself. Again, I think of the simple, graphic symbol of empathy that is suggested by a comparison of the way in which some Palestinians retain keys to abandoned homes in what is now Israel, paralleling the way

in which some Sephardic Jews retain keys from abandoned homes in Spain.

Such changes in conditions and mindset are easier said than done. It requires a Rabin-esque, Sadat-esque, Begin-esque leadership capacity for stepping outside the box of distrust and fear—just as any accommodation with Israel will require the same stepping out by the Palestinians. Barak ultimately lacked it and Arafat in the end certainly lacked it. Did Sharon, ironically and in the end, develop it? The stroke that took him out of the picture as quickly as assassin's bullets took Sadat and Rabin out of the picture left us with only a speculation regarding how far he might have gone along a peace-seeking road. What of Olmert and Netanyahu? What of Abbas—and those who lead *Hamas*?

An important cognate of this, which also intersects the matter of thinking of one's self only and always as the "victim" is the following small matter of past-future thinking. As ugly as the Israeli occupation became in the thirty years between 1967 and 1997, by the end of that time, as the Palestinian Authority took over control of those areas ceded to it by Rabin, Perez and then even Netanyahu, the P.A. operated the prisons with more infamous gusto than the Israelis had: more Palestinians died in *Palestinian* prisons during the first four years of post-Oslo P.A. control of Gaza and West Bank cities than in *Israeli* prisons. The point is that from whichever side of the fence, the protagonists have to examine their own conduct and not only scrutinize what is happening across the barbed wire.

Here is where another paradox enters the picture. One might argue that, if all other parties, near and far, removed themselves from the situation and left the Israelis and the Palestinians to themselves, the situation would have a better likelihood of yielding a successful outcome. But strangely, while that may or may not have been true a century ago or even half a century ago, it certainly is not true now, for two reasons. First, because the problematic of the Middle East, even where only the Israeli-

Palestinian corner of it is concerned, is not limited to Israel and the Palestinians; and second, because of the overly large volume of fear and distrust that has been built up over the decades between Israelis and Palestinians.

With that double issue in mind, (and this is another circular sequence of necessary developments), the other Arab states must come forth and put their signatures where their mouths have been. Thus beyond Egypt and Jordan, Syria and Iraq, the Saudis and the Libyans must make it clear that they have abandoned their decades' long hostility toward the State of Israel. Obviously Syria is particularly significant in this matter. It is arguable that Syrian unwillingness to follow Jordan and Egypt toward peace discussions with Israel even when progress toward peace between Israel and the Palestinians was in place helped maintain the necessary sparks of antagonism that, with the failure of Camp David and Taba, became a conflagration. But there is also strong evidence that Hafiz al-Assad was thinking toward peace as he lay, ultimately, dying of cancer: would he have gone forward or backward had he lived?[169]

I recognize that this will bring back into focus the matter of the Golan Heights and that the fear and distrust factor from the Israeli side at the thought of returning the Heights to Syria would require major psychological surgery (even as I have heard repeated military analyses by *Israeli* military experts arguing that, with Israel's current level of military technology, the Golan is not what it was before 1967 as a potential security threat; and even as it must also be noted that virtually none of the terrorist activity against Israel has come from across the Syrian border in the past more than forty years), and it is highly unlikely that without a discussion of the Golan the Syrians will come to the table of negotiation. What this means, then, is a major gesture of peaceful aspiration on the part of the Syrians, to convince the Israelis that giving up what, real or not, most view as a large strategic advantage, is in Israel's long-term interest.[170]

What that means in pure Arabic terminology is this: *salaam,*

not *sulh*. We have returned once more to the issue of definition. For both of these terms may be translated into English as "peace," but whereas the first implies a full peace, the other does not. *Sulh* implies something between a cease-fire and a full peace; it implies a temporary peace until such time as war becomes an option. *Salaam* derives from the same root as the word "Islam" and with the root meaning of "submission" it is a powerful statement of a serious interest in peace (see above, 10). To the extent that *salaam* is understandable as cognate with the Hebrew word *shalom*, it implies "fullness" and not the mere absence of armed conflict that is suggested, for example, by the Latin word *pax*, which yields the English word "peace."

It is obviously essential for Israel to feel that the arrangements arrived at with the Palestinians, the Syrians and other Arab states fall into the category of *salaam*. Put in other terms, it is essential that these states, all of which are Muslim, declare themselves capable and more than merely grudgingly willing to accept a *dhimmi* state within their midst. Thus peace and security for both Israelis and Palestinians involves more than just themselves within the region.

The Arab states need to do more than accept Israel's existence; they need to embrace Israel's legitimacy so that, like the Palestinians, they denounce and not merely renounce terrorism. Arab leaders need to support the proposition that not only Israel, but also the Palestinians and the Syrians need to be willing to compromise if all sides are to walk away from the negotiation table with something substantial.

There is more, less visible to Western eyes but crucial: the sort of anti-Semitic (i.e., anti-Jewish) bombast that continued to pour out of the Palestinian and Arab—particularly Egyptian—press between the time of the Wye Memorandum and the collapse of the Camp David-Taba talks must unequivocally stop. Particularly when we consider that the media in most of the places under discussion are state-run, this is not only *not* a matter of repression, it is a matter of altering public perceptions about

Jews and about Israel in a positive way, rather than reinforcing the negative imagery that has prevailed for so long.[171]

More will be required of the Arab states as a practical measure. The wherewithal to create the infrastructure of Palestinian statehood will necessitate the sort of financial help that was promised and not fully delivered after Oslo, albeit not only from the Arabs. It will require a more pro-active interest in the fate of everyday Palestinians. An obvious sort of gesture could and should be offered by the Kuwaitis, for example, who as a practical matter could re-employ all of those Palestinians who were expelled at the time of the first Gulf War, thereby slicing significantly into the economic shape of myriad Palestinian communities.

Interestingly enough, of course, the beginnings of what I have just prescribed for the Arab states was actually put into play toward the end of 2001 and the beginning of 2002. The Saudi plan, put forth by Crown Prince Abd'Allah of Saudi Arabia called for full normalization of relations between the Arab nations and Israel in return for full Israeli withdrawal from the occupied territories. The proposal even called for adjustments that would, in incorporating some settlements into Israel, thicken the country's narrow waist, for which comparable territory, perhaps bordering Gaza, would be transferred to Palestine. The Plan was unanimously adopted at the Arab League's summit in Beirut in March, 2002. But by then the Israelis were in the midst of the Sharon administration, obsessed with the explosion of the new *intifada* and under no pressure from any allies to consider the plan, and it was rejected.

Indeed the one ally whose pressure might have pushed Israel to look at the Saudi proposal with serious eyes—the United States—was not willing to push. And strangely, given the history of the last 130 years or so, and the overall negative impact of Western involvements in the Israeli-Palestinian, Arab-Israeli and overall Middle Eastern picture, this proposal will necessitate the involvement of the West—particularly the

United States—as well. As the frequently referred to "sole super-power" on the planet, the United States is in a unique position to do what it so successfully did during the Clinton years: act as a go-between to help the Israelis and the Palestinians think and talk together. But there are at least two prerequisites to our ability to function that way again. The first is changing an attitude and a policy that was reflected in President Bush's refusal to meet with Chairman Arafat.[172]

We can hardly act as a go-between if we ourselves refuse to talk with one of the principals! We can hardly expect the Israelis to step beyond their own fears and distrusts regarding the Palestinians if we simply corroborate their most negative view of the Palestinians as enemies, rather than as partners. Happily, between when I wrote these last few sentences and the present, that shift seems to have already been accomplished: Barack Obama has made it abundantly clear that the United States under his administration will both function cooperatively and not dictatorially where our allies are concerned, and reach out with words and gestures to all protagonists on the global (and not just the Middle Eastern) stage.[173]

But neither can we expect the Palestinians—or the rest of the Arab and Muslim world—to accept us as mediators if they perceive us as one-sided in our view of the situation. That we are perceived this way and that we in fact operate this way on an official governmental level is not only corroborated by our unwillingness even to speak with the Palestinian leadership. It is demonstrated by the absolute carte blanche we ceded to the Sharon government (and its Olmert-led successor) to do as it will with regard to the Palestinians. (This will presumably change, now, too, with the Obama administration in its relationship with the new Netanyahu administration).

We support Israel for two theoretical reasons. The first is that Israel is the only democracy in the Middle East; it is our only natural ally and our only consistent ally. Stated from a larger perspective, it *is* the outpost its founders hoped it would be, of

Europe (America) and the West in the Middle East. Whatever its demographics, its governmental, economic and societal infrastructures mirror our own and thus it offers a natural focus for our sympathies.

The second reason, in the post-September 11, 2001 era, is that we have become capable of seeing ourselves mirrored in a different, more negative way, every time we read or hear of a suicide bomber blowing himself up at a Jerusalem bus stop. We perceive the Israelis to be fighting the same war against terrorism that we are—and since, in our unilateral arrogance during the Bush-Cheney-Rumsfeld years, we determined to fight that war our way and without cooperation from most of our European and other allies, Israel's role as parallel to our own is even more accentuated.

There is a series of ironies that these two sources of natural alliance offer when we place them within the larger picture of Israel-American relations and the significance of those relations for the issue of Israel-Palestine relations. The first is this: many experts will argue that the "realer" reason behind American support for Israel, particularly as, in the Bush-Cheney years it largely became blind support, is the Jewish lobby on Capitol Hill. While that view is quite accurate as far as the present moment is concerned—the Jewish lobby is the most successful on the hill at the current time—it does not explain the history of American support except by retrofitting the present onto the past. American Jews were not overly supportive of Israel until 1967, as I have earlier noted.[174] They feared that Israel might upstage the Promised Land that they had found here, particularly by the 1950s and early 1960s, and they feared the accusation of double loyalty, in spite of having found a land of such extraordinary promise here.[175]

When President Truman met with Chaim Weizmann prior to the United States' recognition of Israel's statehood, he did so virtually in secret and without enthusiasm; recognition and subsequent support came other than through a lobby or love.

Nor were American Jews organized yet as a lobbying force in any case. In the 1950s they were beginning to become seriously involved in the process of candidate-support and to develop the skill of translating such support into elected officials' support of their (the Jews') agenda. It would be some time before that involvement and that skill would emerge as significant and before that agenda would push support of Israel to the top tier of Jewish concerns (think, for example, of the struggle against denominational prayers in non-denominational public schools that came before concerns for Israel did in the early 1960s.)

Moreover, the beginnings of American support for Israel both predate the existence of the State and came to Israel in the larger context—there are always larger contexts in this narrative—of the Cold War. During World War I, more than a generation before the State of Israel existed, the U.S. government sent aid to the Jews of Palestine and conversely, one of the "Hebrew" battalions that helped in the defeat of the Ottoman Turks was organized in America. Mordecai Ben-Hillel HaCohen wrote in his diary at around this time: "The entire national enterprise in Palestine has fallen on America's shoulders."[176] In the aftermath of the War, in spite of the overt central position of the British (and secondarily, the French) in the region, America's significance was already being recognized: Ben-Gurion, who would emerge more than twenty years later as Israel's first Prime Minister, was already directing his efforts on behalf of the Zionist movement to the United States, rather than to Great Britain, in the 1920s.

On the one hand, America's interest in the region was already piqued in the late eighteenth and early nineteenth centuries because of coffee—a growing beverage-taste fire that the Ottoman Turks had kindled in Europe as they extended their dominion westward in the sixteenth and seventeenth centuries, so that coffee shops began in Budapest and spread to Vienna and thence to Paris. Barely was the United States a presence in the world (by which time Ottoman power was receding from Europe) and the taste was beginning its spread on this side

of the Atlantic: and the Middle East seemed to be the source toward which to turn in order to fulfill the need for it. By the mid-nineteenth century, as we have seen, the American interest had become religious.[177]

By the time the British and French were jockeying for final predominance in the region, in the 1930s, the United States was also beginning to awaken to the issue of oil. In the aftermath of World War II American interest was driven by the strategic concerns of the Cold War. These included but were not limited to the growing question of how to prevent the Soviet Union from access to the enormous oil reserves that were by then known to reside beneath various surfaces in the region, from Iraq to Saudi Arabia—the consequences of which concern are repercussive up to and through both the Gulf War under Bush the Elder and the second invasion of Iraq under Bush the Younger.

But also with the development of the Cold War that coincided with Israel's birth, the United States began to worry that Israel (whose birth and infancy had been strongly supported by the Soviet Union) might join the Soviet bloc. So it developed a special fund with which to disseminate American books, periodicals, films and music to Israel (as well as to several other countries). CARE packages were delivered to Israel, and shortly before the first Israeli parliamentary elections, the American Export-Import Bank agreed to extend a $100 million loan—an enormous sum at that time—to Israel to assist with immigrant absorption and development projects. As much as this pattern of American patronage soon became the norm, an Israeli might worry that, with the collapse of the Soviet Union as a counterweight to its own power, the United States might rethink it alliances (as, one might say, the second incursion in Iraq has demonstrated pretty well, albeit not with respect to Israel).

Having reviewed this, the fact is that the United States has, by now, established a long track record of supporting Israel, both in United Nations votes and other international fora and in dollars loaned or granted outright to the Jewish state, which

put it in a unique position (a position notably ignored by Bush the Younger) to apply pressure to the Sharon government, and to push Sharon's successors Olmert and now Netanyahu in a way that a state like France or Britain hardly could.[178] What kind of pressure? The kind that links American fiscal support with a shift in Israeli policy, away from the construction of state-supported settlements in the Territories and toward renewed and serious discussions with the Palestinian leadership, toward expressing recognition of the validity of a Palestinian state and away from offering bits and pieces of semi-autonomy that leave room for neither infrastructure nor self-esteem. Pressure not intended to be punitive in the absence of such a shift, but that speaks eloquently and forcefully about the future of Israel, both physical and psychological, with regard to both security and spiritual well-being.

There should be two objections to this proposal beyond the fear and distrust problem. First, that even a viable Palestinian state offers a logistical problem given that its two parts, the West Bank and Gaza will be separated by Israel. I would argue that, under the sincere peace conditions that this plan envisions, untrammeled passage across that stretch of Israeli territory—across a double border that, at the outset will be a double point of nervousness and tension—can in the *long* run become as uncomplicated as the passageway that winds through the Pyrenees between Spain and France or that marks the transit between the Netherlands and Germany in the aftermath of the shaping of the E.U.

But I would not wait for that long run to eventuate, and for several reasons would propose a slightly different solution. It is modeled on the experience of India and Pakistan, which were shaped as modern states at around the same time that Israel was being first shaped. Having primarily Muslim Pakistan divided, into Eastern and Western Pakistan by primarily Hindu India proved disastrous for decades, until finally a decision was arrived at to disconnect the two Muslim states from

each other, leaving one as Pakistan and renaming the other as Bangladesh. Why not do the same with non-Jewish-dominated Palestine? Instead of a two-state solution, then, I am proposing a *three*-state solution.

This proposal would offer several advantages. Firstly it would eliminate the majority of the logistical complications pertaining to the communication between the two Palestinian parts of a two-state solution. The notion that has been floated by any number of individuals—most recently, in the popular press, by way of Daniel Klaidman's January 12, 2009 *Newsweek* article, "A Plan of Attack for Peace"—of creating "a land corridor connecting Gaza to the West Bank and allowing for the free flow of people and commerce between the two" seems ill-conceived as an on-the-ground practicality. That plan effectively cuts Israel in half: how do Israelis then flow from north to south of the corridor? There have been other proposals, for extensive tunnels or bridges connecting the two sides of a Palestinian state, but these, too, are a logistical challenge.

More to the point, two separate states for Palestinians would accord more realistically with the current facts on the ground: *Hamas* controls Gaza and *Fatah* (so far, anyway) controls the West Bank. Creating two separate states would allow each of these antagonists to develop according to its own strategies and plans. Moreover, from a psychological viewpoint, at least some of those Palestinian and other Arabs who still rankle at leaving an intact Jewish state carved out of the western part of the erstwhile Palestinian Mandate might be more effectively persuaded to focus on peaceful building than violent destruction with not one but two states on which to work.

As a practical matter from the perspective of Israeli security, one might assume that the vast majority of Palestinians and their PA leaders on the West Bank are willing and ready to think and act in favor of peace and to move toward normalized relations both with Jordan and with Israel—and with the world within and beyond the Middle East—but that *Hamas*,

embedded in Gaza, remains more intransigent. The three-state solution would make it possible for Israel to focus in one way, toward normalized relations, with the West Bank, *Fatah*-led Palestinians, and in another way, with defense measures a more central issue, with the Gazans. *Hamas* and its intransigence has a greater chance of being isolated and its ugly intentions—if they remain ugly—thereby undercut if it is completely disconnected from the West Bank; the possibility of being voted out by the Gazan Palestinians themselves, it seems to me, would increase.

The notion of a three-state solution neither complicates nor simplifies the mundane issues of garbage collection and mail delivery. Nor does it further complicate or simplify the matter of Israel's Security fence/wall—except that, should the West Bank relationship move toward greater normalcy while the Gazan relationship does not, it is much simpler to construct or maintain such a fence on the Gaza border than along the Green Line. Nor does it simplify or complicate the issue of the settlements on the West Bank. I reiterate my suggestion for these, that they not be dismantled, but that their inhabitants become citizens of Palestine as there are Arab Palestinian citizens of Israel—even dual citizens of those two states.

Finally, the three-state solution does not affect the issue of Palestinian refugees seeking repatriation to what is Israel in any way differently from how a two-state solution would. If Israel were willing—as for the past decade its leaders have asserted that they are[179]—to allow a limited "law of return" to apply to some Palestinians—an international court could seek to adjudicate the claims over the next three or five or seven years of those coming forth either to ask for return rights or compensation.[180] But as I have observed above,[181] the number of those claiming to have "always" been in Israel's part of Palestine is much smaller than a close look at the history of the region in the last 150 years suggests. Others would be resident in one of the two new Palestinian states, and still others would be finally

accorded citizenship in Syria and the other states where they have resided as stateless persons for so many decades.[182]

The second objection to this proposal is that the role of the United States may sound as patronizing as ever the British and the French sought to be a century ago. To this second objection I would respond that Israel—and Europe and half the world—has followed and swallowed the lead of the United State for three-quarters of a century; that the culture and socio-economics of the United States has swallowed Israel and Europe and half the world on many levels, from MacDonalds to Democratic values, for better and for worse. Certainly Israel has embraced the U.S. in many ways other than as a client state and its patron. So to invoke the Americans as a force to push the Israelis out of their box of fear and distrust and to push the Palestinians and the Arabs out of theirs is perfectly appropriate. It merely requires the interest and the will on the part of an American leadership committed to long-term peace in the region and not (by paradox, given the involvement I have prescribed) to American hegemony.

There is, in fact, another irony in this. Israel learned democracy from the United States, and as of this writing, particularly but not only with regard to the issue about which I am writing, Israel practices democracy much more efficiently than does the United States. In the U.S. one heard virtually no public debate during the Bush years regarding Israel or regarding Israel and the Palestinians. Not only was speaking out in disagreement with the Bush administration on *any* issue treated by that administration and its champions as treasonous—as anti-American. But to speak out against the blind American support of Sharonist policies which were blind both to the moral infrastructure and to the future survival of Israel was to be perceived as anti-Semitic (if the speaker was not Jewish) or as treasonous (if the speaker was Jewish).

To be sure, there have been and are and will be anti-Semites who attempt to cloak their animosity toward Jews behind anti-

Zionism or, a few years ago, anti-Sharonism and more currently, unqualified horror at the Israeli attack on Gaza without any references either to what provoked the attack or the effort exerted by Israel to make it less of a horror. But it is also true that there were strong *supporters* of Israel at the time of Sharon (and since that time) who were (are) ultimately anti-Semitic; and Jews and non-Jews alike who were and remain loyal to and in love with the State of Israel because of which love and loyalty they were or are critical of its stance vis-à-vis the Palestinians.

In the first case, for example, there are members of the Christian religious right, including many of those closest to and most supportive of President Bush. Their rhetoric would suggest that their strong support of Israel derives not from philo-Semitism, but rather from the conviction that the Second Coming must be preceded by the ingathering of the exiles. This means that the rapture will follow the return to Zion of all the Jews. Its corollary is that the Jews will then participate in the rapture, having recognized the Christhood of Jesus—or be swallowed up with everyone else whom the Apocalypse swallows up, in the event that they fail to see the Light of His Return for what it is. So their Zionism is in fact a function of their supercessionist perspective.

In the second case are not only Americans who do or would speak out, were they given a forum in which they would not be excoriated. This category also includes—and this in particular underscores the "realer" democracy operative in Israel than in the United States at this time—a growing array of Israelis from different walks of life, including soldiers and scientists, former cabinet ministers and head of the Shin Bet (Israel's internal security services), to say nothing of professors and doctors, lawyers and journalists, who have spoken and/or written in no uncertain and often extremely angry terms against the policies of the Sharon administration and its successor with regard to the Palestinians, or more pointedly, about the policies that the Sharon government actually inherited and refined from its

predecessors (and did or did not pass on to the Olmert and Netanyahu administration).

So I am referring here both to the right and to the obligation to speak out in calling to our own government for attitude change, and for that change on the part of our government as a complement to the words, actions and thought-pattern changes that I am suggesting as necessary for Israelis, Palestinians, the Arab world at large—and, for that matter, the European and Middle Eastern Christian and Muslim worlds at large.

That there are American Jews who, while Bush was still president, were already becoming more vocal with regard to championing Israel's cause other than by pushing the administration to accord her carte blanche on any and all fronts, is evidenced by the emergence shortly before the last presidential election of a Jewish organization called *J-Street*, made up primarily of and intended to appeal to American Jews concerned about Israel's survival, but who see that survival as under-served by Bush administration-style politics as I have briefly described them with regard to the Middle East. This symptom of a surging, grass-roots effort to enact exactly the sort of attitude change that I am describing most recently, in late May, 2009, called for American Jews to impress upon President Obama and Secretary of State Hillary Clinton that they must stand firm with the just-then visiting Israeli Prime Minister Netanyahu with regard to an absolute freeze in West Bank settlement construction.[183]

That the Obama-Biden-era atmosphere invites debate on this as on other issues, as opposed to the Bush-Cheney-era preference for pre-shaped dogma that tolerates no disagreement is also evidenced in the March-April, 2009 of *Moment* magazine, a left-of-center Jewish publication that covers politics, culture and a range of diverse kinds of issues. In that issue, two opinion pieces from opposed sides of the spectrum appeared—separately, not on facing pages, so that they were simply two different pieces with two different viewpoints. Gershom Gorenberg's brief piece entitled "It's Time for American Jews to Speak Up!"

asks whether "American Jews [will] dare to ask the same question that are regularly asked by the Israelis themselves... will
they listen to their own opinions? Will they dare to voice them
publicly and without embarrassment?... I'd like to believe that
[party line-towing Jewish American leaders]...doubt the wisdom
of expanding West Bank settlements, or question the attempt
to ban two Arab parties from Israeli elections, or feel qualms
about the firepower that Israeli forces directed at civilian areas
during the war in Gaza. But if they have those doubts in private
they don't agree with themselves in public."[184]

In the same issue of the same magazine, David Frum's
opinion piece, "Force: An Inconvenient Truth"—drawing that
subtitle without irony from Al Gore's book and video documentary on Global Warming—notes how, "[d]uring the Gaza
war, many American Jews were gripped by... self-destructive
sympathy... They anguished as much (or more) over the suffering inflicted by Israel's defensive actions as by the danger
and terror of *Hamas'* aggression." Frum turns to a quote—from
his "friend and co-author, Richard Perle... [who] likes to repeat
a story of an encounter with a peace protester. 'War solves
nothing,' the protester said. 'Well,' Richard answered, 'it has
a better record than social work,'"—in order to underscore his
point that force is the only solution to this problem. After the
Gaza war, "*Hamas* has been relatively quiet." He argues that
Israel, pushed to make peace at any price over the years, lest
time run out on her, has continued to flourish, while refusing
to accede to such pressure, while "Israel's enemies, by contrast,
fell farther and farther behind."[185]

I will not judge whether Frum's hawkish perspective is a
valid existential one for Israel in either the physical survival
sense, or the moral and psychological sense in which Israel
might be measured by more than her technological achievements. I won't judge whether Gorenberg is stepping out on a
dangerous or naïve limb by his commentary. The reader can
probably deduce well enough by now what my opinion would

be on this. My point, though, is that the juxtaposition of these two radically different perspectives in a public forum of sorts bespeaks a willingness on the part of the publication's editor and publisher to promote such discourse, however controversial, because of the perception that Israel and everyone else is better served by discourse than by silence.

So much for the right and obligation to challenge and not to acquiesce on the part of Jews and of attitude change on the part of the American administration. But I am also talking about opposing a double standard that views Israel with different obligations from those of other countries, including our own, for relating to near and distant neighbors. It may be fair to criticize Israel's security fence—or at least aspects of it—but only if one is equally vocal about the vigilante-patrolled fence that separates the United Sates from Mexico, designed not to keep out suicide bombers but those seeking no more than a livelihood on our side of that border.

It may be fair to express dismay at the crushing weight of the Israeli attack on Gaza, but only if one expresses dismay at the two years of continual rocket attacks into southern Israel that preceded that attack and also takes note of the Israeli efforts to minimize the weight; one ought to note the times when Israeli soldiers exhibited the opposite of restraint, but only if one acknowledges the myriad times when Israeli soldiers exhibited restraint and/or expressed grief at the damages that they perpetrated—and only if one also expresses outrage at the fact that Hamas has forced scores of Gazan children into forced labor to dig smuggling tunnels between Gaza and Egypt, and at how many dozens of children have died doing such work.

It is interesting, in passing, to observe how the Arab world at large was remarkably subdued in its verbal response to the Israeli Gazan incursion. Did they hope that *Hamas* would be dismantled? If so, was it because of their concern for the spread of *Hamas*-like ideology to other parts of the Arab world, where other regimes would be threatened? We may well recall that

part of the reason that the Saudis permitted the encampment of American and other non-Muslim troops on their soil during the first Gulf War was the fear of the regime-toppling instability that Saddam's incursion into Kuwait might generate. Given the pre-Black September trauma that the Kingdom of Jordan had experienced at the end of the 1960s, the Saudis can surely recognize the potential provided by *Hamas* for regime-threat.[186] Or was it because of their sense that *Hamas* was a fly in the ointment of furthering the Israeli-Palestinian peace process? Did they *get* the issue of the Israeli perception of all of those rocket attacks into southern Israel? That relative verbal restraint offered quite a contrast to the response of much of the world beyond the Middle East. The potential configuration of positive and negative inputs into the peace process is as unpredictable as so many other aspects of this narrative.

Notes

[157] The United States, since the collapse of the Soviet Union, has been—or has the potential to be—the most influential outside participant in the Israel-Palestine dialogue.

[158] I must also add that, both when I first wrote these words in 2004 and reviewed them in 2007, the Israeli and American leadership were different from what they are now, in 2009. To wit: Ehud Olmert has been succeeded by Bibi Netanyahu (again) and George Bush has been succeeded by Barack Obama. In the first case the change may be a cause for concern; in the second case the change may be a reason for hope.

[159] See above, 77. "*Merkaz ha'Rav*" means "the Rabbi's Center"—*the* Rabbi meaning Rabbi Abraham Isaac Kook.

[160] In part his sermon, apparently delivered in great anguished tones, continued: ". . . and where is our Hebron? Do we forget this? And where is our Shechem? Do we forget this? And where is our Jericho? Do we forget about this too?!. . . Is it in our hands to relinquish any millimeter of this? God forbid!!"

[161] La Guardia, Ibid, 287. The italics are mine.

[162] See above, 72.

[163] See the perspective discussion of this last point in Dennis Ross, *The Missing Peace: The Inside Story of the Fight for Middle Eastern Peace*, especially 25-9, 44-5, and 797-9.

[164] Telhami, Ibid, 62.

[165] The strategy of victimization is discussed with regard to the Palestinians by Ross, op citum, 42, 775-6. As it applies to the Arab world in general, see Albert Hourani, *A History of the Arab Peoples* (Cambridge, Mass: The Beltknap Press/Harvard University Press, 1991). Hourani also talks of the tendency to romanticize one's history as a characteristic particularly endemic to the Arab world. The strategy of victimization—and the tendency to look outward rather than inward for causes of failure and/or disaster—as it applies to the Arabo-Persian, Islamic world at large, is also taken up at length (it is the core theme of his book) by Barry Rubin in his *The Tragedy of the Middle East*, (Cambridge: Cambridge University Press, 2002). Of these three works, Hourani's is the most unassailable, since he is himself an Arab and one of the deans of historiography of Arab culture and history; Ross's will be unassailable by many, given his role in the peace negotiations in which his objectivity was presumably paramount—but as an outsider will be viewed suspiciously by many in the Middle East; Rubin's indictment is the strongest and certainly his absolute objectivity, in spite of his powerful prose and compelling presentation of both concept and detail, the

most suspect for some, given that the Global Research in International Affairs Center that he directs is located in Israel. His book reminds me of La Guardia's, but from the other side of the fence and with a larger arena of focus. (And he is quite clear that the Israel-Palestine and Israeli-Arab conflicts are only part of a much bigger morass).

[166] See above, 136.

[167] I am well aware of the irony—indeed I intend to be ironic—of raising the issue of the "Jewishness" of the "Jewish" State in this manner, since the debate about that issue has been a constant in Zionist history, from the discussions of Herzl and Ahad Ha'Am and their generation regarding what and where the state should be, to the debate regarding the right to be automatic citizens of Israel by way of its Law of Return, for Jewish children of non-Jewish mothers and Jewish fathers from the former Soviet union, or for converts to Judaism whose conversions were not performed by Orthodox rabbis.

[168] *Tikkun olam* means "fixing/repairing the world." It is a rabbinic phrase that came to be particularly strongly emphasized in the sixteenth-century mystical movement surrounding Isaac Luriya in Safed and enjoins Jews to improve the world, however minimally; each is obligated to leave it a better place than it was when s/he was born into it.

[169] See the last paragraphs of the article by Kevin Peraino, "How We Got to This Point," in the January 12, 2009 issue of *Newsweek*, 34-5. In it the author effectively summarizes observations contained in three recent books, Daniel Kurtzer's and Scott Lasensky's *Negotiating Arab-Israeli Peace*, Patrick Tyler's *A World of Trouble: The White House and the Middle East—from Cold War to the War on Terror*, and Martin Indyk's *Innocent Abroad: An Intimate Account of American Peace Diplomacy in the Middle East*.

[170] In the last few years it has become more widely known that Rabin was willing to give up the Golan Heights in exchange for a serious peace initiative from Syria, so one might even say that there is a precedent of sorts.

[171] See, for example, the scurrilous article by Nasi Ahmad in the Palestinian Authority daily *Al'Hayat a'Jadida* of 7 November, 1998, that begins with the words "Corruption is a Jewish trait worldwide, so much so that one can seldom find corruption that was not masterminded by Jews or that Jews are not responsible for." Or the rhetorical question asked in the Egyptian weekly, *Roz al'Yusuf* of 24 August, 1998 "Is Israel waging chemical and biological warfare against the Arab states and Islam?" (by passing on imported blood units infected with AIDS, hepatitis and bilhariza to Arab and Third World nations). Or the nasty article by Dr Hassan Ragav in the 14 July, 1998 issue of the Egyptian daily, *al'Akbar*, asserting that "the Zionist movement is a racist political movement" and going on to deny the Holocaust. Or more recently, the anti-Jewish rant by the Egyptian Cleric, Muhammad Hussein Ya'qub,

broadcast on January 17, 2009 on *Al-Rahma* TV across Egypt—which aside from its horrifyingly hateful content ("...Jews... whose ancestors were apes and pigs...") also exhibited stunning ignorance both of Jewish ideology (... the Jews say that Uzair is the son of God...") and of history (...They [fight and kill us] for the sake of their religion...").

[172] While it is true that, since the time of writing this narrative, Arafat has gone from the scene, this does not mean that the American administration's attitude toward the Palestinian leadership significantly changed. Again, however, that attitude clearly *has* changed as we move toward the summer of 2009 and the second 100 days of the Obama administration.

[173] Indeed, as I write, President Obama is about to travel for six days through parts of the Arabo-Islamic Middle East, stopping in Riyadh to meet with Saudi leadership and in Cairo to offer a public address.

[174] See above, 131 and 133.

[175] The discussions of the "dangers" to the United States of an overly influential AIPAC—particularly as and when those discussions ignore lobbies such as the Cuban-American lobby and its success at holding American foreign policy vis-à-vis that Caribbean island hostage— smack of just that sort of implied accusation (double loyalty). The primary text discussing this issue in recent years has been the March 23, 2006 *London Review of Books* article (originally written for the *Atlantic Monthly* but not published by them) and subsequent book by John J. Mearshimer and Stephen M. Walt, *The Israel Lobby and U.S. foreign Policy*. The primary weaknesses of the accusatory thesis are first, that the authors single out AIPAC, rather than presenting it in a comparative framework that, to repeat, could well examine the activities of the anti-Castro Cuban-American lobby with regard to the issue of holding US policy hostage; and second, that they ignore the fact that our political system was designed precisely to give interest groups the opportunity to be heard in the halls of governmental power, without drawing a line with regard to success at that endeavor. Their thesis places the old wine of the "dual-loyalty" saw in a new bottle.

[176] Mordecai Ben-Hillel HaCohen is quoted in Segev, *Elvis*, p 52.

[177] See above, 60 and fn 41.

[178] Indeed times and conditions have changed and not changed! One recalls how the British and the French, as Israel's primary allies, collaborated with her in the 1956 Sinai Campaign—who now, for good reasons, are both far too distrusted by her to be able to exert much influence on her—and how it was pressure from the United States, now more than ever in a position to exert friendly influence on Israel, that at that time caused all three to withdraw from Egypt.

[179] At least until the re-advent of Netanyahu: I wrote these words before the recent election, and don't know where he stands on this issue.

[180] This is in part what Klaidman, among others, suggests in his earlier-referenced January 12, 2009 *Newsweek* article with regard to refugees and a "law of return"

[181] See above, 106-7.

[182] This is also discussed by Klaidman, among others.

[183] The May 28 email to *J-Street*'s constituents noted that "Clinton said yesterday that President Obama 'wants to see a stop to settlements—not some settlements, not outposts, not natural-growth exceptions.' This is exactly the sort of leadership we need from the President and Secretary of State if we are going to achieve a two-state solution to the Israeli-Palestinian conflict—the only way to truly secure Israel's future as a Jewish, democratic homeland." The email goes on to urge recipients to "make sure the President knows pro-Israel, pro-peace Americans support his strong line on settlements, both for Israel's and America's sake and security. Click here to send the President a message telling him you support his 'Freeze means Freeze' approach to Israeli settlements..."

[184] Gorenberg, a Jerusalem-based journalist—it is significant that he lives in Israel and not the United States, since he cannot be accused of making his comments from 10,000 miles away—among other things noted that hammering the Gaza Strip had the opposite effect that it had intended: "Among Palestinians, support for the hardline *Hamas* grew...In Israel, the suicide bombings of the second intifada had a similar effect." And he commented, "For diplomacy to succeed abroad, Obama will need support at home. He'll want the support of the Jews in particular... The first time [he] asks something from Israel... will [Jewish leaders] have the courage to support an initiative that is essential to Israel's future?" See *Moment* Magazine, March/April 2009, 12.

[185] Frum contends that "sometimes in politics, the only thing to do is the dumb thing, not the smart thing. Your neighbor throws a rock at you. The smart thing is to walk over, find out what's bothering him, and see if you can resolve the disagreement without escalating the violence. Then he throws another, bigger rock. And another. And another after that. At that point you have to recognize: I guess we're in a rock-throwing competition, dumb as it is. He hits me, I hit him harder... How does this end? I don't know." It is a compelling argument, if one assumes that the conditions that precipitated the Israeli-Palestinian conflict may be reduced to this paradigm—that the Israelis are simply next door to rock-throwing neighbors. A Palestinian might object (and we might debate the objective validity of the objection) that the house in which the Israelis live is one from which the neighbor next-door had been unjustly evicted. What then? See *Ibid*, 18.

[186] Non-Muslim troops on sacred Muslim soil presented a serious religious problem.

Chapter 13

The Larger Contexts of Peace and War

Let us circle back to one of the emphases offered at the outset of this volume: the Middle East is a web the threads of which would be tangled even if we could eliminate or solve the Israeli-Palestinian relationship. Let us assume, for the sake of argument, that the Israel-Palestine problem *were* solved; that a pair—or better, a trio—of secure and viable states were to shift into place side-by-side, and even that their interaction evolved in a fully positive and productive manner for both of them. What, then, of the region overall? Surely the tightest knot in the tangled web would be untied, but the web would remain a tangle requiring continued delicate maneuvering to unravel. One need only sweep across the region (and let us define the region in broad rather than narrow terms for this purpose) and realize how the web of confused and conflicting definitions, aspirations and interferences militate against simple disentanglement.

The situation in the Middle East is more complicated than Israel and Palestine, Israel and the Arabs, or the complexities of Islam, Christianity and Judaism. It includes the ethnic struggle between Arab and non-Arab entities (Iraq vs Iran, Syria vs Turkey, even Egypt vs Jordan or Libya—to say nothing of the Kurds within Iraq, or the Kurds within Turkey, in which last case *neither* side is Arab—or the Arabs in the Sudan) as much as it involves intra-Arab conflict between Islamic and Christian populations (Syria and Lebanon) or intra-Islamic conflict between Sunni and Shi'i populations (Iran and Iraq; Iraq within itself).

It is interwoven with socio-economics (as in the objection on the part of some of Ussama Bin Ladin's followers to the ongoing impoverishment of so many Saudis while an inner circle continues to swallow up billions in oil revenues). Its politics are complex. Even within the limited context of the Palestine Liberation Organization we see this in its range of different sub-organizations. Beyond the PLO are more than a dozen other Palestinian liberation organizations, and the PLO, while it has become virtually synonymous with *Fatah* is dominated by but not limited to *Fatah*. Some of these organizations are Muslim; some are Christian. Some seek a peaceful solution to their conflict with Israel; some simply and unequivocally want Israel destroyed. The identifying nomenclature of Palestinian organizations has shifted in the last decades and the last few years, (the *Fatah*-dominated PLO became the dominant component of the Palestinian Authority in the wake of the 1993 Oslo Accords, but the PA is not merely a continuation of the PLO or of *Fatah*). This shifting nomenclature is particularly apparent where the more distinctly anti-Israel groups, such as *Hamas* and *Hizb'allah*, are concerned.

Within Morocco the struggle between a secularizing Islamic monarchy and a rising fundamentalist faction, interwoven with the question of how to maintain a dynamic balance between the constitutional and monarchic sides of the constitutional monarchy that governs the state has increased the level of violence

and chaos in that country over the past decade and a half. Morocco's next-door neighbor, Algeria, has provided some of the wherewithal for that violence by breeding the fundamentalists who concern both the Moroccans to the west and the Tunisians to the east of Algeria. The Tunisians are equally wary about the intentions of the neighbor to *their* east, Libya, whose leader, Mu'amar Qadaffi has only recently begun to re-seek a place among the constellation of nations beyond the region, and whose support of terrorism has yielded disputes both with Tunisia and with Egypt, aside from complicating relations with Europe and the United States. All of these complexities derive from a combination of political and religious issues.

Egypt itself has at times seen itself as ethnically Arab and even as a leader of the Arab world—as, briefly, under Nassir, who not long after the revolution of 1952 finally removed the British presence, even forged a United Arab Republic that joined Egypt and Syria together in 1958, as we have noted earlier. At other times, as when Nassir's successor, Sadat, signed a peace agreement with Israel in 1978, Egypt has viewed itself as other than Arab. To its south, the Sudan is, as I write, the location of the worst racial and ethnic genocide anywhere (at this moment) on the planet, which is being meted out against the Christian and Animist blacks of the south, in and around Darfur, by the lighter-skinned Muslims of the North and their Arab allies.

Jordan may to some extent have rid itself of its Palestinian problem, first by the conflagration of Black September in the early 1970s and later by the peace treaty with Israel in the 1990s, in which the Hashemite Kingdom renounced all interest in the West Bank. In both cases King Hussein was trying to lessen the sense of threat to his throne deriving from the ethnic matter of his family ruling over a Palestinian population while itself being non-Palestinian. Israel inherited the problem on both occasions. First, because the PLO and its entourage relocated to Lebanon when Hussein drove them out of Jordan, which made that the locus of anti-Israel activity and ultimately the object of Israel's

problematic 1982 invasion.[187] Second, because the unsolved West Bank Palestinian problem remains both unsolved and one that is essentially an Israeli problem now, from which Jordan is free.

If the Syrian-Lebanese border is quiet, it is because the United States and our allies allowed Syria to swallow Lebanon in all but name in the aftermath of the first Persian Gulf War. But Syria's borders with Turkey and Iraq are rarely silent. Part of that derives from ethnic hostility (the Turks are neither Semites nor Arabs), part of it is religious (part of the Iraqi community bordering Syria is Shi'i; the Syrians are primarily Sunni), part of it is ethno-religious: the Kurds, who have never had their aspirations for political self-determination, promised since World War I, addressed, are located largely in the northern and eastern areas of Syria, where she borders Iraq and Turkey, respectively.[188] And the Kurds are themselves not a monolith; there are in Iraq, for example, at least two major and mutually antagonistic factions.[189]

In Iraq the Kurdish region encompasses not only the Zagros Mountains within its territory, but more importantly, most of the Mosul oil fields in which the British and the Iraqis in turn have been so interested. Indeed the British had considered creating a Kurdish state after World War I in order to protect the Mosul-Kirkuk oil fields—and promised this to the Kurds in that region—but the conflict that this would have brought about with the French as well as with Russia and Iran caused them to abandon the idea.[190]

By 1967, after the June Arab-Israeli War and under the regime of Colonel Abdul Salam Muhammad Arif, the Kurds and Iraqis seemed to arrive at a *modus vivendi* in which the former retained autonomy in the mountains and the latter were ceded control of the Mosul oil fields. This tacit agreement was made more formal in March, 1970, and by then included oil revenue-sharing between the Iraqi government and the Kurds, but already by January, 1972 new fighting had broken out between the two sides. More recently, of course, the Kurds have

suffered genocide attacks at the hands of Saddam Hussein, while in Turkey they have engaged in terrorist activity against the Turkish population and regime. On and across the borders of all three countries, (Iraq, Syria and Turkey), they have not been the *source* of complications but *part* of the complications.

By the time that the Baghdad regime had worked out an arrangement with the Kurds in the late 1960s and early 1970s, "Iraq" had changed hands several times. Having deposed and assassinated King Faisal II in 1958, Brigadier Abdul Karim Kassim assumed control of the government. At that time he sought to assert himself as the leader of the Arab nation. In this he opposed the claim of Arab leadership asserted by Abdul Gamal Nassir and Egypt—but the issue became moot when he was executed in his own apartment in 1963 by the court martial instituted by the National Council of the Revolutionary command. He was then succeeded by Colonel Arif, whose support came from the Ba'ath Party. One might assume that this would have meant good relations with Syria, also by then controlled by the Ba'ath party—but the party of the same name in Syria at that time (the mid-to-late 1960s) preferred independent socialist development in each Ba'ath-led country, while in Iraq, Arif's notion was pan-Arab, including Egypt.

While Arif was in Damascus discussing a unity plan, the Syrians with whom he was negotiating—al'Bitar and Michael Aflaq—were discussing a plan with his Deputy Premier, Salah al'Sa'adi, behind his back, that would create an economic Syrian-Iraqi merger that would exclude Egypt. Al'Sa'adi ended up expelled from Iraq, Aflaq and al'Bitar flew to Baghdad and attempted to seize control of the Iraqi government in the name of the international Ba'ath Party, the Iraqi army expelled them, restored Arif and his government to their positions, and the Ba'ath party was banned from Iraqi politics.[191] Thus where relations between Syria and Iraq are concerned, the situation is not helped by the intra-Ba'ath complications that have affected their respective and mutual histories in the last half-century or

212 ◆ Untangling the Web

so. Simply put, part of the tension between Syria and Iraq in the past two generations has been based on the fact that each is led by a branch of the Ba'ath Party and each has asserted that it should be the true leader of that party. Nor was this issue improved with the assumption of power in Iraq by Saddam Hussein.

Iraq is better known to the world for other relationships than that with Syria, however. In 1980 Saddam's troops entered into a protracted war with Iran which would last for eight years, at the end of which he could claim victory since it was the Iranians who actually sued for peace. But both peoples were exhausted, their resources decimated. Saddam's forces gained enormous experience and confidence in this war, during which he also experimented with chemical and biological weaponry—both against the Iranians and against the Kurds in Iraq itself. Two matters of particular note are relevant to our discussion. The first is the role played by the United States in the eight-year war. Since barely two years earlier the Iranians under the Ayatollah Khomeini had taken American hostages and released them after an extended period of tension and difficult negotiation, and since the Ayatollah's regime had been consistently antagonistic toward America in its rhetoric, it is not surprising that the U.S. took the Iraqi side and provided much of the weaponry that brought Saddam his success—at least initially.

For actually, a more detailed look at the United States' position during the war reveals that, in its middle phase, when it appeared that Iraq was gaining a decisive advantage, and in spite of the strong public stance against Iran, the Reagan administration began secret negotiations to supply Iran with arms in exchange for assistance in negotiating the release of a second group of American hostages—in *Lebanon*. So arms began to make their way to Iran from the United States in the form of antitank missiles, in 1985. As this narrative is consistently caught in the matter of how tangled the web of the region and its subsidiary threads are, the following somewhat bizarre datum

should perhaps not seem so bizarre: the missiles that were sent to Iran were provided through Israel.[192] By the following year, when Iran seemed to be gaining the upper hand, and particularly after the Iranian forces conquered the Iraqi Faw Peninsula, near Kuwait, the United States began to worry again, not as much about Iraq as about the threat to oil shipments coming from and through Kuwait. Thus not only did American support swing back more clearly toward Iraq, but by 1987 Kuwaiti ships began to fly American flags and therefore boasted the protective support of the U.S. Naval forces in the Gulf.

Yet another matter of particular relevance to our discussion is that Saddam, at the end of the war, represented himself as the champion of the Arab world against "the Persian menace." With this in mind, having exhausted his funds and incurred enormous debts in the course of the war, and also aware of the power of his army, Saddam turned rapidly after its end to the other Arab states, and to Kuwait and the Saudis in particular, with a demand for financial support and relief. In a long note to the Secretary General of the Arab League on July 15, 1990, Iraq's Minister of Foreign Affairs, Tariq Aziz, wrote in part:

> Before the war Iraq was one of the main oil producers, with about 2.6 million barrels a day. . . [but] Iraq's losses during that period [1980-85] rose to $106 million.

> In point of fact this sum has gone into the coffers of the other oil-producing countries of the region. . . A simple calculation is enough to show that Iraq's "debts" to Kuwait and the Emirates are easily compensated for by the surplus profits they made, thanks to their increase in oil production during the war.

> The question we must ask is: since Iraq took on all the responsibility for defending the security and dignity of the Arab nation and for protecting the wealth of the countries in the Gulf—which would have fallen into foreign hands if Iraq had lost—must it still, despite everything, consider the aid it was given as a "debt"?

> . . . How then can we continue to consider the amounts given
> to Iraq by brother Arabs as debts, when it contributed many
> times those amounts from its own treasury, and its youth
> gave its blood in defense of Arab land, dignity, and wealth?

Aziz emphasized Arab unity many times in his note, commenting that "if only there existed a feeling of being part of
Arabness and a desire for the security of the Arab nation,"
which feeling he observes to be lacking, the situation would be
a happier one for all concerned. It is symptomatic of the complicated world of Arab politics, and of a long history of ethnic
and political as well as religious and cultural strife militating
against the desire of Arab unity not only that Aziz could see
the bitter reality of that lack, but that the intra-Arab negotiations that began in 1990 to prevent the Iraq-Kuwait war failed.

Once Saddam began increasing his war-bound rhetoric,
there are many places in which one can see this failure taking shape. When intra-Arab diplomacy was still hopeful and
active toward preventing the Iraqi invasion of Kuwait and its
consequences—and a summit meeting was still scheduled to
take place in Jeddah—the Kuwaiti Emir wrote to his brother,
Crown Prince Sheikh Sa'ad al-Sabah, in part: "It is noteworthy
for us to keep in mind our national interests; therefore don't
listen to whatever you may hear from the Saudis or Iraqis in
regard to brotherhood and maintaining Arab solidarity. Each
has his own interests to cater to."[193] That sensibility is reflected
in nearly every phase of the negotiations undertaken in their
various stages to prevent the war from taking place.

Part of Saddam's rhetoric with regard to Kuwait focused on
an assertion that Kuwait was a natural and historical part of
Iraq and that therefore, were he to "liberate" it from the Sabah
family and bring it back under Iraqi governance he would merely
be restoring the integrity of his land. Two interesting historical
data come to mind in this. First, that on the one hand Saddam
was right, in that Kuwait was an artificial contrivance of the
British; but that on the other hand he was wrong, since Iraq

itself was similarly an artificial contrivance of the British from the same period, and "Iraq" had never in its history existed as a unified entity of common ethnicity with distinct borders.[194] Second, that Saddam was not the first Iraqi ruler to assert this. Back in 1961, Abdul Karim Kassim had claimed sovereignty over Kuwait by means of the same sort of claim: that that oil-rich area had always been and topographically still was a natural part of Iraq. At that time, the British, Egyptians and Saudis allied together to prevent the Iraqi take-over.

In 1990, Iraqi troops swiftly invaded Kuwait, driven by Saddam's lust for conquest and its concomitants, multiplied by his frustration regarding the response (i.e., non-response) to his demands of other Arab states and also the mixed signals from the United States regarding what its response to an attack on Kuwait would be. When the invasion of Kuwait arrived, the Egyptian Foreign ministry put out a statement condemning it, which provoked shock from Jordan's King Hussein: "This destroys everything. And it gives all chances of broadening the conflict."[195] If half the Arab world was shocked by the Iraqi invasion of Kuwait, the other half was concerned about the American response that would surely follow. The majority of the Arab League's twenty-one foreign ministers adopted a resolution condemning the invasion and demanding that Saddam Hussein withdraw his troops from Kuwait unconditionally. Seven—Djibouti, Jordan, Libya, the PLO, Sudan, Yemen, and Iraq, of course—did not vote for the resolution.

According to King Hussein of Jordan, Saddam had expressed willingness to discuss a withdrawal from Kuwait if a mini-summit of certain key Arab leaders were to be convened— provided that the Arab League did not condemn his actions. Given the adoption of the resolution, the summit could never take place—although, astoundingly, Saddam was apparently shocked that the summit which had indeed been scheduled for August 4, was cancelled even after his invasion and the publication of the resolution of condemnation. It is perhaps one

among the symptoms of his irrationality that he should have been so surprised.

The resolution also called for Western Powers not to deploy troops on Arab soil. It would take one week for the United States to turn that point of view around. A key element in the about-face was the achievement of Soviet support for co-active intervention in the situation. The mere attempt to gain that support reflected two related developments. The first was that, with Gorbachev in charge, the Soviet Union was rapidly moving at this precise movement toward *perestroika*. The second, informed by the first, was that the decades-long American goal of keeping the Soviet Union out of the Middle East had suddenly shifted: Secretary of State James Baker's strategy of *involving* the Soviets went against a dogma that had been in place since the Truman administration.

A further key element was to get the Saudis to agree to host American troops. The American satellite images that showed concentrations of Iraqi troops in Kuwait and near the Saudi border were ultimately sufficient to convince King Fahd to agree to permit the temporary stationing of American troops on Saudi soil—and a secret protocol was agreed upon: that when events permitted, the American troops would be removed, but permanent bases would be established for multinational troops in the nearby Emirate of Bahrain and in Kuwait itself, once it had been freed.[196]

The third key element in rendering the deployment of Western troops on Arab soil feasible was the configuration of that multinational force: it included Arab and Muslim states, thereby eliminating the possibility for Saddam to present the impending conflict as one in which he represented the Arab and Muslim worlds against an infidel and/or foreign imperialist enemy. Two issues here are relevant for considering the question of how the larger tangled Middle Eastern web might become disentangled by peace. One is the very fact of such an alliance: it signifies the possibility that countries with countervalent interests, if

they find common interests stronger than those that are antagonistic, can work together. In theory, at least, not only the United States and this or that Arab or Muslim state, but even Israel and those states (or, as the case may be, the Palestinians who don't yet have a state) could work together if they found sufficiently compelling common interests.

The second relevant issue is that, if we once again take one step further back in Middle Eastern history, to February, 1957, we find that the most apparently implacable of Arab Muslim enemies, the Hashemite Crown Prince Abd'Allah of Iraq and King 'Abd al-'Aziz Ibn Sa'ud of Saudi Arabia—the latter had dispossessed the family of the former of its kingdom in the *hijaz*, but the mutual enmity of these families went back centuries— were meeting in Washington, DC and, under the patronage of President Eisenhower and secretary of State John Foster Dulles, agreeing to an alliance in order to fend off the Arab revolution that threatened both. This also speaks to the United States' ability to function as a go-between, if the will and the wiles are there, in the context of the most delicate of conditions.[197]

But even as these key elements needed to oppose Saddam Hussein and the myriad details that made them up were shifting into place, negotiations with him continued. It is not clear whether, as they began to achieve success in shaping a far-flung alliance against Iraq, the American leaders of the coalition wanted a negotiated settlement or became increasingly eager for a military confrontation which would afford the opportunity of dismantling Saddam's now considerable (after his eight-year war experience against Iran) military infrastructure. Certainly the adoption of a UN-sponsored resolution on November 29, 1990 calling for a precise date of Iraqi withdrawal from Kuwait has been interpreted by some as an indication that the window for negotiations was being rapidly closed.

On the other hand, President Bush (Senior) announced the following day that he would send Secretary of State Baker to meet with Iraqi Foreign Minister Tariq Aziz to facilitate negotia-

tions. Remarkably, such a meeting only took place by the skin of its diplomatic teeth—on January 9, 1991 (six days before the UN Resolution had demanded Iraqi troop withdrawal)—since for the five weeks between that time and President Bush's call for a meeting the two sides could hardly negotiate a time and place for a negotiation meeting! Pierre Salinger asserts that "a top Iraqi source told me that all that was needed to set up conversations involving Tariq Aziz, George Bush, James Baker and Saddam Hussein was for Bush to pick up the phone and call Saddam Hussein to discuss it with him. This was part of Saddam Hussein's mentality."[198]

This assertion leads simultaneously in several possible directions. Since Salinger doesn't specify his source, but leaves it vague, can we take this as true? Salinger is a respected, veteran journalist and historian, so can we trust him and can we trust his judgment and might we understand the vagueness of his reference as protective of his source? Is his source to be trusted as honest? Salinger apparently believes so. If the statement is true, then what of "Saddam's mentality"—is that *his* mentality or *"Arab"* mentality? In either case, if it is so, how far should the President of the United States be willing to go in catering to that mentality in order to avert a military conflict? If the statement is true and President Bush chose not to pick up the phone, was that his *own* mentality of dislike or distrust of Saddam or his sense that if anyone should pick up the phone it should be Saddam, calling Bush, and not the other way around? Or did he not wish to avert the military confrontation either for internal reasons (a re-election effort not all that far away and waning popularity) or external reasons (American hopes to dismantle Iraq's military power and therefore alter the balance of power in the Middle East)?

If one quotation from one book among the scores that discuss the first Gulf War can yield such a plethora of possibilities without any certainty, and one considers that the first Gulf War is only a part of this much larger arena of complication, then at

the very least we must be struck once again by the impossible complexities of the tangled web of the Middle East overall.

In any case, the January 9 meeting between Baker and Aziz which took place in Geneva, lasted more than six hours, during which the world waited and, due to the unexpected length of the meeting, began to hope that perhaps a diplomatic solution was being worked out. It wasn't. Aziz had come to Geneva to assert that the January 15th deadline for Iraqi troop removal be lifted: "We can't negotiate with them unless they do."[199] Baker handed Aziz a letter to be given to Saddam, but reading it, Aziz refused to deliver it. Aziz later asserted at a press conference that "the language in this letter is not compatible with the language that should be used in correspondence between heads of state." Again: is this so? If so, was the language insensitivity a function of American insensitivity or Iraqi hyper-sensitivity?

The First Gulf War and Its Aftermath

By January 10 the United States had decided that, unless for some reason Saddam actually withdrew his troops from Kuwait, the attack on those troops would begin on January 17, 2 A.M. Baghdad time. The aftermath of that moment—and the provisional ceasefire arrived at six weeks and four hours later—was that the military capability of Iraq had been crushed and its infrastructure more or less ruined. More than that, the Arab world that had placed itself on both sides of the coalition fence was more shaken and divided than it had been in a long time. A number of American and Western military bases came to populate the region. But Saddam remained both uncaptured and, when he resurfaced, unrepentant, and as time went on, whatever positive aura had accrued to the United States for its role in the war began to fade.

In the aftermath of the Iran-Iraq conflict, and after it the Iraq-Kuwait conflict and the Persian Gulf War; and in the decade following that conflict through the concatenation of events

that carried from the attacks on the Pentagon and World Trade Center buildings on September 11, 2001 to the invasions of Afghanistan and Iraq—in the course of this time, Iran regained some of its military potency and found itself included on the second President Bush's short list of nefarious states. But in the aftermath of our second invasion of Iraq (in 2003), capture of Saddam (in 2004) and dismantling of any and all parts of a potential Iraqi infrastructure, Iraq's neighbors such as Saudi Arabia and Jordan grew concerned that the currently ambiguous shape of Iraq could adversely affect them. It is not merely the fact of instability that worries them, but specifically, that the majority Shi'is might find common ground with the Shi'i Iranians, creating a block of power potentially destructive to them.

Within Iran, the hardliners who are disinclined to seek rapprochement with the West—and part of whose unequivocal ideology is the denial of Israel's right to exist—are more firmly entrenched in power than ever, corrupt, engaged in rigging elections and controlling all aspects of infrastructure. Iran has been a consistent supporter and funder of *Hamas*, *Islamic Jihad* and *Hizb'Allah*—groups devoted to Israel's destruction. And Iran, in spite of signing the international anti-nuclear proliferation treaty, has been seeking the opportunity to develop a nuclear weapons program, claiming that, since its isolation during and after the eight-year-long war with Iraq, it requires it own sources of nuclear power in order to function effectively. Such a possibility is considered by Israel in particular to pose a fundamental threat to its existence.

Thus the condition of Iran is linked to that of Iraq and in turn to that of Saudi Arabia, Jordan, Syria and ultimately to that of Israel—regardless of the outcome of the Israeli-Palestinian problem. The tangled web is tightly wound indeed. And one key to disentangling it is most distinctly the United States. We are the power which, in spite of our shortcomings, still has the most overwhelming capacity to effect positive change in the region.

On the one hand, the Arab world has ignored or championed

the most "internal" of issues—the Palestinian cause—as that world's constituent elements have felt inclined, for whatever reasons. The Saudis have spent millions of dollars on the Palestinian cause; the Kuwaitis threw out thousands of Palestinian workers in the context of the Gulf War, eliminating an important means of Palestinian socio-economic infrastructure—albeit not located within Palestine itself.[200] On the other hand, this entire narrative has exploded in the past generation beyond the most "external" of Middle Eastern bounds: on September 11 it reached half-way around the world. The stakes, to say the least, as I write, have broadened exponentially. It's not just about Israel and the Palestinians and it's not just about the Middle East but about the world at large.

The theology that pitted Islam and Christianity against each other in the Medieval *reconquista* and Crusades, and that focused both faiths in the post-medieval struggle between the Ottomans and Europe, became an oil-based interest in a politically and socially backward Near East over a century ago on the part of the Prussians and thus the British and the French. The ensuing competition led to the First World War. That oil-based focus from the outside world into the world of the Middle East is continued most obviously in our own era by the United States. It is American oil interests that both primarily governed our intervention in the Persian Gulf more than a decade and half ago and motivates our continued presence in Saudi Arabia. It is that presence that so enrages Bin Ladin and those like him: Muslim fundamentalists spiritually descended from *wahhabi sunnis* who gnash their teeth at the notion of all those infidel feet striding back and forth across the soil bearing "the two holy mosques (Makka and Madina)"—while also ostensibly fretting at the oppression of too many Saudis by the we-take-it-all-for-ourselves royal family.

At the same time that our troops are in effect protecting not only our own oil interests but the Saudi royal house, the members of that house necessarily tightrope walk with regard

to supporting our government's attempts to form a coalition like that assembled by the Senior President Bush that would pit moderate Christians and Muslims against fundamentalists and "legitimate" governments against terrorists. We *are* engaged in a third world war. Like World War I, its starting point is a confusing interweave of religious, ethnic, political and socio-economic issues that begin in the Middle East and the interaction between Western Civilization and that corner of the world. Like World War II, the enemy is a force and its followers intensely committed to fulfilling delusional dreams of fixing the world by ridding it of elements it regards as impure and of dominating whatever survives.

The fact of the matter is that most of the principals in this discussion, whether they say so explicitly or not, do wish to be like us Americans in a range of socio-economic and cultural ways, and so our positive influence potential is great. One can observe this desire from the detailed discussion of it as it pertains to Israel by Israeli journalist-historian, Tom Segev, in his *Elvis in Jerusalem*, just as one can observe it from a personal story related in a public lecture by Fareed Sarouq.[201] Sarouq is a South African Sunni Muslim, an activist in the anti-apartheid movement who studied for eight years in the very *madrasa* in Pakistan that later became best known for producing Taliban fighters. He was in a position to witness the following moment that he described in his lecture: while a Taliban leader was being interviewed by the media, one of the Taliban body guards quietly pulled an American television cameraman aside to ask him how he could get a visa to the United States and a Green Card. Sarouq's point at the time was how pervasive American TV is: that the market-driven expression of what America is had captured even this most implacable enemy of America. For the purposes of this discussion what is significant is simply how we capture the world.

Which yields two questions. The first, cognate with the point of Sarouq's observation, is "what *are* we?" At our best

we offer hope to the entire world regarding the possibilities to improve one's condition in the world, regarding individual rights and communal responsibility and respect for difference between individuals and communities with respect to religion, race, ethnicity and a host of other attributes. At our worst, we are arrogant and overly-certain of our ability to *dominate* the world. We *can* be—and in the years that have followed the attacks on us of September 11, 2001, which began with so much sympathy for and with us on the part of the world, we *have* been—beyond arrogant in our assumption that we can operate as lone rangers with respect to terrorism and its concomitants.

This sensibility pertains both to actions and to words: When George W. Bush, in finally responding to the events of September 11, continued—five times within a short period of time—to use the word "Crusade" in referring to how the United States would engage the terrorists from the Middle East, the very term carried with it the same sort of association to Arab and Muslim ears that Western ears would carry were they to hear a leader from that part of the world refer to opposition to America in terms of *Jihad* (as Ussama Bin Ladin did indeed do, but the point is that he does not represent all Arabs or all Muslims any more than Dick Cheney represents all Christians or Westerners).

Which United States will move forward toward the future?

This is a difficult question to answer—I was writing these words as the United States hurtled toward the November confrontation between Bush-Cheney and Kerry-Edwards, and the very nature of that confrontation and the American response to it indicates how difficult it is to answer that question. I am rereading them in the aftermath of the past November confrontation between Obama-Biden and McCain-Palin and four months into the Obama-Biden era, and the question has still not arrived at a simple answer.

I recall that, in reading in the newspaper in the days following September 11, 2001, how struck I was by both the poignancy and the irony of stories about those with cell phones who were

trapped in the Towers, some of whom spoke for as much as forty-five minutes to loved ones before their world literally collapsed—to say nothing of those on board doomed flights who also knew that they were doomed. Poignant because we know that they knew that they were doomed. Ironic because that brief moment imbued each of those individuals with a future-seeing and therefore prophet-like quality: briefly, the consummate terrorist act produced a large supply of Moses-and-Muhammad-like everyday people who knew in advance the hours of their deaths.[202]

That extended agonizing moment is the other side of Arthur Miller's essay of nearly six decades ago, in which he observed how tragedy on the stage in the second half of the twentieth century is defined by everyday Willy Lomans, each of whom dies the non-descript death of a salesman—but to whom we can all thereby relate—rather than by ancient Greek tragic figures like Oedipus: great mythic kings and heroes the staged bringing down of whom so satisfied the Athenian audiences of twenty-five centuries ago. But I bet that not a single one of those in the Towers, as they watched their deaths approaching, thought of themselves as Moses-(or Oedipus)-like, as any more than the everyday people we all are—yet to those around us, each unique and very special.

Not so Pat Robertson and Jerry Falwell. I also recall how these two scions of the Christian religious Right had a televised dialogue a few evenings after September 11, in which they casually pointed the finger at groups of Americans (gays, lesbians, the ACLU—I don't recall every group they mentioned) whose lifestyle is not theirs and accused them of bringing God's righteous wrath upon America. (They didn't mention Jews, of course, but surely Jews should be included in that list, by definition.) One can only be horrified at the cruelty and the arrogance of these men. That in a time when thousands of our fellow-human beings were grieving over the horrifying and sudden loss of loved ones; that at a time when the vast majority of even hardened

enemies were joining hands in prayer and determination; these men could cast stones is as despicable as are the acts of Ussama Bin Ladin and his suicide squads, if more subtly so.

Like Bin Ladin, Robertson and Falwell have forgotten that they are *not* Moses or Muhammad, to whom, according to traditional Judaism, Christianity and Islam God spoke directly; they are not prophets and conduits of the Word of God. They are men gifted, at best, with conviction and a certain charisma that hits a note with some. With their stone-throwing—I am not sure that they are so peculiarly innocent as to have earned the right to cast the first stone—they have shown the rest of us that they are madmen, no different in *conception* (albeit different in substance, no doubt) from the Bin Ladins of the Islamic world. And on the large front, *which guise*—that of would-be Moses and would-be Oedipus or that of Willy Loman's simpler dignity and the humility of those who perished in the Towers and the Pentagon and in a Pennsylvania farm field without accounting themselves prophets or heroes or even martyrs—will this country offer to the world in the years that follow?

So the second question is: how can we use the charisma that we command in the world to our advantage, and the advantage of the principle parties whose interests are so interwoven and intertangled in the Middle East and elsewhere. The answer to this second question is informed by the answer to the first. And they are enormously important answers. The future of the United States and the world depend on it. Hopefully the Obama/Biden-led America will fulfill its promise of inspiring us toward cooperation and leadership, not domination and egoship.

Notes

[187] It may not be so surprising to learn that the Israelis were initially hailed by the Lebanese as liberators—but they made the error of overstaying their welcome, so that when they finally left, their departure was a source of joy and offered a sense of victory to the mixed Lebanese-Palestinian array of communities whence Israel departed.

[188] The closest the Kurds have come to an independent polity, interestingly enough, was in 1945. After leading a revolt that went nowhere for two years within Iraq, Sheikh Mustafa al'Barzani led his followers in that year to Mahabad in northern Iran, that had been established with Soviet support as a Kurdish Republic. But when, at the insistence of both the UN and the US the USSR withdrew from Iran in 1946, Mahabad collapsed; al'Barzani and his followers left for Soviet Armenia.

[189] Ethnically, the Kurds are related to the Persians (today's Iranians); their language is related to the Persian branch of the Indo-Iranian branch of the Indo-European family tree of languages (of which English—and French, German, Russian and Greek, among others—is part). Their presence in the same region from antiquity is attested by the very naming of Book Three in the early fourth-century BCE Greek writer Xenophon's work, *The Anabasis*, as "The March to Kurdistan."

[190] That area was in any case promised to the French according to the dictates of the Sykes-Picot agreement, but it seems that the British hoped to get away with not honoring that part of the 1916 accord.

[191] For more details, see Eugene M. Fisher & M. Cherif Bassouni, *Storm Over the Arab World: A People in Revolution.*

[192] This would not have been bizarre at all a few years earlier, since the Shah's Iran was on good terms with Israel, but for the Ayatollah's Iran, which had eliminated the Israeli Embassy and consistently spouted heavy anti-Israel rhetoric to have been saved from Iraq by means of American arms and Israeli intermediation would be remarkable were the Middle East not so consistently unpredictable.

[193] This is quoted by Pierre Salinger and Eric Laurent in their *Secret Dossier: The Hidden Agenda Behind the Gulf War*, 65.

[194] See above, 89. In antiquity, what is now Iraq was variously part of the Assyrian and Babylonian Empires, swallowed up by the Medo-Persian Empire and Alexander the Great in turn, and subsequently part of the renascent Parthian and Sassanian Empires in turn. Its general topographic contours were what defined it for the Greeks, who called it Mesopotamia (meaning "between the Rivers") due to the dominating role played by the Tigris and Euphrates Rivers in its life. By the seventh century CE it was dominated by

the Arab Muslims and became the seat of the Abbasid Empire for several centuries, was swallowed up by the Persians again and then became part of the Ottoman Empire, which it remained until the British took over.

[195] Salinger and Laurent, 113.

[196] Ibid, 136.

[197] I am deliberately ignoring two issues here. One is that the alliance in the end failed, because the attempt to bring in a third monarch, Muhammad V of Morocco, failed, and the other two apparently chose not to go it alone. Two, that there is an unhappy irony in a meeting in the US capital, named for the leader of the American revolt against a monarch, in which American support was being offered to two monarchs against the revolt of a people whose situation in 1957 might be said to have mirrored the American situation in 1776. This irony leads us to the question I shall raise at the end of this chapter: what *are* we Americans as we move about the world diplomatically and militarily?

[198] Salinger and Laurent, 204-5.

[199] Ibid, 210.

[200] The expulsion of Palestinians is not so surprising when one keeps in mind that Yassir Arafat, as leader of the Palestinians, had openly supported Saddam Hussein in 1990 in the latter's decision (and follow-up!) to invade Kuwait.

[201] The lecture was delivered at Chautauqua Institution, Chautauqua, NY, on Wednesday, August 18, 2004. Tapes of that lecture are available from Chautauqua Institution.

[202] I am alluding to the passages in Deuteronomy (31:14 and 32:15) that note that Moses knew in advance the moment of his death, and the rabbinic tradition that emphasizes that he was the only individual in history to know the day of his death in advance.

Epilogue

I remind the reader that my primary emphasis has been on the complexities of the past and not on the present. There is no place in the world where the present more quickly and emphatically *becomes* the past than the Middle East. Between the time when I began to write this book—between, even the time I *finished* the manuscript in its first version—and the time I am writing these words, small but important changes in the region and the world focused upon the region will have altered how we might think about or discuss the present. The more so the future. Even the last paragraph of the previous chapter, in referring to "the charisma that we command in the world" no longer applies as it did when I wrote it; the United States is now engaged, in part, or should be engaged, in the process of re-claiming our charisma in the world, as we have approached, among other things, our *next* presidential election and elected Barack Obama to succeed George Bush. That reclamation pro-

cess may or may not have begun truly to succeed by the time readers have these words before them. With that in mind, we still are drawn irresistibly forward, toward:

Hope, Despair, Memory and Forgetting

The future of the world depends on many different things, especially in an era where the world is interconnected by the tangled web of technology; in which events happening on the one side of the planet can be observed virtually instantaneously from the other side and in which a desperate madman hiding in the mountains of Afghanistan can effect the destruction of the two mighty towers of the World Trade Center without ever leaving his cave.

With this in mind it might be worth considering four concluding (as opposed to final) issues for this brief narrative. The first two pertain to the specifics of Israeli-Arab relations and the third and the fourth to the Middle East at large.

Within the Arab-Israeli aspect of the overall tangled web, the Israeli-Palestinian problem is the centerpiece of complication. That issue itself is, as we have observed, complicated by aspects of the problems of definition and aspiration that we have sought to unravel across the broader terrain. Key among those aspects is the functional distinction among three groups of Palestinian Arabs, as we have seen: those who dwell east of the Jordan and have been citizens of the Kingdom of Jordan for seven decades; those caught in the aftermath of the first Arab-Israeli war who have been dwelling in Gaza and the West Bank who are most frequently the functional reference point of the word "Palestinian;" and finally those who remained or returned to the State of Israel after that war who, since 1949 have been most frequently referred to as Israeli Arabs.

Within the framework of Palestinians in the West Bank and Gaza, we can derive hope from entities such as *Windows*, a non-profit joint Israeli-Palestinian grassroots peace organization

that, since 1991, "has promoted acquaintance, understanding and conciliation between people from both nations, through educational programs, media and art," and which "ignore[s] the ups and downs of the political arena, . . .overcome[s] the sadness and anger that acts of violence make us feel, and . . . keep[s]. . . busy doing the work we know how to do—creating constructive and equal dialogue between Palestinians and Jews."[203] Such an organization is part of the vanguard of the struggle to write the future history of this corner of the region in terms very different from those of the past.

In a different way we may derive hope from an array of often unheralded artistic enterprises, both those which reflect cooperation across the Green line and those which simply reflect the will to shape the positive and the creative within the morass of so much negativity and destruction—or on the other hand to use art as a means of addressing issues beyond the realm of political and military discourse. Thus my eye was drawn to two recent articles by Daniel J. Wakin in back-to-back issues of the *New York Times*. One focused on 16-year-old Dalia Moukarker and others like her, in the West Bank city of Ramallah, who have been drawn to and managed to study—assiduously—Western Classical music (she plays the flute). The other focuses on 18-year-old Shehade Shelalde, also of Ramallah, who turned his natural hand skills in the direction of music: he has his own musical instrument repair shop in a garage. "In a place all too familiar with the sounds of gunfire, military vehicles and explosions, he said, '*Al Kamandjati* ["The Violinist"], a school founded by Ramzi Aburedwan, a French-trained violist raised in a Palestinian refugee camp taught us to hear music.'"[204]

One of the keys out of the morass is the recognition and respect of the *humanity* of the Other. This is what so many Israelis and Palestinians—and Arabs and Kurds, and Persians and Arabs, and Turks and Armenians, and Shi'is and Sunnis, and Muslims, Christians and Jews—have had difficulty doing and need to do. Music, that requires no words in the myriad

languages that populate the region, is among the most magnificent of carriers of our humanity, and among the most poignant of articulators of hope.

So is the cinema, and there have been recent Israeli movies that, as Eric Alterman observes in an opinion piece in *Moment Magazine*, "boldly go where few politicians dare."[205] Two films that Alterman particularly notes are *For My Father*,[206] that tells the story of Tarik, "a would-be suicide bomber, who falls in love with an Israeli girl estranged from her Orthodox family"; and *Lemon Tree*,[207] "based on the true story of a Palestinian widow who defends her lemon tree grove when a new Israeli defense minister moves into a house adjacent to her land..." and his advisors "decide that terrorists could take cover among the aromatic trees and declare the grove a safety threat." (It is as if Chekhov's *The Cherry Orchard* has been squeezed through a dying process and come out a completely new color.) Neither film ends happily; both offer a range of competing complications, but the bottom line is that one sees a suicide bomber through a sympathetic lens and the other sees the "vaunted Israeli justice system as a kangaroo court when it comes to the Territories"— and both think outside the box of political convention.

More recently, a museum devoted to the presentation and discussion of the Holocaust opened in April, 2009—on Holocaust Memorial Day—in an apartment in Na'alin, a Palestinian village better known for the weekly protests taking place within it against the Israeli security fence that divides the village in half. One of the residents of Na'alin and a leader of the fence protesters, Ibrahim Amira, commented at the time of the museum exhibition opening, that "if leaders on both sides know and remember what Hitler did, maybe we'll have peace."[208] And he might have added: protagonists on both sides of the fence (pun intended) need to think about the real suffering of those on the other side.

The second, related issue, derives from our noting the inherent self-definitional—identity—complications for Israeli Arabs,

which necessarily escalated as a complication in the course of the decade that leads from Oslo to the present.[209] Having to a range of extents come to recognize themselves as Israelis in the course of nearly sixty years of citizenship, their sense of identity as Palestinians, rather than—or in addition to—their sense of identity as Israelis suddenly began to take shape both in the hopeful era of the seven-year-long peace process and in the nine-year-long reversion to violence between the end of the peace process and the time of this writing. How exactly to feel and how to define their fitting in has become intensified by the events of this period. There is irony here, since what I am describing echoes in large part the condition of many Jews just over a century ago, when confronted by the birth of Zionism and by the ongoing question of how to define themselves vis-à-vis the host countries of which they had been more or less full citizens for the century since Emancipation—France, England, Austro-Hungary, even to a more limited extent, Prussia—and how that self-definition was being affected, ca 1900, by the shaping of a Jewish nationalist movement.[210]

With such unresolved complications in mind it is encouraging to encounter not only organizations within Israel such as *Shalom Akhshav* (*Peace Now*) which, among other things, work to promote cooperative efforts involving Jewish and Arab Israeli communities and individuals on a range of cultural, social, economic and political fronts; or such as *Seeds of Peace*, which seeks to change the mentality of fear and distrust in the next generation by intense cooperative programs that target Jewish, Christian and Muslim, Israeli, Palestinian and other Arab youth in various countries in the Middle East and bring them for an extensive period to a camp in Maine (in the United States). There their interaction can be nurtured away from the immediate difficulties of their native environments.[211] But there are also organizations such as the joint Arab-Jewish dual-community effort *Givat Haviva-Wahad al-Salaam* which has flourished for decades now. This last effort involves a neighboring pair of

villages—one Jewish and the other Arab—in a series of active programs of cooperation and active (not merely passive) peaceful co-existence.

So, too, it is worth noting that in the aforementioned film, *Lemon Tree*, the co-writer, Suha Arraf, is an Israeli Arab, and the star, Hiam Abbass is a renowned Israeli Arab actress. The film is by definition a joint Jewish-Arab Israeli enterprise. So, too, where music is concerned, on the one hand one recognizes the importance of an institution such as the Barenboim-Said Foundation, established by the Israeli conductor and pianist, Daniel Barenboim, who has long been a vocal advocate for Palestinian rights; and Edward W. Said, the Palestinian-born American intellectual. The Foundation opened a center in Ramallah in 2006 to provide lessons there and coaching in nearby towns and villages. On the other hand are the complications: that some Palestinians perceive the idea of an orchestra made up of Israelis and Palestinians trained through the Foundation's schools and teachers inherently off-base because of the political reality of the Israeli-Palestinian relationship. So even threads of hope in this tapestry are not colored simply.

Differently encouraging, though, is the story of the victory by the Arab Israeli Bnei Sakhnin team in the Israeli State Cup soccer championships in June, 2004. This meant that Bnei Sakhnin would represent Israel in the European UEFA Cup Tournament. More to the point, "'this is what's called the New Middle East and this shows the Arabs are here and they are an integral part of Israeli society,' said Bnei Sakhnin's Arab Chairman Mazin Ghanim after his team beat HaPoel Haifa 4-1 in Ramat Gan Stadium before 30,000 cheering fans."[212] The article reporting this story goes on to observe that "Bnei Sakhnin is seen as a model of co-existence with six Jewish players mixed among the Arab players—joined by four players from four different countries." Moreover, "for most Israelis, Sakhnin is known as the town which hosts annual 'Land Day' commemorations for six Arab Israeli demonstrators killed by the police during pro-

tests against land confiscation in 1976. It was also in this town of 23,000 that 13 Arabs were killed by the Israeli police during demonstrations of support to the Palestinians in the early days of the *intifada*, three-and-a-half years ago. But with last week's game these incidents have faded to the back burner." In the late night celebrations, Jews and Arabs were joined together, their sports heroes common property.[213]

The story of the Bnei Sakhnin soccer team brings to mind the dictum that I offered at the outset of this narrative and to which I return (this is the second of my four concluding but not conclusive issues): that the key to a transformation of the Arab-Israeli arena from a non-stop war cauldron to a zone of peace is the ability to engage in two acts simultaneously. The first is *not to forget and to acknowledge* the long history of agony that each side has experienced in general and at the hands of the other. The other is *to forget every ounce of it*; to remain cognizant of the past while abandoning it as a shackle to our abilities to build from present to future, so that we *can* build, unshackled. The Arab martyrs of Bnei Sakhnin will not cease to be remembered, but if the memory of the ugliness that led to their martyrdom can be moved to the side of the stage in favor of beautiful moments such as this one, then ". . .a lot of good can come out of this."[214]

The Bnei Sakhnin story also brings me to the third inconclusively concluding issue, as the use of the phrase "The New Middle East" evokes discussions such as that by Daniel Pipes in November, 1998, of "The Real 'New Middle East'."[215] Pipes discussed how, in the aftermath of the collapse of the Soviet Union and the advent of the Peace Process signaled by the Oslo Accords, the matter of "who is my enemy" and "who is my friend" (including "my enemy's enemy") became reconfigured. In his discussion—which included Greece by way of Cyprus in his definition of the "Middle East," reminding us that our very terminology is subject to change through the course of this narrative—"if all goes as scheduled, Russian ships will

begin delivering $400-million worth of advanced surface-to-air missiles, CAM-300s to Greek Cyprus in late November. Greek Cypriots insist that they must have this powerful weapon to balance Turkish air superiority over the island."

The Turks warned the Greeks that they would prevent deployment, if necessary, by force; Athens warned the Turks that it would come to the aid of the Greek Cypriots if the Turks carried out their threat; the Turkish foreign minister asked then-Israeli Prime Minister Benjamin Netanyahu for help in preventing the missiles form reaching Greek Cyprus; the Greek Cypriots asked the Russians to exert pressure on Israel not to get involved. Meanwhile Greece itself solidified its ties to Russia as well as with Syria, Armenia and Iran—none of which has been a natural ally of the others in the past—and offered increasing support to the PKK (Kurdish Workers Party), the leftist movement whose terrorist activities had led to the death of at least 30,000 Turks between 1984 and 1998.

Meanwhile the Turks, aside from reinforcing relations with Israel, augmented their military ties to Jordan and moved troops toward the Syrian border. Pipes goes on to observe that the potential for further allies for the Turkish-Israeli-Jordanian alliance could include Kuwait and the United Arab Emirates as well as groups exiled from Syria, Iran, Iraq and Libya, and furthermore Christians in Lebanon and Sudan. Conversely, the Greek-Syrian-Iranian alliance could also include the Palestinian Authority, Muslims in Lebanon and possibly even Iraq, with whom "relations are even improving, [although Iraq] has nearly always been on bad terms with Syria and Iran alike, and the same holds true for relations with Libya and Sudan."[216] As for the Kurds, depending upon their country of residence their alliances would likely vary.

The two main points that Pipes makes are that the reconfiguration extends its filaments of connection beyond what has for most of the past century been thought of as "The Middle East;" and that "the logic of 'my enemy's enemy' can override

even such powerful fundamentalist factors as shared religion or ideology."[217] Concerning this analysis one might make two comments. The first is that we might recall that the very terminology that labels the Near or Middle East as "Near" or "Middle" has itself undergone change since the beginning of the last century, when British colonial vocabulary still understood the "East" as having three zones—far, middle and near, in which India and its environs constituted the "Middle East" (and that it was from India that the troops arrived to defend British prerogatives in Mesopotamia in both world wars), yet now we hardly think of that neighborhood as part of the Middle East at all. The Muslim world might extend as far as the Philippines, but the Middle East peters out in our current thinking beyond Iran—or at least beyond Afghanistan (I intentionally equivocate; we have come full circle once again to the problem of definition). So reconfigurations that extend beyond where current or recent vocabulary leads is not really so surprising in the discussion of this region.

The second comment one might make is that whereas Pipes' discussion ends with both negative and positive conclusions—increasing arsenals and shrinking incomes, increasingly hardened attitudes toward Israel and the intensification of Islamic fundamentalism, new rogue regimes on the one hand; a new Turkish-Israeli-Jordanian alliance on the other hand—in principle the fact of reconfigurations where other than iron-clad religious or political or ethnic ideology governs positions is a reminder of the hope that, under the proper conditions, individuals and peoples can think outside the boxes of entrenched views of fear and mistrust.[218]

Which leads to the fourth point that I would make in concluding this discussion. If there is a truism regarding the Middle East, it is its unpredictability. Nobody but a divinely-inspired prophet would have predicted the shaping of such alliances fifteen years ago. If we backtrack further, two or three years before 1993 nobody could have anticipated the Oslo Accords or the progress made and almost made in the seven years that

followed Oslo. Nobody could have imagined, in the aftermath of the War of Attrition that led up to the 1973 Yom Kippur War an the aftermath of that war that Anwar Sadat would visit Jerusalem just a few years later and begin a peace dialogue with Menachem Begin—much less that the two would develop such a strong personal relationship.

Who would have thought, for that matter, that in the aftermath of the June, 1967 war, with the Israeli victory over the Arabs, a course for further conflict was being set from two directions and two forces that played relatively minor roles in that conflict up to that point, but which became the two most salient sources of conflict between that time and now? I am referring to the revolutionary Palestinian guerilla movement on the one hand and the Jewish national-religious movement on the other, both of which have provided the lion's share of the extremists who have made a final peace so elusive in that corner of the Middle East.

And in remembering that the tangled-web chaos of the Middle East is not limited to that corner of it, and considering perhaps the most obvious other primary flashpoint in the region—Iraq—I love the following small historiographic irony. Barely had Joseph Braude finished writing his book, *The New Iraq*,[219] and by the time it was actually published—he must have finished it in 2001 or 2002, as it was published in 2003—the second Gulf War was being planned and then begun by the Bush-Cheney administration. Braude's narrative addresses the question of how to rebuild the country in the aftermath of the first Gulf War, not only for the benefit of its own inhabitants, but of the entire region and the world, both the West and the East.

Braude's text begins with the words "This book is not about Saddam Hussein." It goes on to discuss the rich ancient, medieval and modern history of what we now call Iraq; the complications of maintaining the richness of that identity during the 23 years of Saddam's power; and a formula for reconstruction based on a combination of inherent, internal historical elements

of identity and judiciously applied lessons from outside. The book eloquently and cogently fulfills its promise to be a book about Iraq apart from and in spite of Saddam, about "an Iraq beyond Saddam Hussein, an Iraq that preceded him and that will remain long after he has been relegated to the margins of history."[220]

The irony is that the invasion being planned unbeknownst to the author virtually while he was shaping his narrative would indeed relegate Saddam to the margin of history and make the question of how to fashion a non-Saddam Iraq—a post-Saddam Iraq—a reality. It is almost as if the author *was* engaged in the sort of prophecy to which I referred a few paragraphs back. His discussion became in a sense *more* relevant than it was when he composed it—whether in 2004, when I was first writing *this* narrative, having recently read *his*, or in 2009 as I update and review my *own* words prior to publication. The disposition of a new Iraq remains open and unclear, after the capture and execution of Saddam and the various levels of transformation to which Iraq has been subject—including the very notion of trumpeting a national sense of "Iraq"ness by many of its inhabitants and their leaders that was inconceivable even a generation ago. It remains open and unclear in the aftermath of the transition to a new American administration.

On the other hand, it is true that the "New Middle East" of Pipes' description is already old, now, in 2009, when the winds of hope that were still blowing so strongly at the time of his article—as the Israeli-Palestinian peace process, among other things, was still inching bravely forward—have shifted. The *newer* Middle East has reverted to the cycles of violence and distress that were the staples of the Old Middle East in the decades—or centuries—before 1993. But the potential is enormous, should the positive outgain the negative—should a handful of leaders with vision push forward and help redirect the Middle Eastern peoples toward an *intifada* of the self-destruction which their current leaders seem to favor. The combination of human and

natural resources necessary to shape an astounding future is there. Yet grasping those resources remains as tricky as taking up residence in wind-blown sand-castles.

But if anything can happen and if twists and turns, knots and dissolutions of the tangled threads of the Middle East are spectacularly unpredictable, then without being sanguine one has the right to hope that, as the threads are unraveled, if misunderstanding can give way to understanding without supposition of solution, then fear and mistrust can also give way to fruitful dialogue. Antipathy can be replaced by empathy and peace is not absolutely beyond reach. To return to the Socratic-Platonic reference in the opening paragraph of this volume, it is by constant cross-examination and dialogue that we may be able to come closer to the truth of peace.

Then, Now and Now Again

I wrote the last of these paragraphs in the early autumn of 2004 when large questions of hope and despair lay before the American people regarding the upcoming elections scheduled for November of that year. Nearly five years have passed since then, but as I review my text there is little that I would alter for most of this narrative beyond the occasional detail, since the lion's share and primary purpose of the narrative was and remains to disentangle a tangled historical web toward coherence (without presuming to thereby eliminate its confusion).

Although there have been obvious and important changes in the region in the past five years, none of them affects either my historical sweep or my limited preaching toward a hopeful future. But there have been changes, of course. Thus in my discussion of what Israeli Prime Minister Sharon might do from his side, two obvious developments have affected that discussion from the Israeli perspective. One might have anticipated Sharon's unilateral decision to withdraw his troops and his settlers from the Gaza Strip, since even though that move seemed surprising

to many, to others it reflected that truism regarding the Middle East: the only thing predictable about it is its unpredictability.

More difficult to have anticipated or to digest was Sharon's sudden withdrawal of himself from the stage of history due to his medical condition. In the wake of that event, Ehud Olmert was elected by the Israelis, pushing forward a political stance that asserted its reflection of a new Sharonist agenda, of concerted unilateral efforts toward peace with the Palestinians, should bi-lateral efforts continue to shrink rather than grow. But now Olmert, in turn, is gone, and Bibi Netanyahu has once more ascended to the Prime Minister's office with an avowed preference for negating the idea of a Palestinian state.

On the other hand, in the aftermath of Chairman Arafat's death, the Palestinian side of this equation has also sustained two obvious question-inducing developments. The first is the inability of Arafat's elected successor, Mahmud Abbas (Abu Mazen), to stem the ongoing mood on the part of enough Palestinians to respond to the Israeli withdrawal from Gaza not with their own peace initiative, but with more anti-Israel violence. Thus while waiting to see whether and how the Israelis might have in mind, from their side, to further extend the process of withdrawal from pre-1967 Palestinian territory, the Palestinian Arabs have seemed determined to demonstrate that they simply have no interest in peaceful coexistence with Israel. This general tone was reinforced by the Palestinian elections of a few years ago, which brought *Hamas* into official political power in Gaza.

Is this simply due to unwillingness? Is it due to frustration with what the Gazans perceive as Israeli obtuseness and American one-sidedness? Is it a function of feelings developed since 2000, or since 1967, or since 1948 pertaining to an existential sense of despair? Has *Hamas* held the Gaza Strip hostage since 2007 or do Gazans want *Hamas* and its ideology in charge—in defiance of Israel, the Arab world, the world at large? At what point does defiance for its own sake become a synonym for self-destruction?

To date, there has been little to suggest a desire on the part of *Hamas* to shift from being a revolutionary force—calling for the destruction of Israel and trying to effect that destruction through violent activity—toward being a political partner in dialogue. That disinterest in dialogue has, in fact shown itself even within the Palestinian context—so that there has been sporadic civil war within the Gaza Strip—and certainly the more so with respect to Israel. Hundreds upon hundreds of rockets have rained down upon southern Israel's towns from Gaza, which activity culminated with a massive Israeli reprisal attack on Gaza with powerful human-cost consequences for the Palestinian Gazans, as we have observed. Thus the issue of trust—or rather, of mutual mistrust—to which I referred above could not be more uncertain.

As I write this most recent of updates the endpoint of these events is not yet clear. Binyamin Netanyahu, in his capacity as the new Prime Minister of the State of Israel, has very emphatically called for the current Pope—Benedict XVI, who just visited the Middle East in early May, 2009—to speak out more strongly against the continuous calls by Iran's president for Israel's destruction.[221] On the one hand, Netanyahu's urging resonates back to the time of the Holocaust, when Pope Pius XII failed—as many but not by any means all historians argue—to speak out against Hitler's avowed plan and execution of that plan to destroy all of European Jewry (particularly given Iranian President Ahmadinajad's consistent denial that the Holocaust happened, and his rhetoric referring to the destruction of Israel—and the possibility that he might be able to accomplish that end through nuclear weaponry in the near future). On the other hand, the brief conversation between Pope and Prime Minister and the urging made immediately public followed on the heels of the Pope's visit to a Palestinian refugee camp and his call for the creation of a Palestinian state. Thus Netanyahu's statement may be understood as a demand for even-handed papal statements.

Meanwhile, shortly after the Pope's visit to Israel, Palestine

and Jordan, Netanyahu himself journeyed, visiting the White House for a meeting with President Obama. That visit prompted an array of public responses from American Jewish groups and their leaders, ranging from expressions of dismay that the new president might stray from the policies of the Bush-Cheney administration in the Israeli-Palestinian situation to those encouraging a distinct departure from them.[222]

In the concatenation of immediate past events leading to this present and its myriad complications, there is a peculiar symmetry to the Sharonist unilateral decision to build a fence between Israel and its Palestinian neighbors and that to withdraw from part of the territory of those neighbors. It remains unclear as to where Israel would have wished to go next on both these fronts had Sharon lived, but for the moment that question seems almost moot, since there has been no evidence of pushing the same envelope from the Palestinian side in the last five years.

On the other hand, the matter of Israel's security and survival once again raised its head during that period, in a different way—in the form of the 2006 kidnapping of three Israeli soldiers, one on June 25, by *Hamas*, from Gaza and two, on July 12, by *Hizb'Allah*, from Lebanon;[223] and the war between Israel and *Hizb'Allah* that ensued following the kidnappings. That war has yielded further food for thought on several fronts.

First, the notion of a well-armed and well-trained force that is not a state, dedicated to the destruction of Israel, offers a new thread in this tangled web, and another version of the earlier question: with whom does one negotiate a peace? Second, the fact that *Hizb'Allah* was being armed by Iran and arguably Syria suggests general and not merely localized complications and underscores the idea that the instability of the region has far-flung sources. If on the one hand the current Iranian president has offered a fairly consistent flow of neo-Hitlerian rhetoric where Israel and the Jews are concerned, on the other there have been suggested hints of Syria's willingness to return to

the negotiation table after an absence of more than eight years. Third, nor is it clear as to how far the Lebanese themselves are willing and interested in going with regard to pushing for a peace with Israel and/or a relationship with *Hizb'Allah*.

Fourth, as a matter of *perspective*, whereas most sources report these kidnappings as a provocative pair of acts yielding Israeli responses, at least one Arab American source, Rashid Khalidi, asserts that *Hamas* had, after taking power, "for eighteen months observed a cease-fire in the face of... [various] provocations (other factions were not so restrained, firing rockets into Israel). However, after a major spike in Palestinian civilian deaths and the particularly provocative Israeli assassination of militant leader Jamal Abu Samhadana, whom the [*Hamas*-led Gazan] PA had just named to a security post, Hamas finally took the bait and responded with the capture of one Israeli soldier [Shalit] and the killing of others. The predictably ferocious Israeli response... finally provoked Hizballah (or perhaps gave Hizballah and its allies, Iran and Syria, the presumptive opportunity they had been searching for)."[224]

Thus Khalidi ascribes all of the rocket-fire into southern Israel to groups other than *Hamas*, and views the conflict with *Hizb'Allah* in Lebanon in 2006 to be tied to Israeli actions in the wake of the *Hamas* electoral victory in the Gaza Strip (rather than provoked by the kidnapping of Goldwasser and Regev). He does not footnote either of these assertions, but the point is that the perspective he offers is radically different from that of most others, and it is difficult to ascertain with objectivity who possesses the absolute facts of the matter, as in so many aspects of this tangled web of webs.

*　　*　　*　　*　　*

But to return to the question of the American role in sliding toward a solution to the problematic of the Middle East: that question continues to be unanswerable. There didn't appear

to be great hopes for a positively-nuanced American involvement as recently as a year ago, since whatever credit may have been built up with the Arabo-Islamic world in different ways—through the alliance organized by the first President Bush during the period of the first Gulf War and the efforts made by the Clinton administration to bring the Israelis and Palestinians toward peace, and even in pure sympathy terms in the aftermath of the 9-11 catastrophe—were squandered by the second President Bush.

The latter's extraordinarily ill-conceived push into Iraq to depose his father's erstwhile enemy, (without having completed the more legitimate American "mission" in Afghanistan, where the Taliban was *not* only not fully dismantled but is apparently once again on the rise!) coupled with a steady diet of misinformation that recalls Goebbels in Germany in the 1930s, fed both to the American people and to the rest of the world, all but erased that credit. Four months out from the Bush-Cheney era we are still challenged with regard to how precisely to regain that credit while rebuilding a leadership role that can appeal to the various sides of the various conflicts that define the region.

Who can truly gauge how many tens or hundreds of thousands have died in the pursuit of the dual chimeras of objects and ideas that were never in Iraq in the first place—such as Weapons of Mass Destruction and ties to the Taliban—and assertions that redirecting our efforts away from the unfinished business of Afghanistan and the pursuit of Ussama Bin Ladin there would make us safer or the inhabitants of the Middle East freer? By turning so many erstwhile friends and neutrals into enemies, both within and outside the country, both within and beyond the Middle East, the Bush-Cheney-Rumsfeld administration effectively eliminated its capacity, at least for the time being, to be part of the solution to a diverse and far-reaching problem.

By pretending—or, perhaps, in simple, spectacular ignorance, genuinely imagining—that the questions of the Middle East and of our relationship with it have a simple, weapons-

based answer, we have created problems where there weren't any beforehand, (or at least expanded smaller ones into larger ones), enabled many of those who are part of the problem to speak and act as if they are not, and licensed some of the latter to act as if the problem is simply Israel and the Palestinians and the uneven position of the United States in that *part* of the conflict. Most obviously, by eviscerating Iraq we have empowered Iran, to the potential destabilizing detriment of the entire region and potentially the world: we opened a door through which Iran and its venom-spewing president have strode, to assert a power-wielding role in the region, with no intact Iraq to threaten that role.

But the new Administration, for a number of reasons that do not require stating here, offers some hope that the time of positive American involvement may have returned. At the very least, there is a window of opportunity through which President Obama seems eager to climb.

Furthermore, where that last key-but-not-singular issue—the Israeli-Palestinian issue—is concerned, there continue, even since 2004, to be small signs of hope that receive few headlines. I was privileged to attend a conference held in Jordan at the end of 2005 that brought mostly Israeli and Palestinian women—with a large outsider population from Europe, the Americas and other parts of Asia, and among these, a handful of men—to articulate a call for Israeli-Palestinian peace. A range of viewpoints was put forth. Disagreements were aired vociferously. Emotions were not held in check or angers suppressed. But most of the 300 delegates to the conference *listened* to each other, recognizing that to have their own stories heard they needed to hear those of others.

Perhaps the most hopeful element within the varied hopeful elements was the presence of a group of mothers from both sides of the fence who have lost children to the conflict—Palestinian children killed by Israeli soldiers; Israeli children killed by Palestinian suicide bombers—who have determined that their

children's memories can only be honored by their becoming the cutting edge of peaceful co-existence; that an endless cycle of vengeance and bloodletting will yield nothing; that their common enemy is all of those individuals and groups on both sides who stand in the way of peaceful co-existence. They are a fragile plant, but a tough one. Their convictions must prevail if there is to be a future and not just a continuous reshuffling of an endlessly pain-filled past.

But one cannot and should not forget the mantra with which this text opened: the complications of the Middle East web extend well beyond the problems of the Israelis and Palestinians, or even the Israelis and the Arabs at large. As the vast literature covering the myriad aspects of the region, its problems, its continuum of pasts, presents and futures, continues to expand at breakneck speed, we must continue to doubt those who offer black and white encapsulations and overly simple solutions.[225] We must continue to question—to cross-examine, in Socratic *elengchos* terms—ourselves and each other, and continue to hope for a day when the unpredictable might take positive shape.

Notes

[203] The first quote comes from *Windows'* mission statement; the second from the first page of their Newsletter, *Open Window* (September, 2003/Issue 7). The organization, appropriately enough, has two addresses: 35 Trumpeldor Street, PO Box 56096, Tel Aviv-Jaffa; and Near Jamal Abdul Nassir Center, PO Box 104, Tul Karem.

[204] The two articles appeared on June I and June 2 respectively, on the front page of the Arts Section. The first is entitled "Minuets, Sonatas and Politics in the West Bank," and the second, "In the West Bank Turmoil, the Pull of Strings."

[205] This is the same issue of *Moment* to which I called attention above: March/April 2009, 16.

[206] It is directed by Dror Zahavi and written by Ido Dror.

[207] Directed by Eran Riklis and co-written by him with Suha Arraf. Arraf also co-wrote *The Syrian Bride*.

[208] He is quoted in a small article on page 12 of the April 23, 2009 issue of *Washington Jewish Week*.

[209] See above, 136-40.

[210] See above, 72-3.

[211] *Seeds of Peace* focuses more broadly than on the Middle East, at kids on different sides of any number of problem spots across the planet, but in recent years the Israeli-Palestinian and larger Israeli-Arab issue has been its most consistent and steady focus.

[212] Quoted in an internet article, http://www.jewishtoronto.com.

[213] One ought to recall the proposition by Daniel Gavron that the Israeli Arab population is a key potential factor in making the peace process work. See above, 139-40 and fnn 117 and 124.

[214] *Ibid*. The words were spoken by Muhammad Darawshe, a prominent Israeli Arab, who was present at the soccer game.

[215] Daniel Pipes, "The Real New Middle East'," *Commentary*. (November, 1998, Vol 106.No.5), 25-29.

[216] *Ibid*, 26.

[217] *Ibid*, 27.

[218] Indeed, the shifting of the sands of coalition relationships among the various Muslim and Arab states continues and will continue into the foreseeable future, based on "resistance" to the West and the United States (most

obviously at this writing, Iran, Syria and Palestine) versus politically friendly to the U.S. But within some states friendly to the U.S. (Israel, Jordan, Cyprus, Turkey, Egypt, Saudi Arabia, Yemen, the Gulf States and Pakistan) there are strong political opposition parties who are part of the axis of "resistance" (Egypt, Yemen, Jordan and Pakistan).

[219] Joseph Braude, *The New Iraq: Rebuilding the Country for Its People, the Middle East, and the World.*

[220] *Ibid*, x.

[221] This reference to Iran should remind us that, while my primary emphasis in terms of contemporary Middle Eastern issues has been Israel-Palestine and the larger Arab-Israeli picture, and my secondary emphasis has been on Iraq, Iran is a web of complications on its own, ranging from its empowerment through the evisceration of Iraq to it potential as a nuclear threat in general to its Holocaust-denying and Holocaust-reminiscent rhetoric vis-à-vis Israel.

[222] See above, 199-200 and fnn 183, 184, and the references to *J-Street* and to Gershom Gorenberg's *Moment* magazine article, for two examples of the latter.

[223] Gilad Shalit was captured by *Hamas* and, as afar as anyone knows, is still alive and in captivity. Ehud Goldwasser and Eldad Regev were captured by *Hizb'Allah* and died during the attack in which they were taken captive or were killed later. The remains of their bodies were sent back to Israel in July, 2008 in exchange for five *Hizb'Allah* prisoners and the remains of 199 Lebanese and Palestinian soldiers. The so-called "Second Lebanon War" that resulted from the two northern kidnappings last over a month, yielding about 1000 dead, most of them Lebanese civilians.

[224] Khalidi, *The Iron Cage*, XVI.

[225] Yet another intriguing observation with regard to the shifting sands of alliances came forth in an early November, 2006 article by Alon Ben-Meir in *The Globalist* (November 10). Ben-Meir suggests that the threat of a Shi'i alliance between Iran and the Shi'is of Iraq (*both* steadily re-empowered by the United States' incursion into Iraq during the past six years) could cause moderate Sunni states, in particular Saudi Arabia, to seek an alliance with Israel, as the only regional power with the capacity to stand up militarily to Iran's growing bellicosity. Syria could and would be part of that alliance, which, would seek to undermine Iranian support of Palestinian extremists while supporting the Palestinian moderates and Israelis to ally themselves with each other against the extremists—together with Egypt and Jordan, of course, and with a Syria returned to the Peace Table with Israel. Consider the implications of Ben-Meir's suggestion for the web we have been unraveling: the Shi'i identity in the first case is seen to trump the Arab/non-Arab

identity that otherwise should (and has, in the past) made Iraq and Iran simple antagonists. In the second case, Sunni identity also trumps Arab/non-Arab identity. Moreover, Muslim identity as well as Arab identity would be trumped by concluding an alliance with Israel, because in the larger scheme of the region's complications, Israel is less of a threat to the survival even of Syria and certainly of Saudi Arabia than Iran has become in combination with Shi'i Iraqis. Thus the issue for us is not only one of common enemies producing a new configuration of (potential) allies, but of being reminded of the expansive geopolitical terms in which one must consider the region encompassed by our tangled web.

Bibliography[226]

Abu Ju'ub, Ghassan, and Kurt Schetelig, "The Jordan River: Natural Flow and Current Composition by the Riparian Countries," in Zereini, Fathi, and Wolfgang Jaeschke, eds., *Water in the Middle East and in North Africa*. Berlin: Springer Books, 2004

Allan, Tony, *The Middle East Water Question: Hydropolitics and the Global Economy*. Mew York: I.B. Tauris Publishers, 2001

Armstrong, Karen, *A History of God: The 4,000 Year Quest of Judaism, Christianity and Islam*. New York: Ballantine Books, 1994.

———. *Jerusalem: One City, Three Faiths*. New York: Knopf Publishers, 1996.

———. *The Battle for God*. New York: Knopf Publishers, 2000

Avineri, Shlomo, *The Making of Modern Zionism: The Intellectual Origins of the Jewish State*. (New York: Basic Books, Inc., 1981)

Avneri, Arieh L., *The Claim of Dispossession: Jewish Settlement and the Arabs 1878-1948*. (New Brunswick, NJ and London: Transaction Books, 1984)

Ball, George W. and Douglas B. Ball, *The Passionate Attachment: America's Involvement with Israel, 1947 to the Present*. (New York & London: W.W. Norton & Co, 1992)

Barnett, Michael N., *Dialogues in Arab Politics*. (New York: Columbia University Press, 1998)

Bar-On, Mordechai, *The Gates of Gaza: Israel's Road to Suez and Back, 1955-1957*. (New York: St. Martin's Press, 1995)

Bergstraesser, Gotthelf, *Introduction to the Semitic Languages*. (Winona Lake, Indiana: Eisenbrauns, 1983)

Berkovits, Eliezer, *Faith After the Holocaust*, (New York: Ktav Publishing House, Inc, 1973)

Bill, James A. and Robert Springborg, *Politics in the Middle East* (Third Edition). (New York: HarperCollins, 1990)

Braude, Joseph, *The New Iraq: Rebuilding the Country for Its People, the Middle East, and the World*. (New York: Basic Books, 2003.

Bryson, Thomas A., *American Diplomatic Relations with the Middle East, 1784-1975: A Survey*. (Metuchen, NJ: The Scarecrow Press, 1977)

————. *Tars, Turks, and Tankers: The Role of the United States Navy in the Middle East, 1800-1979*. (Metuchen, NJ: The Scarecrow Press, 1977)

Burke, Edmund, III and David N. Yaghoubian, *Struggle and Survival in the Modern Middle East* (Second Edition). (Berkeley: University of California Press, 2006)

Carey, Roane and Jonathan Shainin, Eds., *The Other Israel: Voices of Refusal and Dissent*. (New York: The New Press, 2002)

Chafets, Ze'ev, *Heroes and Hustlers, Hard Hats and Holy Men: Inside the New Israel*. (New York: William Morrow & Co, 1986)

Cleveland, William L., *A History of the Modern Middle East* (Third Edition). (Boulder, CO: Westview Press, 2004)

Curtis, Michael, Ed., *People and Politics in the Middle East*. (New Brunswick, NJ and London: Transaction Books, 1971)

Davis, Moshe, Ed., *The Yom Kippur War: Israel and the Jewish People*. (New York: Arno Press, 1974)

Dothan, Shmuel, *A Land in the Balance: The Struggle for Palestine 1918-1948*. (Tel Aviv: MOD Books, 1993)

El-Nawawy, Mohammed and Adel Iskandar. *Al-Jazeera: The Story of the Network that is Rattling Governments and Redefining Modern Journalism*. (Boulder: Westview Press, 2003)

Field, James A. Jr., *America and the Mediterranean World 1776-1882*. (Princeton, NJ: Princeton University Press, 1969)

Finnie, David H., *Pioneers East: the Early American Experience in the Middle East*. (Cambridge, MA: Harvard University Press, 1967)

Fisher, Eugene M. and M. Cherif Bassiouni, *Storm over the Arab World: A People in Revolution*. (Chicago: Follett Publishing Co, 1972)

Fleischner, Eva, ed., *Auschwitz: The Beginning of a New Era? Reflections on the Holocaust.* (New York: Ktav Publishing House, Inc., 1977)

Foad, Dr Baher, *Islamic Concepts: Evidence from the Qur'an.* (Cincinnati: Zakat and Research Foundation, 1989)

Friedman, Thomas, *From Beirut to Jerusalem.* (New York: Doubleday, 1990)

Fromkin, David, *A Peace to End All Peace: The Fall of the Ottoman Empire and the Creation of the Modern Middle East.* (New York: Henry Holt & Co, 1989)

Gabriel, Richard A., *Operation Peace for Galilee: the Israeli PLO War in Lebanon.* (New York: Hill and Wang, 1985)

Geyer, Alan, *Piety and Politics.* (Richmond, VA: John Knox Press, 1963).

Gibb, H.A.R., *Mohammedanism.* (Oxford: Oxford University Press, 1962; paperback edition of the 1949 original)

Goitein, S.D., *Arabs and Jews: Their Contacts Through the Ages.* (New York: Schocken Books, 1974)

Goldschmidt, Arthur, Jr, and Lawrence Davidson, *A Concise History of the Middle East* (Eighth Edition). (Boulder, CO: Westview Press, 2006)

Halabi, Rafik, *West Bank Story: An Israeli Arab's View of Both Sides of a Tangled Conflict.* (New York: Harcourt Brace Jovanovich, 1981)

Handy, Robert T., ed., *The Holy Land in American Protestant Life, 1800-1948.* (New York: Arno Press, 1981)

Harkabi, Yehoshafat, *The Bar Kokhba Syndrome: Risk and Realism in International Politics.* (Chappaqua: Rossel Books, 1983)

Hasan, Sana, *Enemy in the Promised Land: An Egyptian Woman's Journey into Israel.* (New York: Pantheon Books, 1986)

Hertzberg, Arthur, Ed., *The Zionist Idea.* (New York: Atheneum, 1970)

Herzog, Chaim, *The Arab-Israeli Wars: War and Peace in the Middle East from the War of Independence through Lebanon.* (Revised Edition) (New York: Random House, 1984)

Heyman, Philip B., *Terrorism and America: A Commonsense Strategy for a Democratic Society.* (Cambridge: MIT Press, 2001)

Hoch, Gary, "The Politics of Water in the Middle East," in *Middle East Insight.* 9.3 (1993), 17-21

Holt, P.M., *Egypt and the Fertile Crescent 1516-1922: A Political History.* (Ithaca: Cornell University Press, 1969)

Hourani, Albert, *A History of the Arab Peoples.* (Cambridge: Harvard University Press, 1991)

Huntington, Samuel P., *The Clash of Civilizations and the Remaking of the world Order.* (New York: Simon & Schuster, 1996)

Indyk, Martin, *Innocent Abroad: An Intimate Account of American Peace Diplomacy in the Middle East.* (New York: Simon & Schuster, 2009)

Karin, Michael and Ina Friedman, *Murder in the Name of God: the Plot to Kill Yitzhak Rabin.* (New York: Henry Holt & Co, 1998)

Karetsky, Stephen and Peter E. Goldman, Eds., *The Media's War against Israel.* (New York: Steimatsky/Shapolsky Press, 1986)

Kark, Ruth, *American Consuls in the Holy Land, 1832-1914.* (Jerusalem: Magnes Press, 1994)

Khalidi, Rashid, *Resurrecting Empire: Western Footprints and America's Perilous Path in the Middle East.* (Boston: Beacon Press, 2004)

————. *The Iron cage: The Story of the Palestinian Struggle for Statehood.* (Boston: Beacon Press, 2007)

Khouri, Fred J., *The Arab-Israeli Dilemma.* (Syracuse: Syracuse University Press, 1977)

Kliot, Nurit, *Water Resources and Conflict in the Middle East.* (London: Routledge, 1994)

Kurzman, Dan, *Genesis 1948: The First Arab-Israeli War.* (New York and Cleveland: New American Library, 1970)

Kurtzer, Daniel C. and Scott B. Lasensky, *Negotiating Arab-Israeli Peace: American Leadership in the Middle East.* (Washington, DC: U.S. Institute of Peace Press, 2009)

La Guardia, Anton, *War Without End: Israelis, Palestinians and the Struggle for a Promised Land.* (New York: St. Martin's Press, 2003)

Laqueur, Walter, ed., *The Israel-Arab Reader: A Documentary History of the Middle East Conflict.* (New York: Bantam Books, 1970; revised and enlarged edition).

————. *A History of Zionism* (London: Weidenfeld & Nicholson, 1972)

Latourette, Kenneth, *Missions and the American Mind.* (Indianapolis: National Foundation Press, 1949)

Lewis, Bernard, *The Arabs in History.* (New York: Harper & Brothers, 1960)

————. *What Went Wrong? Western Impact and Middle Eastern Response.* (New York: Oxford University Press, 2002)

Lowi, Miriam R., *Water and Power: The Politics of a Scarce Resource in the Jordan River Basin.* Cambridge: Cambridge University Press, 1993

Lunt, James, *Hussein of Jordan: Searching for a Just and Lasting Peace.* (New York: William Morrow & Co, 1989)

Makdisi, Ussama, *Artillery of Heaven: American Missionaries and the Failed Conversion of the Middle East.* (Ithaca, NY: Cornell University Press, 2008)

Mansfield, Peter, *A History of the Middle East* (Second Edition, revised and updated by Nicolas Pelham). (London: Penguin Books, 2004)

McLaurin, R.D., Mohammed Mughisuddin and Abraham R. Wagner, *Foreign Policy Making in the Middle East: Domestic Influences on Policy in Egypt, Iraq, Israel and Syria*. (New York and London: Praeger Publishers, 1977)

Mearsheimer, John J. and Stephen M. Walt, *The Israel Lobby and U.S. Foreign Policy*. (New York: Farrar, Straus and Giroux, 2007)

Memmi, Albert, *Jews and Arabs*. (Chicago: J. Philip O'Hara, Inc, 1975)

Merlin, Samuel, *The Search for Peace in the Middle East: The Story of President Bourghuiba's Campaign for a Negotiated Peace Between Israel and the Arab States*. (Cranbury, NJ: Thomas Yoseloff, Publisher, 1968)

Miller, Aaron David, *The Much Too Promised Land: America's Elusive Search for Arab-Israeli Peace*. (New York: Bantam Books, 2008)

———. *The PLO and the Politics of Survival*. (The Washington Papers/99; Washington, DC: Center for Strategic Studies, Georgetown University and Praeger Press, 1983)

Morris, Benny, *Righteous Victims: A History of the Zionist-Arab Conflict, 1881-2001*. (New York: Vintage books, 2001)

Ochsenwald, William and Sydney Nettleton Fisher, *The Middle East: A History* (Sixth Edition). (New York: McGraw Hill, 2004)

Oren, Michael, *Power, Faith and Fantasy: America in the Middle East, 1776 to the Present*. (New York: W.W. Norton & Co., 2007)

———. *Six Days of War: June, 1967 and the Making of the Modern Middle East*. (Oxford: Oxford University Press, 2002)

Palmer, Leonard R., *Descriptive and Comparative Linguistics: A Critical Introduction*. (London: Faber & Faber, 1972)

Pappe, Ilan, *A History of Modern Palestine: One Land, Two Peoples*. (New York: Cambridge University Press, 2007; Second Edition)

Peters, Joan, *From Time Immemorial: The Origins of the Arab-Jewish Conflict Over Palestine*. (New York: Harper & Row, Publishers, 1984)

Pollack, Kenneth, *The Persian Puzzle: The Conflict Between Iran and America* (Washington, DC: Brookings Institution, 2004)

Porath, Yehoshua, *The Emergence of the Palestinian-Arab National Movement, 1918-1929*. (London: Cass, 1974)

Quandt, William B., *Camp David: Peacemaking and Politics*. (Washington, DC: Brookings Press, 1986)

Rabinovich, Itamar, *The Road Not Taken: Early Arab-Israeli Negotiations*. (New York: Oxford University Press, 1991)

Ro'i, Yaacov, *From Encroachment to Involvement: A Documentary Study of Soviet Policy in the Middle East, 1945-1973*. (New York: Halsted Press, 1974)

Ross, Dennis, *The Missing Peace: The Inside Story of the Fight for Middle Eastern Peace*, (New York: Farrar, Straus & Giroux, 2004)

Roucek, Joseph S. and Michael V. Belok, *The U.S. and the Persian Gulf*. (Malabar, FL: Robert E. Krieger Publishing Co, 1985)

Rubin, Barry, *The Tragedy of the Middle East*. (Cambridge: Cambridge University Press, 2002)

Rubenstein, Richard, *The Cunning of History: The Holocaust and the American Future*, (New York: Harper and Row, 1975)

Sacher, Howard Morley, *The Course of Modern Jewish History*. (New York: World Publishing Co., 1958). An updated edition was put out by Vintage Books in 1990.

Salinger, Pierre and Eric Laurent, *Secret Dossier: The Hidden Agenda Behind the Gulf War*. (New York: Penguin Books, 1991)

Segev, Tom, *Elvis in Jerusalem: Post-Zionism and the Americanization of Israel*. (New York: Henry Holt & Co, 2002)

―――. *One Palestine, Complete: Jews and Arabs under the British Mandate*. (New York: Henry Holt & Co, 2000)

―――. *The Seventh Million: The Israelis and the Holocaust* (New York: Hill & Wang, 1993)

Shehadeh, Raja, *Occupier's Law: Israel and the West Bank*. (Washington, DC: Institute for Palestine Studies, 1988)

Shipler, David K., *Arab and Jew: Wounded Spirits in a Promised Land*. (London: Penguin Books, 2001)

Shlaim, Avi, *Collusion across the Jordan: King Abdullah, the Zionist Movement, and the Partition of Palestine*. (New York: Columbia University Press, 1988)

Silberman, Neil Asher, *Between Past and Present: Archaeology, Ideology, and Nationalism in the Modern Middle East*. (New York: Henry Holt & Co, 1989)

Silberstein, Laurence J., Ed., *New Perspectives on Israeli History: The Early Years of the State*. (New York & London: New York University Press, 1991)

Sinai, Anne and Allen Pollack, Eds., *The Hashemite Kingdom of Jordan and the West Bank*. (New York: American Association for Peace in the Middle East, 1977)

Stauffer, Thomas, *Water and War in the Middle East: The Hydraulic Parameters of Conflict*. (Washington, DC: The Center for Policy Analysis on Palestine, 1996)

Stillman, Norman A., *The Jews of Arab Lands: A History and Source Book*. (Philadelphia: The Jewish Publication Society of America, 1979)

Tamir, Major-General Avraham, *A Soldier in Search of Peace: An Insider's Look at Israel's Strategy in the Middle East*. (New York: Harper &Row, Publishers, 1988)

Telhami, Shibley, *The Stakes: America and the Middle East; the Consequences of Power and the Choice for Peace.* (Boulder: Westview Press, 2002)

Thomas, Lewis V. and Richard N. Frye, *The United States and Turkey and Iran.* (Cambridge, MA: Harvard University Press, 1952)

Tibawa, A.L., *American Interests in Syria, 1800-1901.* (Oxford: Oxford University Press, 1966)

Timerman, Jacobo, *The Longest War: Israel in Lebanon.* (New York: Random House, 1982)

Tyler, Patrick, *A World of Trouble: The White House and the Middle East—from Cold War to the War on Terror.* (New York: Farrar, Straus & Giroux, 2008)

Vogel, Lester, *To See a Promised Land: Americans and the Holy Land in the Nineteenth Century.* (University Park, PA: Pennsylvania University Press, 1993)

Williams, John Alden, *The Word of Islam.* (Austin: University of Texas Press, 1994)

Wolf, Aaron T., *Hydropolitics along the Jordan River.* Tokyo: United Nations University Press, 1995

Ye'or, Bat, *The Dhimmi: Jews and Christians under Islam.* (Cranbury, NJ: Associated University Presses, 1985)

Zeitlin, Solomon, *The Rise and Fall of the Judaean State,* (vols I and II; Philadelphia: Jewish Publication Society, 1962)

Zipperstein, Steven J. and Ernest S. Fredrichs, Eds., *Zionism, Liberalism, and the Future of the Jewish State: Centennial Reflections on Zionist Scholarship and Controversy.* (Providence, RI: the Dorot Foundation, 2000)

Notes

[226] Two things should be noted with regard to this bibliography. The first is that it is far from comprehensive, and perhaps not even weighted with regard to perspectives on the varied matter encompassed by it, but consists of books that I have found useful in achieving a better-rounded understanding of the tangled web. The second is that any number of works cited here is significantly skewed one way or another, so that the fact that they are listed here should not be interpreted as an endorsement of their contents and/or points of view. It simply means that they offer information that is useful one way or another.

Timeline

BCE

ca 2000 Abraham the Hebrew and the first *muslim*

ca 1450 Moses, leader of the Israelites

ca 1000-965 reign of Israelite King David

ca 965-30 reign of Israelite King Solomon; building of the First Temple

ca 925 division of Israelite Kingdom into Israelite North and Judaean South

853 reference to Prince Gindibu Arabi in Assyrian inscription of Shalmaneser III

ca 720 swallowing up of Northern Israelite kingdom by Assyrians

586 Destruction of First Temple by the Babylonians (Chaldaeans); exile of uppercrust Judaeans

538 Return of Judaeans (not all) from exile under Achaemenid Medo-Persian patronage

ca 530 references to *Arabaya* in Achaemenid Persian documents

ca 490 reference to *Magos Arabos* in Greek playwright Aeschylus' *The Persians*

444 Traditional date for redaction (final written form) of the Torah

ca 330 fall of Achaemenid Persian Empire to Alexander the Great, whose rule extends from Libya to India

323 Death of Alexander the Great; beginning of "Hellenistic" Period

ca 300 Seleucids in power in Syria and beyond, Ptolemies in Egypt and beyond, Judaea in between, sometimes subject to or allied with one or the other

168-5 Successful revolt of Hasmonaean-led Judaeans against Seleucid rule

37 Death of last Hasmonaean ruler

37–4 rule of Idumaean-born King Herod "the Great" over Judaea

4 Loss of Judaean independence; establishment of Roman procuratorial system

CE

26–36 Procuratorship of Pontius Pilate

70 Destruction of Second Temple

ca 100 definitive schism within Judaeanism, birth of Judaism and Christianity

132–5 Bar Kokhba Revolt against the Romans

140 canonization of Hebrew Bible

325 Council of Nicaea under Emperor Constantine; official embrace of Triune Christian as *religio*; Arian Christianity termed heretical

354–428 St. Augustine, shaping of key Christian concepts

ca 390 Under Emperor Theodosius, Christianity becomes official religion of the Empire

397 Synod of Hippo approves canon of New Testament

476 Romulus Augustulus deposed; end of Western Roman Empire

517–25 Dhu Nuwas, Jewish king in Yemen

570–1 Birth of Muhammad

610 Muhammad experiences his first revelations

622 Muhammad's *hijra* from Makka to Yathrib/Madina

624 Muslim victory over the Makkans at Badr; expulsion of the Jewish Banu Qaynuqa tribe from Madina

627 Muslims repel Makkans at the Battle of the Trench; extermination of the Jewish   Banu Qurayza tribe

628 Muhammad's successful attack, siege and subjugation of the Jewish oasis of Khaybar

630 Makka submits to Muhammad

632 Death of Muhammad; Abu Bakr succeeds him as first caliph

633–8 Arab Muslim conquest of Syria and Mesopotamia (Iraq)

639–42 Arab Muslim conquest of Egypt

653 Caliph 'Uthman establishes standard version of the Qur'an

656 Murder of Caliph 'Uthman; first civil war in Islam

661–750 Umayyad Caliphate in Damascus

ca 685–90 construction of Dome of the Rock in Jerusalem

711–18 Muslim Berber/Arab conquest of Spain with widespread Jewish support

750–1258 Abbasid Caliphate in Baghdad

813–33 Caliphate of al-Ma'amun; beginning of Muslim cultural Golden Age

929 Umayyad ruler of Spain assumes title of Caliph, asserts equality with Abbasid Caliphate in Baghdad

969 Fatimid conquest of Egypt

1007–19 Persecution of Christians by Fatimid Caliph al-Hakim; destruction of church of Holy Sepulchre in Jerusalem (rebuilt by Hakim's successor)

1012–19 Persecution of Jews by al-Hakim

1054 Great Schism between Eastern (Orthodox) and Western (Catholic) Churches

1061–91 Normans take Sicily from the Muslims

1071 Battle of Manzikert: victory of Seljuk Turks over Byzantine Christians

1085 Christians recapture Toledo (Spain) in *reconquista*

1090 Almoravids conquer Muslim Spain

1096–99 First Crusade led by Count Raymond IV of Toulouse

1099–1187 Latin Kingdom of Jerusalem

1147–60 Almohads conquer Maghrib (Northwest Africa) and much of Islamic Spain; heavy persecution of Jews

1147–9 Second Crusade led by Holy Roman (German) Emperor Conrad II and French King Louis VII

1171–1250 Ayyubid Dynasty established in Egypt and Syria by Salah ad-Din (Saladin)

1187 Salah ad-Din defeats Christian Crusaders at the Horns of Hattin

1187–92 Third Crusade led by English King Richard Lionheart, French King Philip II and Holy Roman Emperor Frederick I

1193 Death of Salah ad-Din

1201–4 Fourth Crusade; Sacking of Constantinople

1215–21 Fifth Crusade led by King Andrew II of Hungary, Duke Leopold VI of Austria and John of Brienne

1220 Founding of Templar Knights organization

1228–9 Sixth Crusade led by Holy Roman Emperor Frederick II

1248–54 Seventh Crusade led by King Louis IX (Saint Louis) of France

1250–1517 Mamluk empire in Egypt, Syria and Palestine

1258 Baghdad captured by Mongols, end of Abbasid caliphate and beginning of Ilkhanid dynasty; no distinction between Muslims and *dhimmi*s

1260 Mamluks turn back Mongols at Ayn Jalut

1270 Eighth Crusade led by Louis IX

1271–2 Ninth Crusade led by English Prince Edward, (later King Edward I)

1291 Sultan Khalil retakes Acre, ending French presence and era of "Great Crusades"

1380–1405 Timur Leng (Tamerlane)'s conquests across Middle East and India

1391 Jewish refugees from Spanish Catalonia and Majorca arrive in Tunisia and Algeria

1405–1506 Timurid dynasty in eastern Persia and Afghanistan

1438 First *mellah* (Jewish quarter) established in Fez, Morocco

1453 Ottoman Turks capture Constantinople; end of Byzantine Empire

1492 Expulsion of Jews from Spain; many Jews take refuge in Ottoman lands

1497 Expulsion of Jews from Portugal

1501–1614 Expulsions of Muslims from various parts of Spain

1501–1722 Safavid Shi'i (Shi'ite) Dynasty in Persia (Iran)

1517 Ottomans conquer Mamluk Empire; Jewish cultural and economic revival throughout Middle East

1526–1857 Mughal (Moghul) Dynasty in India

1529 First Ottoman Siege of Vienna

1571 Battle of Lepanto: stunning naval defeat inflicted on Ottomans by European allies

1574–95 Reign of Ottoman Sultan Murad III: reintroduction of the sumptuary restrictions for *dhimmi*s

1683 Failed Ottoman siege of Vienna, first of several key Ottoman defeats in Europe

1738 John Wesley founds Methodist Church as break-away from Episcopal Church

ca 1750 Wahhabi movement begins in the *hijaz*

1768–74 Russo-Turkish War; Ottoman Turks defeated

1785 John Lamb conducts first American diplomatic mission to the Middle East

1788 John Ledyard, first American to explore the Middle East, arrives in Egypt

1798–1801 Napoleon occupies Egypt

1801–4 Wahhabis capture Makka and Madina

1805–48 Mehmet (Muhammad) Ali independent ruler of Egypt under nominal Ottoman Suzerainty, but first shaper of concerted Arab political nationalism

1810 British annex the Ionian Islands

1818 Mehmet Ali turns on his erstwhile Wahhabi allies

1819 First American missionaries to the Middle East: Levi Parsons and Pliny Fisk

1821–29 Greek War of Independence from Ottoman Turkey

1822 Massacre of Greeks of Chios by Turks (25,000 killed, 50,000 enslaved of total population of 100,000)

1823 Pliny Fisk establishes first American school in the Middle East

1830 France invades Algeria

1831 First American Ambassador to the Middle East, David Porter, arrives in Istanbul

1831–40 Egyptian occupation of Syria and Palestine

1837 American evangelist Harriet Livermore sets sail for Palestine

1839 *Khatt-i Sherif* improves civil status of *dhimmi*s in Ottoman Empire

1842 Cyrus Hamlin opens a school just outside Istanbul, later evolves as Robert College

1844 Restorationist and US Consul Warder Cresson sets sail for Palestine

1851 Clorinda Minor arrives in Palestine to establish an agricultural school to provide Jews with the skills necessary for statehood

1853–56 Crimean (Russo-Turkish) War; French and British troops occupy Greece

1856 *Khatt-i Humayan* grants equality to non-Muslims in Ottoman Empire

1860–1904 Theodore Herzl, founder of modern Zionism

1862 Daniel Bliss offers proposal to open the Arab world's first modern university: the Syrian Protestant College (later American University in Beirut)

1866 George Adams recruits 166 Americans to form a colony in Palestine

1866–69 Unsuccessful revolt of Greeks on Crete against Ottoman Turks

1868 Egyptian leader Isma'il recruits American Civil War vets to modernize his army and strengthen Egyptian-American ties

1869 Suez Canal opened

1873 Persian Shah offers and later revokes Reuter concession to British company for railway and mining activities

1881 French occupation of Tunisia

1882 Britain occupies Egypt; first European (mostly Russian) and Yemenite Jewish agricultural colonists in Palestine

1883 Tunisia declared a protectorate of France; Samuel Benjamin heads first US official mission to Persia (Iran)

1886–1973 David Ben-Gurion, first Prime Minister of the State of Israel

1890 Persian shah sells tobacco concession to British company

1897 First Zionist Congress in Basel

1902 American naval theorist Alfred Mahan coins the phrase, "Middle East"; Ottoman Sultan Abdul Hamid II engages Prussian firm to build Baghdad railway

1904–14 Second Aliyah of Jews, mainly from Russia and Poland, to Palestine

1908–9 "Young Turks"—Ottoman Turkish army officers—depose Abdul Hamid II

1909 American State Department creates a Division of Near Eastern Affairs (NEA)

1912 Henrietta Szold founds the women's Zionist organization, Haddasah

1913 First Arab Nationalist Congress in Paris

1914–18 World War I

1915 British High Commissioner in Cairo, Sir H. Mcmahon, asserts British support of Arab independence to Hussein, Sharif of Makka

1916 Sykes-Picot Agreement articulates British and French vision of dividing political administration of the Middle East after World War I

1917 The Russian Revolution; Declaration by Lord Balfour of British embrace of the concept of a Jewish state in Palestine

1919 At the post-war Paris Peace Conference American President Wilson tries vainly to secure independent national self-determination across Middle East

1919–22 Greco-Turkish War

1920 Post-World War I Paris, London and San Remo Conferences establish French and British Mandates, confirmed by League of Nations in 1922

1921 Iraq becomes independent kingdom; becomes republic in 1958

1922 Egypt becomes an independent kingdom (ending 1914 British protectorate status); Final collapse of Ottoman Empire; founding of secular State of Turkey by Attatuerk

1924 American and European oil companies form the Iraq Petroleum Company (IPC); the US recognizes British mandate over Palestine; Ibn Sa'ud takes *hijaz* from Hashimites

1927 Saudi Arabia becomes independent kingdom

1928 Conclusion of the Red Line agreement, specifying areas for IPC oil exploration in the Middle East

1929 Anti-Jewish riots in Jerusalem, Hebron and six other locations

1933 Saudi Arabia grants the right to prospect for oil to American companies

1933–45 Hitler in power in Germany (and eventually elsewhere); 1939–45 World War II; 1941–5 full-scale Holocaust of European Jewry

1937 Peel Commission Palestine Partition Plan; escalating attacks by Arabs against Jews and reprisals by Jews against Arabs; these would expand the following two years, as would conflicts between the British and the Arabs and of Arabs against Arabs; three major Jewish terrorist attacks against Arabs took place in 1938, in which year there were two further Palestine partition proposals, one British and one Jewish

1938 American engineers strike oil in Damman, Saudi Arabia

1939 British White Paper limits Jewish immigration to Palestine to 15,000 per year for following five years

1943 Syria becomes independent republic (ending 1920 French Mandate); US and Britain compel France to respect Lebanon's independence

1944 Lebanon becomes independent republic (ending 1920 French Mandate)

1945 Establishment of the Arab League

1946 Transjordan becomes independent kingdom (ending 1920 British Mandate); Jewish Agency's Palestine Partition proposal; the US, working through the UN, succeeds in pressing the USSR to withdraw from Iran

1947 United Nations' Palestine Partition Plan; escalation of Arab attacks on Jews

1948 Establishment of the State of Israel (ending 1920 British Mandate), followed by War with neighboring Arab states; Arabs leave Israel from Haifa-Acre, Beersheba, Jaffa-Ramallah areas: 100,000

to Lebanon, 75,000 to Syria, 4,000 to Iraq, 70,000 to Transjordan, 7,000 to Egypt, 190,000 to Gaza Strip and 280,000 to West Bank; Egypt occupies the Gaza

Strip; Transjordan occupies the West Bank; war continues into 1949 and Rhodes Armistice

1948–72 Jewish refugees from Arab lands include 260,000 from Morocco, 14,000 from Algeria, 56,000 from Tunisia, 35,666 from Libya, 29,525 from Egypt, 6,000 from Lebanon, 4,500 from Syria, 129,290 from Iraq and 50,552 from Yemen and Aden

1950 Transjordan annexes the West Bank, renaming the totality under its control the Hashimite Kingdom of Jordan

1951 Libya becomes independent kingdom (ending 1912 Italian, 1945 joint Anglo-French rule)

1951–56 Arab Fedayeen attacks into Israel from Egypt and Jordan (and some from Syria and Lebanon) leave 967 Israelis dead

1953 Egypt becomes republic

1955 Formation of the Baghdad Pact, an American-backed anticommunist coalition; Egyptian blockade of the Straits of Tiran and Gulf of Aqaba to ships seeking ingress to and egress from Israeli port city of Eilat

1956 Israeli military attack into Sinai; French and British attack on Port Said; Morocco becomes independent kingdom (ending 1912 French and Spanish protectorate status)

1957 American pressure causes full Israeli withdrawal from Sinai

1962 Algeria becomes independent republic (ending 1842 French colonial governance)

1967 Six-day June war between Israel and her Arab neighbors

1967–73 sixteen Israeli settlements founded in the West Bank, with total civilian population of 1,150; 44,000 Arabs who fled the West bank in 1967 return there by 1972

1969–70 Egypt's War of Attrition against Israel

1970 "Black September" campaign of Jordanian King Hussein against PLO after the latter culminate a two-year-long campaign of autonomy within Jordan with an attempt to seize political control; thousands of mostly Palestinians are killed between September and July, 1971; relocation of PLO command center to southern Lebanon

1971 Creation of the United Arab Emirates (UAE)

1973 October "Yom Kippur" War between Israel and her Arab neighbors; Saudi Arabia spearheads an oil boycott against the US because of its support of Israel

1974 Coup in Cyprus is followed by Turkish invasion

1975–90 Lebanese Civil War

1977 Egyptian President Anwar Sadat speaks before Israeli Knesset at invitation of Israeli Prime Minister Menahem Begin

1978–9 Iranian Revolution deposes Muhammad Reza Shah and brings from exile and into power Ruhallah Khomeini; Iran becomes a republic

1979 Camp David and Israeli-Egyptian Peace agreement; 52 Americans taken hostage in Iran; an American rescue attempt the following year fails; Saddam Hussein becomes president of Iraq

1979–89 Soviet occupation of Afghanistan

1980–88 Iran-Iraq War

1981 Hosni Mubarak becomes president of Egypt after assassination of Anwar Sadat

1982 Israeli War in Lebanon against PLO; relocation of PLO command center to Tunisia

1983 Terrorist attack on military installation in Tyre, Lebanon leaves 241 US Marines and 30 Israeli soldiers dead

1986 In response to terror attack on American servicemen in a Berlin nightclub, US President Reagan bombs Tripoli, Libya

1987–91 First Intifada of Palestinian Arabs in Gaza and West Bank against Israeli Occupation forces

1989 Death of Ayatolah Khomeini in Iran

1990 Iraq invades Kuwait

1991 First Gulf War; 30 of the scud missiles fired by Iraq make it to Israel; post-conflict, the US convenes a Peace Conference in Madrid, seeking a comprehensive Arab-Israeli peace accord; population of Jewish settlers in West Bank and Gaza reaches 103,855; 137th Jewish settlement established on West Bank on August 5

1993 The Oslo Accords, following secret Israeli-Palestinian negotiations, are signed on the White House Lawn; over the next four years negotiations continue, leading, among other things, to the creation of a Palestinian National Authority (PA) and the extension of its administration to most of the West Bank and Gaza Strip

1994 Peace Treaty between Israel and Jordan

1995 Jewish extremist assassinates Yitzhak Rabin

1996 Nineteen American soldiers killed in a terrorist attack on Khobar Towers housing complex in Saudi Arabia; the Taliban establish rule over most of Afghanistan

1997 Election of reformer Muhammad Khatami as president of Iranian republic

1998 President Clinton brokers interim Palestinian-Israeli peace agreement at Wye River Plantation; responding to al-Qaeda attacks in east Africa, the US bombs presumed terrorist targets in Sudan

1999 Abd'Allah II becomes king of Jordan after death of Hussein; Ehud Barak becomes Israeli Prime Minister, pushes Israeli-Palestinian negotiations ahead

2000 A suicide bomber kills 17 sailors aboard the USS *Cole* near the Yemen coast; beginning of Second (Al-Aqsa) Intifada; Bashar al-Assad becomes president of Syria after death of his father, Hafiz al-Assad

2000–1 Collapse of final Israeli-Palestinian negotiations at Camp David and in Taba

2001 Ussama bin Ladin and al Qaeda orchestrate terrorist attacks on World Trade Center in New York City, the Pentagon outside Washington, DC, and an unspecified target for which the intended plane went down in Pennsylvania, killing nearly 3000 people altogether; Ariel Sharon elected Israeli Prime Minister

2001–2 The United States declares war on the Taliban and topples the regime in Afghanistan; President Bush's strategists coin the phrase "axis of evil" to refer to Iran, Iraq and North Korea; Sharon send tanks into West Bank cities, killing between 500 and 1500 Palestinians; Palestinian suicide bombers become increasingly active in Israel; Israel begins building a security fence, cutting off much of the West Bank, to end terrorist attacks

2003 President Bush announces a "road map" for resumption of Israeli-Palestinian negotiations, but with no follow-up (he subsequently refuses to receive Arafat at the White House); claiming that Saddam Hussein had been associated with the al-Qaeda terrorists and possessed Weapons of Mass Destruction, President Bush and a handful of allies invade Iraq to topple Saddam's regime; over the next six years the regime collapses, Saddam is captured, tried by an Iraqi court and executed, Iraq is reduced to internecine chaos involving Sunni and Shi'i Arab Muslims and Kurdish Muslims; by 2009 well over 4,000 Americans had been killed and countless Iraqis

2004 Sharon announces a plan to unilaterally withdraw from Gaza Strip, also announcing construction of new houses in West Bank settlements (violating "road map"); Arafat dies in Paris

2005 Palestinians elect Mahmud Abbas to succeed Arafat in presidential election; Sharon offers to evacuate troops and Jewish settlers from Gaza Strip and to re-open peace talks, if Abbas closes down *Hamas* and other groups accused of terrorist activity against Israel; *Hamas* and *Islamic Jihad* verbally support Abbas' plea to Palestinians

for a ceasefire; Sharon effects Israeli withdrawal from Gaza and dismantling of Jewish settlements; Iraqi Shi'is and Kurds form a new government after long negotiations; former Lebanese prime minister Rafiq Hariri assassinated in Beirut; Egyptians demand that President Mubarak open scheduled presidential elections to opposition candidates; US begins to put pressure on Iran to end its nuclear research program

2006 Sharon has a stroke and falls into a coma; Ehud Olmert becomes Israeli Prime Minister; Gazan Palestinians overwhelmingly vote *Hamas* in as new leadership of Palestinian Authority; Abbas and *Fatah* are reduced to clinging to power in the West Bank Territories

2007 Civil War primarily in Gaza Strip between *Fatah* and *Hamas*; beginning of steady stream of rocket attacks into southern Israel from Gaza Strip, which, apart from a brief period of ceasefire, continue through the end of 2008

2008–9 Month-long Israeli military attack on Gaza Strip to decimate *Hamas*; hundreds of Palestinian civilians among those who are killed

2009 Binyamin (Bibi) Netanyahu is elected Israeli Prime Minister, with a stated perspective that does not favor Palestinian statehood; newly-elected US President Barack Obama visits Middle East in June, speaking publicly in Cairo

2010 In late May, a flotilla of six small ships, largely from Turkey, try to break the Israeli blockade of Gaza and are intercepted by the Israeli navy. One ship violently resists being boarded; in the ensuing fight, nine activists are killed and seven Israeli commandos are wounded. Turkish-Israeli relations are strained but the Arab media response, as with the Israeli attack on Gaza the previous year, is muted. In the fall, American-sponsored peace talks resume between Israel and the Palestinians without positive outcome; controversy continues regarding expanding or limiting Jewish settlements around Jerusalem. Questions expand regarding Iran's actual or potential nuclear arsenal: concern is raised by both Israel and a number of key Arab states; a report emerges in November asserting that claims regarding the arsenal are fraudulent as other reports doubt the claim of this report. Al Qaeda emerges in Yemen, provoking concern that "Yemen may be the next Afghanistan." Iraq appears to move toward stability; US troops continue their presence, in lesser numbers in Iraq; they have now spent as much time in Afghanistan as did Soviet troops three decades earlier.

Index

FOR THE BEST IN PAPERBACKS, LOOK FOR THE 🐧

LOKING DOWN ON

LEADERS

A BIRD'S EYE VIEW OF BUSINESS AND BOSSES

IAIN J. MARTIN

ISBN: 1490544054
ISBN-13: 9781490544052
Library of Congress Control Number: 2013911714
CreateSpace Independent Publishing Platform
North Charleston, South Carolina

Contents

Dedication

I gratefully dedicate this book to the worst and the best leaders that I ever worked for.

Thank you Philippe, Barclay, Ali, and Willie—for demonstrating, in copious quantity and glorious consistency, what excellent leadership is not!

And my sincere thanks to Eddie and Dave for consistently showing, under fire in the management trenches, what caring and courageous real leadership should be.

…and to all my other bosses who were neither worst nor best, but who meant well and tried hard.

….and to my own executive coach of twenty-seven years ago, his name now forgotten, who helped me to globalise my career and to learn leadership things that I still use every day of my life.

LOOKING DOWN ON
Leaders — the

Prologue

I sn't *that* a strange title for a book on leadership? Why did I call it that? Well, there are more than eighteen thousand leadership books on Amazon.com alone, most of them with sober, academic-sounding titles. I wanted something a bit different.

Looking Down on Leaders also just seemed pretty cute to me. It might have been the nice red wine I was drinking at the time…or maybe it was the way the "L" words rolled alliteratively off the tongue.

Then again, the title could have got your Amazon-browsing attention because we're supposed to look up to leaders, not down. I read recently that Barack Obama uses this counterintuitive trick in his speeches. If it works for him…

Here's how the name first came to me. I was sitting in the wine bar of the venerable Institute of Directors in Pall Mall, London. I was gazing around me at my third generation of business leaders and wondering, "Do they truly *inspire* people to look up to them? Are they all the Level-Five Leaders that Jim Collins describes so well in *Good to Great?*"

My eye settled on one pinstriped forty-something, with the smooth born-to-be-a-leader look of privileged upbringing, who was lounging

arrogantly, arms and legs widespread, at a table with three companions. Another colleague approached the table and, without even looking at him or sitting upright, the forty-something held out his hand for the new arrival to grasp.

"Well," I thought, "if that's how he treats his peers, how on earth does he treat his staff? Do they look up to him? Does he look down on everybody?" He didn't command my respect, for sure. The words "Looking Down on Leaders" came to mind at that precise moment.

But here's the real reason for the title. I am an executive coach. I lead a team of sixteen absolutely exceptional people around the world who, having had successful executive careers, now exercise their talents as CEO advisers for our clients in Europe, the United States, and Asia.

As coaches, we often advise clients to take the bird's-eye view, to smoothly glide above the maelstrom of everyday management life and see the big picture. I'd like to illustrate the bird's-eye view with this story...

One sunny Monday morning, I called a client with whom I had scheduled a two-hour coaching meeting. This man, a highly intelligent young chief legal counsel, had lived in beautiful Zürich, Switzerland, for three years and had never been outside the city. He travelled all the time on business (if you don't, you probably think it's glamorous). His usual daily routine was airport-plane-taxi-office-hotel and 3:00 a.m. e-mails from his boss in a time zone ten hours away. Does that sound familiar?

So this world traveller had never had the time to escape his corporate straightjacket and look into the distance. Today was going to be different! We agreed to meet at the railway station, not his office. Through the city's peaceful suburbs and shadowy pine forests, we took a winding twenty-minute train ride up to Zürich's local mountain, Uetliberg. We crunched up the gravel path to the summit and looked down on the bustling city. The glacial-green waters of Lake Zürich vanished into the misty distance as the sun rose above the rugged peaks of the Northern Alps. To the north, tiny white aircraft sketched lacy vapour trails in the deep-blue sky as they

departed Switzerland for faraway places. To the south, Pilatus, the Dragon Mountain of Lucerne, bathed in the pink glow of the summer morning.

"Look down there," I said. "Look at how the ferries on the lake dock right in the centre of the city. See how the local trams are stopping by the harbour as the boats come in."

"Follow the tramlines to the station where they connect with local and international trains," I continued. "Observe how the road system integrates with all of that."

"You're taking the bird's-eye view of Zürich's transport network. Now imagine that this is your business strategy. See how all the elements integrate to form a grand corporate plan."

"From now on," I advised, "stand above the daily grind of travel and meetings and look at your business in a different way."

His mental outlook, his physical health, and his strategic contribution to the corporation grew from that day on.

That is my job: looking down on leadership and helping others see the wider context of their roles in global business.

ABOUT THIS BOOK –
grab a glass, sit

down, and enjoy!

I like books that I can pick up in quiet moments, enjoy what I read, and put back down at any time. I learn much more about "real leadership" from interesting stories than from impressively worded theories.

This is not a leadership textbook or a coaching manual. It is a collection of short stories and personal comments on business and bosses. In this book, I have shared my experiences from forty-five years of corporate life and coaching senior business executives around the world. Some have been comical, some were tragic, and all have been educational. I have recorded thoughts from my first (professional) career, my second (managerial) career, and my third (making a difference to the world) career. Along the way, I've poked some gentle fun at myself and my fellow executives and coaches. I know that you won't be offended, because, if you were oversensitive, you wouldn't be reading this book anyway. If it sometimes gets too personal for comfort, remember that laughter is the best medicine. Have a good laugh at yourself, and learn from others' experiences, as narrated herein.

As I planned the book (though *planning* is a big word to describe my ad hoc approach to writing), I asked myself, "Should it be a serious tome on leadership or executive coaching to join the many worthy texts on those subjects?"

"No," I decided. "I don't have the time or the patience to do all that research and name all my sources. Besides, what busy executive has the energy and motivation to read such a book from start to finish, in linear fashion?"

The last thing hard-pressed business leaders need is yet another earnest and academically rigorous tome on leadership or coaching. There are enough of those already…and real leadership is much more of an art than a science, anyway. This book is just a gentle ramble through the buzzing, steamy global business jungle.

And I thought, "Life isn't linear. And, as a coach, I am always advising executives not to think about business strategy as a straight-line exercise." A truly inspiring business strategy starts, spontaneously, with a 4:00 a.m. vision—from the heart and not the head—and only then proceeds in a more logical way. My business life is, as yours, often a set of disjointed and varied events, running in parallel or overlapping each other. I have written this book in the same way, so that you can open it at any time, read whatever you feel like, and close it again.

As I wrote, my spiritual guide and alter ego introduced himself. I called him MacMentor, for the obvious reasons that I am a Scot and my firm provides coaching and mentoring services to senior executives in global companies.

MacMentor's job is to sum up the learning from the stories and make an occasional observation along the way. You will find MacMentor's words of Scottish wisdom somewhere in nearly every chapter.

Why do I often start a chapter in a non-business setting or with a funny story?

"Well," MacMentor says, "we should always see business in the overall context of life, and a sense of humour often helps us get serious things in sensible proportion."

That's one reason. The other reason comes from my own experience. Some years ago, I was struggling with a really complex business issue. I couldn't see the solution because I was too close to the situation. One weekend, when the deadline was fast approaching, my partner and I hopped on an easyjet flight from Geneva to Nice. We lay back on the beach in the warm spring sunshine—and the answer popped into my head in a flash.

And now, as I do the final edits on this book, I am sitting on a sunny terrace, looking down on the images of emerald-green palm trees and white cotton-wool clouds reflected in the mirror-blue waters of Lago Maggiore. Back in my office last week, I thought that I had finished, but now new ideas are wafting into my head like the breeze-blown ripples on the lake below.

As a coach, I help clients take the bird's-eye view of business and bosses. Looking down on business from a different angle shows you the wider picture and the way to reach your destination. That's why, for example, I set the scene, in the chapter on background discussions, in a hot and steamy equatorial jungle. Another story starts off in the dentist's chair, because that's where I was when I thought of it. Yet another chapter sets a narrative on principled negotiations in Istanbul's Grand Bazaar.

So here's a book that you can open up, dip into, and enjoy in any order at any time. I wrote bits of it as each idea occurred to me. So I just let it slide out of my head and run onto the page as it came. Sometimes, the ideas came with my morning shower, and my handwritten notes were blotted and hard to read. Occasionally, I had a moment of inspiration at 4:00 a.m., and my weary bedside scribbles were almost unintelligible. At other times, I would (slowly, because I have dyslexic fingers and only use two and a half of them on the keyboard) type a few paragraphs at my desk in Zürich when I got bored doing some tedious administration (an alpha male feature—low threshold of boredom. We just hate doing admin, don't we?). Often I had notions in the back of a plane on yet another flight to somewhere.

If you've never heard of The Morale Curve, The Hollow-Cube Organisation, Excel Leadership, Soft Is Hard and Hard Is Soft, The Chief Honesty Officer, or The Twenty-First Century Factors of Production (and you probably haven't unless I've coached you, because they are my inventions), then I hope that this book will amuse you and give you some useful stuff to think about.

I have seen, heard of, and lived some interesting experiences in leadership around the world. The truth can often be stranger than fiction. You will guess, as you read, no doubt, that I sometimes invented the character's names. Some of the stories are composites of two or three real people with similar experiences. From time to time too, I employed a more entertaining false name, for no better reason than to raise a little smile.

You'll find some themes repeated in several chapters because they arose naturally in the context. Some things are relevant in many aspects of leadership.

Perhaps you will see yourself in some of these stories. Hopefully you will find some good ideas to help you in current challenges or to prepare you for future ones. If you find this book, in the words of the BBC's founding charter, "Informative, Educational, and Entertaining," please let me know on macmentor@ijmartin.com and/or write a customer review on Amazon.com—because feedback is just as important to us coaches as it is to business leaders.

Read this book as I wrote it—bit by bit, in no logical sequence…when you get bored at your desk, when you have a few minutes relaxation in your armchair on a rainy Sunday, sitting in yet another airplane, or whenever. Just sip a glass of your favourite "medicine" and enjoy the journey through my leadership life!

Now move on to the Twenty-First Century…

THE TWENTY-FIRST
Century Factors

of Production

"Our people are our greatest asses"

So read the final draft of our group's annual report, as I did a last-minute check at the printers. A Freudian slip, perhaps?

"Our people are our greatest assets." How many times have you read that in the chairman's statement in the annual report? So, isn't it funny that people are also the most neglected asset in the corporate balance sheet? In fact, very rarely, if ever, do you see the business's "greatest assets" listed at all in the balance sheet.

This has always struck me as odd. In my student days at Glasgow University, my economics professor, a disciple of Adam Smith, used to tell us that the factors of production were land, labour, and capital. In today's capitalist economy, land has ceased to be a key factor. You can manufacture almost everything in some far-off country where land is plentiful and has little economic value. Indeed, many businesses, such as banks and software companies, sell products that barely need land at all. So, today, the twenty-first century factors of production are slightly different—they are leadership, labour, and capital. Or, I use the words: leaders, people, and money.

11

Today we have a global capitalist economy where the Money God reigns and people don't matter. These two essentials get highly unequal weighting in the minds of most corporations. Leadership, I mean real leadership, is grossly underrated.

I always find it strange that, when times are hard, companies invest in making the machinery more efficient. They overhaul the transport fleet for fuel optimisation, and they double the insulation in the factory roofs. But when it comes to their most important asset—people—they treat them as disposables. Instead of investing in training and coaching people, they make them redundant and throw years of knowledge, experience, networks, and customer relationships into the corporate dustbin.

Executive antifreeze

What do you do with your car in November? (Southeast Asia readers move on to the next paragraph.) Do you put antifreeze in the engine, or do you wait until it's 8°C below freezing in January? Obvious, isn't it? You prepare your car engine for the winter's challenge in advance to avoid a cracked cylinder block—the cost of waiting too long is high. Yet, when it comes to preparing our "greatest assets" for the challenge of business downturns, what do we cut first? Yes, you guessed it—training and development budgets! Makes no sense to me! Apparently, in the minds of senior management in many companies, a cracked block is too expensive, but a "cracked bloke" can be thrown to one side, even in mid-career and after twenty-five years of loyal service.

It's somewhat reflective of today's transactional world, isn't it? Relationships have no value. People are disposable. Keep them, use them, don't invest in them, and when they fail, get rid of them. Yet developing people is the best investment we can make. I heard a great quote once, I forget where, but I wish I'd thought of it myself: Don't ask yourself, "What if I train them, and they leave?" But ask instead, "What if I don't train them, and they stay?"

The Holy Trinity

But here's the good news. Some corporations have heard the message, and others are catching on. Here's an example of one who gets it!

A former GE star very successfully leads one of our favourite clients, a Swiss-based global corporation with $40 billion revenue. His Holy Trinity, as he calls it, comprises himself as CEO, the CFO, and the CHRO. I call this team the boss guy, the money guy, and the people guy—the high priests of a well-led business and an excellent illustration of the twenty-first century factors of production!

Others on the executive board are extremely important too, naturally, but no major business decision is ever made without extensive consultation among the members of the Holy Trinity. It is essential, of course, that the three members of the Holy Trinity and the others on the EB are highly strategic thinkers who place people alongside money as the keys to success and who try to be the best examples of real leadership to the corporation.

MacMentor says "This is a twenty-first century model for others to follow!"

Four Reasons I

Hate "Coaching"

Blue-suits coaching

No, I don't hate my job…but I dislike having to use the word "coaching" to describe it. The word is far too general, and the profession is much too inclusive. In our fifteen years of business, I've heard of date coaches, sitting coaches, breathe-your-way-to-success coaches, colour-your-way-to-a-brighter-future coaches…even potty-training coaches. Any man or woman who loses a job today can hang out the shingle and be a coach tomorrow.

Self-styled executive coaches are often people who have never been executives. One such person defiantly told me that she had been a personal assistant to an executive, so she knew how executives thought. Besides, she also had a nicely framed executive-coaching certificate. She had earned this during a hard weekend at one of the myriad coaching institutes founded by people who have figured out that it is much more profitable to establish a coaching school than to provide coaching services. Can you imagine learning to drive a car just by reading a book about it? How can people imagine that they can coach executives if they have never driven an executive desk?

Global coaching partnerships often turn out to be loose associations of coaches connected by LinkedIn and their surreal ambitions to fool the client. Grandly named "Brainleaders" (Brainleaders, logically, must have "brain followers" somewhere, but who would admit to being one?) can easily, via skilled use of social media, create high expectations of, and deep disillusionment in, the coaching profession. In an occupation where the entry barriers are so low, no wonder the styles and the standards vary, and the reputation is poor.

True, since I facilitate the learning of others using certain techniques, I am a coach. I can't deny it. But there's a world of difference between what my team of coaches does and what life coaches or psychologist coaches do. We call it our "blue suits as opposed to white coats" approach and "experienced-based" coaching. We style our programmes "Going for Gold in the Business Olympics." Simply put, as people who've spent a long time in business leadership, we offer that experience to other business leaders, and we help them learn through us. Our aim is to help business succeed through excellent leadership. And our coaching helps "winners in business" to be even more successful.

Four reasons to hate "coaching"

Coaching senior executives is a serious business and a hugely satisfying one for a successful coach. Much depends on the outcomes in terms of bottom-line benefits and the dissemination of excellent leadership through all levels of the organisation. And yet, so many coaching conferences (actually, "conferences" are passé; everything is a "summit" today and almost every little coaching firm styles itself as an "institute") submit their high-paying attendees to nonsensical, time-wasting interludes. In a couple of those learning occasions, I've been hijacked by Hula-Hoops, mugged by maple leaves, side-lined by samba sessions and bored brainless by bongo drums.

Let me explain. I rarely go to coaching conferences these days. I prefer to go to events on other topics like corporate governance, global finance,

and strategic HR—in fact, almost any relevant subject except coaching. But in my early days of coaching, I felt the need to attend coaching conferences to learn and to associate with fellow professionals. Let me tell you about my first coaching conference.

I didn't mind that I was the only one wearing a business suit and tie. I was fine with being surrounded by large, softly upholstered people wearing sackcloth and Jesus sandals. I was (almost) OK with the proposed agenda at my first coaching conference in Switzerland's scenic Interlaken. I thought that "Playing with Coaching" was a pretty cute title for the first agenda item—until I walked into the room wearing my best blue pinstriped suit, my polka-dot silk tie (It was a sevenfold tie. I just mention this to feel a moment of superior knowledge.), and black lace-up business shoes.

Hula-Hoops and twirling ladies

"Ohmygawd" was an expression I had never used before, but it escaped my lips uncontrollably as I entered that adult kindergarten. I was surrounded by dreamy-looking ladies (I mean that they looked as if they were dreaming, not that they were the women of my dreams) twirling ribbons on the end of sticks, and barrel-shaped men futilely trying to defy gravity by sustaining the orbit of revolving plastic Hula-Hoops around their generous middles.

"Ohmygawd," I whispered again, as I reached for my Blackberry to invent an urgent client call.

"Don't go yet!" gaily twittered the limp-wristed host. "You haven't tried the Ping-Pong!"

"Ohmygawd" rose to the surface for a third time, as a drowning person does just before going down for the last time. "I didn't know that Interlaken had a mental hospital," I thought as I gazed up at the north wall of the Eiger mountain just outside and considered jumping off it. "How could I have made such a mistake? I'm sure the notice outside said 'Coaching Conference'!"

It did! I read it three times more to make sure that my eyes were telling the truth. "Playing with Coaching" meant exactly that. I was, as the saying goes, in the wrong movie. I retreated in shock to my hotel room to write e-mails. At the appointed time, I went back to the conference room for the second session.

Maple leaves

This time, there were seats in the room. "Great!" I thought. "A proper conference at last"—until I saw the maple leaf on the seat. It wasn't a real maple leaf. They couldn't get any maple leaves in Switzerland in April, so we all had to pretend that the big, brown things on our seats were real maple leaves. A Danish lady took the stage. She looked like someone from this planet, but she spoke as if she came from another one.

"Aha!" I thought. "Now I know what these leaves are…and I think she's been smoking them."

For the next ninety minutes, the lady treated us to an exposé on how trees dig their roots into the soil, how they extract the goodness so they grow nice, big leaves that fall to the ground and renew the earth, and then they grow into new leaves and…

You get the picture? I did, repeatedly, for one and a half hours before lunch. "Ohmygawd" rose to the surface for a fourth time, in defiance of the laws of drowning. "But all is not yet lost," I tried to convince myself. "The last session of the day should be good. I've heard that this guy is one of the world's best coaches, so at least I should learn something now."

Samba school

The "world's best coach" was from Latin America. I should have known what was coming when he started up the samba music.

"Now," he said to the audience. "I want you all to stand up." Yet another agonised "Ohmygawd" emanated from my mouth.

"Everybody put your left foot out to the side!" My elegantly brogued left foot slid out to the side.

"Now bring it back, and put your right foot out and bring it back." The samba music quickened.

"Put your left foot out in front, bring it back, and put your right foot out…" He went on. It reminded me of the man who wrote the famous Hokey Cokey song. When he died, the undertakers had a terrible time putting him in his coffin. First, they put his left foot in, then they put his left foot out, then they put his right foot in, and they shook it all about… you know the rest.

Up on stage, the rhythm throbbed fast and furious. And, before our very eyes, the world's best coach was doing the samba dance. Four hundred people (actually, three hundred and ninety-nine…I sat down) were dancing a kind of samba shuffle with the chairs, their neighbours, or the coach in front of them.

"Ohmygawd" was in no way close enough to covering the situation now.

I didn't learn a thing about coaching that day, but I learned a lot about "coaching."

So that, I hope, explains three of the reasons I hate the word "coaching." For the final reason, bongo drums, walk with me into the following scenario.

Bongo drums and Master Beaters

I'm in the Mövenpick Hotel in Zürich. It's December 2012. It's 9:15 a.m., and I have just braved arctic temperatures and deeply rutted frozen snow to hear the legendary Ram Charan and the eminent Dave Ulrich speak to a senior HR conference. I walk into the conference room…and my heart sinks!

Neatly arranged in front of the audience is a row of Japanese samurai drums. Behind is an assembly of orchestral timpani and brightly coloured bongo drums. "Ohmygawd. Here we go again!" I thought. "This is why the 'people business' is not taken seriously." It's also why serious business too often regards coaching as a bad joke.

So guess what happens next? Some androgynous guy with a weak falsetto voice and no tie tells the audience, "Now we are going to spend the next thirty minutes discovering together the power of teamwork. We are going to *drum* together! Isn't that *exciting*?"

Can you imagine what Jack Welsh would have said to that?

So next, Ram, Dave, and I beat a hasty retreat (and not a drum) to the adjacent coffee lounge. From the conference room pulses an insistent rhythmic "bongo-bongo" sound, like a well-known Italian politician's sex party. The andro with the weak voice proceeds to spend the next hour (not the thirty minutes that he promised) getting people to beat drums in time. This is supposed to show all those high-level HR executives the power of teamwork...a ten-second lesson that those mature "people" people would have learned years ago! Now, I admit, the andro is actually an expert at beating the drums. Indeed, I'm thinking of him as a Master Beater (or something that sounds like that)!

That waste of time took one hour of valuable conference time. Prorated to the conference fee of three thousand dollars, this added up to the most expensive coffee break I have ever had. And the opportunity cost of not having face time with our clients was much more.

"No wonder," MacMentor comments, "that coaching doesn't get the respect it should in the executive board room!"

Coming up next - prevention is better than cure…

PREVENTIVE COACHING
and the Extraction

Industry

Filling in the name

I've just been at the dentist, hence the title of this chapter. Not the dentist, actually—he's a highly qualified, highly charged (to be precise, it's me that is highly charged, he's highly fee'd and highly dynamic) Swiss-German super-surgeon. To be more exact, I've actually just visited his dental hygienist. She's a blonde, blue-eyed German with an Australian accent. "I've spent too long in Osstrylya, mate," she said to me today. "Strewth, Sheila, it's infectious!" I thought. She reminded me of the old story about the general in the Australian Army who paid a morale-lifting visit to a field hospital. Lying in a camp bed and cursing his bad luck was a wounded trooper. "Buck up, man!" boomed the general. "You didn't come here to die!"

"Nah," replied the trooper. "I came here yester-die!"

Coming back to my hygienist, I asked, "What's your name, Sheila?" "It's Eunida," replied Sheila, or at least it looked like that to my tired eyes, as I checked out her ID badge. Why don't women just wear their name badges on their foreheads? You really can't keep looking at a woman's chest long enough to focus clearly on her name, can you? It's embarrassing at

Swiss networking events to have to constantly stare at women's lapel badges. In America, it would probably lead to a harassment charge!

So, let's call my hygienist Eunida Goodbrushin, just for the sake of a cheap laugh.

Brace yourself for risk

I've always been lucky with dentists. My last dentist, before he retired, was a great Scottish guy in Geneva called "Risk." Wonderful name for a dentist, isn't it? But, joking aside, his family name really was Risk. One of the questions that we ask about our clients in feedback interviews is, "Does he (or she) take too much risk or not enough?" Well, in Geneva, I used to take just about the right amount of Risk. I visited Dr. Risk regularly— every six months—to avoid future problems. And that's the whole point of this chapter, which I'll come back to shortly.

But staying for the moment on the topic of names and occupations, there's a funeral director's firm in Twickenham, near London, called "Wake & Paine." Yes, that really is its name…and I have the photographs to prove it. Normally, first you have the pain, and then they hold the wake. But with this undertaker's firm, they combine both processes in the interests of efficiency. You are welcome, at any time, to contribute other such occupational name combinations. I'm thinking, just to get you started, of a crematorium director called "E. Burns." I knew a lawyer in Geneva called Crook, so how about a law firm called "Robb, Steele, and Cheetham?"

Eunida Goodbrushin

"Just lie back and make yourself comfortable," said Eunida Goodbrushin. She might have added, "…on our nice plastic-coated dental chair while wearing your heavy wool business suit." She didn't need to. I was sweating already, having just glimpsed her stainless steel instruments of torture neatly arranged before my eyes.

"Just lie back and relax," she crooned in that deceptively soothing style that all medics have just before they inflict terrible pain on you. Now,

I don't know what you think about in the dentist's chair. Before I go, I always tell myself that this is a good investment of time, effort, and pain. I ask myself, "Should I go for a checkup and a 'good brushing' now, or wait until I have a toothache and get it fixed then?" The debate is often finely balanced, given my busy schedule, but I always decide in favour of preventive dentistry in the end. The analogy between this and preventive coaching, as opposed to remedial coaching, is incredibly subtle. But as you are in the "top 2 per cent" of the intellect business, I am confident that you will quickly get the point.

So, the biannual inner debate having resulted once more in a preventive visit to Eunida Goodbrushin, I was now lying back on her plastic-coated chaise longue. It's a funny thing about personal space and eye contact. It's also a cultural issue that's been the subject of a lot of good research. According to Wikipedia, "Penetration of the intimate zone is strictly reserved for lovers, children, and close family members." It doesn't know about those Hong Kongers who hover over your shoulder at bank automats in Tsim Tsa Tsui, desperately trying to glimpse your bank balance on the screen.

Wikipedia doesn't seem to know about Eunida either. Her blue-masked, blonde-fringed face was hovering like the angel of death about ten inches above mine. I had a choice between gazing dreamily into her deep-blue Germanic eyes or into the bright-blue LED lights hanging from the ceiling. Being superbly correct British and not hopelessly romantic Italian, I chose to gaze into the LEDs. Normally, I'd be thinking of something to distract me from the pain of having my unanaesthetised gums scraped off my jawbone. Often, I think (a long way) back to my last game of rugby before leaving school. I was determined to go out in a blaze of glory, so I scored three tries, collected a cracked cheekbone, and led the team to a glorious victory over our opponents.

But rugby wasn't doing it for me today. The old adrenaline just wasn't flowing. Instead, my mind was centred on the concept of preventive treatment. I have regular check-ups because I don't want to wake up at 4:00 a.m.

with a violent toothache. Equally, I don't want business leaders to wake up before dawn with headaches about their business or their own leadership performance. If they're going to wake up in the early hours, I just want them to be seeing a vision of how their business might be in five or ten years' time.

Talent-retentive coaching

In an earlier chapter of this book, I introduced the concept of "executive antifreeze." I came up with the term because, in countries in the northern hemisphere with four seasons, you put antifreeze in your car engine in October, before the cold season starts, and not in January when it's too late to prevent serious damage. When I mention executive antifreeze, I'm talking about coaching business leaders to prepare them for future challenge. To put it another way, coaching is a highly effective preventive treatment to ensure that problems don't arise in the future.

It's much harder to make the case for coaching, especially in times of budget cuts, when nothing bad has happened—much easier for an HR manager to persuade the boss to fund coaching when things are going wrong. That's when coaching moves from "discretionary spending" to "mandatory expenditure." That's a big advantage for headhunters. When you fire a senior executive, you just have to replace him or her. You've no choice but to pay a search consultant between 25 and 33 per cent of the incoming replacement's total first-year reward package. Recruiters are in the realm of "must spend," whereas coaches operate in the "discretionary" zone. And so corporations spend huge amounts on search fees to replace dismissed managers, when a much smaller investment in preventive coaching would have avoided the problem in the first place.

The cash savings on fees is obvious, but even more dramatic benefits lie in retaining, not losing, a number of intangibles. With preventive coaching, the executive stays and performs better in the organisation. His or her customer relationships don't go to the competition, nor does all the hard-won knowledge and experience. Preventive coaching enhances

relationships with bosses, peers, and reporting staff, and bad things don't happen. It's strange, but true, that we avoid preventive coaching, but we never question why we have police forces. Policemen and policewomen keep us safe and prevent bad things from happening. And yet, only a small number of enlightened organisations see clearly that preventive coaching avoids those 4:00 a.m. corporate headaches that keep business leaders awake at night.

The hidden costs of "just in time"

I think it's mainly the fault of the negative "problem-fixing" image of coaching that stops otherwise smart people from considering the use of executive coaching as a value-adding strategic tool. Back in the early 1980s, American insurers stopped paying for a whole range of psycho-therapeutic interventions. Deprived of a large slice of fee income, many clinical psychologists in practice turned to the so-called "new" concept of coaching, to replace lost earnings. I believe, in truth, that coaching is as old as leadership itself…that is, it's thousands of years old. There is no such thing as "new" in leadership—only new theories and new research studies. Leadership itself is ancient and timeless. Just think of old-time leaders, like Moses and Alexander the Great, who led their people across the high seas and continents and into battle. What they did, and how they did it, was in essence no different than what level-five leaders do today.

Psychology, the study of behaviours, is a fascinating subject for amateurs like me. I love to sit and watch other people during our shopping expeditions in Zürich or Manhattan or Singapore. Clinical psychologists, however, are conditioned to detect problems. Seeing a problem in every executive, they are there to fix it. "When all you've got is a hammer, everything's a nail," goes the old saying. That approach over the last thirty years has led to the image of coaching as a remedial science. Not all psychologists, of course, are clinical practitioners. Organisational psychology puts a sense of order into chaotic corporations. Brain science, the study of zonal-brain activity in a range of situations, uses MRI and related technologies

in an additive approach to understanding behaviours. I even sometimes use their findings in layman explanations of why the thinking process in talking aloud to a coach is different, and more effective than just thinking internally. However, I express it in ordinary language. I abhor the self-styled "experts" who pick up a little knowledge from textbooks and short courses and turn it into a spurious kind of service offering in order to make a fast buck. If you're going to mess around with someone's psychology, you'd better have seven years of intensive formal training and a great deal of practice, just as in other branches of healthcare.

I believe too that the expert with the "hammer" overdoes the "nail" in dealing with leadership. In my view, executive coaching is much more of an art than a science. Its true value comes when corporations use coaching to prepare executives for future challenge. This preparation-for-challenge coaching is, by definition, preventive coaching.

When my firm began coaching executives fifteen years ago, all we got was remedial mandates. The phone would ring.

"Hello, Iain. We have another one for you. We're about to fire him (or her) but we wanted to give him (or her) one last chance."

And they thought that this was enlightened business management. It was, too, for its time. Unenlightened companies just fired the executive, regardless of cost, loss of reputation, and disruption. But the sad thing was always that these last-chance phone calls would come to us when it was almost too late. The company had already incurred huge losses. Employees were already upset and badly managed. Customers were, at that stage, disappointed and moving to the competition. Vendors were already adding the "ass**le premium" to their prices. We're very proud to say that, in all those mandates over fifteen years, where clients hired us for remedial coaching, we have never yet lost a client executive. Though they were often on the verge of dismissal, coaching turned the situation round to the extent that the clients later won promotions at least once, and sometimes more.

Here's a typical story of how leaving it almost too late caused unnecessary disruption and how remedial coaching saved the day.

Kumar's story

Kumar was a bright and ambitious human-resources executive who had achieved much in his early career. In his early forties, Kumar had reached a high level in one of his group's most important business divisions. His bosses had allowed him to believe that he was a star with an even bigger future. In reality, Kumar was making enemies as well as friends. His privileged upbringing and cultural prejudices caused him to act in an arrogant way with his peers and his staff. Even worse, his over-confidence had brought him into conflict with some of the most senior business leaders in the group. He was hardly aware of this, however. His bosses knew that he had caused problems, and they had hinted at those in his annual appraisals. Typical of those who have to convey difficult news, they had wrapped up the warnings in subtle hints and between-the-lines messages. Kumar's self-belief led him to filter out the bad news, leaving only positive reinforcement of his own self-worth.

The big crunch came when Peter, his functional boss, attended an executive board succession-planning meeting. Peter confidently put Kumar's name on the table as his most likely successor. "Over my dead body!" was the mildest comment from around the boardroom table. The CEO's interest was aroused, and he asked for some explanations. For the first time, the reality of Kumar's behaviour was exposed. Within a few minutes, from being the boss's heir-apparent, Kumar's employment in the group was now under serious threat. At that point, Peter called me.

"The reaction to my proposal was so violent that I can't leave him in his current job," explained Peter. "The problem is, though, that none of the other divisional heads will take him now," he went on.

"What do you want us to do?" I asked.

"I think you're going to have to help him find another job outside the company," said Peter.

We are good at helping executives make "elegant exits" from the company. Peter knew that, because we had provided this kind of career-transition coaching to one of his colleagues the year before. He had left, with

great dignity and minimal disruption, to be the CEO of another company that was much more suited to his ambitions.

"Fine," I said to Peter. "I can agree to working on our Plan A and Plan B in parallel. We can do feedback and coach Kumar on his behaviour. Then we can help him manage his image in the company and start to change perceptions. That's Plan A. At the same time, we can help him to prepare an exit strategy and coach him in the skills he will need to make an elegant exit. That's Plan B."

Peter agreed. After a frank discussion with Kumar, we interviewed a number of his colleagues, gave him our usual clear and direct feedback, and coached him in changing his behaviours. In parallel, we helped him learn the skills of career transition. We covered influencing, self-presentation, image management, and networking...all the same skills, in fact, that he needed to succeed in his current corporation.

This story had a happy ending. Kumar changed his style dramatically and fed on the rewards that this brought to do even better. He worked hard at changing the perception that others had of him. Just eighteen months later, Kumar's name was back on the succession plan, and he received three promotional offers, within six months, from other business divisions.

Happy ending—but at a cost!

Nice conclusion!

"But," MacMentor says, "just think of how much bad feeling, disappointment, and expense the company could have spared if it had been more direct in Kumar's earlier feedback and if it had offered him preventive coaching!"

The good news is that after fifteen years of preaching "executive antifreeze" to client corporations, approximately two-thirds of our mandates are now primarily for preventive coaching, usually with some preliminary leadership improvement coaching to start off on the right basis.

Panic-driven remedial coaching, in our business, has largely given way to a much more enlightened, strategically planned "preparation for challenge" approach. In this, we work in close partnership with the client's management team to ensure excellent leadership and a full pipeline of talented successors for the future.

"If you can't, you must" read on…

The

CEOptimist

Positive coaching for positive action

"There are no problems, only opportunities," says the CEOptimist. Here's a message to HR leaders and CEOs— how about coaching for opportunities instead of problems? Or, at least, how about more of the former and less of the latter? Coaching for opportunities means, in my mind, helping executives learn the leadership and business skills they need to be fit for their next challenge. Coaching for problems refers to the old-fashioned, but still valuable, coaching to help someone with problems that have already arisen.

The CEOptimist as (cheer)leader

When I was a group controller, I worked for an American CEO called Victor. Victor enjoyed an apt name for such a positive person. It may be that his good-news name had shaped his adult personality and his over-optimistic outlook. There are many "Victors" in this world, but I never heard of anyone called "Loser." Now there's a good field of study for the psychologists!

33

Victor's oft expressed mantra was, "There are no problems, only opportunities!" Nice, positive thinking, if a little bit unrealistic. The group, at that time, was breaching covenants all over the place and was losing money on most of the "really promising acquisitions" that Victor, our CEOptimist, had purchased.

Eventually the board had to fire Victor because he was presenting the company with so many "opportunities" that the company was fast going bankrupt.

That reminds me, for some vague reason, about the "wise" mantra of Anthony Robbins, the famous motivational coach.

"If you can't, you must!" chants Anthony.

Nice one, Tony! Tell that to the poor guys who ran over hot coals shouting "Cool moss! Cool moss!" in one of your motivational coaching programmes and ended up with burned feet as their reward. Or try saying it to the thirty guys from KFC's Australian franchise who were hospitalised with Kentucky Fried Chilblains in a similar demonstration of blind trust. Despite popular belief and motivational mantras, faith does not usually defy physics!

I say, if you can't, then figure out how you can, or do it differently— don't (figuratively speaking) run over red-hot coals just because some guy, sitting safely out of the heat with his shoes on, says, "If you can't, you must!"

Georg's story—Germany's answer to Don Quixote

Georg was a typical example of how this philosophy works in business life. Georg was one of my senior clients in a corporation where the executive board (EB) was unhappy with its CEO because he was always travelling and rarely accessible for his direct reports. Georg's colleagues were all urging him to speak to the CEO about it, on behalf of the entire EB. You can just imagine them saying to Georg, "Go on, then—if you can't, you must! Tony says so. You can do it much better than we could!" And this in a business where shooting the messenger would have been a kinder fate.

Georg, my client, being a Germanic kind of Don Quixote, was determined to use his next scheduled CEO meeting (fifteen minutes per month for each EB member) to be the voice of his EB colleagues "in the interests of the company." Wisely, though, Georg decided to consult me first. He then thanked his colleagues for their faith in him, but politely declined the messenger role.

Why do we have policemen when we have no crime?

Georg's story makes me think about all the arguments for the payback from coaching—it's often the things that *don't* happen that make coaching valuable. Like having policemen, in a way!

Victor's phrase, "There are no problems, only opportunities," however, has stuck in my mind. Ever since we established our executive coaching company, I have tried to encourage clients to use coaching as preparation for challenge, as opposed to using it to sort out problems. For one thing, the positive nature of this spin on the service we provide made the idea of coaching much more appealing to executives who disliked the old notion that coaching is psychology based and is only good for fixing problems.

Preparation for challenge

Mostly, though, preparing someone for a bigger, or different, role through experience-based executive coaching is just sound common sense. You don't start to manufacture in a new facility without careful planning, preparation, and trial running. You don't launch a new product on the market without intensive focus-group feedback and designing the offering to best suit the customer. You don't (I hope) teach your children to swim by swinging them by their legs and tossing them headfirst into a two-metre-deep swimming pool.

So why do so many corporations throw valued executives into the deep end of the pool in sink-or-swim gambles? It is inconsistent, like so many "people" things, with best practice in every other aspect of business.

Ken Tucky's story

One of our clients recently acquired a large company in Bluegrass country. It was successful in its own domestic market but had little presence outside the United States. As part of the company's well-managed integration, executives appointed Ken Tucky, a senior finance manager from the newly merged subsidiary, to a line management role in a difficult foreign region.

Ken is a good professional in a head-office functional role. But Ken has already suffered from lack of some interpersonal skills, which will be an even bigger challenge in the new job unless he deals with them before he moves. He doesn't speak the local language and has never worked in that particular culture. In addition, Ken has never before had bottom-line (or any kind of line) responsibility before.

Now a typical corporation would just throw Ken into the job and, inevitably, a host of problems would soon emerge. Some very good Harvard research in the early nineties demonstrated that first impressions do count. It takes six months or more to change your mind after a first meeting of just three minutes. Imagine, then, how much longer it would take to undo the damage that Ken could do if the company throws him, unprepared, into a new market, a new job, and a new organisation as the country head! Yet, this is what most companies do. Just think of the loss of customer relationship, staff morale, and everything else. No wonder executives fail.

I am delighted to report that the company is handling this real-life challenge in a very enlightened way. Ken, the new country manager, has started work with an executive coach from an excellent global coaching company (ours). She speaks the local language, understands its culture, has been a country manager herself in a global organisation, and has the maturity and experience to prepare Ken in advance and to hold his hand through the difficult first six months of his new assignment.

The last-chance saloon

Happily, the message is getting through, and more and more companies are using coaching to prepare executives for all kinds of challenge,

whether it is a forecast downturn in their markets, economic recession, or a new job assignment. Fifteen years ago, when all our coaching work was remedial coaching, the "last chance" call from HR would arrive and we'd charge off to save someone's career.

This was not the best way to help a valued, experienced manager who had made a mistake and was about to be fired for it. Imagine all that business experience and technical knowledge, those trusted customer relationships and in-house networks walking out the door, cardboard box with his or her personal possessions in hand, and going straight to the competition (or, even worse, the unemployment line). Not to mention the cost of severance pay and the huge head-hunter fees incurred in hiring a replacement that might, or might not, turn out to be better in the job.

We're proud of the fact that we have never lost a last-chance client in fifteen years. The problem has always been remarkably easy to turn round with solid feedback, some plain speaking, and good coaching. Our clients have not only stayed with their company but have mostly won promotions soon afterwards.

The Gospel according to Charles

I remember one typical example. I got a call from Bob, the CEO of a large American group. He was having problems in his top team. One senior executive, Charles, had been a brilliant people leader in a region outside the United States. His business results had been excellent and his people, all five thousand of them, adored him. But when Charles was promoted to head office, problems started. His colleagues, all smart, ambitious, and (naturally) politically wise executives, were complaining that Charles was preaching at them, telling them how to run their business and generally sticking his nose in where it wasn't wanted. As usually happens, bad vibes from one direction gave rise to pushback, and a downward spiral of bad feeling set in, to the point where the top team was becoming dysfunctional.

Bob's solution to all this, however reluctantly, was to fire Charles. Twenty-five years of experience, relationships, and knowledge were about

to cross the street to the competition! Fortunately, the CEO called me for advice instead. I visited the corporate head office and arranged to interview all the key players in this organisational drama. In the "C" suite, they call us the chief honesty officers because we are very clear and direct in interviewing and discussing feedback.

With my CHO hat on, I asked some penetrating questions about the top team's perceptions of Charles, my client.

"He's preaching leadership at us!" they told me. "We're all highly seasoned top managers. We think that he's making a power play for the top job," they went on. "He doesn't seem to value our own experience and abilities."

Charles was creating the impression that he knew much more than they did about the ways of the world outside the United States, and he was being an all-round "pain in the ass."

I put those views to Charles during my visit to head office. He was astonished.

"Look," he said, "I know that I have more global experience than my colleagues. I'm just trying to pass on my own hard earned lessons for the good of the corporation. I want to help them grow from my own experience."

When I explained that his colleagues interpreted this as preaching, Charles was quite shocked. But he bought in to the need to change his style. We then began to work on different ways to disseminate his hardwon experience to his colleagues without causing resentment.

In parallel, I talked again to the other top team members. I explained Charles's horrified reaction and stressed that his objective was purely innocent—he was not trying to score points or play games for the CEO role. I said that his sole intention was to help them and the corporation, however clumsily he had tried to do so. This created a new, and more positive, perception in their minds, and immediately the atmosphere began to improve.

Bob never did fire Charles. Just six weeks later (this was America, remember?), Charles was promoted again to one of the biggest jobs in the global group.

MacMentor advises, "It's great to spread your wisdom, but, in leadership, style counts just as much as content."

The Chief

Honesty Officer

The silent killer

"Always tell the truth, but don't kill yourself with honesty!"

It's a familiar marketers' philosophy. After all, if they're selling coffee, they will highlight the taste, the lifestyle image, and how well it goes with a nice smoky malt whisky from Islay. Actually, that last bit is not strictly correct. I think that they should, but I'm biased. I'm Scottish. The marketing guys won't go out of their way to say that coffee can keep you wide awake at night, will they?

If you wake up in the early hours, I'm hoping it's with a brilliant vision for your business—not just because you drank strong coffee the evening before. Over the years, sad to say, too many people leaders have taken marketers' advice literally. When it comes to performance appraisals, the boss will usually tell you the truth and nothing but the truth. But he or she will avoid telling you the whole truth—and it's usually the bit you don't know that kills you, or, at least, keeps you from realising your full potential in your career.

Too many chiefs

You know how, in US-styled corporations everywhere, they always have a "C" suite? They have, as you well know, chief executive officers, chief technology officers, chief financial officers and, in enlightened organisations where people really matter, chief human resources officers too.

Sometimes, it seems, they have too many chiefs and not enough Indians. This is a particularly sore point in Silicon Valley, where everyone is a chief and all those brilliant and talented Indians have to go back to Bangalore. The antiquated US immigration laws force them to leave, just as they are adding valuable business experience to their ability to juggle terabytes and user-friendly interfaces into yet another highly commercial social-networking product.

The alphabet soup of the "C" suite

So, in the "C" Suite, I am the chief honesty officer of the organisation.

In amongst this alphabet soup of CEO, CFO, CTO, CHRO, and all those other "C"s of this and that and their EAs and PAs, what happens to honesty? You know about honesty…that's when someone tells you the truth. The truth—unadulterated, honest, get-to-the-point truth that you need to know is a rare commodity in the modern business world.

I always thought that, as a leader of people, my job in the annual appraisal round was to set the context by briefly praising the qualities of my staff members, and then focusing on the areas where they were not performing as well as they could. Sometimes, at least until they got used to my style, some people would be a little offended that they were portrayed as less than perfect in my review. I never just criticised; I tried to depict the precise issue that they needed to work on. I always finished with ideas to help them grow and offered help of some sort (maybe coaching or a training course or something similar). I may have upset one or two, but I have had some really brilliant young leaders leave my company and go on to high positions elsewhere.

Outsourced honesty—the I. J. Martin way

This is a core element of our coaching service offering—really precise, constructively critical comments on a client's executive's performance as leader of business and people. It's "outsourced honesty," offering the hard messages about leadership shortcomings, and ways to deal with those, that business people find it hard to give. Sometimes the boss just doesn't have the time to dig deeply into the situation. Often, he or she lacks the ability to ask the right questions. Usually, the boss is reluctant to provide really hard comments because he or she has to work with the executive every day and it's embarrassing to speak forthrightly when the boss has to face that person on a daily basis. And always, always, it's so easy to get it wrong and destroy the subject's confidence and damage the relationship.

When we are holding a feedback discussion with a client, our report is usually about twelve pages long. It's almost all text and contains absolutely no page-filling bar charts or line graphs that take too long to assimilate, are often unreadable, and are rarely referred to afterwards.

No, our feedback reports are all words, apart from some simple performance scores in an Excel sheet. It's an exception report and, since five members of our team are qualified management accountants, we know how to write exception reports. Only 5 per cent of those words are about the positive attributes of our client.

We tell them, "You're in a very senior job. They pay you well. You know how good you are—you don't need me to tell you that. What you need to know is what you don't know. And what you don't know may have been quietly killing you for years."

I think I understand W. Edwards Deming, the man who, amongst many other things, revolutionised manufacturing efficiency in Japan and made its industry a model for the world. He counted annual performance appraisals as one of the seven deadly sins of management. It was, in his view, counterproductive. He felt that the process motivated people to try to seek rewards within the system for short-term gain, rather than trying to change the system.

Get me the next million-dollar bonus!

I get what Deming meant. I once met a banker (who else?) who told me that one of his colleagues had won a seven-figure bonus the previous year. The banker's bonus was "only" half a million dollars, and his colleague wasn't half as smart as he was, so he didn't think it was fair.

"I want you to coach me to get much more than him this year," he said.

Now, elsewhere in this book I discuss coaching in the United Nations and mention that when the bottom line is human lives, we in our coaching team get even more than usually motivated. I agreed (naturally, since we are a business) to coach this banker and help him get a bigger bonus than his colleague.

Following his annual performance review, he got his bonus. In addition, he was promoted to the group management board. But he paid more than our usual fee because we built in the "ass**le premium." (That's a technical term we use. We generally charge the same fees for all clients. But when clients act arrogant or are just generally greedy and unappealing, we add the "ass**le premium" to compensate for the extra effort…and just to make them pay for being who they are.)

Appraisals and Deming

With appraisals, the choice is to do them as everyone does or not to do them at all, as Deming argued. I don't agree with him. I believe that appraisals have an important role, provided that you do them in a constructive way that is designed to build excellent leadership within the organisation. In doing so, you are laying the foundations to change the system, which is what Deming wanted. We see our role as leadership coaches and mentors to be exactly that—moving leadership along the path of excellence. Our feedback reviews function as an important tool in this cause.

It's amazing how often we ask a client, "Did the boss tell you this?" and the answer is "no." But when we ask the boss, "Did you tell him this?" The answer is "yes"… and neither the boss nor the client is telling a lie.

They all really believe they are telling the truth. The boss hides hard comments in the coded message that he or she tucks between the lines. The receiver of bad news has to decode the message and understand the hint. Meanwhile, our client, usually an alpha personality (I'm an alpha male too, with an ENTJ profile, according to my Myers-Briggs tests), has a rather robust ego. Frankly speaking, he or she is somewhat vain about his or her abilities. Robust egos do not equal full understanding of negative, coded messages. In this time-honoured way, people keep on making the same mistakes. They don't get the message, and the boss often finds it easier to fire people than give them the plain, old, honest truth.

And now, MacMentor says, ask yourself this: "In my last annual review, did I really pick up all the hints? Was my boss being truly open and honest? What is the thing I don't know that is killing me or holding me back from realising the career heights that my abilities truly deserve?"

Is now the time to consult the chief honesty officer?

Good things falling apart

Our feedback process is fundamental to our success as executive coaches. We invest more of our time and more of our clients' money in interviewing people for feedback, writing a report, and discussing it with our client than any other coaching firm I know. When we ask clients at the end of a programme, "What was most useful in our work together?" the feedback report always gets a mention.

Underlying our feedback is a process of deconstructing and reconstructing behaviour (being careful not to destroy the client's confidence or change good behaviours). All our clients are extremely able people—they just want to be even better (or get a bigger bonus, if they're big-time

45

bankers). To achieve this, we need to remove some self-perceptions in order to replace them with more accurate assessments of the client's leadership abilities.

As Marilyn Monroe once said (yes, that Marilyn Monroe of the skirt-swirling, blonde bimbo fame) "Sometimes good things fall apart so better things can fall together." She wasn't such a dumb blonde—or, at least, her scriptwriter was not.

Even in national regimes where telling the truth gets you shot, or did in recent times, I am nearly always pleasantly surprised by how candid the feedback we get from interviewees is. Most interviewees are mature, experienced people who just want our client to be a better leader. It would not help if they only gave us rave reviews about our client. It does not help, either, if they use the interview as a vehicle for revenge by giving only low scores and unbalanced comments. I usually say to clients, "Don't give us your best friend for interview; give us your worst enemy."

Helga's story

"Don't nominate people for feedback who will be too nice about you. Give me someone who really doesn't like you."

I said this to one very smart young lady in a US corporation at its regional headquarters in Europe. "Young" is a relative term. Helga was in her mid-forties, but in a very senior job. She was highly ambitious, and she wore that ambition on her sleeve. In every meeting, Helga would sit close to the boss and dominate the discussion in an effort to impress. She was not fooling the boss, who was a wise and experienced marketing executive. In fact, Helga's behaviour was holding her career back because she was annoying her peers and demotivating her team.

When I said, "Give me your worst enemy to interview," she immediately nominated Bruce, a male colleague in US headquarters who quite literally and palpably hated her. In the course of my interviews in the United States, I met this man. I could see why Helga had nominated him as her worst enemy. I didn't like him either.

To my surprise, though, given the bad feeling between them, Bruce proceeded to offer some well-balanced, deeply considered comments. His scores were not out of line with the relationship, many being below average with the occasional "one out of five" thrown in. But when I asked him, "Why did you say that?" and "What can she do to win 'four out of five' from you?" Bruce's responses were always carefully measured and critically constructive.

Finally, after a rich and rewarding one-hour interview, I ventured to say, "Bruce, you really don't like Helga and she doesn't like you, but do you know that she admires many things about you and really wants to collaborate better?"

Bruce was surprised and deeply reflective for a few moments. "Well, you know, I just told you some things that she could do to change. She's very good at business and very smart. No doubt, I'm not perfect either, but I think we can get along better if she just works at those things I mentioned."

Back in Europe, I told Helga, "You might be surprised, but Bruce gave me the best quality feedback of all ten of your nominees. He didn't give you high scores, but he had thought honestly and deeply about the interview in advance, and he gave me a lot of really good advice to pass on to you."

Helga was indeed surprised. "Well!" she exclaimed. "I didn't expect that."

I went on to say, "You know, Bruce respects you in many ways. He thinks you're smart and good at your business. He believes that, if you change in certain aspects, you two can get along together."

"What can I do to reach out to him?" asked Helga.

"Here's an idea," I said. "How about choosing three things from your feedback report that you really want to change and asking Bruce to observe your behaviour on those three points? Get him to discuss them with you after every meeting and see if you have managed to change, at least in his opinion."

Helga did exactly that. After every meeting, she asked Bruce how she had done in her three areas to improve. Bruce gave her a score out of

five and offered his helpful comments. Pretty soon, Bruce was engaged in Helga's success and helping her change her off-putting ways. Helga and Bruce will never be best friends, but they are now pretty good collaborative colleagues. And, I'm happy to tell you that Helga's over-ambitious behaviour has changed radically. As often happens in life, when she stopped trying, Helga got the success that she yearned for. The boss, her peers, and her staff all noticed and appreciated a different kind of Helga.

Last time I met her, Helga proudly told me, "I got that promotion I really wanted! I also stopped smoking six weeks ago and I haven't touched a cigarette since." As a coach, I'm not sure what I'm most pleased about: Helga's promotion or the fact that she's given up her dependence on the "deadly weed." Either way, with a little help from her friends, she did it her way. She is a client to be proud of.

Monologues with your computer

Now this story underlines an unexpected benefit of good objective feedback, conducted face-to-face, that we never foresaw when our team began coaching back in 1998.

To get this benefit, it's essential not to do feedback the way most organisations do it. How was your last appraisal organised? Did the HR department send out a multiple-choice questionnaire by e-mail and ask you to complete the questions before some deadline date? Given that there is no other affordable way to get feedback if you have a hundred thousand employees, I still argue that the process is full of flaws and that your most important assets, your senior executives, deserve something a lot more specialised and personalised.

I hate multiple-choice questionnaires. Last year, I was presented with the question: "Would you prefer to spend your vacation a) on a crowded beach or b) in a quiet forest?" My response was supposed to provide some psychologist deep and meaningful insights into my personality.

I didn't know how to answer the question. What if the beach is crowded with muscular bullies kicking sand in my face (shades of the old Charles

Atlas bodybuilding adverts back in the 50s…when I was just a boy, I hasten to add)! What if the beach is the Copacabana in Rio, and it is crowded with tiny-bikini-clad Brazilian beauties? (Here I mean that the bikinis are tiny, not the Brazilian beauties.) What if the quiet forest is warm and tranquil and in the heart of Switzerland's alpine loveliness? But it might be freezing cold, swampy, and alive with man-eating mosquitoes!

This was a multiple-choice questionnaire. It was also a monologue with a computer screen, not a dialogue with an intelligent person. I had to choose a) beach or b) forest. I had done what everyone who has to complete an appraisal questionnaire does. I had left this tedious task until it had moved, on my personal time-allocation matrix, from being "not important and not urgent" to being "not only urgent and important, but there will be serious consequences if you don't finish this in the next five minutes!"

I randomly punched one of the responses and put myself in the hands of the psychologists.

Does this sound familiar? Is this really the best way to learn how people are performing and the most efficient way to advise your key assets how to improve? Not in my opinion! A monologue with a laptop screen and answering questions that only pose even more unanswerable questions doesn't seem to me like the best way to do performance reviews. Much better, is it not, to just sit down in the privacy of a quiet room and ask people some simple questions? Those questions often pose more questions, but, unlike the laptop monologue, these are the subjects of a lively dialogue with an experienced and objective coach.

The unexpected benefit

As we question interviewees about our client, they start to question themselves and wonder how others would rate them as leaders—the first step in the path to their own development.

Interviewees also question whether they themselves could do something to change the working relationship with our client.

The benefit? If just half of those interviewed for feedback start to work on their own leadership and adopt one or two different approaches with our client, the team's dynamic improves quickly and dramatically.

MacMentor says, "Ask your CFO if he'd approve a project with infinite return on investment. This huge side benefit has zero cost because the coaching fee has already paid for it."

Turn over to look down
on a flat world…

CANCEL THE
Meeting—I forgot

my wedding

Looking down on China

Sitting in my twenty-sixth-floor office near Shatin, I was gazing with huge admiration at my reflection in the window. Well, to be more precise, my reflection was just getting in the way of some beautiful scenery outside. It was that scene which captivated me, not my own image. Before me soared a craggy mountain, clad in lush green forest. High above, the sky was deep blue and the sun was burnished gold. Deep in the shadows below lay a tiny Chinese village. Traditional little whitewashed houses with glazed-tile roofs and ornate red and gold temples surrounded the village water well. In the tiny backyards, flea-bitten dogs of every colour, size, and breed scratched their ears and yawned, while scrawny chickens fussily clawed the earth for tasty insects. The scene was timeless in this "land between," except for the dusty, beat-up Hondas and Toyotas parked outside each house.

Most newcomers to Hong Kong don't know about this "land between". To them, Hong Kong is the main island and the densely populated southern tip of the mainland, called Kowloon. Standing on the famous Peak, they stare in the direction of China and believe, as I once did, that the

border lies on the summit of the distant mountain range. But beyond those mountains, before you reach the real border with China, lies the "land between"; the New Territories. Satellite cities such as Shatin, Fanling, and Tai Po are themselves major conurbations. Further east are the beautiful hills, golden beaches, and tiny islands of the Sai Kung Peninsula. Standing on my hillside terrace on the edge of the Sai Kung Country Park, I could easily imagine that I was back home in my native Scotland on a sunny day. My office near Shatin was in equally lovely surroundings.

Cancel the meeting

That afternoon, as I gazed out of my office window, I was thinking over the meeting I just had with my Chinese colleagues. The loud and insistent ringing of my telephone interrupted my tranquil contemplation.

"Weiiiiii?" I said in my bad Cantonese. "Iain Martin speaking."

"Iain," said the caller, "it's Alfred here." Alfred Wang was our CFO and we had just left the meeting together.

"You know how we arranged a follow-up meeting on Thursday? I need to cancel it. I forgot that I'm getting married," said Alfred apologetically.

"You forgot you're what?" I gasped in disbelief.

"Yeah, I forgot. My wedding is on Thursday afternoon. I can't make the meeting."

"But that's just two days from today, Alfred," I said in bewilderment. "How could you forget it?"

"Yeah, yeah," replied Alfred. "We have so many here—I just forgot this one. But we can meet on Friday instead."

"But what about your honeymoon?" I asked, even more astonished.

"That's not for about six months from now—no problem," explained Alfred, the absent-minded bridegroom.

This little exchange reminded me of the YouTube video of the married man who had forgotten the password to the family computer and called out to his wife.

"It's easy," she said. "It's the date of our wedding anniversary, *darling*!"

"Oh sh*t. I'm in so much trouble now," whispered the husband under his breath.

Alfred's problem, Hong Kong style, was that they have so many ceremonies to celebrate a wedding that it is easy to forget one of them. There's the Chinese ceremony and the solemnisation in church, then there is the civil wedding, not to mention the red dress, the white dress, the black dinner suit, and the white suit, plus hundreds of invitations to family members that you never knew you had. The Chinese like to hedge their bets in religion and family matters, as in all else, so getting married is a complicated and expensive business in Hong Kong. And it gets even more complicated and expensive once the man starts travelling on business to China. I used to wonder why some of my colleagues, when we left Dongguan for weekends at our Hong Kong homes, always had Friday night dinners with "friends" in Shenzhen, leaving me to cross the border alone. It took me a while, but eventually I learned about the "other wife." Six wedding anniversaries, two birthdays, two sets of credit cards with separate addresses...I was surprised that they could concentrate on the thing that paid for it all—their jobs.

The world is flat

It's a small world nowadays. It's made small by fast Internet connections and the World Wide Web. Skype and Facebook have given us global friendships and allowed us to move away from home without losing our social connections. Twitter and LinkedIn have helped us become best friends with people we've never met and probably never will. Global business leaders can hold virtual face-to-face meetings every month with their regional managers without leaving the head office. It's easy to assume that the world is, in Thomas Friedman's words, truly flat. The social science phenomenon called ethnocentrism—when one culture believes that it is superior to all other cultures—reinforces the perceived flatness of the globe. These combined forces create potential for misdirected leadership. This can explain why the head office of a large equipment maker in a small town in Illinois may think, wrongly, that it knows what's best for its

manufacturing team in France. This influence may explain why a London-based healthcare corporation might assume that its way of doing things is also right for a former UK colony in Southeast Asia. It's the reason why the management of a large Swiss bank may have mistakenly believed that it understood the thinking of the Inland Revenue Service in the United States. This imperialist overconfidence, which, sad to say, is still manifest in certain corners of the old British Empire, is most often nowadays associated with the United States. The former Bush/Cheney/Rumsfeld regime inspired a wonderful tragicomical song just after the invasion of Iraq in 2003. It went something like:

"Oh, I've got a bigger bomb than you
And I'm gonna tell you what to do
And if you're not with me, then you're my enemeeee
Cause, I've got a bigger bomb than you."

Happily, the current government has worked hard to change that image of imperialist United States, with much success around the world.

Despite the false perceptions created by global connectivity, a study by the *Economist* magazine a few years ago showed that 90 per cent of executives surveyed in sixty countries believed that their biggest challenge was cross-cultural leadership. The most interesting thing about Alfred the Absent-Minded was not that he had forgotten his imminent wedding, but that I, as an expatriate Brit living in a Chinese environment, was surprised that he had done so. The confluence of national/regional cultures and corporate cultures creates challenges for business. Leaders in global business, to be successful, need all the usual leadership and business skills, but they also need a deep understanding of, and sensitivity to, the dynamics of this turbulent interface. Achieving the right balance for sustainable business success demands some very special skills.

The Garden of Eden and SADP syndrome

But we need to make sure that we separate perception from reality. We define cultures by clichés and perceptions. We encapsulate those by

stereotyping to make the complexities easier to grasp. Here is an old joke that demonstrates my point.

An Englishman, a Frenchman, and a Russian were standing in an art gallery. They were admiring a painting of Adam and Eve in the Garden of Eden. They were speculating about which country Adam and Eve came from.

The Englishman said, "They are modest, they have classical Anglo-Saxon physiques and typically perfect British complexions—they must be English!"

"Mais *non*! Nonsense!" said the Frenchman. "They are both completely naked, and still, they look so beautiful—they must be French!"

"You're both wrong," said the Russian. "They have no clothes, they have no shelter, and they have only one apple to eat between them—and someone is telling them that this is paradise. They must be Russian!"

Translate that into your leadership life. Don't we all think in those over-simplified, stereotypical terms? And doesn't it lead to some serious misjudgements? For example, everybody thinks that the Scots are cheap—that we don't like to spend our money. It's not true at all—we all just suffer from SADP Syndrome. SADP is short for "Short Arms, Deep Pockets." It's not our fault—we inherited it through our "jeans."

And the Dutch! Paul Polman, the Dutch CEO of Unilever, once told me that the definition of a Scotsman was "a Dutchman who learned how to swim."

I like this definition of "national culture":

"Culture is the sum total of learned behaviours of a group of people that are generally considered to be the tradition of that people and are transmitted from generation to generation."

Now, I'm not a social scientist. I largely derive my views empirically from my own observations and experiences. I believe that a national culture is a fluid and evolving thing. I'd even argue that national cultures actually comprise a number of regional subsets. Cantonese people, for example, think and act in very different ways than Beijing and Shanghai people.

Inhabitants of Marseille have different cultural dynamics than those of Paris. The Scots subcultures collectively resemble the northern English subcultures, and these are very different from those of London and the Home Counties.

Cultural anthropologists recognise these differences and collectively label them "cultural relativism." This concept says that different groups act, feel, and think differently, but it does not seek to say that one group is superior to another. Understanding the nature of these differences must precede taking action. One facet of this is in negotiating with people of a different culture. Sustainable, win-win success will come from understanding the reasons for different starting positions and objectives. Only then can you arrive at win-win outcomes that satisfy all parties.

Obvious, isn't it? But how often do multinational corporations with powerful headquarters in the Anglo-Saxon world attempt to understand these key issues before engaging in negotiations with Middle Eastern or Asian counterparts? In Anglo-Saxon cultures, negotiators will be driven by "What has he or she done for me?" If the other party feels obliged to you, it will be easier to arrive at a satisfactory outcome. In Confucian Asia, the driver will be "Who is the other party connected to?" In Latin cultures, it will be "Who are our mutual friends?" whereas in Germanic cultures, the driver will be "Is this consistent with regulatory and legal frameworks?"

Shakin' Stefan, the spreadsheet king

I was the CEO for European operations for a US corporation based in Germany. One day, on my way along the autobahn to start a much-needed family holiday, my car phone emitted a harshly ominous beeping sound.

"Iain, where the hell are you?" It was my group president in New York.

"I'm heading for the airport. I'm going on holiday," I replied.

"No, you're not! Turn round, go back, and start to close down the German operation."

There was no arguing with this man. Back in my office, we spoke again.

"I want it shut down in three weeks—got it?" said the president.

"That is impossible—and the impossible takes a little longer," I told him.

"How long is 'long'?" he demanded. "And what's it going to cost me?"

"Under German law," I said, "these people are protected. It's going to take a year, because we just missed a quarter-end deadline to do it in three months less." I said, "If we buy them out, it's going to cost real money—about $50 million."

"I don't give a sh*t about German law!" he exploded. He wouldn't, because he was safely ensconced in his Manhattan high-rise office and I was the Geschäftsführer of five German entities—with all the legal liabilities that this entailed.

"You've got six months and $20 million max!" said the president as he slammed the phone down.

My German team and I put our heads together and reviewed the German labour laws. At first, the task seemed impossible. But, slowly, we began to explore the factors that would drive the approach of the parties to be involved. We considered the views of the director of the local Arbeitsamt, the regional employment office. We thought about the full-time official of the trade union and the company workers' council. A plan emerged, based on understandings of the motivations of each. The Arbeitsamt could be flexible, if we could guarantee a minimal lasting presence rather than a total closure. The union official needed to appear to be tough to the workforce, but, pragmatist that he was, he was quietly prepared to accept the continuation of a minimum presence, too, provided that we did not publicly embarrass him. The workers' council expressed concern that they would be unemployable in another company, but this was really just a ploy to extract generous severance terms for themselves.

Drawing on our understandings of these different cultural drivers, we entered into negotiations and, within the president's deadline, arrived at the final negotiation. The workers' council was not that smart, apart from

Stefan the Spreadsheet King. Stefan could calculate the worth of our latest offer in a heartbeat—a valued attribute in our fast-moving negotiations.

On the last day, Mr. President called to say, "You've got until 2:00 p.m. your time, or I will close you down anyway." With the prospect of an extended holiday in a German jail before me, I redoubled the effort to agree to the final sticking point—the compensation for workers' council members. Stefan the Spreadsheet King was being difficult...until the call came from the gatehouse.

"Stefan," said the guard, "the police are here. You haven't paid your alimony or your car insurance or your speeding fines. They are here to arrest you."

Stefan went as white as his latest spreadsheet. Taking me aside, he begged me to advance his next month's salary, in cash on the spot, to hand over to the visiting polizei. At first, seeing a probable zero-sum outcome for us in this final negotiation if they put the spreadsheet king in handcuffs, I refused. Well, can you imagine trying to do complicated calculations on a laptop when your hands are tied behind your back? Eventually, though, I weakened and said, "Stefan, I will agree to this...but you must help me come to an agreement by 2:00 p.m. Stop being an Arschloch." (Clue to non-German speakers—*loch* is "hole" in German.)

Stefan got his salary advance from the cashier's office, paid off the police, and returned to the negotiating table. Despite our deal, he persisted in being difficult. But "Shakin' Stefan" was spreadsheet king no longer. He couldn't focus on the debate or his magic formulae correctly. By the deadline of 2:00 p.m., he had produced some palpably wrong responses to our final, final offer. By 2:30 p.m., the deal was agreed, committed to writing, and signed. The Arbeitsamt got to keep some jobs in the town, the union official enhanced his "tough negotiator" image, and the workers' council got a handsome severance package...and I got to stay out of the German jail.

Understanding all the cultural drivers and "walking a mile in their moccasins" were the keys to success in this theoretically impossible scenario.

Cultured corporations

The definitions of corporate culture and national culture do not differ much.

Merriam-Webster's dictionary defines corporate culture as "the shared values, traditions, customs, philosophies, and policies of a corporation." The corporate personality defined by these factors drives the atmosphere and behaviours of the business and its people. A corporation is, however, capable of much faster change to its culture than an entire nation is. A new CEO can change the culture fast because he or she can apply real economic pain to those who don't conform…that is, the CEO can fire them. The culture of an organisation is like an electrical force field; you can't see it and you can't touch it, but its powerful presence is there all the same. Like national cultures, there can be subsets of corporate cultures in different locations and functions. The corporate subculture of a US corporation in Tokyo will probably be different from that of the head office in New York. The subculture in finance and accounting likely would not resemble that of sales and marketing. Sometimes, with weak corporate leadership and a vaguely defined corporate culture, this may lead to conflict. On the other hand, a strong corporate culture may overcome national influences, in some or all aspects. DuPont, for example, under Ellen Kullman's leadership, has a very strong culture of safety, arising out of its origins as a manufacturer of explosives more than two hundred years ago. With much effort, DuPont has managed to impose safety culture in places like China, where, in general, companies place less importance on safety than those in the United States do. DuPont did have a bigger struggle to foster its gender and national diversity cultures in Tokyo, though it was ultimately successful.

Values—the bridge over troubled waters

The key to success in smoothing the currents of this turbulent interface between national and corporate cultures is to make sure that the corporate culture reflects the fundamental values in every human being. Corporate

culture should be designed to work in the personal interests of the employees as well as the business. This is yet another manifestation of the win-win approach to sustainable success. As in negotiation, a mood of mutual respect supports the acceptance of a corporate culture.

"Here are five ways," says MacMentor, "to foster a long and happy marriage between national and corporate cultures":

1. Top leaders must recognise that their own leadership style reflects the national culture of the headquarters' location.
2. They should accept that their ways are not necessarily better or worse than others in different regions of countries—just different.
3. They should understand that the preferred style of remote subsidiaries, while different, is no better or worse...but may be more effective locally.
4. They should acknowledge cultural differences and take active steps to open them up for discussion and multi-directional coaching.
5. Finally, we all need to actively build a sincere belief that more creative and better ways of leading can grow from cross-cultural learning.

MacMentor's advice is not new, but as I travel round the world, I see that this turbulent confluence of national and corporate cultures is no less troubled than it was when I was a young manager on my first international assignment. As localisation of expatriates and foreign assignments gives way to globalisation of local leaders, MacMentor shows the way to a more harmonious and productive future.

Getting things done with influence - next…

WIN FRIENDS AND INFLUENCE

People with the

Eternal Triangle

Getting along with influence

"The greatest ability in business is to get along with others and to influence their actions." So spoke John Hancock, a well-known eighteenth-century American politician. His words are even truer in today's "hollow-cube" organisations than they were then.

"Command and control" no longer works in big corporations. Distance from the head office, autonomy of business divisions, and complexities of functions, geographies, and markets all mean that, whatever the CEO says, the employees of an organisation will do just what they want to do in the end.

Organisations have even moved beyond the two-dimensional matrix structure. They are now "hollow cubes," with the CEO sitting in the middle, trying to make things happen. His or her most important tool is the skill of influencing—the core leadership skill that encapsulates most things that are true of a real leader.

Alice Clarr's story

We were sitting at a long rectangular table in the mahogany-panelled boardroom of one of Switzerland's most traditional engineering

companies. "Define 'influencing,'" I said to Alice. Alice is the German chief executive of this $5 billion autonomous business within a bigger group.

"It's the same as persuasion," replied Alice.

"Define 'persuasion,'" I responded.

"It's getting people to do what you want...I guess..." said Alice. Her eyes conveyed a thought forming behind her spectacles.

"So, influencing is getting people to agree with you. Is that what you're saying?"

Alice was looking a little doubtful. She knew I was getting at something, but she was not sure what it was.

"Did you get a call from Johan yesterday?" I asked. Johan is her autocratic regional boss in Frankfurt. Alice nodded.

"What did he want?"

"He wants me to take another five hundred people off the head-count."

"And?"

"And he told me that the board says that we need to cut the workforce to meet our numbers this year."

"How do you feel about that?" I asked her.

"Not great," said Alice. "It makes no sense to fire trained people—we're going to need them again early next year for the big contract we just signed. But he told me that the board is coming down hard on missed budgets," she went on. "So in the end I agreed."

"So he persuaded you to reduce the headcount," I said. "And do you feel good about that?"

"No," said Alice. "I'll do what he wants for now, but I've got a little plan up my sleeve to take them all back in in a few weeks' time as subcontractors."

"How do you feel about the way Johan persuaded you?" I asked.

"Not good," said Alice. "I felt pressured, and I don't like the way he got me to agree."

"So," I said, "It wasn't a win-win discussion where he listened seriously to your views before getting you to agree, was it? What was wrong about the way Johan told you about the headcount reduction?" I asked.

"Basically, he didn't listen to what I wanted to say, and he didn't leave me any options. He didn't actually tell me what to do, but I felt that I didn't have a choice."

Therein lies the difference between persuading and truly influencing—it was essentially a zero-sum outcome. With a different approach from Johan, Alice would have felt listened to, respected, and valued in the debate. She agreed, but at a long-term cost to Johan's influence over her.

True influencing—the key ingredients

Persuading—Sometimes you just have to persuade people to do what you want. There may be no option. Usually, though, persuasion is just a milder form of autocracy. Quoting the board, regulations, or the law to legitimate your own agenda will get people to agree with you one time, but they will find ways to get revenge and their own way the next time, and the next...

Building bridges—True influencing is so much more than persuasion. In coaching clients in this essential skill, I introduce the benefits of bridging. It's a long discussion for another time, but, briefly, bridging is about building networks. You need to have an excellent, active network to be truly influential because otherwise nobody hears you.

- ✓ Networking creates your "warning antenna," so people you know will think about you when they hear about potential problems and warn you in good time.
- ✓ Networking creates your "opportunity antenna," so people remember you when opportunities arise and advise you before anyone else knows.
- ✓ Networking creates your voting constituency so that, when the time comes, people will say, "I know her. She's good at running her business. Let's do what she advises."

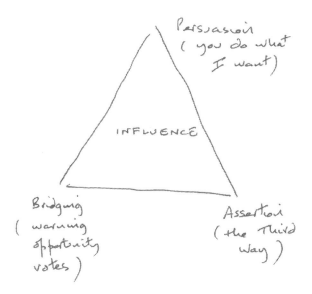

THE INFLUENCE TRIANGLE

Persuasion
(you do what
I want)

INFLUENCE

Bridging
(warning
opportunity
votes)

Assertion
(the Third
Way)

Assertion—Many people think that there are two kinds of business behaviour: aggressive and passive. They don't know about the third way—assertion.

Assertion means respecting the opinions and objectives of other people, and your own, in equal measure. Assertion means having an open discussion, listening carefully to the arguments, presenting your views, and arriving at an outcome that allows all involved to feel satisfied. Assertion has its own special language and behaviours. It's the basis of all win-win leadership negotiations and of a truly influential leadership style. While it may take longer than short-term persuasion, it pays off many times over in the long term.

Wrapping up with Alice

"Alice," I asked. "If Johan had listened carefully to you and explained some valid reasons the board has to insist on cost reductions, would you

now feel better, a bit more motivated? And if he had asked you to advise him on how the company could meet its cost objectives and still, somehow, retain these experienced workers, would you be able to offer a viable solution? "

"You bet I could…on both counts!" said Alice emphatically.

"So how are you going to pass on this news to your own management team?"

She looked thoughtful for some time. "Alles klar!" said Alice Clarr. "Can we have a chat about that?"

"The boss can always get what he or she wants, or at least he or she might think so," says MacMentor. "But it is only through mastering and skilfully using all the skills of influencing that he or she will truly achieve what everyone wants in the most committed way.

REFLECTIONS FROM
the Heart of the

Business Jungle

My walk on the wild side

It was only mid-morning, but already it was 32 degrees Celsius and 95 per cent humidity. Sweat was stinging my eyes and running down my back. I was completely alone, but a thousand pairs of eyes stared at me through the forest foliage. Insects chirped and buzzed all around, and, high above in the treetops, tropical birds called lazily to their mates. At the start of my journey, I had dodged the sticks and stones that two tribes of warring monkeys were tossing at each other in a shrieking, chattering territorial dispute. A small, brightly decorated snake had slithered across my path, glided lazily in a U-turn, and then slid back into the rotting debris of the jungle floor. A few minutes later, a giant monitor lizard had blocked the muddy path as it ambled along without a care. A sparkling stream tumbled over a fallen tree into a murky pool where an inquisitive turtle swam, its black, beaded eyes following my every movement. The sights and sounds and smells of this steaming equatorial forest overwhelmed my senses. I felt a long, long way from civilisation.

And yet, in this primeval forest, I was just a ten-minute taxi ride from high-rise downtown Singapore. This twenty-second century city-state is

71

the most confident and civilised of the Asian megacities. Occasional business visitors and tourists en route from Australia to somewhere else know it as the world's best airport and only ever see a concrete forest of ever-higher hotels and office towers. This energetic, confident, and visionary country hides from them its tranquil heart of dense green forest, enclosing a sparkling blue expanse of gently lapping lake water.

Reflecting on the stark contrast between Singapore's loud and glittering exterior and its gentle, leafy heart as I sweatily strode along the McRitchie Forest trail, I thought about the executives that my team and I coach around the world. Regardless of where they are, and whether they are men or women, the similarities between them vastly outweigh the cultural and gender differences that are the focus of so many leadership deliberations.

Polished pewter

A veneer of self-confidence is an essential tool to get to, and stay at, executive level in organisations. After all, if you don't believe in yourself, why should anyone else? A select few, and only a few, possess the kind of self-confidence that sits on the face like the muted shine of polished pewter. This kind of tranquil certitude is an essential quality of a real leader—someone that others want to follow. This kind of inner tranquillity and belief in the quality of one's owns ideas and strategies allow the real leader to behave modestly and assertively, rather than boastfully and aggressively. This, however, is only given to a few. Most executives, out of necessity and in self-defence, adopt a thin veneer of confidence. In contrast to the depth of polished pewter, this kind of self-confidence is like a thin and glittery surface of chrome, applied over a core of brass. Frankly, most of us in business don't feel nearly as confident as we act and look, but we adopt the persona for self-defence and for career advancement. And, because we're all doing it, we all try even harder, which results in a downward spiral of self-perpetuating superficiality.

And then there are the truly arrogant ones. Oh, how I feel sorry for them! They are not all investment bankers, though some sectors attract

more than their fair share of conceited types. Their arrogant behaviour and aggressive climbing-over-dead-bodies ambitions win them no friends and many enemies. And this conduct is all self-defeating in the end. Sustainable behaviour leads to sustainable relationships and sustainable, win-win successes. But these types of leaders just don't get it until it's almost too late and the last-chance remedial coach comes in to save their careers and the sanity of all those around them.

Did I just write, "Oh, how I feel sorry for them"? Yes, I do. And here's why: I call it over-compensation for early bad experiences. (And now, the psychology-based coaches are crying out, "Don't go there, Iain—you're not certified—don't go there!" But, what the heck! Business is mostly just common sense. And there is, as far as I know, no fancy diploma for common sense—it comes from the "school of life" and not from a coaching college or business school.) Occasionally, arrogance is in the genes, and no coach on earth can manipulate those genes out of some people. Those, in my view, are in a small minority. Most so-called arrogant people in business are really overreacting to early negative experiences and are adopting hubris as a defence mechanism. Over fifteen years of coaching, I've learned to ignore my first reflex impression of arrogant executives. Now, I try to turn the situation round and look for the vulnerable little boy or girl inside. And you know what? Most of the time I find it—some nasty experience or horrible upbringing that left its mark on a nice little child and produced an overbearing monster for the executive workforce. If only we can get past the brash veneer to the gentler heart of the real man or woman…

Corporate seagulls

I had such a conversation only yesterday. It's one of those "almost too late" scenarios where the client has called us in only after much damage has occurred. A senior executive in a global company, a brilliant but undiplomatic man in his early forties, called Claude, has saved his company nearly a billion dollars in the last three years through his first-class professional negotiations. Along the way, he has built a strong and loyal team and also

made some serious enemies. He has no patience for those oxymoronic "I'm from head office—I'm here to help you" politicians. You know the type, don't you? They've never worked a day in an operation, but they have a million opinions about how to run one. I'm not talking, of course, about good line managers who have risen up the ranks to corporate level, carrying a wealth of real-life experience into corporate HQ. I mean simply those who join head office in early career and stay there, never getting to learn real business in "the school of hard knocks."

Have you heard the expression "corporate seagulls"? These are the guys from head office who fly, squawking noisily, into your operation in the early morning, eat all your food, mess all over you, and fly out again at night. Unfortunately, Clumsy Claude has not tried to understand what motivates these "seagulls." Neither has he tried to find some shared values and objectives with them. He has not been shy, either, about loudly voicing his poor opinions of these feathered flocks of HQ colleagues.

The real crisis, though, has just erupted in a meeting with a team of well-known strategy consultants, which the group CEO has recently mandated for a cost-reduction exercise.

"It was impossible," said Claude later, "to listen to these assh*les any longer." He had exploded with impatience at the challenging questions and gratuitous opinions of these bright and confident—but very inexperienced—young consultants. Yesterday, in discussing the messy aftermath with us, our new client showed us that behind his rough, tough exterior lies a vulnerable and decent man who learned only paternal aggression and disapproval in his early upbringing. "I really want to change," he said. "I know there must be a way of dealing with these guys. But I need your help to find it." Claude obviously wants to mend his ways, but at the time of writing, I don't know if we will be allowed the chance to turn the situation round or if the company will fire him first. If only they had offered him "executive antifreeze" before things came to a head!

74

What they don't know won't kill you!

Our coaches have a way of getting to the heart of the difficult situation…and it's what helps me see beyond the brash exterior to the inner person. Some coaches call this "the exploration interview." I think that this sounds a bit "white coat-ish." I prefer to call it our "background discussion"—our blue-suited alternative. In this process, we have an in-depth discussion, in privacy, with our clients about where they are coming from, where they think they are now, and where they want to be long-term. Elsewhere in this book, I write about feedback, which covers the present and future life planning, which deals with the long term. Here, I am referring to the "coming from"—an apt American-English description of the process of describing your origins: the things that shaped your personality and opinions, and the events that you still carry, often needlessly, as a burden into middle age and beyond. As with other parts of the background discussion, I will leave the blow-by-blow account of the process to another time. Suffice it here to say that this intense discussion reveals a lot about the clients we work with.

Nowadays, not much surprises me. People (and our client executives are people too) come in all shapes and sizes and often have issues that they can't discuss with the boss or HR manager. They do, however, trust the sanctimony of our coaching relationship enough to reveal their problems to our coach. Often, that is sufficient to help them deal with the issues, and, if not, they can discuss sensitive matters with their life-experienced coach.

One of our clients—a young, intelligent, and svelte lawyer, has a debilitating and incurable disease, but she daren't admit it to her private-equity-owned company. Her bosses would see it as a weakness and she would risk dismissal.

Another, a very self-confident top executive in a Fortune Fifty corporation, has a son with a serious drug addiction. The son regularly accepted, or stole, money from our client to feed his habit. Eventually, our client had no option but to exercise tough love and deny his son the money he needed to

buy drugs. The son then held up some gas stations, equipped with a hand-gun. Eventually, the police caught him and he went to jail. That episode deeply affected our client's work performance. By sharing it with his coach and with me, we were able to work together to help our client without revealing this family problem, which would have deeply dented his ethical reputation.

Peder's potential

I am working right now with a difficult client from Sweden, called Peder. His business performs better than any other in his group. Peder is a rising star in the corporation—or he would be if he could communicate better by sharing with his peers and showing regard for the feelings of others who report to him. He is rude, dismissive, and uncooperative. When I faced him with these truths in a feedback meeting, he said, "I had no idea that I am like that. But to hell with them. My business is doing just great, and I don't really care." Interestingly, he and I had just had a probing background discussion. I had learned that his upbringing had been very difficult. "My father never told me that I did anything well. I never got praise for anything. All I ever got was, "Why could you not do better?"

In this discussion, Peder talked, reluctantly at first, but with increasing warmth, about his own family. His love for his wife and children shone on his face. His hard blue eyes softened in a tearful mist as he described the happy weekends that they enjoyed at their lakeside cabin. Here, it was clear to me, was a man who had answered rejection and criticism as a boy with a brittle veneer of indifference. The real Peder, the vulnerable and hurt little boy, showed itself only in the privacy of his family weekend retreats. "This," I thought, "is a man that I want to help."

Peder behaves much better in the company now, though it still seems a bit artificial as he learns new ways of opening up to others. He gives the appearance of having "ticked the box" on coaching without really endorsing it. He is now ready for a much bigger job, but his boss is reluctant to promote him until the change seems more genuine. The boss has just

asked me to extend our programme, hoping that Peder will demonstrate an authentic commitment to behavioural change in all his relationships on the business.

"Have we learned anything from this chapter?" asks MacMentor.

I think the lessons are as follows:

Most people are not as confident as they seem. They put up a front, which leads others to do the same, with all-round loss of quality relationship in organisations.

The most arrogant people are usually the most vulnerable and damaged of all and need the mature understanding of a trusted mentor.

The most assured-seeming executives may be hiding a dark secret that they dare not reveal to the corporation, but which, nevertheless, is affecting their contribution.

Don't wait until it is too late to offer experienced mentoring or coaching help. Offer some executive antifreeze now.

And don't, whatever you do, offer half a coaching solution. To save money, companies sometimes propose a short programme. That is a false economy—a "sticking plaster," non-sustainable solution that leaves the executive needing, and wanting, more.

What do you think the lessons are?

Dorotea—the role of communications

in leadership

The yellow brick road

It was a warm and balmy June evening in Geneva. American Citizens Abroad was staging its annual charity auction. The purpose was to help all those needy expats who were trapped between a plummeting US dollar salary and the soaring cost of living in Swiss francs (that is, almost the entire Geneva population of "taxed on worldwide income" Americans). I. J. Martin & Co Ltd, already an up-and-coming name in Geneva in executive circles, had donated a coaching programme to this worthy cause.

There I stood before them, one hand in my pocket, the other holding my notes, describing the delights of our services in a way that, I thought, embodied all the best practices in public speaking. I was wrong! Little did I know that this calm and peaceful scene was about to be violently disrupted. As the auction drew to a close, I left the room searching, as Scotsmen do, for the nearest bar. Suddenly, I was confronted by a blonde, blue-eyed human tornado. "Hello!" exclaimed the tornado as I rocked back on my heels. "My name is Dorotea!"

I was, all of a sudden, transported to *The Wizard of Oz* and 1939 Kansas. Dorothy (sounding remarkably like Judy Garland) was singing in

my head, "The wind began to switch, the house, to pitch, and suddenly the hinges started to pitch." Lowering my arms, which had been raised against pitching hinges and similar flying objects, I heard this supercharged Geneva version of Judy say, "I'm a professional actress, and I want to be a communications coach!"

Dorotea tells the story somewhat differently in her book. She writes, "As I started moving forward—it was as if part of me left my body and hovered above it, watching. I observed myself walk up to him, put out my hand, and say, "Hello, I'm an actress, and I'm wondering if your company could use a communications coach."

Her version sounds very nice, but I have witnesses to verify the human tornado. The floating out-of-body experience sounds credible, all the same, because Dorotea is a unique mix of 50 per cent Italian (the tornado-like energy bit), 50 per cent Swedish (the blonde, blue-eyed bit), and 100 per cent Buddhist (the serenely hovering above her body bit).

Looking around for flying broomsticks and wicked witches, my wary gaze settled once more on Dorotea, the human tornado. "Great!" I thought. "Here is the world's most energetic communications coach, and I'm speechless." Finally finding my voice, I said, "Well, you don't exactly fit our model of former CEOs as coaches. But you can try it out on me and our team first, and if it works, then maybe we could offer your communications coaching to some of our clients…maybe."

That, as they say, was the start of a beautiful friendship. We knew, of course, that an effective communication style was helpful, but over the years since, we have become committed to communication skills as being central to excellent leadership.

Communication is partly about being good at networking. Building bridges to others is an essential component of influencing skills. In today's three-dimensional, hollow-cube organisations, it is influencing, not autocracy, that allows leaders to lead effectively. And we don't have time for long conversations anymore. When was the last time you wrote an e-mail that was more than two hundred words, or a hundred kilobytes, long? Or

even twenty words? Life is too busy. We get too many e-mails and telephone calls. We attend too many (unnecessary) meetings. We really just have time for "elevator pitch" messages and thirty-second water-cooler conversations. We struggle to communicate too much, with too little time to do it.

Your whole life—in thirty seconds

In coaching meetings, I often say to my clients, "So, tell me about yourself...in thirty seconds." After four or five minutes of them rambling on, my eyes go all glassy and my attention starts to wander...and all I've heard is a boring dissertation on the client's work history. At this point, I interrupt and say, "Stop! That's your CV! I can read your CV! Tell me about you—what really matters to you? Do you have values? Do you have ethics? Do you have a partner in life? Do you have children? Do you have any ambitions beyond your job? Are any of these important to you? If yes, tell me about the real *you*!"

It is possible to say all this in thirty seconds. Try writing it down and see how long it takes. Your first effort may need ten minutes. But persevere—with practice, you will find that you can really give a comprehensive account of yourself in thirty seconds. You will get many opportunities to use this personal elevator pitch, sometimes in unexpected scenarios—in bars or golf-club changing rooms—often where the conversation is really an informal and well-disguised job interview or a sounding-out for a business opportunity. I must confess that most female executives and the occasional sub-alpha male offer more rounded thirty-second accounts the first time I ask them to. But the ones I describe above who only list their work history are typical. We've lost the art of communicating.

There was a time, not so long ago, that we scripted carefully worded, handwritten letters to friends and officialdom. They had to be well worded because we only got one chance. Delivery of snail mail took several days for letters within a country, and international airmail took far longer, You could even send an amphibious carrier pigeon from London to Hong Kong

in much less time than it took for a "slow boat to China" to carry your low-cost surface-mail letter.

"You've got mail!"

Now, of course, we have e-mail. I used to be an early adopter of technology. Back in the early 1980s, my company introduced internal e-mail. I thought it was brilliant! I could send a hundred Christmas greetings to colleagues in a few seconds, without getting writer's elbow and numb thumb as symptoms of excessive seasonal bonhomie. The responses should have been predictable, though I didn't see them coming. "Trust a Scotsman to find a money-saving way to send Christmas cards," was the gist of most of them. Not one congratulated me on my brilliant initiative. Corporate jealousy at its worst!

E-mail has become a tyrant. How many did you get this morning? How many of them evaded the spam filter and offered you discounted Viagra? You get what you pay for with discounted Viagra…"50 per cent less" means exactly that…in more than one way!

How many of today's e-mails were cover-my-ass copies, so their senders can say, "Well, I did tell you!" How many were truly needed, clear, crisp, unambiguous, and to the point? Not nearly enough, I'll bet! I'll even bet a bottle of Scotland's finest that most of them were too long, too short, unclear, or downright dangerous. The combination of fast communication and too little time to think often results in a downward spiral. One badly worded message can cause a negative reaction and a hastily typed angry response from you, which leads to an even angrier answer…and so on. Sometimes, when a client raises such an issue in a coaching meeting with me, I will ask, "Where does this other guy sit?" Mostly, he's just across the corridor or downstairs in marketing or in the next building. My highly paid advice then goes something like, "So why don't you just get off your seat and go talk to him face-to-face? You might enjoy the break, your hard-pressed chair will enjoy being seatless, and, you never know, something good might happen if management goes walkabout."

If it's too far to walk, just pick up the phone and speak to a real person, not a computer screen. I've even seen some offices in the United States (like GE's operation in Cincinnati) where people have to take a bicycle just to get to someone else's cubicle…under the same roof! Google has special Google Bikes in its Mountain View headquarters, which lends a new meaning to the phrase "business cycle."

Corporate affairs

Rambling back to my treatise on concise, effective communications, we really need more, not fewer, communication skills in the twenty-first century. A good place to start is with important e-mails.

Here's some really good advice from MacMentor on important e-mails:

"Don't enter the recipient's address until:

1. You've written the message,
2. Checked it,
3. Had it reviewed by a colleague, and
Slept on it."
MacMentor should have spoken to Charlotte.

A friend of mine, a young divorcee called Charlotte, had just embarked on a passionate new romance with a man who worked in accounting in the same corporation. You know what it's like in the first flushes of a new love affair. You think, act, and write e-mails like an imbecile. Actually, I'm being a little insulting to imbeciles. You pour your heart out to this "God of all that is wonderful in a man" and write the dumbest, most embarrassing things. But no matter; it will only be seen by the man of your dreams…unless you e-mail it, by accident, to the entire organisation of

three thousand people. It was the start of a beautiful love affair but the end of a wonderful career for Charlotte.

MacMentor repeats, "Don't ever address that important e-mail until you've gone through steps one through four. And then check, and check again, that the addressee is the intended recipient."

So far, I've only talked about e-mails, elevator pitches, and water-cooler chats because those are the main ways that we communicate these days. But the need for excellent communication goes way beyond such devices. Take investor relations, for instance. I've done this job three times.

It's fun! Part accountant, part marketer, part communicator, the investor-relations executive is a very important member of any publicly listed company or private-equity-owned entity. You need to be skilled at reading and interpreting numbers, so financial-management abilities are essential. You need to sell your corporation to analysts around the world…and they are all MBA graduates with twenty-something agile brains and no experience in business. You need to be good at marketing and selling because you're creating a desire in these twenty-something MBA minds to buy or recommend your equity. And you are facilitating the sale by conveying a sense of current and potential value in your stock. And, because all those skills are wasted in this job if you can't communicate them well, you will fail if you do not have them.

Investor-relations professionals, therefore, need to be excellent communicators. They are not the only ones. Anyone who works in public affairs, regulatory affairs, or corporate affairs (funny how many affairs you see in business, isn't it?) needs excellent communications skills too.

A UN organisation based in Geneva was electing a new director general. If you think that corporate politics are difficult, you should try the United Nations. Every donor country, albeit long on promises but short on delivery, was clamouring to get its own representative elected. The noise

was incredible. Eventually, a long shortlist was agreed upon, and a special UN committee gathered in New York to make the final choice. The final selection step for this UN organisation was a presentation to this committee. One candidate, a diminutive Asian, small of stature and quiet in voice, somehow scrambled himself onto the end of the list—candidate number fifteen, with no hope of success.

Until our human tornado Dorotea arrived on the scene!

This half-Italian, half-Swedish, 100 per cent Buddhist communications coach went into overdrive on articulation, voice projection, and content. Long story cut short, the "no chance" candidate got the job and became a highly effective director general for this important UN organisation.

So here is my big point about communications in business. Real leaders are people that others want to follow. They are real leaders if they first switch on the emotion and creativity parts of the brain. They dream up a vision. They articulate that vision, and they communicate that vision in a clear and compelling way that gets the power and energy of the team behind them.

Somebody in a conference that I attended in New York recently said, "A leader with only a vision is a dreamer. A leader with only a strategy is a worker. A leader with both vision and strategy is a real leader." I paraphrase, but you get the point.

MacMentor says, "Real leaders in any organisation have to be many things, but if they can't communicate effectively, their talents are hidden, their ideas are unheard, the power of the team is disengaged, and the entire organisation loses out."

His message to busy leaders is: Don't think, "I don't have time to learn how to be a good communicator." Instead, think, "I don't have time *not* to!"

Influencing

inside the Cube

A ring of grim-faced soldiers stood around me, assault rifles at the ready, as the rain poured down on their oilskin capes and heavy backpacks. One, the biggest and the baldest one who resembled a camouflage-painted King Kong, needed none of his fearsome weapons to scare me to death. One cold stare from him was enough to make me want to turn and run. That, however, was impossible, because I was knee-deep in sticky mud and surrounded by the lion-like roaring of sixty-four-ton armoured bulldozers, their 50 mm cannons waving just above my head.

This was real leadership in action. The commander-in-chief of the Swiss Armed Forces had invited a group of foreign executives and HR directors to a field demonstration and to discuss collaboration between the Swiss military and the world of business. Years ago, this would not have been necessary. The connections were clear to all and deeply rooted in Swiss society. An insightful book, called *Target Switzerland*, by American author Stephen P. Halbrook, describes the role that the Swiss militia plays in this small, politically neutral country which is surrounded on all sides by its much bigger neighbours. The legendary Swiss democratic system derives from the freedom of all individuals to choose how their politicians lead the country. Every

young man must undergo military training and keep his weapons at home. It was this "armed neutrality" that kept hostile Fascist forces at the Swiss borders for the six terrible years of the Second World War. Today, Switzerland, a stable and prosperous economy, depends no less on armed neutrality to preserve its unique business proposition to the world. It's not really about banking secrecy—that's been grossly exaggerated by jealous neighbours and politically ambitious American lawyers. It is much more about economic stability, sensible taxation levels, self-help attitude, and political neutrality. Yesterday, as I stood in that muddy field beside the Swiss commander-in-chief, Egypt's military leaders were deposing President Mursi in a "democratic coup." I couldn't imagine Korpskommandant Blattman deposing Swiss President Ueli Maurer, nor would it be necessary.

Today though, it is foreigners who often lead Swiss business, not Swiss nationals who have served shoulder to shoulder in the army. Most of them have never performed military service anywhere. In today's harsh global economy, it becomes a major question to release young male employees for extensive basic training and refresher courses each year. Non-Swiss business leaders don't "feel the tradition" and sometimes question the value of the Swiss militia.

The arguments posed by Mr. Blattman and his team are compelling. Training in military leadership closely parallels that in civilian life, though army training is more practical than theoretical. Technical skills, like those in the engineering battalion that we visited, are honed in the field in a demanding military environment. Less obvious, but even more telling, is the role of influencing skills in modern military leadership. The organisation chart may look like the traditional "tree," but it takes real leadership to get these young men to go out in the rain and mud to happily host a group of visiting executives. In the Swiss army, the language of leadership and building a real team comes in four varieties. Military service builds both verbal and non-verbal understanding across internal boundaries in this multilingual nation. In modern Switzerland, immigration has brought a flood of young second-generation foreign recruits who

cannot share the history and traditions of this ancient nation. In business, you can always fire an undesirable employee. In the Swiss army, you're stuck with them and you'd better find a way to get along with the troops. In armies round the world, it takes real leadership from the front, not an organisation chart, to get soldiers to "go over the top of the trench" and stare danger in the face.

The classic org chart

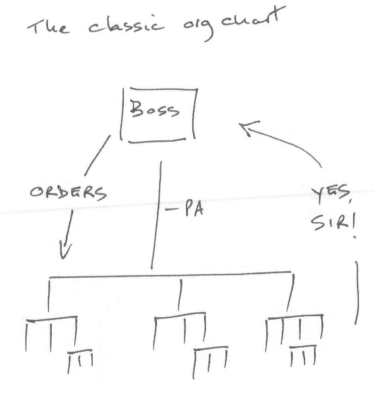

Every time someone shows the organisation, he or she produces a chart like a Christmas tree with many branches. The "angel" at the top of the tree is the big boss—the CEO. The functions and businesses beneath him, or her, are the candles—mere decorations to illuminate the "beauty" of the chief executive above. You can almost believe, because it used to be true,

that the CEO sits at the top of the organisation and issues orders to those on the lower branches. In turn, these people give out commands to those beneath them…and so it goes on, right down the organisation. Of course, that old model no longer exists, not in Germany, not in France, not in Switzerland, and much less than it used to in Asia.

Modern business thinkers talk about the matrix organisation. They imagine a two-dimensional rectangular organisation, with points of contact between people sitting at all points on each side.

The matrix organisation

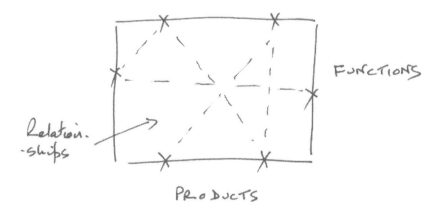

This model worked for a long time, but even that is no longer adequate to describe the twenty-first-century international corporation.

What we have now in most big businesses around the world is a "hollow-cube" structure.

The hollow-cube structure

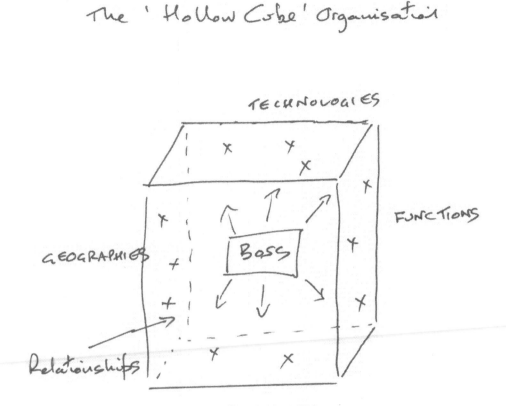

The 'Hollow Cube' Organisation

This is a three-dimensional model with multiple points of contact between people in any position within that hollow cube. The three dimensions are products, geographies, and functions.

How many corporations do you know which have multiple business divisions, within which sit manufacturing, marketing and sales, finance, HR, and other business functions? Expanding that structure to a multi-division corporation with presence in many countries means that you have relationships between divisions, between functions, between customers, and between a whole host of other interconnections. You can even argue that the modern global business model could have more, if it were possible, than three dimensions.

The fourth dimension - the organisational Rubik's Cube.

But even this hollow-cube concept does not really capture the enormously complex structures of mega-corps like Exxon Mobil, Nestlé and J.P. Morgan Chase. I checked Google to find a four-dimensional model to represent the biggest global organisations. When I got to the bit about hyperspheres, vectors and tesseracts, my mathematical courage failed me and I made a hasty retreat back to the safety of three dimensions. Here's a simple 3-D concept that I *can* grasp: some businesses are so big and complex that they comprise multiple hollow cubes, each with its own virtually independent leadership structures.

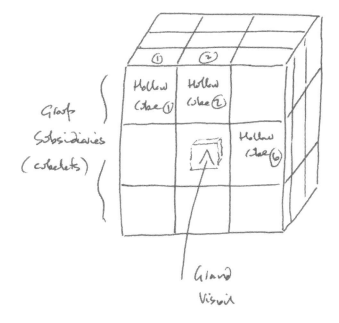

Have you ever played with a Rubik's Cube? Have you ever solved the puzzle? Well, clever you! Wikipedia says that there are only twenty six cubelets in a classic 'three by three' Rubik's Cube, but there are more than forty three quintillion possible permutations. How many zeros is that? If you are a maths genius who knows what a hypersphere is, then you've already said 'eighteen'. The rest of us are still writing it down and counting. Can you imagine the potential anarchy in a mega-corp with fifty, or even one hundred, highly-autonomous business units? Each one is a hollow cube with its own leadership team in its middle. But what stops the global mega-structure flying apart?

The answer is simple. All you have to do is take your child's favourite Rubik's Cube and prise the pieces apart. You will soon see, as well as your very upset Junior, a series of screws and springs that allow the cubelets to move around in all directions without detaching themselves from the Master Cube. At the very heart of the cube, you will then find a three-dimensional crucifix to which every piece is ultimately connected in a firm but flexible mechanical structure. And so it is with well-led mega-corps. Take them apart and you will find the 'screws' and 'springs' that bind each corporate entity into a cohesive whole; the policies, cultures and practices of the Global Corporation. There too, you will find the three-dimensional cruciform heart of the mega-corp; the charismatic leader and his, or her, Grand Vision. GE has its Jeff Immelt, Novartis has its Joe Jiminez and Unilever has Paul Polman with his Sustainable Living Plan…all vibrant demonstrations of the organisational Rubik's Cube in action.

Now the hollow cube and its even more complex big brother Rubik's Cube are a long way from the old structure that I called the Christmas tree. Clearly it is no longer possible for the CEO to sit in the corner office on the fifteenth floor of corporate HQ and tell everybody in that kind of organisation what to do. It just does not work. The poor old CEO may issue commands until he's blue in the face, but employees have a million ways to ignore him and do their own thing. They may appear to follow his

wishes, but people are very skilled at creating a facade, behind which they do exactly what they want until the boss comes to visit.

Now, there's a problem. If the CEO can't issue orders because nobody would obey them, how can he or she get things done in the corporation? This brings me to the one thing, above all others, that gets things done in a twenty-first-century hollow-cube organisation and in its big brother Rubik—and the thing that is central to real leadership—influencing skills.

Corporate politics

Many of my clients, including some very senior people, tell me, "I don't like organisational politics—I don't want to get involved in them." I tell them two things.

I say that "organisational" politics is not the same as "political" politics. The timescales, the levers of power, the objectives, and the mechanisms are different. "Politics" in an organisation is just a shorthand term for "managing interpersonal relationships to achieve specified objectives." The most effective tool for managing such relationships is a set of influencing skills. The scenarios and approaches are fundamentally no different if you are an executive in a $50 billion corporation, an army officer, or the president of your children's school board.

The second thing that I say to my clients is, "What do you mean, you don't want to get involved in politics? You don't have that choice. You are involved in the corporation's politics, whether you like it or not. The only choice you have is to use these politics for good purposes or for your own selfish agenda."

"So, since you are a decent person with admirable objectives for your company, do you think it would be a good idea to have a discussion on how to use politics for a good purpose? Shall we talk about influencing skills?"

It's a conversation that all the coaches in our team have with every client in Europe, the United States, and Asia, because, as I've argued elsewhere in

this book, we are fundamentally alike as business leaders, no matter where we are.

There are UN People… and real people

Ten years ago, I had a call from a very fine man… living proof that very many people really do care about others less fortunate. John, a doctor, ran a clinic with the help of his wife Shirley. The clinic was in a remote village in Bolivia, so remote that they had a two-day walk over mountains and through forest just to get to a road that would eventually take them to the capital city, La Paz. John and Shirley helped hundreds, perhaps thousands, of desperately poor people from the countryside and, along the way, adopted two tiny babies whose impoverished unmarried mothers had abandoned them at the gates of the clinic.

John worked in a United Nations organisation. Now there are two kinds of people in the UN. In Geneva and New York, I say that there are "real people" and UN people. If you want to check this out, just have dinner any night of the week in a restaurant on Second Avenue in New York, between Thirty-Fifth and Fifty-Fifth Streets. Or take the tram from Geneva's Cornavin Station to the Place de Nations in the UN Quarter. I don't mean to be disparaging about UN people. But, if you listen to their conversations, you will know what I mean. Whereas you or I from the world of business will think about stock price, market share, customers, and bottom lines, they have quite different interests and objectives. With UN people, the bottom line is not dollars and cents, but human lives.

UN people themselves divide into two distinct sorts. There are truly dedicated, altruistic people who spend much of the time in the field, in dangerous situations, doing nasty work that you or I would avoid at all costs. They spend the rest of their time at HQ, doing tedious administration and fighting for funding that the donor countries are delighted to promise in front of the cameras, but somehow find it hard to deliver when it's needed.

The other kind of UN people are also dedicated—but not to mankind. Their devotion is to their own agenda, their ideas, and career. Organisational politics is at its fiercest in altruistic organisations. You think you have a tough time with your CEO or the board? Try working in the UN or the Vatican or in your local parent-teacher committee. You haven't lived until you've "enjoyed" one of those experiences!

So John, doing his truly dedicated work with Shirley in that remote village in Bolivia, received a summons to take on a senior management role as head of a public health function at head office in Geneva—thousands of miles, and several worlds, away from that little clinic in the Andes. Grumbling, but obedient to the call, John and Shirley packed all their possessions and the adopted babies and set off on foot and by donkey and chicken-crowded bus and jet plane to Switzerland.

All went well for a while. John ran his department efficiently, and his people loved him as their leader. His effectiveness spread in ripples from Geneva around the world as his work helped, not thousands as in Bolivia, but hundreds of thousands on every continent. John was very happy, productive and, he believed, not involved in the politics of that well-known organisation.

This is where I came in. John had just received a highly desirable job offer that absolutely appalled him. The director general wanted him to be her special adviser in the DG's private office. John engaged me as his mentor to discuss this terrible prospect.

"It's a purely political job," he exclaimed. "I don't want to be involved in politics. I'd rather stay where I am helping save hundreds of thousands of lives!"

"You don't have that choice," I told him. "You're already involved in politics—you just don't know it."

"Here is the only choice you have," I went on. "You can take on this job and apply your talents and experience to saving millions of lives, or you can decline the invitation and deny your skills to many around the world that desperately need them."

"Not only that," I concluded "if you don't take the job, you leave the way open for the other candidate to take it. You know what a schemer and politician he is. He will force his own agenda on the DG and persuade her that it's a good one, and you know that it's really just designed to increase his own importance in the organisation."

"Here's your choice. You can seize this chance to help millions of people, or you can let the opportunity slip away forever."

John and Shirley discussed it intensely that weekend. By Monday morning, John had realised the chance he had to "make a difference to the world" by his experienced and judicious counsel to the director general. He could see that, by refusing that chance, he would allow a self-centred opportunist to block the position for years.

John called me the next day. "I get the point. I am involved in politics. I just don't know how to handle them." John and I then worked together on his influencing skills, applying the principles to discussions about a number of real-life situations. The more he practiced, the better he got.

Ten years later, John is still the highly esteemed, wise counsel in that organisation, guiding and supporting a succession of directors general in their good works around the world.

Funny how, in our coaching firm which helps business executives earn ever more profit and bigger bonuses, the thing that most excites our coaches is the chance to grow the "bottom line" of human lives in that organisation and others like it!

THE UPSIDE-DOWN

Organisation Chart and Wobbly

Bottoms

Management 1.0.1

D o you remember the concept of servant leadership from your Management 1.0.1 lessons?

Servant leadership means exactly that—the CEO exists to serve the organisation, which exists to serve the customer. An American Civil War principle for cavalry commanders said, "Feed your horses, then feed your men, then feed yourself."

Lincoln's hundred horses

I came across this story in General Colin Powell's excellent and highly readable book, *It Worked for Me*. I think about the story every time I see some greedy top executive filling his or her pockets with excessive bonuses at the expense of the shareholders, on the grounds that he or she is "special."

President Abraham Lincoln was sitting at a military telegraph office outside Washington when a message arrived from the battlefield. Confederate cavalry had surprised a Union camp in Virginia and captured a brigadier general and a hundred horses. Lincoln slumped in his chair and exclaimed, "Sure hate to lose those one hundred horses!"

"What about the brigadier general?" asked the telegraph operator.

"I can make a brigadier general in five minutes, but it is not easy to replace one hundred horses," responded Lincoln.

Colin Powell writes about his military days: "My job as a leader was to take care of the 'horses,' get the most out of them and ensure they were all pulling in the direction I wanted to go." Making sure, Powell added, that there were always people ready for promotion to brigadier general in his place.

Coaches support wobbly bottoms

The idea of the servant leader is very simple—the old treelike organisation chart no longer exists. The servant-leader model is an upside-down triangle. At the top of the organisation are those without whom a business would not survive—the customers.

Just beneath them are the good people in your organisation who exist to support your customers: sales, marketing, customer service, invoice clerks, despatch teams, warehouse staff, and others. If they don't do their jobs right, you won't have customers for long, will you? And then you won't have a business!

Under those are all the others who exist only to serve those key people—the support staff. That includes all the administrative folks, like accountants, HR, facilities management, and others whose sole purpose is to make sure that the customer-facing guys are well equipped to serve the top line.

And, under all of those is the man, or woman, who exists (whether he or she believes it or not) to serve the entire organisation—the CEO!

Now that's a rather radical idea, even today—even if we first heard it back in early-1980s management classes. It looks like this:

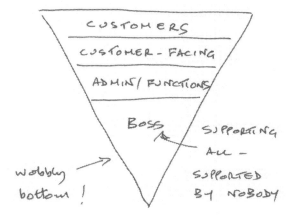

THE SERVANT- LEADER ORGANISATION

(UNSTABLE)

But here's where my own thinking goes a step further. Does anything strike you about the structure above? Yes, it makes sense. But it looks very unstable—it might fall over at any time, as soon as you apply some pressure to it, doesn't it? So what, or who, is it that is missing?

Here's a modified version that looks a whole lot more able to withstand the stresses and strains of modern business life:

THE SERVANT- LEADER ORGANISATION

(STABILISED)

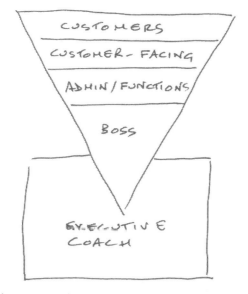

Yes, the poor old CEO at the bottom of the pyramid needs some support to make him or her strong enough to support everyone else in this organisation—an objective, external executive coach.

And that's the end, for now at least, of my elevator pitch for executive coaching.

Coming up now -
dangerous dining,
Dongguan style…

Burger Bradley's

Foreign Adventure

Don't ask, don't tell Asian-style

"What's this, then?" asked Brad. He had speared an elongated, brownish object on his fork. It was about three inches long and half an inch thick with a bulbous, purple-coloured end. The object was glistening in the dim electric light in a slimy sort of way.

"It's a...it's a kind of meat," I answered euphemistically, thinking back to my early days in France, when a waiter described the "andouillette" on my plate (a bunch of sautéed pig's intestines) as a "meat sausage."

Poor Bradley was struggling with the local culture. We were in Dongguan in Guangdong Province, in the Pearl River Delta of southern China. Brad had rarely travelled out of Illinois, though he had gone abroad several times to Iowa, Ohio, and Indiana. Brad's favourite food at home was burgers and fries, and when he took his wife and kids out to dinner, their preferred venue was McDonald's. Occasionally, for health reasons, they gave up red meat and ate Kentucky's finest fried chicken—with fries.

I had met Brad in Hong Kong at the old Kai Tak airport. He had been scared to death when the plane headed straight for Lion Rock before

making a sharp right into its final flight path. Seconds later, he had looked out the plane window and met eyes with a T-shirted Chinese man who was cooking rice in his fifth-floor, neon-lit kitchen. Brad's plane then landed with a bump and a screech of brakes as it halted just yards from the murky waters of Victoria Harbour.

Brad was in shock when we left the terminal and took our places in the endless line at the steaming-hot, noisy taxi rank. We took a taxi to the border at Lo Wu, on our way over to Shenzhen in the pre-handover, real China. Passing quickly through customs and immigration formalities with Brad's shiny new blue passport, we walked briskly down the sun-baked city street, accompanied by a ragged little boy who gripped a hole-filled umbrella. This local urchin, despite my several attempts at dismissing his services, insisted on shading us from the hot sunshine all the way to our waiting company people-carrier.

This was the "Wild East" in early-1990s China. "Don't make eye contact with anyone!" I told Brad. "Just walk fast and get to our meeting point as soon as we can." Paying off our walking sunshade with a handful of renminbi, we boarded our chauffeur-driven van.

Highway to hell

"This is going to be a long and bumpy ride," I told Brad. "They haven't finished building the new expressway yet. They don't have any police on the road, but there have been many hijackings. Our driver's probably got a gun in the car," I told him, "but keep your eyes wide open for someone overtaking us and pushing us into the side of the road."

"The penalty for murder is death by hanging, if they catch them," I explained. "But they get the death sentence for highway robbery, too, so they usually just shoot you so there are no witnesses." I was exaggerating a little, but not too much, to tease Brad. He was looking quite at ease, it so happened. "Not much different from Chicago, then," he said.

We set off on our five-hour journey to the company's operations in Dongguan. We bumped into huge potholes and crawled along muddy

streets through decrepit-looking villages. We passed ragged farmers and their families, bent stiffly over their rice planting. Their dilapidated homes, made of bamboo frames and plastic bin-liners, starkly contrasted with the shiny, new mirror-glassed electronics factories standing side-by-side with their tiny fields. We passed huge tracts of red-clay, bulldozed land in which here and there, perched high on a lonely pinnacle of earth, was the house of some farmer who had refused to sell his little plot of land. In one village, we skirted an overturned truck, painted in the ubiquitous faded Chinese blue colour, out of which, staring wide-eyed at the sky, hung the body of the young driver. A few villagers walked around it, gazing with mild interest at the body, but didn't do anything about it. We avoided numerous elderly peasants, wearily pushing handcarts loaded with boxes and crates, along the wrong side of the highway. Finally, we reached our destination, just in time for lunch.

After a cursory identity check by skinny security guards with dark-blue uniforms two sizes too big for their bodies and teeth three sizes too big for their mouths, we entered the compound. It was huge—big enough to house forty thousand people—and complete with canteens, shops, cinemas, discotheques, a school, and a medical centre. It sounded like paradise for these Chinese immigrant workers, until we saw their dormitories—concrete floor, cement walls, no heating or air conditioning, and iron bunks arranged in tiers of four against each wall. During the long, humid Pearl River summers and the short but cold and damp winters, these seemed like miserable conditions. Until you realised that all this was indeed a paradise for those young girls from far-away Chinese villages. They were working in our factory only long enough to earn a dowry and go home to marry a nice local boy. They were indeed, in those days of female infanticide, just lucky to be alive.

Dining in Dongguan

Brad and I made our way, under polite but careful guidance, to the VIP suite for lunch. Spread before us was a feast for twenty people. Rice,

noodles, pak choi, beef in clay pots, chicken legs, chicken feet, chicken wings—in fact every part of the chicken except the best bits from the breast. (I've always wondered if Chinese chickens actually have breasts, because I've never seen any on my plate. Have you?) All was artfully arranged on large oval plates. We sat down and picked up our chopsticks. At Brad's panicky expression, a fork silently appeared by his side and we started eating.

"So what exactly is this, then?" repeated Brad, as he stared at the long, brown object on his fork.

"It's a bull's penis," I said.

"It's a what?…What…what did you say?" stuttered Brad.

"It's a bull's penis," I repeated. "When they have too many male calves, they de-sex them. You do that in the United States too. Have you never heard of prairie oysters?"

"Yeah," said Brad, "but I never ate any. What are they?"

"Back in the old Wild West days," I explained, "cowboys used to castrate young bulls to keep the numbers down. They cut the 'prairie oysters' off the bull and popped them straight into the frying pan, two by two. Nowadays they go straight to the meat factory to make sausages."

"No way!" said Brad, with a look of utter disbelief.

"Check it out," I replied. "What do you think goes into your low-cost burgers—prime beef?"

By now, Burger Brad was looking askance at his fork, holding what was, in truth, just a very large, brown Chinese mushroom with a thick stem and a wider top section.

"Eat it up—it's protein," I advised Brad. "Here in China, they say that they eat everything with four legs, except the table…and often with eight legs or a hundred legs or no legs at all."

Brad's grimace reminded me of when I was a "new boy" in China. My Chinese colleagues and I often ate out in a local restaurant—one of those huge places with five thousand seats and old ladies shuffling around with dim-sum carts as they tinkled bells to get your attention. We usually ordered roast pigeon, and it would arrive brown and glazed and elegantly

spread out on its back, its breasts neatly sliced, its wings extended wide and its head turned to one side, as if to avoid looking at the open mouths of its immediate future.

"You should eat the head. You're our honoured guest, and it's the best part," invited my companions. In Hong Kong back then, to be the "honoured guest" meant that you picked up the bill at the end. Politely, I declined their generous offer. This little scene repeated itself every week for about three months. Finally, one day, I looked around the table at my Chinese friends and asked, "If the pigeon's head is so delicious, why don't you ever eat it?"

They looked at each other right and left and, in perfect unison, exclaimed, "Oh nooooo! That's disgusting!"

I never trusted them again. And now here I was, doing the same nasty trick in reverse to Burger Bradley.

"Eat it, Brad" I said. "It's only a mushroom. I was just kidding you. But," I continued, "I've seen people round here eat deep-fried cockroaches and beetles and snakes. Now, you should try snake. It's quite good—a bit like chicken, actually."

Brad put down his fork and left the table, heading for the VIP toilet. I never saw him again after that trip, but I'm willing to bet that he never again ate a sausage or a burger, much less a prairie oyster.

"So," asks MacMentor rhetorically, "what three things can we learn from the story?"

First, learn to use chopsticks. You'll be so busy trying to eat slippery mushrooms that you won't have time to think what else it might be.

Second, when in Rome, do as the Romans do. But keep your wits about you, all the same.

Finally, never judge something, or someone, on first appearances. The reality may be somewhat different.

EXCEL LEADERSHIP—

Starting at the

Wrong Place

No budget, no problem!

I came up the finance route, though I had a few formative diversions into new ventures and non-executive roles along the way. I was kind of an oddball accountant, because I was not fixated on budgets. In my very early career, I had worked with a COO called Alex who, beneath his gruff exterior, was a rather nice man. He had, sadly, an unfortunate physical feature—a stiff upper lip and a highly flexible lower one. It was, as they said on the shop floor, a mouth shaped for saying "No"…and Alex exercised it in this way at every opportunity.

Alex was one of those interesting people that you meet in wage bargaining. Another one was Ernie. Ernie the Engineer entertained us all during the annual three-day, five-star negotiating holiday that was obligatory before the trade unionists would sign up to the new deal. When their appetites for Michelin meals and Cuban cigars had been sated, and when our man Alex had uttered his last "No," he and the full-time union official would feel the need to visit the toilet, after which they had a quick "corridor meeting" and agreed to settle the offer. Ernie the Engineer, meanwhile, with a serious face and his tongue entangled in his teeth, would lisp malapropisms such as, "Someone is making allegations about my members, and when I get the alligators responsible…"

Ernie always reminded me of Sean, an Irish engineer colleague from a long time back in my accounting career. Sean once announced to our monthly management meeting that he had been negotiating hard with a vendor company. "It was tough. They were offering us a 10 per cent discount," said Sean with great pride. "But I beat them down to 5 per cent."

I never forgot Alex's mouth that was shaped for saying "no." In my later financial management career, I would see its image every time someone proposed an expenditure for which there was no budget. I would say, "Well, we have no budget for that, but let's find a way to say 'yes.'" If the proposition would make money, that mattered more to me than budgets.

And now, from my coach's seat, I see many managers running their businesses "by the numbers." This is as close to the art of leadership as painting by numbers is to creating a Rembrandt masterpiece.

Excel leadership is not excellent leadership!

People and leadership stand alongside money as today's factors of production. Money and machines don't get things done in business—only *people* can achieve results!

A leader, by definition, is just someone that others want to follow…and who wants to follow a walking, talking spreadsheet? Ideas, not numbers, excite people! Too many leaders in business today are "left-brained leaders." Many managers start in the wrong place with an excellent numbers-rich strategic plan. But how does that excite a team and get its commitment to success? Just think how businesses in general do their annual planning. We start with market data, current year's numbers, the board's share-enhancing ambitions, and the CEO's pet objectives.

Wrong!

Visionary leaders

We must get people engaged! The best way I know is to start with vision—a clear and compelling vision that excites people and gets them behind the leader. Think of some of these great leaders in history—Hannibal, Cleopatra,

Alexander the Great, Boudicca, Jesus Christ, Golda Meir, Buddha, Gandhi, Rosa Parks, Ho Chi Minh, Joan of Arc, Martin Luther King Jr., Genghis Khan, Margaret Thatcher, Lee Kwan Yew—even Adolf Hitler (though he failed the test of worthy objectives)...the list goes on. They all had one thing in common. They had a clear, imaginative, and attractive vision that got people excited. This vision took people past the limits they set for themselves— into territory they'd never believed possible. The leader outlined how they could, together, achieve something glorious. He or she engaged the power of the people in formulating a plan that would get them there and led from the front all the way through. None of that was about numbers, and none of these leaders had ever heard of a spreadsheet.

The role of vision in business leadership

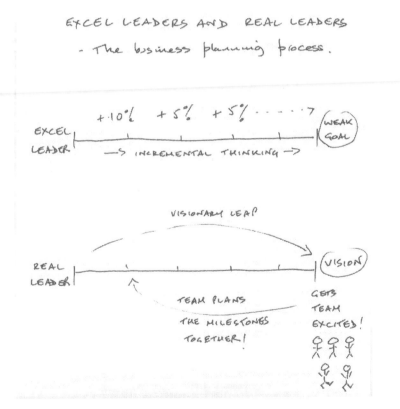

113

The power of the people

Back in the early 1980s, when I was a young chief accountant in a large pharmaceutical company, I found myself in charge of the worst performing finance and IT department in the entire worldwide group. Even worse, it was located in UK's Merseyside, when left-wing militancy was at its worst. The previous finance boss had ruled by fear, and, of course, had gone on to greater things in the company.

The staff members had no self-confidence at all. Now I was not the best accountant or IT guy in the world—far from it. But I could see, as the new boss, that the people had the potential to be much better. I told them:

"You're no worse than anyone else in this company. In fact, I believe that this department can actually be the best in the group and we can serve as a global role model. You have the intelligence, the experience, the energy, and the desire. All you need is to believe that you can do it. My job is to provide the right direction and the resources we need."

It took a few months to completely shake off the inertia and engender some real excitement. But in less than two years, that finance and IT function had routinely become first to finish monthly performance reports, first to complete annual budgets, and first to finish the year-end accounts. We went on to devise a group-wide supply-chain management system, an effective multidisciplinary cost-reduction group, and daily line efficiency reports. We became the first to use e-mail as a business tool. I made sure that the company recognised their efforts. One of my proudest moments was when they all resigned en masse from the trade union, saying, "Why should we pay these union dues, when the boss looks after us better than the union does?"

This team had many proud successes after that—all I did was see the possibilities, help them believe they could do it, and show the way to success. That, I think, is what real leaders do. All the spreadsheet stuff that follows is just the mechanics of doing business.

Bill the Bully—perceptions, reality, and real leadership

"He's brutal with his team, and he's rude to his peers."

That was my introduction to Bill, my new client-to-be. I met him at his company HQ in Switzerland. True—Bill was a big, rough, tough, and scary guy from Australia who was running an Asian business team out of Singapore. He was not just scary to me, but highly resistant to coaching. Usually, I would discuss our kind of coaching with potential clients for an hour. If they were still unconvinced by then, I would give up. "You can lead a horse to water," goes the old saying, "but you can't make it drink." Or as some Americans say, "You can take a guy to the fence, you can tell him it's electrified, but some guys still have to pee on it themselves to understand."

But something about this rough, tough Aussie made me persevere. And, after another hour, Bill conceded. "OK, let's give it a go, but if you're wasting my time, I'll soon tell you."

Good enough for me! Now here's what happened: I interviewed Bill's boss. I sensed that the boss was somewhat afraid of him, though he would never admit it. I interviewed his peers and learned that this Aussie guy, finding himself in a rather gentrified, politicised British business culture, had adopted a protective shell of aggression and abruptness as a defensive measure. I interviewed his "brutalised" Asian direct reports and enjoyed an interesting lesson in cultural stereotyping.

Culture coaching and funny ticks

"In Asia," the culture-coach experts tell us, "You have to be very polite and indirect. You must realise that Asians hate to lose face when you challenge them too hard. They also hate to say 'no.'"

Flora, the teacher at my Mandarin night school in Hong Kong, echoed this when she told our class, "We Chinese don't know how to say 'no,'"… inviting my instant response, "Well, maybe that's why you have so many babies, then!" A wintry Beijing stare ensued. No sense of humour, these Chinese! Flora once confused the class (even more than it was already) by

talking about "funny ticks." We thought that she meant those little strokes you write above Chinese words to tell you to make your voice go up, down, or sideways with intonations. Flora, with her strong Beijing dialect, was actually referring to "phonetics."

I once got into trouble when I was speaking at a coaching conference in Zürich (I don't do that anymore—all these nice, caring, "coachy" people can be absolutely savage when it comes to peer-reviewing one of their own). I said something innocent, such as, "When I was a CEO in China, I found Chinese guys who were more like me than my own brother in Scotland."

Wow, did the room erupt! Cries of outrage and derision emanated from all four corners of the room! One well-upholstered American lady who worked as a culture coach but had probably never been closer to China than San Francisco, said loudly from the back row, "Don't go there, Iain. Don't go there!"

My response, which I thought then was utterly devastating but, with hindsight, was pretty weak, was, "Well, who am I to comment, but actually I've already been there."

I worked for a Chinese company, on local contracts, for six years. I was in a totally Chinese environment for three years and ran a company in Dongguan for a while—just two thousand Chinese and me. I knew many Chinese people who shared the same personal values, had the same thoughts about business, and generally seemed very similar to me in many ways. (I do, however, have to question the inventiveness of a country where the staple food is rice…and which created chopsticks to eat it with.)

By contrast, my Scottish brother is a schoolteacher. He works as a dedicated school headmaster who lives, breathes, and dreams education and has never worked anywhere outside his native land. We were close as boys and have stayed close since, but our career paths and our experiences have gone in different directions. As I said, some Chinese are more like me than my own brother is.

All that culture-coaching stuff derives from reality but is only half true. It ignores the fact that these Asians have been to American colleges, watched Hollywood movies and western television, and have adapted considerably to the western world through centuries of colonial occupation and American domination of global business. They are, if you will forgive the gross generalisation, much more pragmatic and flexible than the textbooks tell us.

As one of our more strategic HR clients says, "I have met plenty of coaches who tell us how different other cultures are, but never one who says how similar they can be." No fees in that, I guess! It's a great subject—the tension between national culture and corporate culture. I've discussed this turbulent confluence of two great forces in business in another chapter.

Perceptions, reality, and real leadership

So, as I was saying about Bill the Bully, my Aussie client. When I interviewed these "delicate" Asian direct reports for feedback on Bill, they told me that he had very big ambitions for their business.

"Bill asks us to achieve highly ambitious targets. He sets demanding deadlines. He makes us believe we can meet them and beat them. But, we're not half-proud when we succeed."

"We've learned that we are better than we thought we were," they went on. "And, when things go wrong, Bill takes all the blame. But when things go right, he gives us all the credit."

"We love Bill—he's the best boss in this company!"

In my view, that's real leadership! Bill did not need to be a better leader than he was already. He just needed to stop scaring his bosses and being rude to his peers. He needed to believe in himself as much as he believed in his team.

In our coaching programme, Bill and I found ways together to build his self-belief and to understand that what had shaped his past had no relevance to the present-day. We worked on ways to change his

outward style, to change the general perception of "a rude Aussie who is brutal to his staff." Perceptions take much longer to change than behaviours, but coaching can support a proactive exercise in perception change.

Bill was so successful in this that, from being a non-runner in every succession plan, his name came top, or second, on the list for every promotional opportunity in the group. The company soon (too early) stopped paying for his coaching support and later, under severe pressure, Bill briefly reverted to his old style. His name disappeared again from the promotion list.

I am glad to report, however, that he soon remembered his coaching lessons, recovered humbly and gracefully, and is now firmly back in the global succession plan.

Excel leadership is *not* "excellent leadership." Real leadership is about waking up at four in the morning with an exciting idea for what might be possible for the business. It's about listening to what your heart and your creative right brain are telling you when your left brain has gone to sleep. It's about telling that vision in a way that gets the team excited and, together, with all the combined energy of the group, devising plans and implementing the vision in a coherent and ambitious strategy."

Visionary leadership—a true story

A key skill of real leadership, and of storytelling, is to take two or three unconnected ideas or themes and weave them into a cohesive, meaningful legend. Here is a true story about visionary leadership in a successful global industrial group based in Europe.

Frank, a member of the executive board, was responsible for corporate strategy. In this role, he was able to take the bird's-eye view of the whole business and was not immersed in the daily pressures and constraints of running a business division. In his early forties, he was learning to become a real leader. His conversations were changing from "I" and "me" to "we" and "us."

Frank conceived an idea, an exciting vision, for the group. By grouping together elements of other business divisions that served the same customers, he thought that they could create a new business. This business would offer a better buying experience. The customer would then have access to a smooth supply chain. It would also create a shared pool of technical experience and knowledge—valuable intelligence that had previously stayed in divisional "silos" that addressed only their own businesses and which did not work across boundaries with others in the group.

This new idea also could lead to significant cost savings in organisational synergies and in greatly enhanced job satisfaction for people in each business. Frank created a vision of an $8 billion business that would secure the loyalty of customers, take bigger market share, and expand the global market itself. It promised incremental growth on the top, middle, and bottom lines.

Very soon, Frank sold his vision and its detailed strategy to the executive committee, the group board, analysts, investors, and, most critically, the team. Three years later, it is fulfilling its performance promises; it's the biggest star in the group and engages the most committed energetic team of people in the business. Frank's vision, and his subsequent leadership of the new business division, has added huge value to his company and his own career. This morning, the board announced Frank's promotion to the role of group CEO of his $50 billion global business.

Managers and leaders

It's been said that managers do things right and leaders do the right things; that managers see "what is" and leaders see "what might be." All that is true. Good managers carry out orders from the top in an efficient way. Leaders do the right things, but the skill of leadership is in knowing what is the right thing to do.

The author John Steinbeck once said that the hardest thing about writing is "breaking the spell of the blank page." Leaders in CEO roles start every day with a blank page. The ability to break that spell, to imagine

something new and impossible for the business, to spell it out and get the power of the people behind it, and to show the way to success—that is real leadership!

MacMentor says, "The lesson is—push away the spreadsheet, switch off the laptop, put aside your preconceived ideas of what is possible, listen to what your customers want, and dream a little. Sell your dream from the heart and let the people turn your vision into value for your business, for your customers, and for all those who hold stakes in your company."

Press on for "Powerful Partnerships"…

Partners Pulling

Together

Powerful partnerships

A doctor once asked his ninety-five-year-old patient, "How do you feel when you wake up in the morning?"

"Increasingly surprised," replied the patient.

Life is about the only thing that is totally a one-way bet. You're going to die; I'm going to die; we're all going to die at some point. The only variables are when and the path we take towards that end. Life, as we live it, is a challenge. We face a constant stream of hurdles. We do whatever we can to make the way smooth by ourselves, but it sure is good to have a partner to help. And, naturally, your partner gains from having a partner too. It's a symbiotic, mutual-help relationship...and that's just as true of personal relationships (no matter what combination of religions or genders is involved) as it is in business relationships.

I often say to client executives, "You don't stop being a husband/wife and a family person when you leave home in the morning, and you don't stop being a business executive when you go home at night." Your life partner is as much a partner in your business success as your deputy, your

team, your peers, and your boss are partners in your home life. We need each other, and we should help each other.

But how often does this partnership go wrong—and why?

The seven-year itch

"The seven-year itch" is a figurative way of saying that, at some point in time, when the honeymoon and the first flushes of hormone-driven love are over, we often start to focus on all the negatives and not enough on the positives. We see readily what is not perfect and we take for granted all that is good about our partner. Then we might look for a better alternative—as if the grass on the other side of the fence is always greener…

Isn't that so in business as well as in private life?

Life is a constant challenge, and we need our partners' help to get to our final destination as smoothly, successfully, and as rewardingly as possible. You need many partnerships in business. You need a partnership with every person who works for you and with you. You need one with your boss, the boss's boss, and the organisation. Isn't it important to do what it takes to make those partnerships work?

Imagine this scenario. You and a friend are on a walking expedition. You're going to walk together to the north pole, with no support team and with all your supplies on a sledge that you will pull along behind you. Off you head out over the ice, dragging your supplies together.

A burden shared is a burden halved! You marvel at the beauty of the sparkling ice floes and stare at the dazzling fireworks of the aurora borealis. Each day, you boldly pull your sledge together over the icy ridges and through deep snowdrifts. What a wonderful thing it is to have a partner to share this with!

But after a few days, you begin to feel that you're doing most of the heavy pulling and that your partner is slacking. This insidious thought grows stronger with each new day until, at last, you begin to believe that you might be much better off without your partner.

But wait! You're a long way from your destination and even further from home. Can you really pull that sledge by yourself? Do you trust your

own navigation, or do you need your partner to check your calculations? Is it not warmer inside the tent at night with two bodies huddled together? What are your choices—ditch your partner or make the partnership work?

In that scenario, the conclusion is obvious. But in business life and in personal life, is it any different? It's not nearly as easy as we think to terminate a partnership, be it a working or a life partnership. There is no guarantee that going it alone, or finding a new partner, will be better than the status quo. Does it not make sense, then, to do your best to make the current partnership work?

Making balanced decisions

What can we do to make it work? Here's a first step to truly appreciate what you already have. Indeed, I find this a handy and simple way to clarify issues of all sorts and then rationalise my decision. It helps me focus on the forgotten positives as much as on the obvious negatives of a situation. As an accountant by training, I like the balance-sheet approach to decision-making.

BALANCED DECISION-MAKING

POSITIVES		NEGATIVES	
	10		8
	7		5
	8		5
	4		3
			1
	29	Net Satisfaction = 7 = 25%	29

I draw a horizontal line across the top of a piece of paper and bisect it with a vertical line down the full length of the page. My old textbooks used to call this "the 'T' account." I head up the left-side column with the word "positives" and the right-side column I label "negatives." Then, I list all the positive and negative aspects in their respective columns. Try it for yourself. The negative side may be much easier for you to do than the positive side. When you are listing the positives, think hard about all the qualities that you once valued in your partner and ask yourself, "Does this person still possess these qualities? Have I become blind to them? Am I taking my partner for granted?" There's a pretty good chance that, if you give this exercise some decent thought, the positives will outnumber the negatives.

What if there are more negatives than positives, though? Ask yourself, "Are both sides equally balanced?" Look again at all the items listed in each column and select the most important one. It can be on either side...it doesn't matter. You can then do a simple "weighting" exercise to clarify the outcome. This is quite literally getting things in proportion.

First allocate a score of "ten" to the most important item on your list. Then consider each of the others, relative to this one, and allocate each one a score from "one" to "nine." You then have a balance sheet with a number value against each item. Now add up all the positive and negative scores and see how the total looks. The balancing figure is the value of your aggregate satisfaction, or dissatisfaction, with your partner. You can even express this as a percentage of the total, to see, in relative terms, the size of that gap.

Ask your partner to do the same exercise, independently, about you. When he or she has finished, it's time to get that bottle of red wine from the cellar, and two glasses, and sit down to talk it through. "Marry in haste, repent at leisure," goes the old saying. It's essential to pick your partner wisely in business and in life. But, once you do, it really helps to lift your eyes from everyday irritations and take the bird's-eye view of your partnership from time to time.

Happiness defined

I once read somewhere—I forgot where—the definition of happiness. Happiness = reality/expectation.

If reality exceeds expectation with a result of 1.1 or more, you are happy. If, however, reality is less than expectation, scoring 0.9 or less, you are unhappy.

This, incidentally, emphasises the importance of managing expectations in leadership, in business, and in life. It is always essential to under-promise and over-deliver. (Try Amazon.com's customer service to see a supreme example of this in action.)

My partner and I founded I. J. Martin & Co Ltd fifteen years ago. The scenario was so unlikely in several ways that our expectation was low. We survived the first five, dangerous, "new business" years; we then made it through another five years of difficult business conditions; and then we persevered through yet another five years in a recessionary global climate.

We often have what I prefer to call "creative tension" moments, which our excellent website designer and other creative helpers find highly amusing. We're having one today, as we debate the style of a promotional campaign for our Asian business. But after all the shouting, we end up with something that resembles neither of our own preferences, but is usually much better for the experience. It works because, in the many calmer moments, our value of what we each bring to the business far outweighs our disagreements. We sometimes scratch our heads in surprise that it has all worked out, but we have happily sustained our business since 1998 through our appreciation of the other and what we each bring to the partnership.

"So," MacMentor advises, "whenever you question the value of your business/life partner, or when you have a decision to make where the outcome is not obvious, draw up a little balance sheet for all the pluses and minuses…and take the appropriate action."

Planning for partnerships—a strategic approach to long-term living

"The only things certain in life," said Benjamin Franklin, "are death and taxes."

I can't argue with either of those, though some of the Top One Per Cent and the Fortune One Hundred corporations try pretty hard to avoid the taxes. What are far less sure about death than they used to be are the "how" and the "when." I'll leave the "how" for another time when I want to write about executive health (not in the mood today—after a twelve-day tour of Asian business hotels, I really struggled with my weekend jog along the Zürich lakeside last Sunday morning).

The "when" is a very different thing from twenty or thirty years ago. A few days back, we passed the fiftieth anniversary of my own father's death at age forty-eight (from "west-of-Scotland disease"…a high-fat diet and unfiltered cigarettes). Back in 1963, I actually thought he was quite old. The age of his demise was far from unusual back then. But nowadays, people are living active and useful lives long after official retirement. I ask my clients to plan to live to at least age one hundred and five. As in their business lives, I get them to take a visionary strategic view of life planning. This approach has many benefits, but it also highlights the risks inherent in any long-term partnership, be it business or personal. After all, you can easily commit to twenty years of togetherness, but nowadays you're making a fifty- to sixty-year promise…or even longer. The risk is that, over time, the partners may drift in different directions, due to lack of structured planning, a focus on the negatives, and failure to communicate with each other.

Lorenzo's life plan

"Tell me about yourself," I asked Lorenzo, "in thirty seconds."

Lorenzo, a forty-seven-year-old senior executive, started on the usual account of his career to date, but I quickly interrupted.

"Tell me who, and what, are important to you," I said. "Start with your wife Nicci and your five children, and take it from there."

"That was the big surprise. She told me that she was kind of thinking about training as a teacher when all the bambini leave home. I had no idea."

"So what's the problem?" I asked.

"But then, she wants us to go back to Milano and teach handicapped children." Lorenzo responded. "I had no idea, and I think she hadn't really thought about it. It was just a feeling she had. Now that we know, we're talking about it to see what we can do to keep us both happy."

"Isn't it better to find out now?" I asked. "Rather than when the children have gone away?"

And then I drew this diagram on the whiteboard.

PLANNING TOGETHER

"Here's the real value in doing this exercise with your partner, Lorenzo." I said "Those who *plan* together *stay* together. Isn't it much better to discuss these differences now and plan ahead to find a solution that everybody is happy with?"

MacMentor comments, "Life is so busy these days, we just don't take time to sit down and plan. But if a visionary strategic plan is important for your business, isn't it even more essential for your long-term life? And isn't it even better when you and your partner plan together?"

Contemplations in
Cattle Class in the next
chapter…

THOUGHTS ON

Leadership at

a High Level

Singapore smiles

I'm thinking high-level thoughts—flying at thirty thousand feet above sea level. It's two o'clock in the morning, but it feels even later, as we fly over the Indian Ocean. The red, green, and white lights of cargo vessels far below, twinkling like tiny jewels of the mysterious Orient, punctuate its ink-black expanse. This first-class business coach is travelling coach class. I'll tell you why in a minute.

I'm travelling on Singapore Airlines, on a direct flight from Singapore to Zürich. Apart from Thai and Emirates, this is probably the most colourful airline anywhere. The stewardesses wear sarongs in one of four colours designed by the famous Pierre Balmain back in 1968. They still look great—some things like real leadership and sarongs by Balmain are just timeless, aren't they?

"Good morning, sir!" exclaimed Susan, the sarong-clad lady at the aircraft's doorway, all dazzling smile and freshly showered after a good day's sleep. Me? I'm hot, tired, and smelling like a quarterback's jockstrap after a long day of meetings and a tedious evening in what passes for a business-class lounge nowadays. My Swiss Senator frequent-flyer card gets me in. It

once got me a nice corner table in a Washington, DC, restaurant when I told them that I *was* a senator. It also got us escorted into the VIP security lane at La Guardia Airport, when my partner announced that I was a senator to the watchful guardian of "privileged access." It's usually good advice to tell the truth and nothing but the truth, but sometimes you should keep the whole truth to yourself.

"Good morning," said Sarong Suzie again. "Just turn right and walk all the way down this nice, long A380. Just when you think you might be taking the garden path to the outside toilet, you will find your nice centre seat amongst all the other economy-class peasants. Have a wonderful flight!"

The pleasures of low-cost travel

No, Sarong Suzie did not really say that. These Asian cabin-crew people come in four colours, according to rank, and they are probably the nicest "hosties" you can find anywhere. They're much better than those grim-faced Teutonics that staff much of what they ironically still call the Swiss national airline. This crew is much better, too, than those androgynous cabin crews of a certain age who shuffle in carpet slippers along the aisles of some American-owned airlines (I'm talking here about US intercontinental flights, not the wonderful internal flights on JetBlue, with those indigo-coloured potato chips and entertaining cabin crew—they are a different breed!).

"What jawanna drink?" exclaimed one of those androgynous American intercontinentals on one of my occasional business-class flights to Philadelphia. "You sure you wanna nutha one?" it grumbled while shuffling off to the galley on aching feet—and this was only thirty minutes out of London!

But not on this flight! After a succession of Singapore Airlines blue, green, red, and purple sarong smiles, I found my seat, stole my neighbour's pillow and blanket before he boarded, and settled back to enjoy some high-level reflections on leadership, a gin and tonic, and a nice little sleeping pill.

Why does the coach fly "coach"?

I promised earlier to explain why I often travel economy class, along with a number of executives whose business-class days are long gone, thanks to corporate savings initiatives.

First, while we are one of the biggest high-end coaching firms anywhere, we are still a relatively small, owner-managed business. Actually, we are two small businesses because our Swiss firm has a sister company in Singapore—and it's really interesting to observe the social and business culture differences, and similarities, between Asia and Europe. Singapore calls itself "the new Switzerland." Now, I hear in Bern that Switzerland should be called "the new Singapore." Well, banning Big Macs and chewing gum on the Zürich trams would be a great start!

Running a small company is an amazing way to learn the business of "business." Nothing can hide behind budgets, committees, and corporate policies. The stark realities of enterprise are staring you in the face all the time. I often think that business schools should not award you your MBA diploma until you have run a small business for a year. It doesn't matter if it succeeds or fails—in fact, Americans would say that you learn more from failure. What matters is what you learn from the experience.

Robert Townsend was the man who took Avis from a small regional car rental business to "we're only second-best—we try harder" global success. He also wrote the entertaining management books, *Up the Organization* and *Further Up the Organization*. Townsend had an intriguing question for candidates during hiring interviews. He would chat with highly qualified MBA graduates for a while, and then he would ask, "And how are you going to overcome the handicap of your education?" Stunned by this contrarian line of thought, the candidates usually had no answer. Then Townsend would explain, in words akin to these:

1. An MBA degree teaches you that you now know everything about business, but a degree is really only a licence to learn.
2. An MBA teaches you how to value things that you can quantify. But, every year, the chairman writes in the annual report, "Our

people are our biggest asset." "How," Townsend asked, "are you going to quantify your greatest asset? The most important asset doesn't even show up in the balance sheet."

3. When you get an MBA degree, you acquire a big bunch of new enemies. Your colleagues, who could never aspire to a business-school education, will now try to drag you back down to their level.

"So how," asked Townsend, "are you going to overcome these three handicaps of your education?"

Like all good questions, this one is easy to ask and very difficult to answer. A clue might lie in the so-called "soft skills" of leadership. A typical MBA programme offers you plenty of hard skills, but very few of the other.

"Hard" is soft…and "soft" is hard

I often argue, "'Hard' is soft…and 'soft' is hard." What do I mean by that?

Simply put, hard skills are concerned with factual issues such as competitor analysis, market segmentation, strategic planning, and financial management. Being factual, the data and the issues are relatively clear and unambiguous, and therefore well within the comfort zone of excel leaders. By contrast, "soft" issues are centred on people—performance assessments, motivation, team building, coaching, and the like. All these things are full of uncertainty and ambiguity and, therefore, are hard to grasp and manage. Ergo, "hard" is soft (easy) and "soft" is hard (difficult).

Townsend might have said, in explanation, "Learning is a lifelong skill." A real leader learns all the time—from customers, vendors, peers, bosses, employees, and the world around him or her. Training your mind to learn important business things in the future should be the main purpose of a business degree. Your studies should offer you a framework in which to rationalise business ideas and experiences. Your studies can also box you in, if you let them. If a degree has simply trained your mind to be inquisitive and open, then it has succeeded. If the degree has merely taught you to think that the only way to lead business is by following standard

textbook formulae, then it has failed. As I have written elsewhere, vision and imagination should precede strategy formulation. If it doesn't, all you can offer your business is the same old uninspiring increments in revenues and margins, instead of leaping to what might be and engaging your team's energy to make the impossible happen.

Townsend, in this imaginary conversation, might have gone on to explain that you can't evaluate the skills and experience of your people by formulae, though HR tries hard to standardise the process. Indeed, some of your most valuable business assets may be those counterintuitive people who disagree with the boss and peers and challenge all the assumptions on which they base ordinary business thinking. These are the people you need to have, but who usually don't score highly on standard assessment formulae.

Townsend might have concluded that the way to get the right things done in a modern, hollow-cube organisation is by influence—and influence is not just persuading people to agree to do what you want. Influence, used in a sustainable win-win way, is one of the "softest," and therefore hardest, of all leadership skills. It's not the graduate business school that teaches you influence—it's the hard school of management experience… with the help, of course, of an excellent executive coach!

Running a small business

Why did I say that you should not get your MBA diploma until you have run a small business for a year?

Unlike most large corporations, in a small business, the twenty-first century factors of production are right there in front of you—leadership, labour, and, most essentially, capital. Entrepreneurs often make poor people leaders—they tend to drive rather than lead—but successful entrepreneurs still exhibit some fundamental leadership qualities.

Foremost amongst those qualities are having a clear and compelling vision, a capacity to work hard and be a role model for commitment, skills of execution, and customer relationships. The capital factor in a small business is crystal clear. It's all about cash! You can make as much paper profit

as you like. If the bank account does not reflect it as cold, hard cash, you're going to fail. Nobody—not customers, not vendors, and especially not bank managers—is going to help you. The only way to manage a small business safely is on a cash basis.

In Switzerland, where we incorporated our business fifteen years ago, it's very difficult to negotiate a small business overdraft. It was, until recently, impossible to run a debit balance on a credit card. We always had to find the cash to pay our card balance every month. Great discipline! My very prudent Swiss partner routinely places cash in a special reserve account for all foreseeable outgoings, so when the time comes to pay the bills, the cash is always there. Thank goodness for this Swiss caution. My "You've got to spend money to make money" mentality would probably have busted us years ago. We tried to do budgets for a little while, but it was a total waste of effort. And, for fifteen years, we have happily survived and grown on a cash-management basis.

Value for money for high-flyers

So back to my initial question: Why does an executive coach who works with top-level leaders often fly economy class? The pejorative "cattle class" is an understatement on most airlines. Many countries that transport farm animals have laws that specify minimum space per "passenger." They also require transporters to provide their animal passengers with regular fresh air and exercise. In human economy class, you have to be a vertical limbo dancer just to leave your seat to go to the toilet on a twelve-hour non-stop flight.

Human rights activists—here's a new cause for you!

The first reason that I often use low-cost tickets, as I explained above, is good cash management.

The second reason is that the cost difference between business and economy class is big. Frankly, it's often hard to justify. Note the number of senior executives who travel economy with their families, if they are not using up their millions of air miles in business class.

When I fly from New York to Zürich, it's just seven hours with a good west-to-east jet stream behind us. The jet stream always travels west to east. That's why it is usually faster to fly from the United States to Europe than the other way. It's something to do with the rotation of the earth and gravitational pull from the north and south poles. Flying seven hours in business class, I'm just digesting a porcelain-and-silver-service dinner when it's "seat belts on and prepare for landing!" time. Back in cattle class, I've had the plastic dinner and plastic wine experience. I've put earplugs in, switched on the noise-cancelling headphones, taken a sleeping pill, and pulled the shades down over my eyes. I've had a few hours' sleep; whereas, in business class, I am frustratingly awake, slightly hung over from the wines and spirits, and just plain exhausted when it's time to land. In economy, I've spent seven hundred dollars and I've had a bit of sleep. In business, I'm tired and out of pocket by another three thousand bucks. That adds up to a very expensive dinner that even an investment banker in the good old days would hesitate to buy.

"So," MacMentor says, "what does this teach us?"

"First," he goes on, "a smile costs nothing. And at two in the morning, it makes a big difference to tired travellers to be greeted with a warm smile and a colourful sarong. European and American airlines, take note!"

"Then," MacMentor continues, "your degree is just a license to learn. You don't know much about real business until you've started up and run a small enterprise. When you have to buy your own desks and install your own computers and manage your cash on a daily basis, then you are learning the business of 'business.'"

"Finally," says MacMentor, "don't be like the accountant who knows the price of everything and the value of nothing. Spend your company's cash wisely—where it will earn you more cash. Don't fritter away your valuable capital on a softer seat and a nice dinner, when a gin and tonic and a mild sleeping pill mean that you won't even notice the difference."

Brian's House

of Horrors

General Computers

Once upon a time, there was a famous computer company called General Computers. It was one of those truly innovative early computer corporations, like Texas, Atari, Commodore, and Sinclair, that had become household names because of their brilliant technology and radical marketing concepts. This famous computer company is long gone. But even now, when you mention its name to people of a certain age, a dreamy smile comes over their faces and they say, "Yes, I had one of those when I was a boy. My GC had 64K of processing power, and that was twice as big as the competition." There are many stories on the Internet about GC's demise, and most of them are true…but those are possibly not the whole story.

One day, a thirty-something executive called Brian crossed the English Channel in search of success on the other side. Little did he know that he was about to step into a corporate house of horrors, the likes of which this well-brought-up young manager never could have imagined. He was about to get some real business education!

Adolf's final days

All was rosy at first. Brian joined General Computers in a role reporting to the local chief executive. Unbeknown to Brian, this poor man, an enthusiastic aficionado of the Adolf Hitler School of Leadership, had broken down under the stress of doing quaint managerial things like "leading teams by example" and motivating people. By the time the hero of our story joined the company, Adolf Aficionado had degenerated to the point where he just played solitaire on his GC256 all day, in full view of the assembly-line teams on all four floors of the operation. He wasn't even good at solitaire, having a win percentage of only twenty-nine and a record losing streak of nineteen games. Adolf Aficionado had to go! And no one was gullible enough to take his place…except our hero, Brian.

"Brian," he heard on the other end of the line. It was the COO, Darren. Darren was a highly international American and one of the best leaders Brian had ever worked for. Darren was calling from his office in Manila. "Brian, I just need to ask you something. You've been in the corporation for ten weeks now. You've seen Adolf in action."

"Action" wasn't the first word that came to mind about Adolf. If Darren had said, "You've seen Adolf's inaction," Brian would have agreed wholeheartedly.

"What did you think about his performance last week at the management meeting in Hong Kong?" Darren asked. "The president was totally pissed with him, and so was I."

"Yes," Brian replied, "I just don't get it. I ran through his PowerPoints last week with him, and I advised him that his presentation was really boring. I cut most of the slides out and redesigned the others. I left him with eight good ones and advised him to just make short comments on each. I said that I'd keep backup material with me, in case there were any tough questions."

"I know how impatient the boss is," Brian continued. "My finance guys and I took him through dress rehearsals over and over until he wasn't doing too badly."

"But," Brian went on, "when we got to Hong Kong, he just ignored all the work we'd done and went back to his old long and boring stuff in his heavy Stuttgart accent. I saw the boss leaving the room at one point, but I just assumed that he was having a comfort break. But then he walked back in and told everybody to come to lunch when Adolf was in mid-sentence. Frankly, though, I wasn't too surprised. Adolf was really bad!"

"I can't let it go on any longer," said Darren. "I've tried everything I know with him. It's just not working. The president says he's got to go, and I agree."

Brian's first CEO role

Brian's long-standing ambition was to be the CEO of a significant company by the time he was forty-five. He was a good finance manager and he had learned a lot about business in various roles, but for him it had really been just his chosen way into general management. Brian, however, did not expect what happened next.

"Brian," said Darren, "I know you worked hard and you've really got a handle on the operation over there in Europe since you joined us. I want you to take over for Adolf. Will you take it on?"

General Computers fired Adolf on Friday afternoon, and Brian stumbled blindly into his shoes the following Monday morning. The expression "poisoned chalice" should have come to Brian's mind, but it didn't…at least until much later in our story.

And so it happened that Brian became a chief executive for the first time in his career, and he happily took on full legal liability for the affairs of several local legal entities at the same time. His enthusiasm was infectious, and the local management team responded positively to Brian's search for excellence. The president, ensconced in his downtown-Boston office suite when he wasn't flying around the world in first-class cabins or private jets, remained a ghostly presence, but nobody ever actually saw him in the European business. Like the Cheshire cat in *Alice in Wonderland*, at the mention of his name, a malevolent grinning mouth and needle-sharp

teeth would appear in the mind's eye of the longer-serving managers. The spectre, however, would fade away like Lewis Carroll's cat, because he never came to town. Brian's naive enthusiasm sparked his wise but wary team to ever-greater heights of operational performance, and the president had other things on his mind, as we shall see momentarily.

And so, Brian and his band of merry men and women happily soldiered on, with output performance growing by the quarter and costs coming down, as line efficiency improved. And then, one day, Brian discovered the sixth warehouse.

The phantom warehouse

To be strictly correct, it was Brian's logistics director, Frank, who found the hitherto-unknown depository.

"Brian," Frank said one day, his voice and demeanour as tense as a tightly wound watch spring "You know our five warehouses here in town? We've just discovered warehouse number six."

Brian was shocked and bewildered. "How can we have another warehouse that we don't know about, right under our noses?"

Brian, Frank, and Martin, the finance director, promptly set off to see this new discovery. The story, as seen through the foggy lens of history, is maybe not completely accurate. Memories fade and details become blurred. Legend has it, nevertheless, that Brian and his deputies arrived at this unknown warehouse to find it packed to the roof with cartons of General Computers products.

To the wheezy throbbing of an old diesel forklift, two warehouse workers appeared from the back of the store. Like Robinson Crusoe and his Man Friday when the ship finally came in to rescue them from their desert island prison, the two warehousemen seemed delighted to see real human beings—three strangers in suits. After some desultory conversation, or so the story goes, the desert islanders asked Brian's team to explain some strange things to them.

"Why do we," they asked "have to take all the General Computers labels off these boxes at the end of every quarter? Why do we then stick new labels on with the name of Computer Paradise (a well-known retail chain in the country)?"

"Why," asked Robinson and Friday, "do we move them from one side of the warehouse to the other? Why do we reverse the whole process a few days after the end of the quarter, then take the CP labels off and put the GC labels back on? Why do we then move the whole damn lot back to where they came from…and why do we do the same stupid thing again, every quarter?"

Brian and his managers, the story goes on, were horrified. They were guessing what the innocent warehouse men did not. These movements were simply cover for falsified sales, reported to financial analysts around the world.

The mystery explained?

Now, a long time has passed and the later dramatic bankruptcy of General Computers has hidden much of what lies behind the story. The legend still persists that Brian had unwittingly uncovered a massive fraud. Almost the entire marketing management team in Europe, it was rumoured, had taken part in a routine falsification of quarterly sales in a publicly listed corporation. Kind, but naïve, souls may believe that they did this in a desperate effort to save the company from going bust.

Others, perhaps wiser or more cynical, or both, noted that these false sales, perpetrated with the collusion of a friendly buyer in Computer Paradise, were never reversed as returns after the end of the quarter. Thus, the rumour goes on, nearly everyone in marketing management, from the president down, got very rich from commissions in quarterly sales and even wealthier, the most cynical suggested, from private sales of the entire inventory that disappeared in the system.

Brian never learned the truth, but he resigned all his CEO roles that day, on a Friday, and he came back to the company on the following Monday as a liability-free independent consultant, to do the same job until he could get himself headhunted out to safety.

A sadder, but a much wiser man, Brian moved on to his next exciting adventure in the big, bad world of business.

Now read Cyril's
adventures in the
Mysterious Orient…

Worm Pie and the

Eater Principle

Opening doors in Asia

Once upon a time, in the mysterious and distant Orient, there was a forty-something European manager—wise in the ways of Western business, but innocent and ignorant about doing business in Asia. Cyril, as this man was called, worked for an Asian corporation. He was based at its head office in a place we shall call "the land beyond." This place was far from the city, over the mountains, and distant from his expatriate countrymen. Cyril was one of only a handful of non-Asians in this faraway land beyond, surrounded by thousands of local Asians. Cyril was happy with his lot and was immersed in the local culture—most of the time.

Cyril soon found that not all was enjoyable. True, he appreciated the vast variety of different local cultures that he encountered in his daily life. He admired the small courtesies that were evident all round him. He was charmed by a little scene on the crowded subway to downtown, when a grey-haired old lady stood up to offer her seat to an older man. Cyril was delighted when, with an elegant sweep of his hand, the silver-haired old gentleman insisted that the lady take her place again. He smiled as the

151

ensuing, polite pushing-and-pulling struggle ended as the old man sat down, the lady leaned on him, and both parties had contented smiles on their faces.

Cyril found other customs in this far-off Asian land to be equally delightful. One day, carrying a heavy suitcase through the border post to another even more distant country, he found his load suddenly lightened as a young lady took the other end to help him. Cyril was amused when waiters in local restaurants offered him "block array" to eat, only to find it was plain old broccoli, Asian style. Cyril enjoyed his morning ritual with the office cleaners, straw-hatted ladies who spoke not one word of any language except their own village dialect. As a well-brought-up European, Cyril was used to holding doors open for women to pass through. The cleaning ladies, by contrast, were conditioned to pay their respects to Westerners by holding the door for any who happened to be in the vicinity. After a few days of smiles and sign language, Cyril and the cleaners reached a noble compromise; one would hold the first door for the other. At the next door, the responsibility would be reversed, and so on, down the very long corridor. Cyril felt he was in Oriental paradise.

Until the day that the typhoon approached! In stark contrast to the old lady/old man scenario, people in every train station were kicking, pushing, and throwing punches in an effort to cram themselves into railway carriages to get to the safety of their homes. Old ladies, geriatric men, children, and pregnant mothers were torn from the carriages to make way for strong, healthy, young, and panic-stricken people.

In time, Cyril observed several such unsavoury scenes from the other side of human nature, but worse, much worse, was the worm pie.

Cyril had travelled far beyond the mountains by this time. He had seen snakes writhing on hooks, ready to bleed into cups of rice wine. He had admired large, oval dishes adorned with artfully arranged black beetles and amber-coloured cockroaches all ready for the deep-fat fryer, but never had he had such an experience as the worm pie.

Cyril was accustomed, by then, to the fourteen-course banquets that he and his colleagues endured at regular intervals. In fact, he rather enjoyed them. But, one day, his chairman decided that, as the culmination of a weekend management workshop, he would treat his managers to a real Asian feast on a remote island.

Dante's Diner and the worm pie

Offloading from the creaking old bus that had transported his colleagues and him from the ferry through dusty village streets and even dustier countryside, Cyril walked by the cobweb-covered window of the restaurant kitchen. It revealed a scene straight from Dante's *Inferno*. Stripped to the waist and gleaming with sweat, a crowd of Asian cooks toiled in the darkened kitchen, illuminated only by the flare of open fires upon which sat yard-wide cooking pans. In a brightly neon-lit private room, Cyril and his colleagues tackled dish upon dish of more and more savoury and unsavoury things. Heaps of black fungus and mushrooms that resembled the offcuts of a mass castration followed glue-like shark-fin soup. Deep-fried grasshoppers with rice followed sea fungus with noodles and then seaweed pudding with ice cream and finally…the worm pie.

Have you ever tried an omelette mixed with garden soil? This is what it looked like. "You're not a real local until you've eaten worm pie," said Cyril's Asian boss. "This stuff costs a fortune. The worms are specially bred for eating." Cyril had heard of the Peter Principle, where people who are competent managers rise to the point where they can no longer perform competently. Cyril was thinking, "the Eater Principle." He had been promoted through several levels of increasingly unsavoury dishes until he had reached his own level of eating incompetency. Taking only a tiny piece of grey-hued, soil-flavoured worm pie in his mouth to boast of the experience later, Cyril the Civil European politely but firmly refused a second serving. Cyril, alas, had shown that he was not a real local. He believed that he had now seen everything that this dark and mysterious land had to offer…until he crossed the border.

Marketers play the wrong hand

After two years in Asia, Cyril thought that he had seen everything. He had witnessed the most charming courtesies and the meanest behaviours. He had eaten things with many legs and things with no legs at all. He had even seen his colleagues carry suitcases full of US dollars across the border, "to our business friends in that bigger land beyond 'the land beyond.'"

One dark day, however, Cyril was asked to do something that changed his view forever. His chairman asked him (when Asian chairmen ask, it's not really a question) to take over a business division of his group. The division was based in a large city, some two hundred miles beyond the border. His job was to exercise control over a badly managed operation, turn it into profit, and sell it to Asian buyers. All went well until, one day, his deputy, Gung Ho, came to his office and said, "We have a problem."

In this distant Asian land, the national government exercised political control, but allowed the regional governments to formulate their own business and tax legislation. It seemed natural, when faced with such a lucrative moneymaking opportunity, for the local governments to create laws that were impossible to observe. "If you can't honour the law, then you will have to find a way to get official permission to break the law," went the line of local thinking. "And the best way to get that permission is to make a generous contribution to my favourite charity—me," it went on.

Now this law, as formulated by the provincial government, required electrical products to be exported, in the customs records, by the kilo. The value of the product did not matter, nor did the nature of the material it contained. Cyril's business regularly exported complex electrical goods containing expensive, but tiny, microchips and heavy, but cheap, metal parts. So Cyril's new company regularly faced a challenge. As part of a listed group, it had audits. The auditors verified that the physical stock accounts tied in with the financial records. The only problem was that the customs records systematically became seriously out of line with the other two sets of data. But this, as our CEOptimist might have said, was no problem, just an opportunity (for someone to get rich). Cyril could

imagine the local customs officials saying, "There is no problem. You give me the money; I give you the customs clearance…no problem!"

Unbeknown to Cyril, at least at first, he employed two marketing managers with rather vague job descriptions. Indeed, all they seemed to do was entertain customers in karaoke bars.

In those days in Asia, the word "entertained" was usually a synonym for "picking up large bar bills." It was the bar ladies who did the entertaining—behind thick curtains in secluded alcoves.

The marketing guys also played card games with government officials, which they routinely lost. Reckless gamblers, those two! They gambled vast sums of money (which they could claim back as expenses), and the customs officials, being excellent card players, regularly took heaps of US dollars off the table.

Cyril, the Western innocent, strode into this strange land, intent on turning round the business and selling it, until Gung Ho, the wise and wily Asian deputy, spoke about "the problem."

"Problem is," he explained, "we have to renew customs license every year, and we always have big difference between customs records and financial accounts. We have two excellent marketing managers," he went on, "who take care of everything…no problem! But," he said, "difference too big, and when you sell company…no can do the card trick this time."

Cyril was in a spot. He thought that he understood Asia. But here was a challenge he had never faced, and he had no idea what to do about it. "No worries," said Gung Ho. "You leave to me. I fix; you don't ask!" And so it came to pass, in that far distant land, that one day, Gung Ho came to Cyril once more and said, "All done. I fixed. You don't ask."

Cyril knew better than to ask. He was soon able to start the negotiation to sell this business. The buyers inherited a clean customs sheet, and Cyril returned to the relative safety of "the land beyond," both a wiser and a none-the-wiser man.

Some years later, Cyril heard a story that might explain Gung Ho's success. It seemed, it was rumoured, that it was possible to borrow several

container loads of products from the competing factory across the street in that far distant land. It was also possible to legally export those products, by the kilo, into "the land beyond." This, it was rumoured, might have reduced the difference in the records by a considerable amount, if enough card games could be arranged and if sufficient karaoke sessions were organised.

It was also possible, the legend said, that the same container loads could be smuggled back into the far distant land. Legend also had it that transportation could be provided by the boats of that country's navy, if enough dollars were offered to compensate for the risk. Product security and land transport, the legend continued, could also be organised, by obliging military personnel, on the same basis. An enterprising marketing manager could then arrange for the same containers to be legally exported again and smuggled back by the same route and again...and again...until the difference became small enough for the usual "cards and karaoke" routine to kick in.

Of course, this was only hearsay. Cyril never did find out how Gung Ho sorted out the "opportunity."

Powerful presidents coming next…

Presidential

Power Misused

Name-dropping in the right places

A funny thing happened to me when I was working in Germany, though the start of the story was not so amusing.

I was commuting weekly between the family in London and the company south of Hamburg when I was working for a United States corporation. We had planned a much-needed family holiday, but I had just had to fly over for one day to attend to some urgent business.

On the way back to the airport that night and halfway up the auto-bahn, my cell phone gave a peremptory ring. (This was 1992. It was the size of a brick in those days, do you remember?) It was the corporation's president calling from New York.

"Turn your car around and go back. I want you to start closing down the German operation—now!" he commanded.

"What?" I protested. "I'm just going off on a week's holiday."

"No, you're not," he said. "Turn round, go back, and do what I told you."

There was no cause for urgency—this was just a needless demonstration of his executive power.

But, three weeks later, we managed to take that vacation in Tunisia. All was blissfully quiet for three days, until suddenly a palm tree beside the pool burst into voice. Actually, it wasn't the palm tree. It was a cleverly concealed loudspeaker high up amongst bunches of unripe dates.

"*Monsieur Martin,*" a voice said. "*Téléphone! Urgent!*"

I hurried, still wearing my less-than-elegant swimming shorts, to the lobby.

"Take the hall phone over there," instructed the anxious desk clerk. It was the boss, calling from New York. We talked for ten minutes about nothing at all, and eventually I asked him why he had called.

"No reason. I just never called anyone in Tunisia before, and I wondered what it would feel like."

"Thanks for nothing," I muttered, as I replaced the handset. The desk clerk looked over.

"I hope it was not a problem," he whispered anxiously.

"No, no," I replied. "It was just the president calling."

His eyes immediately swept over to a large portrait of Ben Ali, the Tunisian president at the time. He stood erect, his hand twitched towards his eyebrow in a half-salute, and he stuttered:

"The...the...the president!"

I looked at the portrait and laughed.

"No, not your president," I said. "It was my president in the United States."

"The president of the United States?" gasped the desk clerk. And he stood to attention and saluted me. I laughed again, but, wisely, said no more.

The hotel moved us that day to the biggest and grandest suite in the hotel, and from then on, every time we walked down the hallway, someone was just ahead of us opening the door to let us through.

"So," MacMentor observes, "that little piece of namedropping (albeit accidental) proved to be rather valuable on that occasion, as it nearly always is."

Sleepless in Sydney

You may find these stories about the president unbelievable because they seem so ridiculous. I have tested these stories often, when executives have complained to me about their bosses and, invariably, they have admitted, "My boss is bad, but not that bad!"

Every word is true. In fact, I have downplayed some aspects and omitted much of the real dialogue—especially the F-word profanities that peppered this man's everyday language. In my amateur view, he was a sociopath, bordering almost certainly on psychopath, who could use silky words wrapped up in a honeyed tone one minute and cut your self-confidence to shreds with a razor-sharp tone the next.

You've read about these types in the news…often when they go to prison convicted of some billion-dollar corporate fraud. You may even have had the misfortune to work for one like this. I've known some bad leaders (as well as some great ones), but this guy stands high above all others (not literally, since he was very short…and that was part of the problem) as the worst.

In the preceding story, I mentioned that this president called me in my car on a German autobahn and cancelled my family holiday at a few hours' notice. There was no purpose—he just wanted to demonstrate his power and to capitalise on the need for salary that any executive with a mortgage, a family, a couple of credit cards, and a car loan has. I think that you can probably empathise with that.

Here's another example of how this man exercised his power needlessly, expensively and, though he probably did not care, at the expense of his own image as the leader of a multibillion-dollar corporation.

We were in a meeting in Düsseldorf. The corporation's top leadership had gathered round the boardroom table—about twenty people, if

I remember correctly. We were in the first day of a biannual three-day review. Someone asked a question about Australia. The president wanted to know some detail of a minor business matter. He was a micromanager in the extreme—a "nanomanager"—with no ability or desire to see the big picture or take the long-term view. Nobody round the table could answer his question. So he ordered his aide-de-camp (a nice phrase to describe his corporate slave, who literally carried his bag) to call the local CEO in Sydney.

"But it's four in the morning in Sydney right now!" said the bag carrier.

"I don't f-ing care!" yelled the president. "Get him on the line…now!"

So the bag carrier called Australia from the room. The poor local boss groggily answered his phone, wakened from a deep, beer-induced sleep. Assaulted by machine-gun-like questions fired by the president in rapid succession, our Aussie friend had no chance of satisfying the boss.

"Get your ass on the next plane," screamed the president…and nobody present thought he was referring to the Aussie's donkey. "Get your ass over here pronto…and you'd better have answers when you come!"

Poor old Aussie had to get his answers from his local team, find a vacant seat from Sydney to Düsseldorf on a twenty-four-hour-long flight, and appear at the meeting before it finished.

On the third and final day of the meeting in Düsseldorf, the conference-room door swung open and the tired, dishevelled, and nervous CEO of the Australian company entered the room, staggering under the weight of his thick files and spreadsheets.

"Get your ass out of here!" said the president in his cold-steel razor tone. "We're done with all your stuff."

It really happened that way. I just omitted some F-words and others in the interests of decency and brevity.

MacMentor comments, "What a sad, useless, and expensive exercise of power by someone who was paid a fortune to lead a famous, but struggling corporation out of trouble and into reward for its shareholders, lenders, and its hard-working team of people around the world."

You won't be surprised to learn that the company went bust less than two years later.

LEADING LADIES AND
"Men from all over

Edinburgh"

Joking about gender

I wanted to start this chapter about discrimination in business with a joke. I know a few, but like everything else about me, my stories are getting a bit close to the "sell-by" date. I thought all I had to do was search on Google and find a good, funny story. What I did find were one or two anaemic jokes about Russians and blondes and a host of dire warnings about telling jokes about discrimination.

So, sorry, folks, there's no kidding in this chapter…just some personal thoughts from the author on discrimination in business and in life in general.

In another chapter, I write about partnerships. I advised that, when you feel disenchanted and annoyed with your partner, then you should do a little balance-sheet exercise. The objective is to focus on, and give value to, the things that are good about your partner and to reduce focus on the things that are negative.

And so it should be with discrimination.

Scotland's multi-coloured history

I was brought up in the West of Scotland where there was, and still is, widespread prejudice in religion…but not between Christian and Muslim or between Judaism and everything else.

Scotland has been, for centuries, a picturesque melting pot of races, religions, and cultures. This is a natural result of its long trading history with the North Sea/Baltic countries and the transatlantic/Far East trades that brought tobacco, sugar, spices, and other commodities through Scotland's seaports. The discrimination I refer to has always been about two kinds of Christianity, with people firmly focused on the differences between Catholics and Protestants, rather than on their common religious origins two thousand years ago.

This senseless divide never made sense to me. As I moved from university to industry, and started to manage people, my eyes were opened to all sorts of discrimination.

"What a waste of management talent and resources!" I thought. "We take the entire workforce population and immediately eliminate half from the talent pool because it's female."

"Then," my thinking proceeded, "from what's left, we rule out people in wheelchairs and people who don't share the same earthworm skin colour as the typical Scottish male. Then we discount Jews, Muslims, Buddhists, Catholics, the too young, the too old, and anyone who has different ideas from ours."

What remained was the usual 2 per cent of the talent pool who looked, walked, and thought just like us Anglo-Saxon males. It was a self-perpetuating, self-defeating exercise, in which we deprived business of some extraordinary resource and lateral thinking.

I once asked the chairman of a well-known Scottish bank (which later crashed in spectacular fashion) whether he really had diversity on his board of directors or if it consisted of "men from all parts of Edinburgh." His reluctant response, not unconnected with the later crash of the bank, was, "men like me." This middle-aged, middle-class protestant Caucasian with

two working legs was not amused, but my question struck home with the audience.

"The Germans"

You find discrimination everywhere, and I think it's largely due to fear of the unknown, which creates an aversion to different customs. Edinburgh distrusts Glasgow and vice versa. Scotland distrusts England. The rest of the United Kingdom distrusts London. New York and New Jersey are not best friends. India and Pakistan are deadly enemies, even though they shared the same nation until 1947.

Part of the unknown is that we do things differently. We have different customs. In Zürich, "The Germans" are not popular. (Generically speaking, of course. Even the Swiss agree that there are many nice individual Germans, but "The Germans" is a different entity.)

One reason for distrust is the influx of Germans in the last few years to Zürich for top jobs in banking, transport, telecommunications, and manufacturing. Even though there are not enough Swiss around for all these jobs, there is huge resentment when a German brings in another German for another senior role. The incumbent Germans, of course, magnify the problem by hiring people who are "just like them," even though there may be a more capable Swiss executive available.

I am a guest in Switzerland. I have lived here for eighteen years, and I never forget the privilege that I enjoy. Being a Scot, I understand the insecurity of a small nation that shares a border with a much bigger one. To understand the Swiss feelings about Germany, you should read a highly informative book, called *Target Switzerland*, by an American named Stephen Halbrook. Until I read it, I had not realised that Nazi Germany had at least twelve major strategic plans to invade Switzerland and that this model of democracy on his totalitarian doorstep constantly infuriated Adolf Hitler.

The main cause for resentment against "The Germans" in Zürich is that their customs and language are quite different from those of the Swiss

Germans. The Swiss German language, Schwiizerdütsch, derives from medieval High German, but it's now just as different from German as the Glasgow dialect is from Standard English. If you've ever been lucky enough to visit that swinging city, you'll know what I mean.

It's all Greek to me!

There's an old story of the Chinese and Greek neighbours. The Greek taunted the Chinese man incessantly.

"Flied Lice; Flied Lice" he would shout, mocking his Asian neighbour's difficulty with the letter R. Infuriated and humiliated, the Chinese man practiced diligently. Finally, the great day came when he shouted in response: "Frrried rrrice; frrried rrrice, you Gleek Plick!"

Certainly, language can unify…but it can also easily cause divisions through misunderstanding. My Chinese boss once told me that learning Mandarin at nightschool would allow me to know just enough Chinese to make a complete fool of myself. It's a commonly heard comment in Hong Kong. He, a Cantonese-speaking local man, born and brought up in a sampan in Mok Kok Harbour, had been needlessly nervous about his personal position in the company ever since I, a Gweilo ("grey ghost") from Europe, had arrived at head office. He was probably right about the language, though. Many words in Chinese sound the same, except that the intonation—whether you make your voice go up, down, or sideways as you say it—can result in a vastly different meaning for the same basic sound.

I had another more amusing experience in Greece when I tried to call Kristina in the local office of a car rental company.

"*Kalimera!* Good morning!" I said loudly and cheerfully in my best "Gringlish for visiting foreigners." "Can I speak to Kristina, *para-kalo?*"

"She is on the telephone!" was the reply, rather abrupt, I thought.

"Well, would you please ask her to call me when she is finished?"

"She is on the telephone!!!" came the louder and more insistent response.

"Yes. Thank you. Would you please ask her to call me when she is free?" I repeated.

"SHE IS ON THE TELEPHONE!!!!!" thundered down the crackling line, followed by some muttered Grecian expletives along the lines of, "Who is this utter fool?"

The penny, or to be more accurate the drachma, dropped at that moment. Kristina was trying to say, in her best *English for British Bozos*, "This is she…Kristina is on the line…to you."

Queuing theory, German style

One especially touchy area in Switzerland is shopping. The Swiss always form neat, orderly, and polite queues. If there is any doubt as to whose turn it is for service, most Swiss will stand back and offer you the benefit of the doubt. Whereas, "The Germans"…! Do you remember studying queuing theory in business school? That's what it is to "The Germans"—just a theory. In shops in Zürich nowadays, it's every man and woman for him or herself—sharp, Teutonic elbows are stretched wide and it is first-come (literally) first-served. An added twist of the knife in the guts of Swiss national sensibilities is that the person behind the counter comes, most likely, from the former Yugoslavia—a migrant who is taking up a nice job that a Swiss could have (even though there are not enough Swiss around willing and able to take it).

Schwaben and Osies

But the borders of our personal comfort zones are much narrower, even, than national frontiers. When I worked in Northern Germany, I really liked the people I worked with and those that met in the town. I once asked my COO:

"Tell me something, Achim. All the Germans I know here are so nice. So, why, when you are all on holiday in Spain, do you always grab the best sunbeds and steal half the breakfast buffet for a cheap lunch?"

"They're not like us Northern Germans," replied Achim. "They're Schwaben from Dortmund and other places down there."

I was witness to some interesting cultural differences in Germany when I worked there. One of the companies I headed up had its base near Magdeburg, in the old East Germany. Gorbachev had taken down the Iron Curtain just ten months before I arrived. The autobahn to Berlin still clearly showed the old border—the slip roads on the eastern side were paved with cobblestones, and all the houses were a uniform shade of Soviet-issue battleship grey. The road maps showed red lines abruptly stopping at points where the fence used to be. Outside the huge concrete blockhouse that housed a major Soviet listening post at the top of the Brocken Mountain, redundant Russian soldiers wandered around, bored, homesick, and deprived of basic rations.

We introduced cashless pay to the Osie (Ostdeutsche) workforce. None of them had a current account at the bank, and they didn't know how to use a chequebook. It reminded me of the man who said, "My wife is very literate—she can't put a good chequebook down until it's finished!" Some of the workers actually did believe that they could keep on writing cheques until the book had no more cheques in it.

My security men were all former East German border guards. Ten months before I arrived, they would have shot to kill if I had tried to cross the border through one of the many forest paths in that area. Now citizens of a united Germany, they were the nicest people you could find. The guard dog, however, was a problem! Unlike its German handlers, it had no respect for rank. I told it many times that I was the boss—it still snarled fiercely and bared its teeth every time I went near it.

In the old East Germany, workers were paid reasonably well, in cash, but had little choice of consumer goods to buy. As a result, they led dull lives but had lots of spare cash in the bank and even more under the bed. When Germany reunited, their savings were converted one-for-one into German Deutschmarks, and, suddenly, the Osies were both wealthy and free to access the abundance of luxury consumer goods in West German supermarkets. It was a remarkable sight to see all those tiny little "Trabbies" (two-cylinder Trabants were almost the only kind of car that Osies could

buy then) wheezing along the autobahn with three-piece suites, fridges, and TV sets strapped to the roof. They looked just like upside-down turtles as they crawled along on their underpowered engines.

Mortgage slaves and career choices

All over the world, it's simply human nature to exclude, mock, or disenfranchise those who are not like us. Psychologists would call it a defence mechanism and say it's part of our fight-or-flight instinct. Anyone who behaves differently is suspect.

Everybody's talking about gender discrimination these days. We're all "leaning in" or "coming out." So much good stuff has been written about sex in business (and I don't include *Fifty Shades of Grey* or its likely sequel, *Fifty Shades of Gay*, in this narrative) that I will not even try to match it. I'd just like to make a few comments from the heart, as the father of a smart, energetic thirty-six-year-old daughter—a lawyer who had to make the classic female career change to a part-time, lower paid job because her son had reached school age and the macho world of law was not accommodating. Like all women in business, Emma has had to be ten times better, to be seen as equal. She might agree with the "not so dumb" Marilyn Monroe who once said, "Women who seek to be equal with men lack ambition." With good luck and much effort, my daughter's new job has turned out to be an outstanding success in a corporate culture that values vision, shared commitment, and teamwork.

Though it didn't happen in my daughter's case, I admire greatly those men who fly in the face of convention and chauvinistic bravado to become househusbands. What courage it must take for these men to endure the macho scorn in the locker room in order to release their talented wives to help this world become a better place. Gender discrimination is not just by men against women. Men who are modern enough to feel an obligation to play a bigger role in the family suffer discrimination by other men who play the macho career game in business. In some business and/or national cultures, if you're not first in to work in the morning, you aren't ambitious

enough or you don't have the corporation's interests at heart. If your car is not the last one in the car park at night, they call you a softie. The result is that men feel pressured more and more to neglect family life at both ends of the day.

I once worked for a man who went right off the sociopath scale. He obliged his senior team to come to his office every evening, when he would crack open a bottle of wine. His reluctant admirers sat round his table, listening to his increasingly verbose words of wisdom. The sessions would end in the early hours, and, often, the boys would just go back to their offices, put their heads on the desk, and sleep for a few hours until the staff arrived for work again. They were more afraid of losing their jobs than losing their families, as many of them did in the end.

Me? I left the office at seven o'clock every night, unless I had a really good reason to work overtime. I soon lost the patronage of the boss, but I kept my family and my sanity and went on to much better things in another company.

But that experience, and others like it, allows me to seriously empathise with men who daily face a dilemma of this nature. Too often they feel compelled to choose the easy short-term option of working crazy hours at night and over weekends, and risk losing their families in the longer term. It's too easy to say that they should face up to the likely consequences, and that they should realise that the company can come and go (or let them go) in an instant.

But you should cherish your family, because it is your family that will be with you through your working career and beyond. I was never perfect, because I was a mortgage slave like others, but I like to think that I could draw a line at some fairly sensible point.

Leading ladies

Women can make superb leaders. We have, amongst many, Meg Whitman of HP, Margaret Chan of the World Health Organization, Ursula Burns of Xerox, Margaret Thatcher, Melinda Gates, Ellen Kullman

of DuPont, Mother Teresa, Michelle Obama…the list of talented, empowered women from all round the world is long. I've coached four African ladies and each was outstanding in her own way, but different from the others. Nadaro, from Senegal, was stately, loud, jovial, and resplendent in her tribal robes. Fatima, from Mali, was studious and gentle. Beatrix, from Kenya, lacked assertiveness, and Tingest, from Ethiopia, made up in energy what she lacked in height. All shared one thing in common—they came from countries where the male sex dominated, but where the women were the real driving force behind progress. Each of them had been cabinet ministers in the governments of their own countries, and they all came to Geneva to add their own special gifts to the betterment of the human race.

Men standing up for women

The list of outstanding female leaders is enormous. And most of them are unknown beyond their field. One of my favourites, a woman who can compete with any man, is Dr. Jill Samuels. Jill led the research team that "accidentally" discovered Viagra when searching for a drug for another purpose (you could say that she was doing her bit to help men stand up for women). Despite this overwhelming evidence of female leadership capability, the norm is still "man follows his career, woman has babies and tries to combine children, housework, and some kind of career with keeping her brain, ambition, and humanity alive." Women still don't have proper choices.

Asia is an interesting region to observe these days, with many anomalies that now challenge the accepted stereotyped image of woman as homemaker. In Singapore, for example, a recent poll showed that 80 per cent of the economically inactive population is female. Of that pool of potential talent, 25 per cent is intending to look for work in the next two years—a notable increase in talent amongst a population of less than six million. In Japan, DuPont was able to instil a corporate culture of safety without a problem, but managers struggled to create a level playing field for women. Now, though, Wal-Mart in Japan (where 70 per cent of women leave work

after having their first child), is building a set of HR practices to encourage the development of female business leaders. "Initiatives like these," Wal-Mart says, "can overcome the traditional practices of society all over Asia."

And yet!

And yet, when it comes to culture inhibiting women as business leaders, don't women have themselves to blame to a great extent?

We have some great female executive coaches in our team (see www.ijmartin.com/team)—women who have fought their way over barriers of gender and race discrimination to be even better than most men in business.

And yet, when we offer a female client a choice of one of those highly experienced and proven coaches, most women executives will say, "No thanks; I'd rather have one of your male coaches."

We blame society for the struggles that women have, to get to the top and stay there (because staying above that glass ceiling is even harder than getting through it).

And yet, what are we doing to change the fundamental assumptions that society makes about the role of men and women in it and to create a level playing field for all?

You'd imagine that women would help other women in every possible way.

And yet, and there is much evidence that supports this, a senior female executive is highly likely to do her best to keep other aspiring women executives down. What deeply rooted instinct drives that behaviour? Is it an inner voice saying, "I had to work damned hard to get where I am today… why should it be any easier for her?" Or is it just plain, old-fashioned insecurity that the younger, perhaps more attractive, female executive may displace her? Or is it some instinct even more deeply grounded in father/daughter relationships? I don't know the answer, but I wish it weren't so!

Some enlightened countries, like Norway, have introduced quota rules to bring the number of female board members into balance with male members of boards.

And yet, many of my female executive friends shun this idea—and I agree. They don't want artificial help to get to the top! They just want this level playing field of opportunity so that their talents can shine out. They want to learn the trade of company leadership and emerge through the ranks on pure merit.

We can "lean in" and "come out" as often as we like. The fundamental problem of discrimination against gender, age, ethnic origins, religion, and all the other kinds of bigotry will not be resolved until everyone has the same opportunity. I mean opportunity to get a good education, to get a job on pure merit, to enjoy the freedom to work late, to not worry about who picks up the kids from school, to earn promotion on the quality of the work done. Until then, business will continue to be run by "men from all over Edinburgh," and we will have squandered yet another generation of talented people who are, in some way, different from the 2 per cent of the population who look, think, and act in the same way.

"Perhaps the best way to manage the discrimination issue," says MacMentor, "is to adopt a balance-sheet approach—that is, to evaluate all individuals for all their merits and demerits, regardless of any other factor. And," he adds, "instead of differentiating people who are, in some way not *like* us, we should treat them exactly as if they *are* us."

In the end we do minorities no favours by having positive discrimination and quotas. In treating them just like us, we must offer a level playing field of opportunity and let them take it from there.

RUNNING A MILE

in Moccasins for

Magnificent

Mediation

Moving arguments

"Idiot," said Michel across the negotiating table. "*Imbécile*," retorted Pierre. The atmosphere in the room was electric. The arguments and insults grew more and more heated. The meeting ended in stalemate, and the trade union officials withdrew to the nearest cafe with Gallic grins all over their faces. Michel and Pierre were not antagonists in a rancorous negotiation over job security—they were both key members of the management team. Michel was head of operations and Pierre was VP of human resources in the important French subsidiary of Globelec Electrical, a major US corporation.

It was late summer of 2007. Globelec, anticipating the imminent global financial crisis, was moving manufacturing operations from its expensive thirty-five-hour working week France to a lower-cost factory in Eastern Europe. Pierre and Michel, with their management colleagues, were trying to negotiate the transfer of more than a thousand jobs from the manufacturing site east of Paris to Slovakia. Progress was slow, primarily because Michel and Pierre couldn't agree on anything, and the unions were threatening to walk out. Michel was a very bright,

but conceited, late-thirty-something INSEAD alumnus, while Pierre was one of those tough, cheroot-smoking graduates from "the school of life" who held MBA degrees in the utmost contempt. Pierre's negotiating style was to insert a burning cheroot in his mouth and hold it two inches from your face in an eyeball-to-eyeball stare until you looked away and backed off. There had never been much *entente cordiale* between these two, but the current disagreement over the relocation plan had descended into a bitter personal struggle for power. Michel was in a hurry. His next promotion depended on the speedy low-cost transfer of operations. Globelec, based in the rural heartland of hire-at-will America, had no idea about French labour laws and cared even less. Pierre's only ambitions, by contrast with Michel's, were to keep his job in Paris and to stay out of jail by honouring, to the letter, the strict tenets of the traditionally protective employment legislation of his proud, revolutionary nation.

Ramón, Globelec's regional president, called me just after this meeting. "Gonna fire these guys if they don't shape up soon! Their personal hate relationship is costing us megabucks, and it's making us look like fools in front of the unions. Got any ideas?"

"Yes," I said. "I've just done a mediation exercise in Moscow between the CEO and COO of a big bank. Now we've started coaching them. We could try the mediation first, to get them working together, and, if it works, offer them coaching to change their ways for good."

"Sounds like a plan," said Ramón. "Finalise the details with my HR guy, and let's get started—soon."

Hot cigars and cold relations

Ten days later, I arrived at Globelec's regional HQ to meet Michel and Pierre, first individually and then together. Pierre, the cheroot-smoking HR man, entered the room. "First, I must tell you," he said in his rasping, heavily accented voice, "my English, she is not so good! We must speak in French."

178

"Mon Dieu!" I thought. "My French, she is not so good either!" *"D'accord!"* I replied in my best Gallic accent. *"On y va!"*

I started by describing my firm's promise of total confidentiality. And, in a pathetic attempt at bonding, I referred to the Auld Alliance—the historic links between my native Scotland and France.

"This *Vieille Alliance*, what good is this for now?" exclaimed Pierre, waving his arms and scattering burning ash from his cheroot over my interview papers. "Let me tell you about this *idiot*, Michel!"

"We've got off to a good start," I thought. "Let's try some mediation questions."

I asked Pierre to tell me all about himself—in thirty seconds. I love this question—so easy to ask, but so hard to answer properly. Most alpha males just ramble on about their CVs, while what I want is an account of their values and long-term objectives. I usually use this question to open up an executive's thinking, but in Pierre's case, his thinking proved to be about as wide as the tip of the glowing cheroot now lodged precariously on his lower lip. Moving on, I asked Pierre to describe his objectives for the business and for himself. When I asked him, "What is getting in the way of your achieving them?" He replied predictably, "That idiot, Michel, of course."

My next questions surprised him. "Tell me about Michel—what are his strengths and weaknesses? Tell me about his family. What is his wife's name? How many children does he have? What are his outside interests? What are his objectives in life?" In this way, I was trying to get Pierre to see Michel as a real person and not just an antagonist in the workplace. Of course, Pierre had no idea, but it made him a little curious.

"Do you see any overlaps between Michel's objectives and your own?" I asked "Can you see any ways in which we can align your objectives with his, in the interests of Globelec?"

Pierre, grudgingly at first but warming to the idea, offered some tentative suggestions. My next question was, "Put yourself in Michel's position. How would he describe you as a colleague, as a manager, as a professional person, and in any other way?"

The theory I was using draws on the old Native American saying, "If you want to know someone, first walk a mile in his moccasins." Pierre was still in the frame of mind, "If you want his moccasins, first walk a mile in them. Then you've got his shoes, and he can't run after you!" But, slowly, like an arthritic escargot, Pierre was moving away from his closed and hostile mind-set.

"How do you think Michel sees the current situation? And do you think he sees any possibility of a better relationship?" I asked. You will note the skilful juxtaposition of open and closed questions. Answering "no" to the second question would have been difficult, so I was sowing the seeds of possible improvement.

"How do you see the relationship?" I asked, as I brought the focus back on him. "Can you see any possibility of improvement?"

Having grudgingly admitted that Michel could possibly see the potential, Pierre would have cast himself as the bad guy if he answered negatively. So, now I had Pierre seeing Michel as a person and not just an enemy. He had just agreed that the relationship could possibly improve. I now took him to the brink of the abyss of failure.

"What might happen if it does not improve—worst case, likely case?" I asked Pierre. Now he could see the downside of mediation failure.

"What is the one thing that could help, in the short term, to make your relationship better?" I asked, leading him into positive thinking and a way out of this unpleasant situation. "What two or three things can we do together to get some quick wins? What can you do personally to help? What can Michel do?"

These questions and Pierre's thoughtful answers were building the action plan. "Summing up," I said with deep relief, as my less-than-fluent French was nearing the end of its linguistic resources, "what can you now commit to doing, and how are you going to do it? When will you start?"

"Finally," I asked, "what have we missed in this discussion? What would you like to add? How do you feel about the situation now?" Pierre's responses, and his demeanour, were considerably more positive than when

he had entered the room. The fiery tip of his glowing cheroot had subsided to a dull grey ash. As he rose to leave, I said, "Try not to worry. I've seen much worse problems ending up happily. You may never be best friends, but at least you and Michel can learn to work together. You described some good things about Michel, and I know that he appreciates some things about you. You share the same values and the same objectives. The main problem is that you don't trust each other. The upside of finding an answer is very high. The downside of failure would be very unpleasant for both of you. Globelec is not going to tolerate the present situation for much longer. But," I continued, "I like you both. I think that you can work it out together and get on with the real job. Let's all get together after I've spoken with Michel and agree on a plan."

Putting more "room" in the room

I spent the next hour with Michel. I asked him the same questions. Neither Michel nor Pierre had any idea about the other's life outside of the office. But, by now, both were seeing that the other was a real person with similar values and objectives. Someone once said that mediation "puts more room in the room" by broadening the perspectives of the protagonists. That's what I had been trying to do. They had put themselves into the other's moccasins and found some shared ground and mutual appreciation of each other's qualities.

The final session brought Michel, Pierre, and me together to review the discussions and finalise the action plan. Both agreed to try it.

In the next negotiation meeting with the trade unions, Michel and Pierre behaved perfectly. They had met earlier and agreed to agree, or agree to differ, in private. In the negotiation, they presented a united front. With their colleagues and the union representatives, they averted the threatened strike. They confirmed a "transfer and compensation" plan that was less generous than the union's demands but more sympathetic than Globelec management's first offer. The relocation to Slovakia eventually went smoothly.

This being a real-life story and not a fairy tale, there was both a happy and a not-so-happy ending. Pierre, the gritty, cheroot-smoking HR man, declined Globelec's offer of coaching. Some weeks after we met, he got into a blazing, cognac-fuelled argument with the regional president and "resigned to spend more time with his family." Michel, by contrast, accepted the coaching offer and worked with us in a coaching and mentoring programme. Last time we heard, he had quite radically changed his personal style and had won a serious promotion to Globelec's regional headquarters.

"So," asks MacMentor, "what three things can we learn from this story?"

First, no relationship is so bad that it can't be improved by helping the protagonists to see the situation from the other side. It helps too if you focus on similarities and shared values, instead of differences and prejudices.

Second, the mediator must always be non-partisan and unflappable. Taking sides and getting emotional doesn't build confidence with either party.

Third, developing some basis for an eventual agreement and getting both sides together to debate them like adults is a good way to align teams and resolve disputes.

Now slide into suit-
ed snakes and smiling
assassins…

FERRARIS WITH NO BRAKES—
psychopaths at

work

Missing morality

I discovered psychopaths last year. Yes, I know that they've existed for thousands of years…I just didn't have a scientific name for some of those weird people that I had met and occasionally worked for (I had many names for them, but nothing scientific). Putting a label on things makes life a lot simpler, doesn't it? At least for me, it clarified the difference between just plain bad leadership and true personality disorders like sociopathy and psychopathy.

Things "went click" for me when I read an excellent book called *Snakes in Suits—When Psychopaths Go to Work*, written by the eminent psychologists Paul Babiak and Robert Hare. It's not intended to be scientific literature, though the authors have won great respect in their professional field. Instead, it sets out to alert us "normal" people to the ways in which psychopaths deceive and manipulate us in business. The book supports their hypotheses with a number of business scenarios in which all of us in business life sometimes find ourselves. It's too easy for us to read a book like this and to imagine that we know someone who sounds like those described; therefore, he or she must be a psychopath. It's like when a hypochondriac

hears the symptoms of some exotic new disease and soon becomes convinced that he or she is its latest victim. Even when I eliminate all those false trails from my mind, though, I now realise, with hindsight, that I have worked with some borderline cases and with a couple or so who were well within the range of psychopath.

With this personality condition, it's not a case of "you are or you are not a psychopath." It's not black and white. There are scientifically grounded grey scales for measuring the degree to which a person is suffering from the condition. Hare's PCL-4 scale, which poses questions designed to assess the degree of sociopathy, ranges from zero to forty. Most people would score less than five. The average for known criminals is twenty-two for men and nineteen for women. A psychopath would typically score thirty or more on this scale. In other words, we are all psychopaths to some extent, but most of us have enough control mechanisms to keep it our own dirty little secret.

I use the word "suffering" because, in a sense, being a psychopath is like being born without a limb or missing a useful organ. The psychopathic equivalent is that these people are born without, or lose at a very early age through conditioning, their moral conscience. Uday Hussein, for example, the elder son of Saddam Hussein, was a sadistic psychopath. He probably inherited the tendency genetically, but any trace of moral rectitude was eliminated at a young age when his father exposed him to sadistic practices of various sorts. I also use the word "suffering" because a lifetime of continual deception, lying, cheating, and abusing others can't be much fun, but psychopaths are compelled to indulge in this behaviour. The ones I have known were not happy people.

Now, this is not an apology for psychopathic behaviour. I'm just saying that psychopaths have no mechanisms to behave otherwise. They can't even see that they are doing wrong, because every event and interaction is internalised and centred on their own interests. If anyone is truly uncoachable (and I believe that many normal business people are unfairly stuck with this label), it is a psychopath. As coaches, we have been party to many dramatic behavioural turnarounds, which others had

dismissed as hopeless cases, but those were not psychopathic situations. I'm not suggesting that we should feel sorry for psychopaths or excuse their behaviour…there have been too many innocent victims who have suffered for that to be justified.

Look right, then left, then right again

Like Babiak and Hare, I'm just flagging up a warning that there are people in the population (and, I would suggest, especially in the business executive population) who are like high-performance sports cars with no brake pedals. So look out as you journey along the corporate career path… there may be a psychopathic, brake-free Ferrari in a pinstriped suit roaring along the street on a collision course with your ambitions.

Brakeless Ferraris have run me over a couple of times in my career. Given that there is a higher percentage of sociopathy and psychopathy in business than in the world in general, I guess I'm lucky not to have had more such experiences. *Snakes in Suits* tells a number of true-to-life stories, and you might recognise situations in one or more of them where you have been unwittingly exposed to psychopathic behaviour. I have a few more to add to these.

Elsewhere in this book, I have told about a formerly well-known company in which the president exercised his power ruthlessly. He had no feelings for anyone in that organisation. He could make you feel like a star today and like something the cat dragged in tomorrow. He routinely played with people's emotions, egos, and the need for a secure salary without regard. He was highly manipulative to achieve his own selfish ends. The president had the most silky and seductive voice that you could imagine. He would have had a starring role in any TV commercial. But his voice could change from one sentence to the next. He had the ability to slice people like salami if it suited his purpose of the moment. Everything he said and did was calculated to enhance his own personal wealth, to ensure a comfortable life and long retirement in the West Indies. This was one of those cases where, at least in the short term, the victims had the last laugh. The corporation

finally went into Chapter 11 protection. When the accountants took over the running of the firm, poor old Prezzie was bumped out of first class into cattle class on every flight he took thereafter. Even if only a temporary victory, it was immensely satisfying to all those who had suffered under this psychopathic tyrant.

Cartwheel management and the smiling assassin

In my earlier career, I had been an accountant. Accountants always work hard. If you see a late-night light blazing in some office block, it's either one of those young legal eagles on the Wall Street treadmill or an average accountant doing the budgets, the monthly report, or the annual accounts. Accountants in industry, like me, had it even harder. I used to have two bosses: one, the local operations director and the other, down in the HQ finance department in London. They were both very understanding…each of them demanded only 75 per cent of my time.

This wasn't a big deal. I was Scottish and raised in the Calvinist ethic where people cooked on Saturdays to allow more time to go to church on Sundays. How I envied those Catholic boys who could go to Mass at 9:00 a.m. on Sundays and have absolution to play in the streets for the rest of the day. We trudged reluctantly off to Sunday school and a long, boring church sermon, followed, for a bit of light relief, by a visit to long-dead relatives in cold and windswept Scottish cemeteries. I had even survived my early-April swimming lessons in a tidal pool on the west coast of Scotland, so a bit of working overtime never bothered me. Not even doing stocktakes at midnight on New Year's Eve in Scotland was a big deal.

But this guy was something else. Let's call him Tommy Hawk—which was just one of the names that we gave him. "Slave driver" was one of the more polite epithets. Tommy's idea of a fun evening was calling in his subordinates to his office after a long day to share a bottle of wine and listen to his endless monologues. He could outlast Fidel Castro and Muammar Al Gaddafi combined, even on a bad night.

Tommy terrorised his wage-slave subjects. I coined the phrase "cart-wheel management" when I first saw him in action. Everything revolved round Tommy, and every decision was his to take…except that he never took any. That would have been politically dangerous! The result was constant chaos, which suited Tommy admirably because he was highly adept at making himself the white knight who rode in on his charger to rescue every situation caused by the incompetence of his tyrannised deputies. I should have realised when I first met Tommy. On my first day in the company, he boasted to me, with great pride, that his nick-name was "the smiling assassin." Much later, he solemnly explained to me that business life was a jungle, that we were all animals, and that only the fittest (that is, the most ruthless and uncaring) could survive.

Tommy Hawk, like almost every psychopath, was able to fool enough people for enough of the time to gain a dazzling reputation with some, but by no means all, of the senior executives in the corporation. It was my bad luck to join the company and to take over from Tommy, while he got pro-moted to head office. For a year or so, it was a constant battle to motivate the fear-stricken team and get them to assume responsibility, while fighting off guerrilla action from Tommy as he invented more and more crises so he could charge up from head office with his sycophantic colleagues (psycho-phants?) to ride to the rescue.

Snakes in Suits describes some good ways to deal with such people. My strategy was to take confidence in the, by then, soaring reputation of my peo-ple and ask to see the "Big Boss." Now, Big Boss had a fearsome temper and was known to throw solid objects around the room in a tantrum. By this time, however, the chance of being struck by a flying director's chair was much less of a concern to me than the impossibility of continuing this constant battle with Tommy the Terrible. To my great surprise and immense relief, Big Boss called Tommy and his pyschophants into his office and warned of serious consequences if they failed to show total support for my team in future. It was a happy ending…and the start of a long period of ever-growing success for the wonderful, but downtrodden, people on my team.

Handy Andy and my lost weekend

Years later, in the early months of my coaching business, we were approached by the thirty-something managing director of a new subsidiary of a venerable Swiss bank. Charming, smooth, polite, warm—this paragon of executive virtue had a PhD in an esoteric subject in the field of exotic financial instruments. He was having a little problem, though. He was struggling to complete a strategic plan for a board meeting. Could we help?

This was Thursday. The board meeting was the following Tuesday. Andy, one of the many names that this young man was known by, needed urgent help. "But," he said, "no problem. It is just a case of polishing up the work I've already done." He would then fly from Geneva to Zürich, and a private helicopter would whisk him directly to the board meeting.

"Simple," I thought. "I'll go over his plan, critique it, and act as coach and mentor in strategic planning over the weekend. I'll make sure that he impresses his board on Tuesday. We asked for immediate payment of our fee, given the short-term nature of the project (we also needed to pay the next month's rent for a very young and cash-light business). Andy turned up at our office with a fistful of used banknotes as down payment and a heap of papers, but no semblance of a strategic plan. Andy, it appeared, was not so handy when it came to doing rather than talking.

Andy sat down beside me, but it soon became clear that he had no contribution to make. His threshold of boredom, fortunately, was very low. At the first excuse, and to my great relief, he soon took himself off to the pub, while I set up the bones of the strategic plan and presentation. The evening dragged on into night, and I found myself rather enjoying the work. I blew out the candles very late that night. Next morning, Saturday, the plan was well underway, but Andy was proving elusive. He was not in my office as planned and was not answering my calls. Regardless, I soldiered on with his plan all day and long into the evening. By late that night, I was sweating and cursing that he had manipulated me into doing his work, instead of allowing me to coach him in how to prepare and present it.

The office doorbell rang sometime after 10:00 p.m. A staggering, red-faced Andy, smelling of sweat and stale beer, was at the door demanding his plan. Things were getting dangerous! I got rid of Andy as soon as I could and carried on into the night. Sunday came and went and Andy stayed out of sight. By this time I was happy that he had not appeared. Bright and early Monday morning, I turned up at Andy's well-appointed office on the most prestigious street in Geneva's Old Town. There sat Andy in his black leather director's chair—scrubbed, fresh, pinstripe suited, and as charming as before. He was in raptures over the strategic plan and enthused by the PowerPoint presentation. I spent the next three hours taking him through it, trying to help him understand the data, and generally trying to coach the uncoachable. "Something is really weird," I thought. "Andy has a PhD in financial sciences, but he has a big problem in understanding even a basic Excel spreadsheet." So I took him through it line by line and made him write a script to answer any question that his directors might ask on Tuesday. He did much better with the PowerPoint because he was a smooth and elegant talker. "So, we're done, Andy. You're all ready for tomorrow's meeting. I wish you good luck. Now, if you'll just make our final fee payment, I'll leave you to it."

"Not until the board meeting's over!" growled Andy with a strong undertone of aggression in his voice. "You'll get paid right after that, if it goes well." I had no choice but to leave, hoping that his private helicopter wouldn't crash and that he would give the board a convincing performance the next day.

Snakes in lawsuits

Andy did well…so well, in fact, that the CEO started to question why Andy, who had disappointed in his first few weeks and had seriously failed to fulfil his PhD promise, was suddenly a strategic genius. In the days that followed, the CEO launched an investigation. His investigators discovered that "Andy" went by multiple names and had moved around from country to country. His original nationality was obscure, and his PhD thesis had

been downloaded from the Internet. Andy was a fake—a very convincing, bullying, manipulative fiction. The CEO laughed out loud when I referred to the helicopter trip to the board meeting. Andy had taken the train, appearing only minutes before the meeting (probably intentionally, lest he get into a conversation that he couldn't deal with).

"So, dear CEO," I said to the boss of this prestigious and honourable old Swiss bank. "What about the balance of our fee?"

"What fee?" he replied. "We never hired you!"

"But we are a very young business and we need that money! And I sweated blood all weekend to help Andy!" I blurted out.

"So, why don't you sue us?" he replied with a shark-like smirk beneath his well-trimmed moustache.

We did. We engaged a lawyer…who turned out to be a college friend of the CEO, and they went off to lunch together after our "reconciliation" meeting. We never got our fee, and we never paid our lawyer. But we did get some satisfaction, as well as a valuable lesson on psychopaths in business. International tax authorities later opened an investigation into the bank and forced it to pay huge penalties for helping foreign nationals evade their country's taxes.

In the end, the experience we gained and the lesson we learned were worth infinitely more than the fee that we lost.

Seductive psychopaths—sirens in suits

My final psychopath-in-business example is still an unfinished story because the perpetrator of the massive $40 million fraud is appealing her sentence. She has, as far as I know, not been diagnosed as psychopathic, but her actions and the situation mirror perfectly many of the stories and scenarios described in *Snakes in Suits*. You may be surprised that this story has a woman in the starring role, because most people assume that all psychopaths are men. I guess that this is because we associate psychopaths with violent crime, and, as usually reported in the media, the criminal is male. We normally don't realise, unless you read *Snakes in Suits* or similar books,

that in our midst on the street or at our workplace are many psychopathic personalities. In reality, there are as many psychopathic women as men, and many of them are in positions in business where they can do a lot of harm to the organisation.

Our "heroine" in the story is called Fanny the Fraudster (her appeal being sub judice, I should not use her real name). Fanny originated in a very poor region of the Middle East, but she invented wealthy parents from Iran and a background of privilege. Fanny also invented several good degrees from respected institutions and forged some impressive diplomas to support the stories. Fanny was apparently very rich, because she lived the high life in every way. Psychopaths are capable of great charm and convincing storytelling. It can be very hard for even experienced HR people to distinguish a highly desirable recruit from a psychopathic candidate. That is why it is absolutely essential, when hiring, to conduct rigorous due diligence before engaging someone. In other chapters, I have referred to people being an enterprise's greatest asset. I urged the reader, when acquiring assets, to carry out careful and comprehensive due diligence. And yet, as in so many ways with the firm's greatest assets, we fail to invest properly. We typically accept academic certificates at face value. We conduct interviews in an amateurish way, asking predictable questions to which a skilled and well-coached interviewee would have excellent pre-rehearsed answers. We carry out reference checking, if at all, in a lax fashion. This is usually because HR people and recruitment specialists are always pressed for time and just need to "tick the boxes" and then move on to the next task.

My biggest hiring mistake

I made this mistake as a very young manager. At age twenty-five, I needed to recruit some geologists at short notice and fly them out to a North Sea oil rig as soon as I engaged them. One candidate was a very nice man. I enjoyed the interview, and he displayed some impressive, and genuine, diplomas of scientific education. He joined the team on the day

of the interview and flew out the next day to the oil rig, a long way offshore from Aberdeen.

One week later, he left the rig strapped into a straitjacket. He was too dangerous to fly out on the helicopter, so the rig master hailed a passing fishing vessel and had him shipped back to Aberdeen. The same day, I received his medical references. His doctor wrote, "On no account must my patient, at this time, be confined in an alcohol-free environment without medication and specialist help." The poor man was seriously dependent on alcohol and, without medication, became violent and abusive. Oil rigs, for safety reasons, were alcohol-free territory. He had unwisely thought that he could cure himself if he just had no access to alcohol. The lesson that I learned that day was, when it comes to your greatest assets, you must exercise the most careful due diligence before hiring.

Fanny fooling around

Most companies don't do this, and Fanny the Fraudster's corporation was no exception. Fanny proved to be a charming, witty, and smart candidate. Her credentials were convincing, and her wealthy origins appealed to the social-climbing chief executive. Psychopaths are very adept at identifying and cultivating influential figures in the corporation. In no time, Fanny was a close friend of the chief executive and was twisting the chairman round her heavily diamond-encrusted little finger. Fanny was officially in a mid-level management position, but she often undertook "special missions." Whenever an official in some obscure country was standing in the way of business, Fanny would fly in and, with a flutter of her long, but fake, eyelashes and perhaps one or two other incentives, the blockage would disappear. Whenever the company needed to know the strategic intentions of a major customer or competitor, Fanny would drive up in her Lamborghini or Porsche to the door of some luxury hotel for a dinner meeting with the key executive. Breakfast would follow dinner, and Fanny would roar off into the dawn light, fuelled with a tank load of competitive advantage.

Fanny's mid-management role allowed her to establish a bank account in the company's name, to which only she had access (yes, the group's head of internal audit, along with a number of others, was later fired). Fanny systematically diverted cash receipts from one specific business activity into a special "Fanny's Fund" account. At the end of the year, Fanny cleared the balance into her private account at another bank. This allowed Fanny to live a lavish lifestyle. She had the biggest house and the fastest cars around. She wore furs and diamonds as if she were born with them. And she explained her way of life by letting on that she had come from a rich family that had fled Iran with all its massive wealth when the Shah was deposed.

Psychopaths engender mixed reviews. Some people, often the most senior in the company, are mesmerised. Even when faced with the obvious truth, these executives will often persist in denial. When a man of a certain age is charmed by a psychopathic younger female, he will often deny to his dying day that he was duped. Others in the business detest the psychopath and try to get him, or her, removed. Nearly always, this backfires and the whistle-blower gets fired instead, or resigns in disgust. Others, possibly the majority, will feel strongly that something is wrong with this situation and correctly identify the person at the source. Too often, however, they lack the charm, influence, and connections of the psychopath. They keep their heads down and just get on with the job.

So it was in Fanny's company. We worked with a number of its senior executives. Not once, until the whole thing was exposed by a new and suspicious regional financial director, did anyone mention Fanny. Instead, they discussed problems arising from her behaviour in different ways. Poor results from Fanny's business division were disguised by the local managing director and chief accountant. They, poor, downtrodden wage slaves, unable to explain the losses, preferred a later dismissal for massaging results than instant firing for underperformance.

"Ask yourself this," says MacMentor. "In any part of your corporation is there chronic underperformance that defies explanation? Does top management protect some charismatic person who is associated in some way with that business? Could it be that undetected fraud is going on?"

Psychopaths make excellent fraudsters. Is there, in your business, a snake, clad in pin-striped suit, working in the shadows (or often hiding in plain sight), and quietly milking the business of a large part of its revenues?

This last story has no happy ending. Indeed, the story is not finished. And, if rumour is true, there is still more to be told in public. The company lost $40 million. Its share price and its credibility were severely damaged. The CEO had to resign. Fanny the Fraudster's husband committed suicide, leaving their young children behind. Fanny sits in jail, pending her appeal against a five-year sentence. Tax investigators are researching related matters.

"In the end," MacMentor comments, "the psychopathic Ferraris with no brakes are bad news for everyone, including the psychopaths themselves. We cannot eliminate this condition in society. All we can do is treat people as our greatest asset, exercise rigorous due diligence when "buying" these assets, and protect our business from the great damage that the psychopathic snake in a suit will inevitably cause, if slack hiring practices allow such a person to infiltrate our organisation."

Everyone's a winner in
the next chapter…

Say "Yes" and

Surprise Me

Talking turkey

I had been speaking on global leadership at an HR conference in Istanbul. I had won a round of applause by addressing the audience in Turkish. "*Merhaba, bayanlar ve baylar!*" I had said phonetically. My local partners had assured me that this meant "Hello, ladies and gentlemen."

I had taken this entirely on trust, though my trust was once deeply abused when I was new in Zürich. We were in the local Coop supermarket in Bahnhofstrasse. ("Railway Station Street" seems a rather prosaic name for the most expensive shopping street in Europe, doesn't it?) Not knowing much Swiss German, I had asked my trusted partner, "How do you say "ostrich meat" in Schwiizerdütsch?" The right answer was *Straussenfleisch*, but I obviously didn't know that. Often, in a foreign language, you can get by if you take the English word and change it a bit. That doesn't always work, though. Someone once asked me what the word for "preservatives" was in French, and I guessed *préservatifs*. She then happily told her French language class that the bread in England was full of condoms.

"*Oesterreicher Fleisch*," my normally trustworthy partner told me, and it sounded convincing. I had missed the glint of mischief in her eye. So I

asked the man behind the counter, in all innocence, for a kilo of "Austrian man's flesh." Compared to Shakespeare's Shylock, I was being rather greedy—he had only demanded half a kilo from his creditor. As bad luck would have it, the shop assistant was a man from Austria. I don't think he would have agreed, in this case, that "the customer is always right."

The moral is, "Never trust your enemies, but, in certain situations, trust your best friends even less."

My presentation in Istanbul was before the famous George Bush press conference "shoe incident" in 2008, as captured in YouTube. I wasn't familiar with regional customs. I thought that I must have said something really good in Turkish to that audience in Istanbul because they all slowly clapped and whistled, and some of them even threw shoes onto the stage. "That's nice of them. But I'm OK for Turkish slippers at the moment, thank you," I thought as I dodged the flying footwear.

So the presentation clearly had gone well, and, afterwards, we went for a stroll to the spectacular Blue Mosque. A very loquacious local man joined us in the street outside, chatting away in accented, but good, English. They are friendly people, the Turks. In Istanbul, they always ask, "Where are you from?" When our New Best Friend asked us, my partner said "Switzerland," and our NBF said, "My sister, he lives in Switzerland." I followed with, "I'm from Scotland," whereupon our NBF replied, "Oh, my brother, she is in Glasgow." If I had said Ulan Bator, I am sure that he would have had a cousin living in Mongolia. We eventually convinced our NBF that we really were not going to buy any carpets. Off he went to tell other visitors about his global family, and we entered that historic and picturesque tourist attraction—the Grand Bazaar.

Bazaar encounter in Maslow's hierarchy

Politely refusing a hundred invitations to, "Just step inside and look—no problem," we strolled idly through the tradition-steeped arched hallways of that elegant, old Oriental shopping mall. We happened upon a little silk-scarf shop whose proprietor's name, written in faded gilt letters

on the dusty window, was "Mustafa P. Pea." In the doorway stood the worried-looking owner, shuffling restlessly from foot to foot. I wondered if his name betrayed his anxious appearance.

"Say 'yes' and surprise me," we heard him mutter quietly as we waved off his hopeful advances. As one, we stopped and looked at each other, said, "Yessss!" and walked into his shop. He was, as he had promised, quite surprised. But swiftly recovering, he pulled out scarves, pashminas, and shawls. Everything was beautifully woven in fine silk by the nimble fingers of southeast Turkish women. It said so on the labels, so it must have been true.

Before we got to the hard bargaining on price, I asked him in my most solicitous voice, "Don't see many tourists around—how's business?"

"Terrible," he said. "Absolutely awful."

"Too bad," I responded, secretly thinking that he had just handed me a huge negotiating advantage. He seemed keen to make a sale quickly, perhaps for the name-connected reason already mentioned. I think that he was on the first rung of Maslow's hierarchy of needs. After much haggling, hand waving, and threatening to leave the shop, we settled on a total price that was satisfying to us, but one that we also felt was fair to this relieved-looking shopkeeper. After all, we believe in win-win negotiation for sustainable success in business.

Everyone's a winner

There's a wonderful book called *Getting to Yes* by Roger Fisher, William Ury, and Bruce Patton. It's clear, straightforward, and easy to read. I often recommend it to my clients. It was first published in 1981, but, like leadership, its tenets are timeless. The third edition is still available on Amazon.com, which rather proves my point. It's not a long textbook—only two hundred pages in my second edition—but books don't have to be long to be good. (*Looking Down on Leaders* is about the same length, so I'm a little biased here.) I base many of my coaching discussions on the principles employed in this book.

"Ultimately a genuine leader is not a searcher for consensus," said Dr. Martin Luther King Jr., "but a molder of consensus." A win-win approach is nearly always the best in the end, not just in negotiations, but in all human interactions. When I discuss influencing skills, for example, I describe how persuasion has its disadvantages. Persuasion implies that you try to get others to agree with your views, or to do what you think should be done. The tactics used in persuasion include "legitimating." In other words, you use external factors to justify your view or your objective and to get others to go along with you. At least one textbook calls this, euphemistically, "proactive influencing." Legitimating uses language such as, "We have to comply with the law on this," or "Regulations say that you should." Quoting Martin Luther King Jr., as I just did, is another version of the same. Business executives are familiar with the chief executive's favourite mantra: "The board believes that…" and "The chairman wants…" Using this legitimating tactic usually gets what you want, but it comes at a price in the long term.

I have, several times, referred to modern organisations as being hollow cubes. Such organisations have some kind of centralised authority. In reality, however, responsibilities for detailed strategy and execution are devolved to global business units, regional managers, and functional heads. Typical large corporations have all three dimensions, and, like an expensive Swiss watch, many additional complications overlaid on top. It becomes difficult for the central authority, the CEO, to get what he, or she, wants because the other people in the organisation can find a hundred excuses and a thousand ways to beat the system. Typically, it's all very subtle and masked by convincing talk and persuasive PowerPoint slides, but it happens all the same.

Blocking the boss behind his back

Here's a simple example in my own recent experience. We have been working for years with a successful global corporation, based in Switzerland. We have coached and mentored more than twenty of its top executives over

the last seven years. Obviously, the group executive team thinks that we are adding value. It seems keen to spread our efforts uniformly throughout the worldwide organisation.

About a year ago, I met the group vice president of human resources in an Asian city. She invited me to dinner, where I would meet the head of Asia-Pacific region and the region's HR director. All was going well in the company of the big boss. The dinner was good, the wine even better, and conversation flowed smoothly and humorously. As we parted company, the local HR director voiced his appreciation of the meeting.

"It's been a pleasure to meet you, John," I said.

"Me too," replied John. "Very interesting."

"So, can I follow up with you, and have a more detailed discussion about the two potential mandates that we have been discussing?" I asked.

"Of course," said John. "Whenever you like. I will look forward to it."

"That was a good discussion," said the group vice president of HR after the regional people had left. "I think they liked you, and I hope you get a lot of business here with us." That night she headed back to HQ in Zürich.

Several days and two e-mails later, I finally got an answer from John, the region's HR director. "You can come to see me if you want, but I can only give you thirty minutes," he wrote.

The meeting took place in a dingy, windowless room. The conversation was as chilled as the air-conditioning, and that was set to its maximum. When I mentioned the potential mandates, the response was vague and evasive. "Well," I thought, "maybe he's having a bad day."

"Can I come back in a few weeks?" I asked. "Meanwhile, let's stay in touch by e-mail."

John's response was unenthusiastic.

Before my next visit to the region, I sent him three e-mails requesting a meeting. Two went unanswered. The third, on which I had copied the group VP, drew a grudging response.

"Yes, I can see you...but only for twenty minutes maximum, and I can't guarantee that I won't need to cancel at the last minute," John wrote.

What would you do in that situation? I simply informed the group VP of HR that her regional director seemed to have no interest in our services and left it at that. She told me later that, when she checked with John, he told a vastly different story.

That's just one example of persuasion having a negative effect. In general, when you get what you want by legitimating, you win the battle but you lose the war. Put yourself in the following position.

It's Friday afternoon. Your boss calls you and says, "The CEO needs your paper on the proposed acquisition. He's decided to talk to the chairman on Wednesday, and he is asking for a load of PowerPoints to summarise the key issues."

"But," you say, "it's Friday. When does he need them?"

"Monday morning," is the swift response. "And he wants fifteen slides, plus backups with more analysis, just in case."

It looks like you've just been given an all-nighter on Friday and a long weekend in the office. Your protest to the boss is ignored. "Sorry, but the CEO says he needs them first thing Monday morning," boss says.

So your boss gets to look good at no personal effort, and you spend the weekend preparing slides that you know nobody will look at. The immediate result is that the CEO gets what he wants. The long-term result, though, is that in the future you stay out of the boss's way on Fridays until you find another job. Meanwhile, your motivation has dropped to near zero.

Is there, then, a different way—a way that does not need legitimating to make it work? I believe that there is, and it uses the same principled mutual-respect approach that *Getting to Yes* describes so well. Many people believe there are only two styles of behaviour in business—aggression and passivity. I promote the third way—assertion. There is a language and a vocabulary of assertion that avoids confrontation without losing its force. The language depersonalises contentious issues and aligns the parties in achieving the same objectives. The behaviour of assertion shows equal respect for your views and objectives and for those of others involved in

the situation. It's not hard to learn. Note the difference between: "You guys really screwed up on this project. What are you going to do about it?" and "This project has gone badly wrong. What can we learn from this and what can we do to fix it?"

MacMentor says, "In negotiations, in business, and in life in general, assertive win-win behaviour, based on mutual respect, is nearly always best in the long run. There is no sustainable value in winning the battle only to lose the war."

Standing on the

Chairman's Desk

Arvin's story

I've written in another chapter about how our coaching is aimed at growing the bottom line. We are inspired by working with World Health Organisation executives, whose bottom line is human life. The more effective our coaching is, the more effective WHO people are in saving human lives around the world.

By contrast, Arvin was one of my banking clients. Now, don't get me wrong. Most bankers I know are nice men and women who just want to do a good job for the boss, get on with their peers, and be effective leaders of their people. Despite all the headline stories about rich bankers, $20 million sign-on bonuses, and enormous salaries, the reality is usually much different and more complex. Especially in Europe (and coming soon to the United States and Asia), public and media pressure is creating a reward system for bankers based more on sustainable business success and less on lucky gambling with other people's money. The reality of a private banker's life is that very wealthy people are usually not very nice people (well, I'd probably be bad-tempered too, if I were sitting on serious piles—of money, or any other kind), and wealth managers are always

online to them 24/7/365. There are, however, a few exceptions to the nasty high-net-worth rule.

Bill Gates had the reputation in Microsoft of having a "throw his toys out of the pram" temper, but he and Melinda are enormously generous supporters of many truly good causes. The culture in Warren Buffett's organisation is harsh and demanding, but he offers a tempting variety of charitable goodies from the "Buffet table." Bono probably has as many anti-Bonos as pro-Bonos in his business life, but he is a highly active do-gooder. Angelina may not always be as "Jolie" as she seems on television, but she is a dedicated and energetic donor and goodwill ambassador for deserving causes.

These Ultra HNW "nice guys" are, all the same, the exception. Many HNWs are rich in tangible wealth and poor in spirit. Have you ever strolled round the harbour in Monte Carlo and envied all those HNWs sitting on the glossily varnished teak decks of their yachts at sundown…frozen margaritas in their hands and frozen Botox masks on their faces? Don't envy them! Feel sad for them instead. Behind the Botox often lurks Victoria's Dirty Little Secret. There's a saying that you should never ask rich people how they made their first million. Don't question the second one either…or the third. Amongst the charming circle of UHNWs that I know about are tax cheats, robbers of United Nations aid funds, CEO fraudsters, and Interpol-evaders. My list includes people who have political opponents quietly disposed of (and one who has them rather less-than-quietly cooked to death in a very large deep-fat fryer). Amongst my second-hand circle of "friends" is also a travel agent who specialises in transporting young girls from Asia to Middle Eastern countries to provide "domestic and related services" to local households, headed by oil-wealthy gentlemen and their less-than-gentle multi-wives.

Marion Haste and the straw men

The following story comes from a source that declined to be publicly named, as he or she was "not authorised to speak for the organisation." Not that it matters much, because the organisation went spectacularly

bankrupt soon after the event. Two of the main characters, however, made their founding fortunes as follows.

The hero of the story was an innocent, young financial controller called Ivan. Ivan was an idealistic young man who had risen rapidly through a variety of financial positions. He had already been a financial controller in another group. He may have been idealistic, but he was not stupid. Ivan thought that his role was to ensure good governance and financial certitude in his new group. He was pleasantly surprised when he got the offer. He was to receive a reasonable basic salary, but the package also included a decent performance bonus and a package of share options that, on maturity, would make Ivan a rather wealthy young man—if the group's performance improved from its current lacklustre state. He was the only employee in the group to enjoy the same reward package as the board of directors.

Ivan was confident that this would happen. After all, he had plenty of real-life operations experience to offer, as well as financial management skills. He would lend his blue chip corporate experience to the businesses, help the group consolidate, and achieve considerable synergies from its portfolio of diverse businesses. Where a division had good management in place, Ivan would lend his objective observations and experienced guidance. Where a division was struggling to succeed, Ivan had other talents to offer. Success, and HNW status, seemed assured.

And so it came to pass…for a year or so. Ivan was influential in business acquisition exercises, helpful to divisional management, and respected when he briefed the monthly group board meeting on corporate performance. One small problem was that his immediate boss, the group CFO, seemed to find it hard to grasp the difference between the profit-and-loss account and the cash-flow statement. Another slight hiccup was that the same CFO was very keen on organisation charts. Almost every week, the group CFO would draw up a new organigram for the corporate headquarters. And, if he didn't like you that week, your name did not appear in the chart. This somewhat Orwellian practice was supposed to send you a message. But, like the boy who cried wolf too often, the message and the CFO

came to be ignored…except by the managing partner of the group's audit firm, whose top priority seemed to be keeping in the CFO's good books. This, as you will see shortly, was not in the interests of the group shareholders, bankers, or the group itself.

The group's estate management function was run by a mid-forties man called Ernest, an oily but charming "third-hand car salesman" type. He reported to the CEO, named Frank.

Yes, you're right about Frank and Ernest. I just made the names up to give you a little smile.

Frank and Ernest were anything but. When Ivan joined the group, the estates manager had just turned a tidy profit by renovating and selling the grand old mansion, in a country park setting, that had served for generations as its headquarters. He had moved the corporate office to an anonymous 1960s-architecture concrete block on the fringes of an ageing "new town" which was situated appropriately close to a well-known facility for the criminally insane. The group CEO was impressed by the possibilities.

Ivan was concerned that this diverse conglomerate was "conglomerating" even more, as the CEO, with board approval, set up a new division. This was now grandly called the property division and it was headed up by Oily Ernest, the car salesman. At this time, the group's gearing was a tidy 3 per cent and the board had no problem in approving this development. The bankers (these were the glory days of freewheeling city-property financing) were happy to extend sizeable amounts of capital. The audit partner was, naturally, ecstatic…because the group CFO had told him to be so.

One day, Ivan received a sounding-out call from Marion Haste, the young (and truly earnest) chief accountant of the new property division. Marion gradually grew more trusting in Ivan and, in a series of private discussions, she revealed that she was coming under severe pressure from her divisional boss to massage the monthly-report data. She was troubled by the fact that the division was engaging in bigger and bigger construction projects all the time. The co-developers were all newly formed companies with no financial history and with obscure names on the boards. Ivan was,

at the same time, monitoring the group's borrowings, which were creeping up as it invested capital into these projects. The group board, influenced by Frank the CEO and the flamboyant car salesman, Ernest, seemed untroubled.

The balloon burst in a spectacular way!

The big-five partner tentatively signed off the annual audit, pending further review of the development projects by an independent panel. At this point, long story made short, the joint projects were nearly all found to be jointly sponsored by the group and a series of insubstantial corporate vehicles, headed by "men of straw." The banks, on hearing of this report, immediately called in the group loans. The "straw men" vanished in a puff of smoke, and the group was left holding enormous liabilities. Gearing rose immediately from 3 per cent to 173 per cent, and it increased exponentially in the weeks and months after. The group was soon insolvent. Creditors shut down corporate HQ. They sold off profitable subsidiaries, and weak performers closed. Within one year, only the group CEO and his PA remained to wind up the remnants of this once grand old corporation.

Ivan moved on, up, and abroad, a sadder, wiser, but considerably less naive man. He lost his pension fund, and his share options were worthless, but the experience was instrumental in his career progressing to CFO, and later CEO, in several countries.

As this was just a fairy tale, with no happy ending, Ivan could just speculate that Frank and Ernest had only been frank and earnest about one thing...their desire to get rich quick. It would never be proved that they, their friends, and their families were the straw men who set up the shell companies as co-developers and ran off with the cash, leaving partially completed buildings around the country.

Did Frank and Ernest finally get their true rewards as a guest of Her Majesty in the nearby "hostel" for the criminally insane? Ivan never knew for sure, but this being an unusual "Once upon a time" story, the answer was, "probably not!"

"So," MacMentor asks, "what's the moral of this story?"

There's more than one, I guess. "Don't trust reward packages that are tied to the group board's earnings," is one. If you are a group controller, you need to be an independent and rigorous upholder of financial ethics. "Don't let the board be swayed by the thought of easy profits," is another, especially if there are external, unknown parties involved. "Don't believe that audit partners are pure and unbiased guardians of shareholder value and are not influenced by the size of the audit fees," is another. I could go on, but you are all smart cookies who can figure it out for yourselves.

Wrapping up with Arvin

Arvin the banker was one of those clients whose bottom line was human lives…at least, one life…his own. His mandate was, "I'm brilliant. My colleagues are dumb. Get me the bonus I deserve." So he paid the assh*le premium. Notwithstanding, he wasn't really a bad chap…fair-ish hair, blue-ish eyes, forty-ish age, Engl-ish…Need I say more? It was fun to work with this "off the wall" personality. Nothing, I began to think, would surprise me about Arvin.

Until he stood on the chairman's desk.

Now, this wasn't just any old common, or garden, variety of chairman but a highly respected pillar of the European banking community who later went on to achieve fame, and notoriety, on the global stage. Charlie Chairman was tall and imposing, even while sitting down.

"Good morning, Arvin," I said breezily, as he entered my office for a coaching meeting. "And what's new today?"

"Nothing much," he said, "except that I stood on the chairman's desk this morning."

"That's nice, Arvin," I replied. "So tell me how the job is going."

"I'm serious," said Arvin. "I stood on the chairman's desk this morning…and I'm proud of myself!"

"Ohmygawd," I thought. "We've never had a client fired before. I guess this is our first."

"Tell me about it," I told Arvin, with a strange sinking feeling in my stomach.

"Well, Charlie called me up to his office this morning. I think he wanted to give me a pep talk or something. I walked in and he was sitting behind his desk—very tall chap, you know."

"Go on," I instructed, my heart sinking lower than a desktop in a kindergarten.

"Well, he told me to sit down. The chair was frightfully low, and I found myself looking up at him," said Arvin. "I wasn't going to fall for that silly old trick, so I jacked up my seat to be at eye level with the chairman."

"Good idea!" I said. "What happened next?"

"He pumped his chair up even higher, so I did the same," said Charlie with a naughty smile on his face. "Then I found that mine was as high as it could go, so I stood up."

"And then?" I asked.

"Well, I saw what ghastly game he was playing when he stood up as well—and he's frightfully tall, you know."

"And then?" I asked again, somewhat afraid of Arvin's answer.

"I stood on the stupid chair, and he did the same," said Arvin, as I groaned inwardly at the inevitable conclusion to this "battle of twits" between two of the finest products of England's boarding-school system.

"So," he exclaimed with obvious pride at his own enterprise, "I got up on his desk and left him no room to join me. I won!" he finished with a triumphal ring in his voice.

The Duke of Wellington might, or might not, have said, "The Battle of Waterloo was won on the playing fields of Eton." But this battle certainly

wasn't, as it ended in an embarrassing stalemate and a literal "climb down" by both parties.

At this point, I remembered something else that the duke once said at Waterloo. Sitting on his horse before the battle started, a young subaltern turned to the duke and said, "I've never been in battle before, Sir. Can you offer me some advice?"

"Piss while you can, my boy," replied the duke. "Piss while you can."

Heeding the duke's sound advice and feeling that my meeting with Arvin was going to be a long session, I took myself off to the toilet—to enjoy a moment of physical and emotional relief and to consider my next smart coaching question.

"So what," MacMentor asks, "have you learned from this 'Arvin the Banker' story?"

Well, I suggest that the duke's advice, literally and metaphorically, is sound. Take advantage of opportunity, because it may not come again.

As for standing on the chairman's desk? Don't try it! Arvin survived that battle, but he lost the war, and he left the bank "to spend more time with his family and pursue other interests" and all the other usual clichés that you hear when someone gets fired.

Coming up - Say "high" to ROI…

O'clock rule"

Switched on for service

A key element of our coaching service for global business leaders is our open access between meetings for urgent matters. I advise our clients, "You don't stop being a family man or woman when you leave home in the morning…and you don't stop being a business executive when you go home at night." If something is urgent or is worrying them, we're available out of hours to speak to. Calls at the weekend and in the evening are not unusual. Our clients travel the world frequently, and we want to be available to them whenever they need some objective and experienced advice. Our team has members based in Asia and the United States as well as in Europe. They are engaged on regional mandates and are available also for clients visiting from other places.

I did have one client who at least considered the idea of calling me in the early hours. Marco was managing director of a BBC radio subsidiary in Switzerland who was facing many challenges in the business side of his operation. He said, "Iain, I find this coaching truly *fantastic*!" (Remember that he was in show business!) "I'd love to do a radio broadcast on my experiences as your client!" The broadcast became a six-part series, repeated

on Sundays. (On Sundays, there's not much to do in Geneva, the home of Calvin, except listen to radio broadcasts about coaching.)

In one of those broadcasts, Marco said something that made me wish I'd thought of it first as an elevator pitch. He said, "You know, my coach told me that I could call him if I was worried about anything—even if it was late at night," he explained to his Sunday-evening audience, which was desperate for something more exciting than dusting the furniture. (In Geneva, on a Sunday, you dust quietly, in case the "noise police" give you a big fine for disturbing the peace.) "I'd never dream of calling him at four in the morning," said Marco, "but if I wake up worried in the early hours, I can go right back to sleep again…because I know that I can call him later and get an answer to my problem."

Thank you, Marco!

Our "five o'clock rule"

I'd never thought of that—coaching as a sleep-inducer. I've never had a client fall asleep in one my coaching meetings…not that I've noticed, anyway. One or two have come close, though. We have a five o'clock rule. If a client comes for a meeting at the end of the working day, then after five o'clock, hospitality comes in a glass. And, if you like, it can have a Scottish flavour, and you even have a choice of "soft and sweet Speyside" or "rough and smoky Islay." They maybe don't fall asleep, but they usually leave our meetings more relaxed than when they arrived. Coaching is always a pleasure. But when it comes in a glass, it is doubly so!

Always online

We are happy to take calls on urgent issues at nine o'clock at night and on weekends. That's what we're here for! In general, the idea of being "always online" is not too smart, but it's a way of life for busy global executives these days, isn't it? You may be in Beijing and it's midnight, but your boss in London "needs to talk to you…now!" When I was a CEO in Europe, my boss in the United States often exercised the right to call me

in the early hours, with detailed questions on our latest operational performance. Most of the time, it was just a senseless exercise of personal power, but I still had to sleep with a stack of Excel spreadsheets beside the bed to be sure to have answers for him.

I once worked with a highly stressed Polish-American executive called Pawel, based in Europe and working for a US corporation. Pawel never left the office until 9:00 p.m., and he always took work home with him. He was frequently on conference calls at midnight and at five o'clock the next morning. He was burned out and inefficient and considering retirement—at fifty years of age. His (second) wife was considering divorce! I persuaded him to leave the office no later than 7:00 p.m. and to come back no earlier than 7:00 a.m. the next day, and never, ever, to work on the weekends. He agreed to try it for one month.

At the end of the month, I asked, "Well, did the corporation collapse because you were working less?"

"Not at all," answered Pawel the Pole. "In fact, I've been very productive since we last met. I finished two major projects and got EC approval… and a slap on the back from my boss too!"

"Well," I thought, "that's a lot better than a slap on the ear." He was now coming to work fresh and rested. Even though he was still working a twelve-hour day, he was much more productive and insightful. He started jogging in the early morning (I'm not especially recommending this—I'm more of an evening exerciser, myself) and he installed a small gym at home soon afterwards.

I hate to use this cliché, but "Work smarter, not harder" has a lot of truth in it.

This "always on" mode is not good for executives suffering from the negative stress that our superiors create for us. If you think that the boss might call you late at night, or if he/she routinely sends you e-mails on Saturday evenings, how are you going to relax and rebuild your brain cells? You will always be tense and distracted. And you will definitely not be visionary and productive. It doesn't help that the boss doesn't call or e-mail you—you'll

then be left wondering if he doesn't value your input anymore. A little paranoia is a good defence mechanism, but more than a little is harmful.

The "five-franc rule"

Another thing about "always on" mode is that it can be very tedious for your life partner unless he or she is equally committed to the business. I know that I have written, "You don't stop being an executive when you go home at night," but really! Is it not time to give it a rest, if only for the sake of your long-suffering partner? Ours is a 24/7 partnership—we work, travel, and live together. I have no idea how it works so well, but it does. We do try to give work a rest, though we are not entirely successful. Some years ago, we introduced a "five-franc rule." You can use dollars—we just happen to live in Switzerland where the currency is francs. The rule is very simple—if either partner mentions work after 8:00 p.m., in goes five francs to the cookie jar. You might need a very big cookie jar until not mentioning work becomes a habit. It doesn't take long, when we're being honest with ourselves, to accumulate enough for a nice dinner somewhere to 'celebrate' the fact that we failed to avoid letting our business crowd out our social life.

I have just advised one senior executive to switch off his Blackberry at 8:00 p.m. every night and all during the weekend. I advised him to tell his boss (a US-based global leader) that he would be doing so in the interests of efficiency. Luckily, he has the kind of boss—a very capable woman—who understands his point. I'm eagerly awaiting his feedback. But I'm willing to bet a bottle of "soft and sweet Speyside" that he will now be more productive, his team will be less tense, and his challenges will all be lined up in nicely prioritised, solution-focused fashion.

"Always online" is bad for executives and bad for business. But that's not quite true of the executive coaches in our team. Of course, we need to sleep, like anyone else, but our motives for working in a third career are quite different from when we ourselves were senior leaders in big companies. We are turned on by "making a difference" through excellent leadership, and global leadership doesn't come in a "nine-to-five" mode. We like

to be available when needed, and, sometimes, this availability can have major benefits for our clients.

I wrote in another chapter about a client who had been removed from his role on a Friday afternoon, with no real warning. He was greatly distressed, and I was seriously concerned for his well-being that weekend. I believe, and he has said, that knowing someone was there and responding with encouragement to his e-mails and text messages was very important to him. It was the start of a highly successful recovery phase. He is in a great place now. But he knows that, if he is ever in trouble again, I am always online for him.

Say "high" to ROI—a Sunday-night saga

Being "always online" for our clients can have very significant benefits in other ways too. I once got a phone call from a client at nine o'clock on a Sunday night. I'd had a good dinner and two glasses of a nice Swiss Merlot, so I was fairly relaxed. My call was from Morris, a regional president of a Fortune 50 corporation. Morris was in great distress, and that in itself was quite unusual for this experienced, mature, and stable executive.

"Iain," said Morris with anxiety in every syllable, "this company is going down the tubes fast, and I can't stand aside and watch it happen."

"What's going on?" I replied.

"The CEO's got it all wrong. Chuck's screwing up big-time, and nobody's got the b*lls (think 'courage') to tell him. They're all scared of being fired. I might be, too, but I have just got to say something."

"Tell me more," I said.

"Chuck's got the wrong strategy. We're losing out on all fronts, and he's too proud to admit it!" he exclaimed.

"How can I help?" I asked.

"Tell me how I can speak to Chuck so he'll listen. He's just going to get mad and yell like he always does…so how can I get the message through?" asked Morris.

"OK," I said, "let's talk this through from the start." We then discussed the problem from the beginning, in small bites, and in a logical sequence.

Morris, who had been frantic at the start, was beginning to calm down. We talked for forty-five minutes. By this time, it was nearly ten o'clock that Sunday night.

"Looks like we have some kind of a plan," I told Morris. "How do you feel about it?"

Morris sounded a lot better than he had an hour earlier.

"Let's sleep on it and talk again tomorrow morning at nine o'clock," I suggested. Morris agreed and we hung up.

Next morning, Morris and I reviewed the rough plan and refined the approach. Morris was in good shape and ready to risk his job. He resolved to call his boss in the United States that night. As bad luck would have it, the boss was away on one of his frequent trips, and so Morris left a message. You know what voicemails are like, don't you? They're just like most e-mails—usually too short, badly phrased, and almost guaranteed to cause problems.

The boss got back late at night, tired and frustrated after yet another unhappy visit to a major customer. It was in the early hours of the morning where Morris was, but that didn't stop Chuck. He called Morris and yelled down the phone at him for an hour.

"What are you saying—I don't know how to run this f***ing company?" was the most polite part of the diatribe. But after exhausting his entire repertoire of insults and epithets, Chuck calmed down enough to say, "If you think you can do it better than me, give me a plan by Friday!" With that, Chuck slammed down the phone.

Morris updated me the next morning, and I advised him to gather a few trusted lieutenants to come up with a broad plan by Friday. Morris and I reviewed the plan as it emerged, with me role-playing a "hostile audience." Come Friday, Chuck called Morris.

"Good plan. Maybe you're right! Get your ass over here Monday, and we'll go through it with the top team."

American bosses do seem to be obsessed with flying donkeys, don't they?

Morris flew over on Sunday night and met Chuck and his senior people the next day. Secretly, they were all delighted that Morris had done what they had not dared to do. Support in the EC was unanimous.

Over the next five weeks, the plan grew into something that resembled a dramatic new strategy. With every additional executive bringing in refinements and some good "devil's advocate" debating, the plan was soon fully polished and ready to make public to analysts and all the stakeholders. The top team was impressed by the unusually harmonious way in which they had planned together to reach a mutually acceptable conclusion. What they did not know, and what they will never know in that corporation, is that some of them were working with one of our coaches. In total secrecy, we were collaborating as a coaching team to ensure that all the inputs from our individual clients were harmonious and that "all the arrows were aligned."

Such is the value of an experience-based executive coach. We've all been in that CEO hot seat. We've all worked in top teams for bosses like Chuck. We've all been in situations where a strategy needed urgent and radical reshaping. Added to this mix was our "inside outside" objectivity and "always online" accessibility.

The corporation announced a major global restructuring of the business. They promised to deliver (and did) an additional five hundred million dollars on the bottom line each year from this new strategy.

When the subject of Return on Investment on coaching is raised, people often refer to the Manchester and Metrix studies on a group of coaching projects that calculated an average ROI on coaching of 600 per cent to the corporations involved. That's impressive, but don't be misled by that high number. The ROI on Chuck's coaching was nearly 40,000 per cent, modestly assuming that our coaching support led to only a tiny fraction of the eventual benefit.

A very experienced HR vice president once told me, "You don't need a fancy business case to calculate the ROI on good executive coaching—you can do it on the back of a business card."

I couldn't agree more!

BUYING IN BERLIN AND Brooklyn—two "due diligence"

stories

Buying in Berlin

I've always thought that people were pretty central to business. Customers are people, employees are people, suppliers are people; even senior leaders are people, though some of them do a good job of hiding it. Without people, you just have a collection of machines, trucks, buildings, and all the other stuff that you see in the balance sheet. But it takes people—the big asset that you never see on the balance sheet—to turn that collection into a living, profit-earning, customer-satisfying enterprise.

So it was that, back in the mid-seventies when I was a very young and only half-qualified management accountant (that was so long ago that engineers still used slide rules, and I was proud when my electro-mechanical calculating machine was replaced by a hotshot new suitcase-sized, valve-powered electronic calculator), I got sent to Germany. I was supposed to help out at a company in which my employer, ICI, was interested. It was only intended to be a two-day visit, with a very vague objective, but just as I was packing my briefcase to get back to Scotland to do my Christmas shopping, my boss called me.

"Iain," he said, "we're thinking of buying the company. Stay on for a bit, and do a due diligence."

Well, the "bit" turned out to be two weeks, and I just made the last plane home for Christmas by leaving the keys in the unlocked company car, running through check-in, and rushing out to the plane, which was on the runway and revving up for take-off (such things were still possible then).

And I hadn't a clue what the boss meant by "due diligence." I had not gone that far in my accounting studies, but I didn't dare tell the boss that I had no idea. The clue was in the word "diligence." It suggested to me that I should check out what we were buying before we paid the money—a reasonable assumption. So off I went round the factory, checking out the inventory and the equipment. I talked to the shop-floor guys as they cooked lunch…long, thick sausages that they called "girlfriend tamers." I still don't understand why.

I examined the order books, studied the last five years' annual accounts, and reviewed the budgets. It then dawned on me that the common factor, and the thing that we were really buying, was the people. Nothing else would become reality without the skills, experience, connections, knowledge, influence, and motivation of the people in the company. And so, I thought, I'd better check out the people too. I discussed the business with Herr Schmid, the founder of the company—one of those driven technical entrepreneurs from communist East Germany who always needed to check out his latest brilliant ideas as soon as he thought of them. The best ideas, of course, always come at four in the morning, and so I also interviewed his poor, overworked, sleepless deputy, Klaus.

I walked around the factory floor and offices and talked to the engineers and the administration staff. The business seemed to be in sound health and a good fit for our corporate strategy. We bought the business, and, in due course, it fulfilled its promise.

Buying in Brooklyn

Some years later, I was the controller of a London-based multinational group. I was convinced by this early Berlin experience, and others, that due diligence had to place the people aspect at the centre of scrutiny. So I set off for the United States at the head of a small acquisition team.

We were looking at a company called Ulysses, Inc., which was in one of our group's business sectors undergoing rapid consolidation. We could see the strategic fit. Discussions on principle, and principal, had gone well. The company was badly managed under the tyrannical grip of the widow of the founder. Ulysses, Inc. was losing money with impressive regularity, but we thought that we could integrate it, achieve synergies, and turn it into profit.

It was snowing and -5 degrees Celsius when I touched down at JFK. The next day was +15 degrees Celsius—but that's New York in January. My buddy, the CFO of the group company that wanted to buy Ulysses, and I checked into our Midtown Manhattan hotel, and then we strolled over to the shimmering glass tower that was home to our financial advisers. They were one of the Big Five, as it was before Arthur Andersen blew up all over Enron. We met the local team, a bunch of young Harvard hotshots with polished shoes, dazzling teeth, and well-oiled hair. These were the numbers guys who were going to check out the data, overheat the photocopiers and the secretaries, and generally upset the entire Ulysses management team with excessive demands for paper, in the hot pursuit of billable hours.

I had suggested to Ulysses, based on Bergen Street in Brooklyn, that we make our own way over from Lexington Avenue to Bergen by subway.

"No way, José," said the Ulyssians. "We're gonna send a driver for you!" Our driver turned out to be an off-duty New York cop, licensed to kill and packing a loaded handgun in his glove compartment.

(As I write this in 2013, I am in New York again. I've just been back to Brooklyn yesterday. I walked down Bergen Street for old times' sake. You could say it has changed a little—somewhat gentrified, to say the least.)

Crack shots in Brooklyn

Back in the eighties, our minders would not even let us walk the two hundred yards down the street to another part of the factory. They drove us there. When we got to the office, we found out why. The fifth-floor boardroom was equipped with bulletproof-glass windows, but the outer pane still had a large star-shaped reminder of the locals' sharpshooting skills, just to underline who was the boss in Brooklyn. Across the street, on the fourth floor of a tenement building, I could see stoves, some pots, and a bunch of rough-looking men.

"That's unusual," I said. "Men in the kitchen doing the cooking!"

I was thinking that every woman's dream is to have three men at the same time…one in the kitchen, one doing the cleaning, and one pressing shirts.

"Don't be naive," said the head Ulyssian. "They ain't cookin' no hamburger. What they's cookin', they be sellin' on the corner of Bergen once it's cooled."

My introduction to crack cocaine, Brooklyn style!

Toothless and Precious

Down below, illuminated in the flattering amber light of a sodium streetlamp, stood Toothless and Precious. Business was slack that night and the weather was mild, so Precious entertained herself, the Ulyssians, the Harvard hotshots, and me by periodically pulling up her sweater to reveal the two things that were the most precious about her. Meanwhile, Toothless kept a keen eye open for passing trucks and potential customers therein. "How did she get that name?" I naively asked the CFO. "Because she ain't got no teeth," he explained as he stared wide-eyed at this simpleminded British guy who was asking such an obvious question. "And, before you ask, I don't know how she lost her teeth…but it might be connected with her specialty service for truck drivers and a mistake with a gearshift."

Waving a fond "good evening" to these ladies of the night, we adjourned the meeting and made our weary, gun-protected, way back

over the Brooklyn Bridge and up FDR Drive to the relative normality of our Midtown four-star hotel. Several days went by. The Harvard hotshots burned out three copiers and the patience of all the secretaries. My buddy and I reviewed the reviews, studied the studies, and due'd the diligence. We interviewed the head Ulyssian and decided that Mrs. President and Mr. Chief Executive were overpaid and underperforming but that the rest of the team was reasonably all right for the acquired business.

Cheap shots and the disgruntled deputy

Then we pulled one of those tricks that you don't find in Harvard's excellent *Getting to Yes* book on win-win negotiating. We made friends with a disgruntled second-in-command. Now I had never thought of doing this before, but it has served me well since in negotiations in Mexico, China, the United States, and several emerging nations. Every day since we'd arrived, Karl the corporate controller had lost no opportunity to tell us that his boss, the CFO, was less qualified, less experienced, less able, and generally less brilliant than Karl was. Karl clearly wanted the boss's job after the acquisition. Privately, we had come to think that Karl and his boss were fighting it out for first place in the "who has the lowest IQ" competition. As the CEOptimist was to teach me later, this was no problem, but an excellent opportunity to gain some inside information to help us in the final negotiation.

Karl, however, was acting coy. He hinted that he knew where the bodies were buried. But he never gave us anything useful to use. Buddy and I hatched a scheme. We would invite Karl the Coy to dinner and play "good drunk, bad drunk." The game was simple. I would pretend to drink but would stay sober, while Buddy plied Karl with burgundy, bourbon, and beer until his tongue loosened. Buddy would booze with him, and I would ask the smart questions about buried bodies.

Entrees followed starters (or, as we would say in Europe, entrees were followed by main courses), each one generously accompanied by copious servings of white, red, and rosé wines. Karl the Coy, all this time, managed

to ingest large quantities of food and wine while keeping his lips tightly sealed about the buried bodies…until the moment came to reveal all! Karl sat back, cigar and a big shot of Kentucky's finest in hand, and opened his mouth.

Out of Karl's lips streamed every dirty little secret and every location of every dead corporate body in the entire organisation. And not one word from Karl the Comatose was intelligible! The good drunk, bad drunk ploy had been far too successful for its own good. There was nothing left to do but bundle the slobbering inebriate into a passing yellow cab and call it a night.

The next day dawned, the final day of the due-diligence review. Buddy the Bad Drunk had a blinding headache and great difficulty in even saying "due diligence." It came out as something like "Jew Jill ingests," which had nothing to do with a wealthy lady from Brooklyn Heights and her eating habits, but much to do with his Bourbon-anaesthetised tongue. Off we headed down FDR Drive, over the Brooklyn Bridge, up Bergen, and into Ulysses. All that remained was a final inspection of the hotshots' report, a final walk round the factory, and a taxi back to JFK.

Management by walking around

When I speak to MBA classes, I draw the letters MBA on the board. Then I insert the letter "W" between the "B" and the "A." I tell the students, "Your MBA is going to be useful, but the best leadership tool of all is the MBWA."

"Management by walking around" is always a good thing to do. In this case it was decisive. I set off on my walkabout with Al, the COO. Now you'd think that Al, as head of operations, would know his operations. Not a bit of it! Al could barely find the exit door to the grounds outside the factory. Walking around to find traces of buried bodies, I spied an iron hatchway on the weed-covered ground. "What's in that?" I asked. "That's… that's…that's…" stuttered Al, as he struggled to read a faded little sign beside the hatch. And Al then named a highly carcinogenic solvent used in

the process. "How much is in there?" I asked Al. "It's probably nearly full," replied the COO.

My dear old mother used to say, "Empty barrels make the most noise." I thought of her as Al opened the hatch and our voices echoed eerily round the patently empty tank.

"That's funny!" said Al in a puzzled voice. "It should be nearly full."

"Funny" wasn't the word I was thinking while I wondered what had happened to the highly poisonous carcinogen that Al had thought was in there.

"Let's try this one here," I told Al, and the lid creaked open. "Another one is empty, Al!" I said, and he looked increasingly nervous. "How many tanks have you got here?"

"About fifteen," responded Al in a less-than-convincing voice.

"Strange," I said. "I've just counted twenty…and there are some more over here. I make that twenty-four…and here's another one in the corner. Let's check them all out." One lid creaked open, followed by another and another…and every one revealed an empty or half-empty tank. Al became more and more nervous. Here were twenty-five tanks that should have been full of poison…and most of them were empty.

"We'd better get an expert to check these out," I told Al.

Buddy and I headed back to JFK and our flight to Europe, greatly concerned about the non-financial aspects of the due diligence that we had, in theory, just completed. The next week, we called in a soil engineer to do an expert study of the risk from these tanks. The result was truly shocking. Twenty-five tank loads of highly dangerous cancer-causing solvent were quietly leaking into the Brooklyn water table. Our "management by walking around" exercise had revealed a huge non-financial risk to our company if we proceeded with the acquisition. We terminated the negotiation immediately.

Six months later, New York State published its latest list of environmental offenders. Number one on the list was Ulysses, Inc. Not surprisingly, it immediately filed for Chapter 11 protection. But, in due course, Ulysses

was declared beyond salvation and was wound up. Al, the COO, retired early, and the CEO relocated to some sunny Caribbean island beyond the reach of American justice.

And Mrs. President? As I write this on the banks of the East River some thirty years later, who knows? She's probably gazing at me now from behind a lace curtain in Brooklyn Heights.

So here's MacMentor's message if you're considering buying a company.

"Harvard hotshots' data analysis is all very well…but when it comes to truly valuing an acquisition, it's the people and walking around and looking under the workbenches and behind doors and in all the corners and using your common sense that really count."

Move on up the Morale Curve…

THE "UPS AND DOWNS" OF
the Swiss Alps and

the Morale Curve

It's what you don't know that kills you

The sun was blazing down. It was early October in Toggenburg, the northern tip of the Swiss Alps. It's just as beautiful, if less known, than the tourist regions of Switzerland. The Churfirsten Mountains, a "dragon's back" of seven jagged limestone peaks, are just as dramatic as the Matterhorn or the Eiger, if not as high. I had started late, but I thought that I had enough time to reach my destination before nightfall.

I like to hike alone at high altitude. Focusing only on where I place my next step on the narrow and dangerous paths, my brain frees itself of all other concerns. I often remind myself that the friendly mountain inns from where I set off are higher than Britain's loftiest mountain, Ben Nevis. Of course, I prepare for foreseeable dangers, so I carry my compass, ropes, torch, and whistle. But, as in business leadership, it's the unknown that gets you into trouble. This day, I had no map for the route I was to follow.

And so, off I went on this October afternoon, on a path that I had never trod before. Below me, encircled by tree-robed mountain peaks, was a vivid turquoise lake. The marmots, already fattened for their long hibernation,

slept safely underground. Cheeky squirrels scampered around, building their food stores for the winter. Far across the deep valley, I could hear the lonely booming of a stag in rut.

At first, the way was easy, but soon the path grew higher and steeper. I crossed a vast area of deep limestone sinkholes, half hidden by dense, green Alpenrose shrubs. I laboured up one slope and down, into the next valley and up again to a yet higher ridge. In due course, I grew tired of the endless climbing up and scrambling down and was becoming a little concerned. In the alpine autumn, the sun sets early behind the mountains, and the temperature in the valleys can plummet by twenty degrees in minutes. The shadows of the peaks were growing longer. Just as I was thinking of turning back on the safe route down, I spotted a familiar-looking outcrop.

"Aha," I thought. "I know that one. Just over that hill is a valley that will take me to the chairlift. I can get to it before it closes."

I was wrong. This was not the place I knew. I climbed a near-vertical rock face, only to find myself entangled in a thicket of stunted trees. All around were deep and narrow fissures in the limestone. One false step and I'd break my leg, alone in the mountains in the late afternoon. Finally, I struggled free and clambered down to the next deeply shadowed valley. To my great surprise and his, I found myself in front of a local hunter, heading out from his mountain cabin, gun in hand.

My guide and saviour! He told me that I was still an hour away from the chairlift. But he kindly showed me the way. I climbed out of that dark and dismal valley, and walked quickly up the narrow path to the final summit. In semidarkness, I reached the chairlift just as the attendant, bemused at such a late arrival, was closing up to retire to his home in the village far below.

The lonely climb to the next job

We do a lot of senior-executive career-transition coaching. We never advertise it, but our clients often ask us to help their executives make an "elegant exit" from the corporation. Good companies care what happens.

They want departing, faithful corporate servants to find the right next job and to be goodwill ambassadors for the business.

It's lonely at the top, but it's much more so if you are no longer there. Job search at a high level is not easy. There are few empty places at the top of the corporate pyramid. Deprived of all the networking structures and internal support services that you have taken for granted over the years, it can be the most isolating and demoralising time in your life. You're on your own—no more executive dining room, corporate credit card, business card, impressive title, big-company name, or company car, and nobody but you to buy the new laptop and install its software. And, the biggest blow of all, you lose your sense of purpose and identity.

It's a rough and rocky upward path, with steep slopes to climb and deep valleys of despondency between. You start off with low morale and a sense of bereavement. If you're lucky, your partner will be sympathetic and supportive, but he or she will feel the same sense of loss, bewilderment, and uncertainty. Essentially, you are out there on your own. We in our coaching team have all been there—we know how it feels. Helping an executive find the right next step gives us huge satisfaction.

It's critical for us to advise our client in realistic terms. "This is probably going to take some time. Looking for your new position is going to be a full-time job. There will be many moments of high optimism followed by deep disappointment. But, if you do it right, and work hard with our guidance, you will probably look back on this time as a turning point in your life."

Scottish swimming lessons and Clive's story

MacMentor says, "What doesn't kill you makes you stronger!" MacMentor never had my Scottish swimming lessons. Our school swimming lessons started in early April in an open-air pool. It was a tidal pool where the Atlantic Ocean swept in twice a day, just in case the water was getting too warm. Well, it clearly didn't kill me, but it sure put me off swimming in anything less than blood temperature.

Clive, from London, had been successful throughout his life. He had never experienced failure. He had been a brilliant doctoral student, a good athlete, a "Sword of Honour" army officer, and a respected business executive.

All went well…until he reached the age of fifty-three!

After twenty-five successful years in his company, latterly reporting directly to his CEO, Clive left to become chief executive of a business in another sector, in another country. It was a tough business, with a domineering executive chairman and many challenges. He had never had the benefit of my Scottish swimming lessons or of MacMentor's advice on "what doesn't kill you."

It was never going to work. Within a year, Clive was out of a job and looking for the next one.

MacMentor says, "One new challenge at a time is fine. Two together is unwise…and three at the same time will probably kill you!"

For the first time, Clive had failed at something, but his life had never prepared him for failure. He grew seriously depressed, and his self-confidence plummeted. Clive asked me to help him with his career transition.

During our first coaching conversation, I tried to prepare him for the inevitable ups and downs of executive job search. I like to talk with a marker pen in my hand. "A picture paints a thousand words," goes the old saying. Taking my pen in my hand, I went to the flipchart and drew the following graph. It still hangs on my wall because everyone who enters my office can identify with it in some way or other.

The morale curve

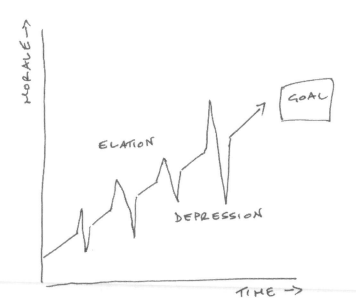

I explained to Clive, "This is how your morale will go in this career transition. It will, over time, go up significantly. I can promise you that you will eventually succeed."

"But it won't go smoothly upwards," I warned him. "You will get some interviews, and your morale will rise. Then you will have a bad meeting, and your morale will fall below where it was before. Then a headhunter will call about an attractive job, and your morale, like this curve, will soar. You will think that this is the job of your dreams. You will get an interview and a second and a third. Then," I said, "one day, it will all go wrong."

This happens often in career transition. The funding for the venture does not materialise. A fabulous new candidate emerges at the last minute. Many things can go wrong beyond your control. Because your expectation has grown so high, the drop in your morale will be all the steeper.

"You just need to persevere, keep on working hard, and rely on me as your guide and mentor. You will eventually get to where you want to be," I advised Clive.

Samuel and Seneca at the crossroads of luck and opportunity

"I've been lucky all my life…and the harder I work, the luckier I get," said the famous film producer Samuel Goldwyn. Seneca, a first-century Roman philosopher, allegedly said, "Luck is where the crossroads of opportunity and preparation meet."

I go a little further in my advice to executive clients. I say, "Luck happens when hard work meets opportunity…but you should create the opportunity yourself." Then we have a discussion about the importance of networking and being proactive.

Clive invested a lot of hard work in his career transition. He created many possible opportunities, which, for one reason or another, disappeared. A business collaboration proposal from a big corporate-services firm excited him greatly.

"Don't get worked up about this one, Clive," I told him. "The ethics of that business sector are not yours. I think they will use your knowledge and connections, but I don't think it will result in a job. And, if it does, sooner or later you are going to feel compromised by the conflict between your ethics and theirs."

Clive listened carefully, and the inevitable happened. When the other party had extracted all they were going to get from Clive, they announced that there would not be a job offer. Clive's morale slumped to the deepest point on the morale curve.

But, prepared by the morale-curve picture and our discussions, he soon got going again on the transition exercise. Clive has just received an attractive offer of a seat on the board of an exciting and fast-growing business—one in which he will fit very comfortably.

MacMentor says three things:

"First, if you have a choice, face one big challenge at a time. Be realistic about the size of the task and your own abilities. It will always be harder than you expect, to find the right job and your resources, smaller than you think."

"Next, whatever your project is—be it a job search, or writing a book, or some other earnest pursuit—look at the morale curve and expect that the path to success will be a rough and rocky, up-and-down slog."

"Finally," says MacMentor, "if you persevere, you will get there in the end. But you must actively create the opportunity to take advantage of good luck when it comes along."

BANDWIDTH AND
"the Last Mile" of

Real Leadership

Blinded by science

"What's the longest word in the English language?" asked William, my daughter's young son. "Antidisestablishmentarianism" came out of the dim reaches of my schoolboy memory.

"Wrong," he said and grinned. A quick Google search brought me to a website that claims the chemical name for the substance Titin contains nearly 190,000 letters. "Wrong again," pronounced William, grinning again. "It's 'smiles'…because there's a mile between the first and last letters."

"How could I have been caught by that old joke?" I asked myself.

Next morning, under the shower, that episode came into mind as I thought of the good news that my nephew had just e-mailed to me. It all began a year ago.

James is one of my Scottish nephews and one of two brothers who are both highly qualified and expert, caring family doctors. James was telling me about his medical practice. "It is," he said, "successful enough, but capable of much more—if only we had the facilities."

"Tell me about it. What is your vision?" I asked.

"Well, we need the new building that's been promised for years. The budget is there—we just need the civil servants to unblock the process. Once we get that, we can have five doctors in their own surgeries. We can also have a physiotherapist and a fully equipped physiotherapy room. Oh, and we can…"

"Hold on," I interrupted. "That's your plan. Tell me what your vision is. What is it that wakes you up at four in the morning, full of excitement?"

"Usually it's a phone call from the local police," he replied. "It's exciting when there's a really juicy murder, and I get called out to do the first examination."

"I understand," I said. "But that's not what I meant. I want you to imagine what might be, not what is staring you in the face. Did you see that movie, *The Magic of Belle Isle*, with Morgan Freeman as the crusty old writer? He's trying to teach a nine-year-old girl to write. He asks her to look down the street and say what she is imagining. She starts to describe the street, the trees along each side, the buildings and the sky, and so on. But he interrupts and says, 'That's what you *can* see. Tell me what you *cannot* see.' That's creativity."

"You're a skilled doctor, James," I continued. "But you are also a highly talented musician and songwriter. Now switch off your thinking brain, and do what you do when you write a new song. But this time, do it for your big, new medical centre."

"What's your dream for this new medical centre? What excites you about the possibilities? Don't just think about incremental improvements. Think big! The difference," I explained, "between a 'manager' and a 'leader' is that managers are concerned with 'what is' and leaders are concerned with 'what might be.'"

"Interesting," he said. "I never thought of it that way. Doctors are just not trained to think in those terms. We deal in facts and scientific evidence."

"Who is the leader in your practice?" I asked.

"Well, it's definitely not the senior partner," he said. "And it's not my other partner. I guess it's me."

"So, if a leader is just someone that others want to follow, who is following you?"

"Good question," said James. "Let's start with Joan—she's my wife at home, but for sure, she's the boss in the office. She's highly disciplined and well organised…and also very frustrated that the new centre is not getting off the ground." James went on to name others in the team—all of them capable, enthusiastic, and just waiting to follow the right dream.

The land of "what might be"

Over the next hour, James and I wandered together through the land of "what might be," until he arrived at a set of imaginative ideas for the new medical centre. Collectively, it added up to much more than his original thinking. His vision had grown into, "To lead the best medical practice in the region, with the happiest, healthiest patients enjoying a full range of health-related services in one easily reached centre…and generating a good income for all the staff, including Joan and me."

A good start," I said. "Now you need to get Joan's views and polish it up a bit."

In my work with senior business leaders, I explain this thinking/dreaming process to my clients with a diagram. This is what I showed James.

ACHIEVING THE "IMPOSSIBLE"

VISION / DREAM   (what might be)

ENGAGEMENT   (excite the team and plan together)

KEY OBJECTIVES / MILESTONES

STRATEGY   (EXCEL $)

TACTICS   (EXCEL ¢)

EXECUTION   (P o L $$$)

"This is what real leaders do, James," I said. "They don't just think incrementally. They imagine 'what might be' and articulate it in a way that excites and engages the team. Then, with the power of the team behind them, they define the milestone achievements that they need to get to the vision, and they plan the way forward. This is how real leaders achieve the inconceivable—by dreaming the impossible, convincing the team, and working together to reach the goal."

At that point, Joan joined us, took one doubtful look at James's excited face, and asked, "What are you two up to?" With her added energy and practicality, James and she quickly fleshed out a persuasive and business-like vision for a brand-new multi-purpose medical centre, complete with an

in-house dispensing pharmacy, a junior-doctor training facility, and a fully equipped physiotherapy suite.

"Now, James," I advised, "you and Joan will have to extend this vision into three or four key objectives and a detailed strategy. When you've done that, you need to sell it to your team. Then you have to convince local government to get moving. And, the biggest hurdle, you need to get qualified as a training practice."

"That's the toughest one," said James. "Nobody ever gets qualified at the first attempt…but we'll give it a try."

That discussion of last year came back to me in my morning shower, as I thought of his "good news" e-mail and little William's schoolboy "(s) mile(s)" joke.

"We got certification as a training centre!" he had written. "First time, too—I never heard of anyone getting that before. Not only that," his e-mail had gone on, "the committee gave us a huge compliment on our leadership—Joan's and mine, that is. And it gave us top marks on the quality of our team and our strategic plan. They loved our vision—I don't think they'd ever seen one before—and they totally agreed with our key objectives."

"Well done. That just leaves the civil servants, then," I had said in my reply, as I wished him good luck.

The last mile

"What role did I play in all that?" I asked myself under the shower. "James is a highly qualified and very experienced doctor. Joan is a well-educated senior nurse, as well as an excellent administrator. What did I contribute to the process, if anything?"

"I provided 'the last mile,'" I suddenly thought. "I supplied the last link in the chain between their talent and experience and the creation of their dream. Isn't that what coaches do?"

At the office later, I did a quick Google search. Wikipedia defines "the last mile" as the final link between a city's communications network

and your home telephone. It stimulated me to think in a way that I'd not thought before. I could see, in business terms, that the last mile is the link between the end user (our executive client) and the external environment (the rest of the team, the corporation, and the global community). The last mile of leadership is about receiving the messages that the world around you is sending. It's hearing the messages from your networks—your warning antenna, your opportunity antenna, and your voting constituency. These are three key elements of the influencing skills that leaders need to succeed in today's hollow-cube organisations.

If the last mile is missing, and if you're not listening—truly, actively listening in a way that everyone feels—then you're not getting the messages you need to succeed.

It works the other way as well. If you're not good at communicating, if you're too busy to do it or you just don't feel the need, then everyone else is missing your potential contribution to the team, to the business, and to the act of making a difference to the world at large.

"So," MacMentor says, "Here's how a coach can help build 'the last mile' for clients."

"First, it's about helping leaders extend their thinking of 'what might be,' helping them create a compelling vision, and supporting them in being the bridge between that vision and excellent execution."

"Next, good coaching helps busy executives become excellent listeners. Active listening turns an executive into a first-class receiver of valuable information about the team, the business, and the market. Creating a global network, and nourishing it constantly, provides the last mile when the leader hears, before anyone else, about early-stage problems and new opportunities. The last mile creates the support that leaders need when it comes to moving from vision to implementation."

"Not only that," says MacMentor, "it works in the other direction too. When a leader learns to be an excellent communicator of his or her vision, strategy, and plan for execution, the team and the wider community become committed supporters and a powerful mechanism for change. When communications in all directions—whether in e-mail, verbal, or any other format—are clear, and when regular testing of understanding becomes a habit for all concerned, the messages, the objectives, and the strategies greatly enhance the team spirit."

"Real leaders make sure that they have well-built last miles, with plenty of bandwidth for hearing and communicating vital messages."

"How big," MacMentor asks you "is *your* bandwidth today? How good is *your* last mile? And what are you going to do to make them bigger and better *now*?"

LOOKING DOWN
on Leaders—the

Epilogue

So that's it, at least for now.

All my stories and thoughts have slid out of my brain and onto paper and found their way into this book. Everything I wrote is based on true stories. I have invented nothing. All these experiences, silly and serious, happened more or less as I have described. I may have added some cosmetics—a touch of verbal rouge, a dab of glossy lipstick, or a bit of dramatic eyeliner, just to make the stories a little more attractive—that's all.

I hope that you found something in the book that was educational, informative, or entertaining—or some combination of those three. If you did, tell all your friends. If you didn't, tell me but nobody else! If what you have read has aroused an interest in experience-based coaching, you can read more about it at www.ijmartin.com.

Thank you for reading this book. I hope we meet again someday.

Bouquets and

Thanks

Did you buy this book to read the acknowledgments? Of course not!

So, since customers come first...and second, third, fourth, and fifth...I put this section at the end and not right at the start. That makes my gratitude to all who helped with this book no less sincere.

My biggest bouquet is for my partner, Marlene Uetz, for being who she is. Her loyalty, encouragement, ideas, and critiques are priceless. Without her timely coaching and mentoring, this book would have stuck at one of the low points on my authorship's morale curve.

Jimm Meloy, Our Man in Manhattan, gets the bridesmaid's bouquet. He has encouraged, cajoled, nagged, and threatened me for years to write this book. If you haven't enjoyed it, it's mostly his fault. As a successful author himself, Jimm has provided me with endless information, advice, and coaching in the course of my writing. Without Jimm, I'd still just be talking about it.

Colin Jamieson is the skilled artist who patiently captured the essence of my alter ego, MacMentor, in a variety of moods. He artfully brings the saying "A picture paints a thousand words" to life. He's not guilty of

the diagrams though…I drew them all myself—can you tell? That's how I sketch them on the whiteboard in coaching meetings.

Some of our global team of excellent executive coaches had special influence on parts of the text. Ian Kleinman, Monty Style, Mike Weitzel, John Tracey, Mireille Quirina, Henry Ferguson, and Tim Farrell offered valued comments and encouragement. All the members of our global team added their collective wisdom and lifetime experiences as coaches and business leaders…and the pleasure of their company.

Emma-Jane Williams served as an excellent role model for the chapter on leading ladies and as our legal adviser. Jenny Chandler and her CreateSpace team have been perfect examples of the Amazon.com customer-service ethos.

Finally, this book does not just draw on my own life. It capitalises on the collective experiences, suffering, achievements, skills, and wisdom of all our clients and of everyone that I have had the pleasure, and in a few cases the pain, of working with over the years. I thank them all for the privilege of knowing them.

If you have enjoyed the book, tell me on macmentor@ijmartin.com and I will tell them. Now write a customer review on Amazon.com and go on Twitter, Facebook, and LinkedIn—to all your friends on social media—and help them, too, enjoy this bird's-eye view of business.

Contents in Detail

30416598R00152

Made in the USA
Charleston, SC
14 June 2014

ally and exclusively on artefacts and literature of the ancient Greek and Roman worlds. In the late eighteenth and early nineteenth century this was replaced by a more general interest in 'old things', which was reflected in the founding of institutions such as the Society of Antiquaries, in the gradual emergence of dealers in 'curiosities' and in the growing interest that attached to auction sales of such material. Although collections of curiosities had occasionally been formed in the past, such as that of Elias Ashmole in Oxford, these had seldom included old plate except in the form of mounted artefacts or natural curiosities. With the exception of family heirlooms or bequests to colleges, livery companies or the Church, it had always been accepted that plate should be in the current style and a significant part of the business of goldsmiths had consisted in regularly refashioning outmoded or worn plate in the newest style.

Rundells have been credited with a marketing innovation that was symptomatic of this change in attitudes: having bought a quantity of surplus old royal plate in 1808, they offered it to some of their leading clients instead of melting it down to be remade as would have been the usual practice.[7] The interest that was thus aroused in imposing antique plate accordingly created a demand for styles that could not readily be supplied by old pieces and which was consequently met by new plate in antique taste. One of Rundells' customers for the royal plate was the collector William Beckford (1759–1844), who purchased two pairs of William and Mary sconces and wrote in 1808 that 'the old pieces from the Royal silver are divine'. He needed more, however, and had no hesitation in ordering the goldsmiths to make up the set with a number of exact copies.[8]

It was in the response of other manufacturers to this new demand that Rundells met with some of their liveliest competition. One of the leaders of the historicist field would appear to have been William Pitts, who was responsible for a number of dishes embossed in seventeenth-century style, made both to Rundells' order and for other retailers. But the most interesting figures of the latter part of the first quarter of the century were the retailer Kensington Lewis and his goldsmith Edward Farrell. Lewis was evidently a colourful figure who posed as something of an authority on antique plate and was equally at home whether dealing in old plate or new.[9] In 1816 he made at least two major antique purchases at Christie's sale of the Duke of Norfolk's plate, and the plate made for him by Farrell ranges in character from close copies of genuine seventeenth-century pieces, which Lewis presumably had in stock, to unmistakably, if eccentrically, contemporary designs.

*Monteith bowl, silver-gilt, 1820, maker's mark of Edward Farrell;
16 in. diameter (Gilbert Collection, Los Angeles).*

Lewis's greatest coup, and that on which his commercial success largely depended until 1827, was in attracting the patronage of the Duke of York. The Duke was perhaps the greatest collector of silver of the period, and between about 1816 and his death he ordered an enormous quantity of plate from both Rundells and Lewis. Orders from the latter included objects in a wide range of styles, such as rococo revival, the seventeenth-century embossed style and magnificent sculptural candelabra. But his extravagance was on such a scale that his executors took the unusual (for the royal family

unprecedented) step on his death of arranging for the sale of practically his entire collection at auction in an effort to pay off his debts. For Lewis this was a disastrous turn of events and he was forced to buy back many of the items which he had supplied in an attempt to support his market. Some plate which he bought at a cost of about 12s. an ounce had originally been supplied to his patron at more than twice the price; in other cases the discrepancy was larger still. Lewis continued in business for a number of years after losing his patron, but on a much less flamboyant scale, and thereafter Farrell's work was largely restricted to novelties and products such as tea services decorated with highly embossed scenes derived from Dutch seventeenth-century genre painting.

The developing interest in antiquarianism during this period was naturally also reflected in the growing number of connoisseurs interested in forming collections of such material. Among the most notable of these might be mentioned Horace Walpole (1717–97) and Ralph Bernal (d. 1854), but of particular interest from the perspective of contemporary silver was William Beckford, whose vast gothic mansion of Fonthill was one of the most remarkable buildings of its time. Beckford filled Fonthill with his collection of paintings and antique works of art, but he also commissioned considerable quantities of new silver with which to complete the decorative effect. The earliest dates from about 1781 and, while of exceptionally fine quality, was typical of the fashionable style of the time (see p. 240). His more idiosyncratic commissions date from the early nineteenth century and include both solid plate and an extraordinary quantity of mounted vessels, both new and old. Although his collections were largely dispersed after the sale of Fonthill in 1822, a large part of them was inherited by his daughter, Euphemia, through whose marriage to the Duke of Hamilton in 1810 a group of about fifty pieces have come into the possession of the National Trust for Scotland at Brodick Castle.[10] The early nineteenth-century pieces at Brodick, extraordinarily various though they are, are distinguished by three main characteristics: a consistently high quality, a sense of delicacy and precision and a frequent use of heraldic charges in the decoration. All these features point to an unusual degree of involvement by the patron with the objects that were made for him. Throughout his life he was obsessed by his ancestry and with his unrequited yearning for a peerage. This was reflected in the decoration of Fonthill and also in his plate, much of which is engraved with charges from his arms, such as the ermine cinquefoil or the Latimer cross, decoratively incorporated into the design. He seems to have entrusted dealings with the goldsmiths to his friend Chevalier Gregorio Franchi,

Beaker mounted as a jug, porcelain and silver-gilt, 1820,
maker's mark of James Aldridge, made for William Beckford; $4\frac{1}{2}$ in. high
(National Trust for Scotland, Brodick Castle).

though his keen personal interest is constantly evident in their correspondence. Although he did commission plate from the larger retailers, such as Rundells and Vulliamy and Co., many of his more original commissions were given to smaller concerns, such as those of James Aldridge and Samuel Whitford.

In one sense Beckford was deliberately trying to recreate the world of the Renaissance prince with his 'Schatzkammer' or treasury of precious objects. In that sense he might well be considered an eccentric and little more than a fascinating tributary from the main stream of the history of English plate. Certainly that is how he was perceived by many of his

Bowl, porcelain and silver-gilt, 1816, maker's mark of James Aldridge, made for William Beckford; 3 in. diameter (National Trust for Scotland, Brodick Castle).

contemporaries, and when William Hazlitt visited Fonthill prior to the sale he acidly described it as 'a Cathedral turned into a toy shop, an immense Museum of all that is most costly and, at the same time, most worthless in the productions of art and nature'.[11] But in his use of different materials, in his concern to break the mould of the acceptable repertoire of form and decoration, his patronage might well be regarded as a prelude to some of the dominant themes of Victorian silver.

Few buyers of plate, however, were able or prepared to pay the high fashion charges inevitably incurred by the more elaborate objects supplied to the Duke of York or William Beckford. The essence of the revolution in

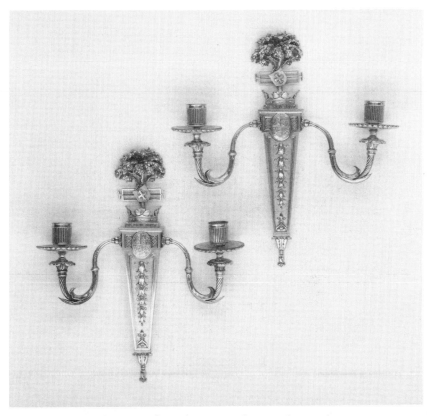

Pair of sconces, silver-gilt, 1804, maker's mark of Paul Storr,
made for William Beckford; 13 in. high
(National Trust for Scotland, Brodick Castle).

the trade which occurred in the late eighteenth and early nineteenth century is that mass-production methods lowered the cost of plate and made it available to a wider public. The advantages were enormous. Spinning, which had first been developed by Sheffield plate manufacturers, was by the 1820s widely used for silver and enabled hollow ware such as teapots and cups to be raised more quickly and thinly than by hammering. The commercial application of Huntsman's hard crucible steel as early as 1760 was constantly extended and made it possible to produce strong dies from which clear impressions could be struck in silver. John Culme quotes an account of a stamping shop in Elkington's factory in Birmingham in which 'an enormous stamp ... converts flat discs of metal thirty inches in diameter by the action of the falling hammer of the stamp ... [into] enormous salvers, dishes and

Chamber candlestick, silver-gilt, 1810, maker's mark LL in script; $6\frac{7}{8}$ in. high
(National Trust, Attingham Park, Shropshire).

meat covers'.[12] But the disadvantages are felt in lower standards of design and workmanship. This was a problem that was increasingly felt as the century progressed and which is discussed at greater length in the next chapter.

Ten

THE VICTORIAN ERA: CRAFT AND INDUSTRY

As recently as 1951 it would have been considered a fair assessment of contemporary attitudes that 'although a nostalgic appreciation for the pretty whimsicalities of the early Victorian period appears to be growing, it is as yet scarcely awarded the honour of academic research or serious aesthetic consideration'.[1] Nowadays such a view is difficult to equate with what is increasingly perceived as one of the most fascinating periods in English silver. The attitude that prevailed until recently was, of course, just part of a more general aversion to all things Victorian which resulted not only in the melting down of large quantities of silver, but the destruction of many country houses and other buildings which would now be considered important examples of nineteenth-century architecture.

Part of the reason for this aversion was the sense of stylistic confusion that characterizes much of the period; another was the evident dominance of the machine, which seemed the antithesis of craftsmanship. But it is a view that fails to do justice to the complexities of the period and to the fact that industrially manufactured silver represented only one aspect, albeit numerically the most overwhelming, of the whole picture. For it is a period of extraordinary contrasts, between the charming and the pompous, the original and the imitation, the beautiful and the banal. Undoubtedly, the greatest tension was between the forces of mass production and individual craftsmanship. Contemporaries were well aware of these contrasts, which were, if anything, heightened by the interaction of artists and entrepreneurs and by the deliberate, almost academic, exploration of new theories of form and decoration which were encouraged by factors as different as parliamentary committees and enlightened patrons.

The middle part of Victoria's reign (1837–1901) has been called the period of the 'battle of the styles', but even by the end of the first quarter of the century it was clear that there was no real consensus over style, or

Milk-jug, silver, 1840, maker's mark of Benjamin Smith the younger
(Victoria and Albert Museum, London).

even a 'typical' style that tended to predominate over others. Publications such as Knight's *Encyclopaedia of Ornament* (1834) and Owen Jones's *Grammar of Ornament* (1857) made a wider range of decoration available to nineteenth-century silversmiths than had existed before, but also reflected the fact that demand for such diversity already existed. In many respects, indeed, the features that are generally regarded as typically Victorian were all evident in embryonic form during the first quarter of the century.

The most obvious of these were stylistic eclecticism; a fashion for large sculptural plate; a dominance of large factories and industrial methods of production; and a tendency for developments of form and ornament to evolve out of a process that had more of the character of a public debate than ever before.

Soup-tureen, silver, 1819, maker's mark of Paul Storr, 1819, $7\frac{3}{8}$ in. high
(Victoria and Albert Museum, London).

The dominant source of inspiration during the first two decades of the century had been ancient art, whether Greek, Roman or Egyptian, though a freer spirit of eclecticism had begun to show itself after about 1810 with the historicizing plate made for Rundells and Kensington Lewis. During the second quarter of the century a number of quite different styles were promoted simultaneously and with almost equal success, the most important of which were the naturalistic style and the gothic and rococo revivals.

If any one style could be said to typify the second quarter of the nineteenth century, it would be naturalism, for although far from universal, this was undoubtedly the most original of the various stylistic experiments

of the period. Evolving out of the use of classical acanthus foliage that figured so prominently in formal Regency plate, it differed fundamentally from the latter in that form and decoration were treated in such a way that, not unlike the rococo at its most fully developed, the decoration became logically integral to the form so that it became impossible visually or

Vegetable dish, silver, 1829, maker's mark of Paul Storr; 9 in. high
(National Trust, Anglesey Abbey, Cambridgeshire).

logically to distinguish between the two. This has been characterized as an 'organic' approach to style and as 'the form becoming the ornament'. A cream jug of 1840 by Benjamin Smith the younger, in the Victoria and Albert Museum, has all the essential features of the style: the classic vase form has given way to one in which the lines have been softened and the entire form treated with a sense of organic growth, of which the decoration is an integral part. Similarly, a covered dish of 1829 by Paul Storr at Anglesey Abbey shows the influence of the style, with its melon-like cover and large vegetable finial. Flaxman seems to have played a decisive role in this innovative movement. Some of his most important designs for Rundells,

such as a candelabrum centrepiece of 1812 in the royal collection, show a marked departure from Piranesiesque classicism, with features such as florally entwined branches and candle sockets in the form of open flowers.

A less innovative but equally striking form of naturalism was one in which the aim was not so much to give a sense of living nature as to produce objects that directly copied it. Influential in the development of this style was the publication in 1833 of Knight's *Vases and Ornaments*, which shows vessels formed from sea-shells and the like, supported by clumps of foliage growing up from the base. Within a year of its publication, retailers such as Kensington Lewis were already exploiting its potential. But as with many printed pattern books from the sixteenth century onwards, its author was as much crystallizing and disseminating a fashion that already existed as publishing entirely fresh ideas. Rundells in particular had been producing silver in this naturalistic vein for some years, having almost certainly been influenced by the rocaille pieces by Nicholas Sprimont in the royal collection, of which they were asked to supply replicas. Garrards were also leading exponents of the style, among the most dramatic expressions of which is their pair of candelabra of 1841 at Brodick Castle, which are formed as four discomfortingly lifelike entwined snakes. Grander still is Flaxman's great wine cooler in the Tower of London, which was supplied to George IV in 1822 and which is modelled as a giant clam shell, presumably cast from a real one, and which is supported by rearing seahorses.

Almost the antithesis of the naturalistic style, the gothic revival was pursued with equal vigour over the same period, and again it was the extraordinary versatility of John Flaxman in collaboration with Rundells that was responsible for its first major success. The so-called National Cup was designed by Flaxman and made in 1824 for George IV. Its stem is inspired by fourteenth-century plate such as the King John Cup,[2] and the decoration of the bowl is comprised of the national emblems of England, Scotland and Ireland, with the figures of St Andrew and St Patrick set into gothic niches and the finial formed as St George and the dragon. But the gothicism of the National Cup is more romantic than historical, and the appeal of the more studied gothic silverware of the second quarter of the century hinged essentially on its perceived 'appropriateness', especially in the field of church art. This notion was a powerful force throughout the Victorian period, particularly in architecture. Gilbert Scott's design for the façade of the Foreign Office, for example, was rejected as inappropriate for a building that represented Britain's imperial position in the world (though it did very well when eventually reused for St Pancras Station); a classical

*Candelabrum centrepiece, silver-gilt, 1812, maker's mark of Paul Storr; 28 in. high
(Royal collection. Reproduced by gracious permission of Her Majesty the Queen).*

building was chosen for that repository of the works of man, the Victoria
and Albert Museum, while a gothic one seemed proper for that of the
Natural History Museum. Similarly, few classical churches were erected
after 1830, the gothic style being deemed to be of a more godly nature
than that of pagan antiquity.

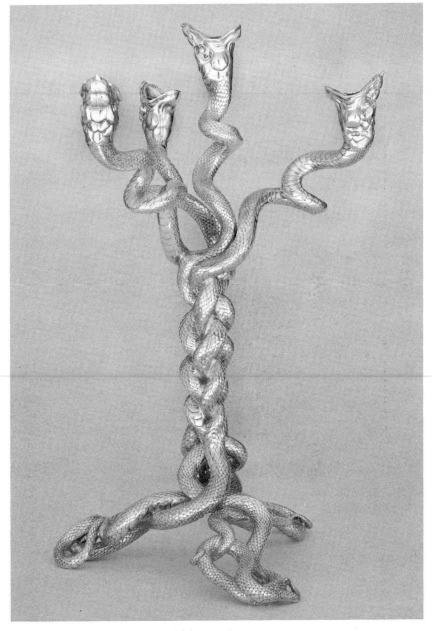

*Candelabrum, silver, 1841,
maker's mark of Robert Garrard; 22½ in. high
(National Trust for Scotland, Brodick Castle).*

The National Cup, 1824, maker's mark of John Bridge,
designed by John Flaxman; 19 in. high (Royal collection. Reproduced by
gracious permission of Her Majesty the Queen).

Dish, silver-gilt, silver and enamel, Birmingham, 1847,
maker's mark of John Hardman & Co., designed by Augustus Pugin; $16\frac{1}{8}$ in. diameter
(Victoria and Albert Museum, London).

The most influential figure in decorative arts of the gothic revival was Augustus Pugin (1812–52), who is said to have been discovered at the age of fifteen, copying drawings and engravings in the Print Room at the British Museum, by John Gawler Bridge. He was immediately engaged by Rundells to design church plate, and most of his designs for silver continued to be in this field until his death, although he did design a certain number of secular pieces, such as a dish of 1847 in the Victoria and Albert Museum. From 1838 most of his work was for the Birmingham firm of John Hardman

Claret jug, silver and silver-gilt, 1851, maker's mark of Joseph Angell; 13½ in. high (Goldsmiths' Company).

and Co. It is characterized by great precision, a fine sense of line and a careful observation of surviving medieval metalwork. His approach, however, was essentially historicizing; he had little interest in innovations of form and indeed condemned the almost inevitable fact that much contemporary plate in the gothic style consisted of 'gothic detail simply applied to a given surface'.[3] But that such plate could be of considerable artistic interest is clear from some of the silver produced by Joseph Angell during the 1850s, such as a remarkable claret jug of 1851 in the collection of the Goldsmiths' Company, in which a general sense of the gothic is suggested by the form, although the decorative scheme as a whole is only faintly reminiscent of the Middle Ages.

The style which seems to have enjoyed the widest and most long-lived popularity of all during the nineteenth century, however, was the rococo revival. Although not coming into vogue on a large scale until about 1815, its origins can be traced to at least the beginning of the century. By the middle of the second decade, Paul Storr was already producing grand rococo silver for Rundells, much of it to royal order, from sources such as François-Thomas Germain, Nicholas Sprimont and Paul Crespin, but as the century progressed there was a growing tendency for debased examples of the style to be produced in the larger factories in an increasingly sloppy and poorly designed manner. The popularity of this style, more than any other in Victorian silver, was a reflection of the greatly expanded market for silver in the mid nineteenth century and, to be fair to the society responsible for its production, it was far from being without its contemporary critics. The *Art Union* complained in 1846 that 'there is a degree of slovenliness engendered by the fact that designers of this kind of ornament know, if they can fill up an angle or a square with two or three large scrolls, throw in a few unnatural flowers and a lot of scrollwork, it will pass current as Old French'.[4]

A similar opinion was expressed in more satirical terms by Dickens, in his description of the silver dinner service that graced Mr Podsnap's table in *Our Mutual Friend*:

Hideous solidity was the characteristic of the Podsnap plate. Everything was made to look as heavy as it could and to take up as much room as possible. Everything said boastfully, 'Here you have as much of me in my ugliness as if I were only lead; but I am so many ounces of precious metal, worth so much an ounce; – wouldn't you like to melt me down?' A corpulent straddling epergne, blotched all over as if it had broken out in an eruption rather than been ornamented, delivered this address from an unsightly silver platform in the centre of the

table. Four silver wine coolers, each furnished with four staring heads, each head obtrusively carrying a big silver ring in each of its ears, conveyed the sentiment up and down the table, and handed it on to the pot-bellied silver salt cellars. All the big silver spoons and forks widened the mouths of the company expressly for the purpose of thrusting the sentiment down their throats with every morsel they eat.[5]

As late as 1890 the phenomenon was explained in unambiguous terms by the *Jeweller and Metalworker*, which observed that 'silversmiths do not seem anxious to abandon the Louis XV style, although the revival of that pretty fashion has had a very long run already. It is true that the public encourage them more and more, especially the parvenues, the wealthy bourgeois, who have made their fortune in lines where even the word art is absolutely unknown. They have heard of the reigning style, and, anxious to show their good taste, they absolutely refuse to look at any article in silver which is not offered to them as a remarkable specimen of the rococo.'[6] A more accurate description of Mr Podsnap's position could hardly be imagined.

The general weakening in quality and design that was evident during the second quarter of the century must be seen to some extent in the light of the decline of Rundell, Bridge and Rundell from their position of virtually unchallenged supremacy during the Regency to the final winding up of the firm in 1842. An unpublished manuscript in the Harvard University Library[7] by George Fox, a long-term employee of Rundells, attributes a number of causes to this decline, in particular the death of George IV and an ensuing vacuum of royal patronage, together with Philip Rundell's retirement in 1823, accompanied by the withdrawal of his capital. Hitherto Rundells had been immensely capitalized which, according to Fox, 'enabled the House to execute Orders of the greatest Magnitude and also to accommodate their Customers with unlimited credits so that no house in London up to that time had been able to compete with them with any chance of success'. Some of his most interesting remarks, however, concern the way in which the firm had capitalized on the shortage of silver during the Napoleonic wars and the effect of their conclusion: 'One of the first effects of the transition from War to Peace was the very great and sudden fall in the value of the precious Metals[.] Gold which had been as high as £5-10 per oz. fell to the Average Price of £3-17-10 1/2 per ounce Standard and Silver fell from 7/- per oz. to about 5/2 per oz.' The large stock of gold and silver which the firm carried inevitably hurt them very badly, since it was impossible for them to pass on their losses to their customers.

The field which Rundells had led and in which their departure presented the greatest opportunities was that of grand display plate. From the 1840s onwards the most important manufacturers of large-scale silver were Storr and Co. (which evolved during the next few decades into Storr & Mortimer, Mortimer & Hunt and finally Hunt & Roskell), Garrards, the Birmingham firm of Elkington and Co. and, later in the century, C. F. Hancock & Co. All these manufacturers placed the same emphasis on the fundamental importance of the design department, and in most cases attempted to attract a prominent sculptor to head the team. The most important figures around the middle of the century included the sculptors Edmund Cotterill of Garrards and Alfred Brown of Hunt & Roskell. It was in the prominence given to the design and modelling departments that Rundells' greatest legacy to the Victorian era lay, but it was also inevitable that such an approach to design led display silver to develop a strong sculptural character. A colourful account of the Hunt & Roskell workshop is contained in Beatrix Potter's journal, describing her visit in 1881: '... there was one more thing to see, the designing. In we all went, a little sized studio with skylights, surrounded by curtains, one of which the Frenchman unceremoniously pulled aside to let us in. The work on hand was a large centrepiece, a drawing of which stood on an easel, while the artist was busy at a plaster model.'[8]

The piece in question was the centrepiece of the Ismay Testimonial, which was presented by the managers of the White Star Shipping Line to Thomas Henry Ismay in 1885 and which was designed by G. A. Carter. It has all the character of a public monument on a reduced scale. But in resembling a monument it is at one remove from the type of presentation silver that was especially popular around the middle of the century and of which Cotterill was one of the leading exponents. These were much closer to pure sculpture and tended to have subjects of a patriotic nature or which were derived from sources such as Shakespeare's history plays and the novels of Walter Scott. There can be no doubt as to the popular appeal of such designs, many of which were published in the press, and indeed the *Illustrated London News* proclaimed in 1850 that 'in no branch of the Fine Arts have the artists of this country made greater progress than in the art of modelling [silver] statuettes ... It may indeed be called a national art, and a national manufacture.'[9] But this 'national art', which was probably the most prominent aspect of the British stands at the Great Exhibition of 1851, was not without its detractors. The painter Richard Redgrave, Inspector General for the Government Schools of Design, complained in 1857 that

Centrepiece from the Ismay Testimonial, parcel-gilt, 1881,
maker's mark of Hunt and Roskell, designed by G. A. Carter; 25 in. high.

'many centrepieces, racing cups, and testimonials are treated merely as groups would be by the sculptor',[10] and the *Journal of Design* complained in 1850 that 'all beauty of form, all excellence of modelling, is lost in the glitter of the metal where burnishing is employed, and the compositions that would have been truely works of art in bronze become almost toylike when thus wrought'.[11]

The enormous popularity of large sculptural centrepieces was a reflection at one end of the market of a phenomenon that was equally marked throughout. The decline in the price of silver and its greater availability

after the exploitation of new mines in Mexico combined with the rapidly expanding middle class to create a greater demand for silver than had ever existed before. Whereas the market for testimonials had largely been created by corporate and political wealth and the desire of companies or political parties to make lavish presentations to their chief executives or representatives, that for domestic silver was mainly in the hands of individuals who wished, much as owners of plate had always wished, to enhance their status through silver. The mid nineteenth century consequently witnessed an enormous expansion in demand for useful as well as decorative plate. While extravagant services such as Mr Podsnap's were certainly produced in large quantities, the greatest growth in demand was not so much for dinner services, which had been superseded in many people's eyes by china ones, as for the matched tea and coffee service and services of flatware. Both these were produced in enormous quantities from the middle part of the century onwards, and an indication of the extent of the demand is given by the fact that one London producer of the mid century advertised a range of no fewer than fifty different patterns of tea services. The key to such large-scale production lay, of course, in mechanization. John Culme[12] quotes a description from 1890 of the process used by the Rhode Island firm of Gorham Company for making silver spoons. It was complicated and involved many stages, but the most significant point is that it was carried out almost entirely by machine, and the procedure in mid nineteenth-century England can hardly have been very different.

An inevitable consequence of these patterns of production was increased specialization; another was a decline in quality. By the beginning of the nineteenth century, Matthew Boulton's company had retired completely from producing silver and made only Sheffield plate; testimonial and large-scale silver was concentrated in a small number of firms, and flatware was almost entirely in the hands of Francis Higgins & Sons and Chawner & Co. The most dramatic example of specialization, however, was that of Elkington & Co. in the field of electroplate. George Elkington had been one of the first to recognize the potential of electroplating as opposed to the fused principle of Sheffield plate. He sponsored the experiments of John Wright and Alexander Parks into plating base metal with silver by electrolysis, and the process was patented by Elkington in partnership with Wright in 1840. Demand was enormous; licences were sold to various other manufacturers, such as James Dixon & Sons and Christofle in Paris, and Elkingtons made such profits that they rapidly rose to be one of the largest producers in the country, both of electroplate and of solid silver.

The most important difference between Sheffield plate and electroplate was that with the former the plating process was done before the object was formed, which made complex relief ornament, let alone sculptural decoration, impossible. With electroplate, on the other hand, the object was entirely formed first, then plated. This gave it the great advantage of enabling worn pieces to be replated; it also enabled electroplate to be made in exactly the same forms as fashionable sculptured silver, and the taste for such objects to filter down to a much lower level of the market. Electroplate was consequently regarded as an ideal means of spreading taste and bringing quality within the means of the masses, but even before its appearance on the market, concern was being voiced about a general decline in the quality of design that had inevitably followed in the wake of mass production.

By 1835 this concern had reached such a level that a Select Committee of the House of Commons was appointed to 'inquire into the best means of extending a knowledge of the arts and of the principles of design among the People (especially the manufacturing population) of the country', the most immediate effect of which was the establishment of the first government School of Design. The report of the Select Committee, published in 1836, was only one of a number of publications around the middle of the century that both criticized contemporary design and suggested various, not always mutually compatible, remedies for the shortcomings. The most fruitful and influential of these was the work of a remarkable civil servant, Henry Cole (1808–82), whose energetic efforts were to lead in the short term to the Great Exhibition of 1851 and later to the establishment of the South Kensington Museum, which came in due course to be known as the Victoria and Albert Museum.

Cole began publication in 1841 of a periodical known under the pseudonym of 'Felix Summerly's Home Treasury'. In response to the widening gulf between extravagant commissioned testimonials and the coarseness of ordinary domestic plate design, he contended in an editorial that 'we desire to see *good Art cheap* ... Art should not be content to minister to the taste of the few alone ... its healthy influence should be felt among *the million* ... grace may be produced as cheaply as deformity. Expensive and intricate detail does not necessarily belong to elegance of form and design.'[13] In 1847 he went further and set up an organization which he called 'Felix Summerly's Art Manufactures', the aim of which was to focus the attention of artists on the design of ordinary domestic plate and 'to revive the good old practice of connecting the best art with familiar objects in everyday use'. He succeeded in securing the co-operation of a number of leading

manufacturers, notably Hunt & Roskell and Benjamin Smith Junior. An illustration of the alternative to the purely sculptural silver attacked by Richard Redgrave is a small christening mug which the latter designed under the auspices of Felix Summerly's Manufactures in 1848 and which is embossed with a frieze of angels protecting a kneeling child. The symbolism

Christening mug, silver, 1865,
maker's mark of Harry Emmanuel, designed by Richard Redgrave; 4¾ in. high
(Victoria and Albert Museum, London).

is obvious enough, and in many ways it is the exact equivalent of the sort of sentimental Christianity contained in Dickens's earlier novels. But viewed as an example of sculpture combined with useful form, in a way that alludes both to the function of the vessel and that is compatible with its function, it epitomizes the aim of the venture.

Felix Summerly's Manufactures may be seen as the prelude to a number of the most significant artistic developments of the latter part of the century, notably, from the point of view of the silver industry, those led by Christopher Dresser (1834–1904) and Charles Robert Ashbee (1863–1942). But of more immediate importance was the part he played in the events leading up to the Great Exhibition. Under Cole's and Prince Albert's direction, the Society of Arts organized a series of exhibitions of contemporary manufactures between 1846 and 1849, the success of which encouraged the Prince to suggest one on an international scale to be held in London in 1851.

The exhibition was well supported by the main English manufacturers of silver, notably Hunt & Roskell, Garrards and Elkingtons. Pride of place

on the former two stands was given to sculptural testimonial pieces that represented patriotic or romantic subjects; other exhibitors showed a variety of pieces in historicizing styles. But the exhibition was held at a time when the battle of the styles was still far from over, and opinions as to the merit of these extravagant pieces differed widely, perhaps the most thunderous

Tea service, silver-gilt and enamel, 1851,
maker's mark of George Angell; height of coffee pot 12¾ in.
(Victoria and Albert Museum, London).

response being that of the *Morning Chronicle*, which pronounced that 'what we want are canons of taste, laws of beauty, principles and axioms of propriety ... The exhibition shows that we are most skilful mimics, that we know how to reprint classics, that we can restore everything. But what do we create?' Nevertheless, it is difficult today to appreciate the enormity of the impact of the series of international exhibitions that followed over the next thirty years. The 1851 exhibition attracted over 6 million visitors, that in 1862 about the same; the Paris exhibition of 1867 admitted over 10 million, while no fewer than 16 million were reported as having attended in 1878. Their power to focus attention on developments in taste and design was therefore immense, and manufacturers responded by producing special pieces on speculation. One of the most imposing of all was the Helicon Vase, made by Elkingtons for the 1871 exhibition[14] and which in fact remained unsold until 1877. But a particularly interesting departure was the series of enamelled vessels produced by George Angell, such as a four-piece tea and coffee service which was made for the Great Exhibition and which is now in the Victoria and Albert Museum.

The decline in purely sculptural testimonial plate that is evident after the middle of the century is in part doubtless attributable to the lambasts of critics such as the *Morning Chronicle* and Richard Redgrave. But it must also in some measure be associated with the presence in England of two remarkable artists, Antoine Vechte (1798–1868) and Léonard Morel-Ladeuil (c. 1820–88), who worked respectively for Hunt and Roskell and Elkingtons. Vechte first met J. S. Hunt in Paris in 1847, and the latter was so struck by his talent as a chaser that he commissioned the Titan Vase which was later acquired by the Goldsmiths' Company. The extraordinary impression made by the vase encouraged Hunt to commission further works from Vechte, who from 1849 to 1862 worked exclusively for Hunt and Roskell in London.

Of equal importance to Vechte was the presence in England of his pupil, Morel-Ladeuil, who worked for Elkington and Co. from 1857 until his death. His first publicly exhibited work was a *repoussé* table shown at the 1862 exhibition in London, but his subsequent works included objects such as the Milton Shield of 1867, the Pilgrim Shield of 1868 and the Helicon Vase of 1871. These works were distinguished by their marked literary qualities and their sophisticated chasing. In his technical command Morel-Ladeuil was by no means Vechte's superior, but the relatively low relief of his designs was particularly characteristic; it invited the eulogy of George Sala that 'he can paint with his hammer'[15] and distinguished his work from that of his master by its obvious inspiration from Renaissance goldsmiths' work. The Milton Shield in particular, although iconographically entirely of its own time, is clearly inspired by an embossed steel shield of about 1570, attributed to Pierre Redon of the Fontainebleau School.[16] Moreover, the techniques reintroduced in both Vechte's Titan Vase and much of Morel-Ladeuil's work, of damascening and contrasting highly polished with oxidized surfaces, were both revivals of sixteenth-century techniques and led the way towards a new taste for silver in the Renaissance style which became increasingly influential during the latter part of the century.

The Renaissance revival would arguably have happened anyway, for reasons that are discussed below, and the main significance of Vechte and Morel-Ladeuil lay in the influence they brought to bear on the development of sculptural silver. During the 1860s and 1870s the other most prominent figures in the field were another Frenchman, Albert Wilms, who worked for Elkingtons, and H. H. Armstead, who by 1862 was working principally for C. F. Hancock & Co. Both responded to the criticism of purely sculptural design by re-emphasizing form. In Wilms's case this meant introducing sculpture as a support for the vessel, in a manner that was reminiscent of

Titan Vase, silver, silver-gilt and oxidized silver, modelled in Paris in 1847 by Antonie Vechte for J. S. Hunt; 29¾ in. high (Goldsmiths' Company).

The Milton Shield,
silver, silver-gilt and oxidized silver, Birmingham, 1867,
maker's mark of Elkington & Co.,
modelled by Léonard Morel-Ladeuil
(Victoria and Albert Museum, London).

Centrepiece, silver-gilt, Birmingham, 1872, maker's mark of Elkington and Co.,
designed by Albert Wilms; 14 in. long.

the Parisian goldsmith Jean Baptiste Claude Odiot's late eighteenth-century
neo-classicism, while Armstead's approach was to unite the vessel and
sculptural form in a way that was much closer to Vechte. One of his most
important designs, the Tennyson Vase of 1880,[17] is obviously derived from
the Titan Vase, both in its general design and the balance of high relief and
overall form.

It has been observed that 'in England after the late 1860s, the silver
industry was in decline'.[18] In terms of the trade as a whole, of its representation at international exhibitions and of volume of production, that

is certainly true, but in terms of new departures in design it was as interesting as a period, if not more interesting, than that discussed at the beginning of this chapter. The various movements that went to make up the artistic character of late nineteenth-century goldsmiths' work, disparate though they were, were subject essentially to three channels of influence. The first

Decanter, silver, silver-gilt, glass, semi-precious stones, maker's mark of Richard Green, designed by William Burges; 11 in. high (Victoria and Albert Museum).

was the historicist trend that had never been far from the surface and which towards the end of the century became complicated by a growing force in the market, namely the enthusiasm among a growing body of collectors for medieval and Renaissance works of art. The second reflected the extraordinary sense of revelation that swept Europe and America after the

opening up of Japan to outsiders in the 1850s; and the third traced its antecedents in the quasi-moralizing writings of Henry Cole and others and its descendents in the parallel movements that were led on the one hand by C. R. Ashbee's Guild of Handicrafts and on the other by the marketing strategy of Liberty and Co.

The leaders of the medieval movement during the latter part of the century were William Morris (1834–96) and William Burges (1827–81), and the work of both was coloured by a more romantic vision of the Middle Ages than Pugin's. Their style accordingly made no pretensions towards archaeological exactitude, but was instead loosely inspired by certain aspects of medieval art, especially the romanesque, such as the combination of different materials and techniques, while drawing freely on the repertoire of ornament.

Although particularly interested in goldsmiths' work, Burges was not a goldsmith himself and much of his more intricate work was carried out by a Danish goldsmith, Jes Barkentin, who worked in London from 1860. His most important client was the 3rd Marquess of Bute, whom he met in 1865 and who commissioned him to rebuild Cardiff Castle. The Marquess had an equal passion for medieval art and instructed Burges to design all the interiors and furnishings for the castle as well. But the growth of antiquarianism and the increasing number of wealthy collectors during the nineteenth century also opened up the opportunity for a different kind of historicizing silver altogether, which was made with fraudulent intent. For obvious reasons, the nineteenth-century fakers, some of whom were extraordinarily skilled craftsmen, are less well documented than their more honest contemporaries. Indeed, some of the most brilliant, such as Salomon Weiniger of Vienna or Reinhold Vasters of Aachen, have emerged only fairly recently and their recognition has inevitably led to the reassessment of objects in private and public collections which had previously been thought to be major works of art from the sixteenth century or earlier.

No faker as brilliant as Vasters has yet been identified in England, although they almost certainly existed. On the other hand, there was a concerted industrial popularization of this antiquarian interest in the form of large quantities of domestic silver in Renaissance styles, such as the so-called 'Cellini pattern' ewer. This was a reproduction of a sixteenth-century pewter model, not in fact made by Cellini, but by the French craftsman François Briot. The tendency during the nineteenth century to associate the name of Cellini with almost any elaborate goldsmiths' work of the sixteenth was symptomatic of the naïve state of that particular branch of art history,

and is reflected as much in the hopelessly bad fakes of the period as in the crude pastiches of Renaissance styles that were marketed in the same way as the gothic and rococo styles throughout the period.

It was partly recognition of the decline in the quality and design of industrially produced silver that led to one of the most significant and prophetic developments in the late nineteenth century, namely the industrial aesthetic of Christopher Dresser. Dresser was a botanist, but was also deeply interested in the industrial arts. In 1848 he attended the Government School of Design, and over the next thirty years published a number of influential books, such as *The Art of Decorative Design* and *Principles of Decorative Design*. During the 1870s he produced series of designs for Elkingtons, Hukin & Heath and James Dixon and Sons. In response to what he considered to be the misplaced dominance of ornament in contemporary silver, his designs instead placed emphasis on pure form and the role of the machine. Partly making a social point and partly an intellectual one, they were deliberately conceived with the aim of minimizing costs in order to make 'good' design available to the widest possible market. But in doing so he went far beyond the kind of cooperation between artists and industry that Henry Cole promoted, and developed an entirely new aesthetic which was characterized by an austere, almost brutal functionality, a minimal use of metal and a concern to emphasize the method of construction and the nature of the material by devices such as the prominent use of rivets and screws.

Dresser was a complex figure, and his pioneering role in the design of metalwork is in curious contrast to his equally passionate interest in the arts of Japan, which he did much to encourage in England. In 1882 he published *Japan: Its Architecture, Art and Art Manufactures* which stimulated the interest in oriental art that had gradually been gaining momentum since Japan opened its doors to Western trade around the middle of the century. So often a pioneer, one of the first English silver manufacturers to take a serious interest in Japanese styles was Elkington and Co. English manu-facturers were at a disadvantage in this style, since the hallmarking laws made it illegal to combine other metals, such as damascened iron, with silver. The lead in 'Japonaiserie' was consequently soon lost to American firms such as Tiffany and Company; nevertheless, throughout the 1880s Elkingtons produced a special line of wares which were superbly decorated with parcel-gilt decoration in the Japanese manner.

Of all the contrasts and tensions that made the Victorian period so complex, the most fundamental was that between the advocates of the machine and its opponents. At the end of the period this was brought into

'Cellini pattern' ewer, electroplate,
made by Elkington and Co., c. 1860; 11 in. high
(Victoria and Albert Museum, London).

stark relief by the conflicting ideologies of Christopher Dresser's industrial aesthetic and the aims and aspirations of the Arts and Crafts movement. C. R. Ashbee was the leading figure in the movement, the silversmiths of which included John Pearson, John Williams, William Hardiman, Gilbert Marks and Nelson Dawson. The first three all belonged to the Guild and

Egg steamer, silver and ebony, Sheffield, 1884,
maker's mark of H. Straford, designed by Christopher Dresser; $7\frac{7}{8}$ in. high
(Victoria and Albert Museum, London).

School of Handicrafts, which Ashbee set up in 1888 at Toynbee Hall in the East End of London. In many ways Ashbee's concerns were similar to Dresser's. He founded the Guild 'with the object of making useful things, of making them well and making them beautiful; goodness and beauty were to the leaders of the movement synonymous terms'.[19] Most silver produced by the Guild of Handicrafts had a simplicity of form and sense of line that in many ways foreshadowed the art nouveau style, but more important was the fact that it was made entirely by hand. Ashbee had a deeply romantic view of the Middle Ages, and invested the idea of craftsmanship unsoiled by the machine with a kind of religious virtue.

It would be tempting to close on the impression that with C. R. Ashbee the story had been brought full circle and that the craft had returned to the

sort of innocence in which it was found at the end of the Middle Ages. The myth is one that exercised considerable attraction, and with life for most being dominated by the squalor and filth of the late nineteenth-century city, it is easy to understand why. Liberty's catalogue for 1899 exploited it to the full by claiming that 'in this [hand-hammered] feature of the work

Tray, silver parcel-gilt, Birmingham, 1877,
maker's mark of Frederick Elkington & Co.; 14 in. long.

... there is an echo of those more leisured days when the craftsman not only loved his art for its own sake, but was able to devote his life to it with comparative indifference to the pecuniary result of his labour of love'. But a myth it was, and a particularly transparent one too. The innocent medieval craftsman had never existed in the sense in which he was imagined. Although no less of an art for being so, the art of the goldsmith was, perhaps more than other crafts, governed by economic reality, and in the end the Guild of Handicrafts was driven out of business by other firms who were able to imitate its work at lesser cost. Ashbee's ideological rejection of the machine enabled other manufacturers to undercut his prices with machine-made goods that imitated its appearance.

The most successful of these were Omar Ramsden, who entered into partnership with Alwyn Carr in 1897, and the London retailers Liberty and

Beaker and cover, silver and enamel, 1903, maker's mark of
Nelson Dawson; 10 in. high.

Co. The former, both during and after Carr's involvement, produced a wide range of silver, much of which was of a medieval character. Most of Ramsden's silver bears the Latin signature 'Omar Ramsden me fecit', which is, of course, a charming and deliberate 'echo of those more leisured days' and an allusion to the signature on the famous early medieval Alfred Jewel in the Ashmolean Museum. But such an evocation of homely hand-crafted techniques was a deceit, albeit a perfectly harmless one. Ramsden was not himself a practising silversmith, and the hammer marks on his silver were deliberately added to the object after it had been made by labour-saving, mechanized means such as spinning.

The most important artist associated with Liberty's was Archibald Knox, and the wares which were produced under his direction were primarily in the art nouveau style and often decorated with enamel. The name under which they were marketed, Cymric ware, again served to allude to Celtic art, with all its romantic associations of unhurried craftsmanship, even though the goods were in reality made as much with the aid of machine as by hand.

While the closing years of the nineteenth century and the early part of the twentieth were marked by a number of interesting developments in the craft, they made relatively little impact on the trade as a whole. For the majority of manufacturers most domestic silver tended to take the form of reproduction of antique styles, such as Queen Anne and early Georgian, and there was relatively little attempt in England to form and market a 'modern' style. This must be seen, in part at least, as a consequence of the growing interest among the buying public in antiques. For not only were well-off people now much more fully committed to domestic wares in other materials than they had been in the past, but when thinking in terms of silver they were now much more inclined to look to old pieces, which could now be considered as investments, than to patronize modern silversmiths.

In recent years the Worshipful Company of Goldsmiths has done much to revitalize the flagging craft, both by the example it has set with its own collection of contemporary silver and by its organization of trade fairs. But the absence of servants to clean silver, the fear of burglars and the relatively high price of modern hand-made silver in comparison with its antique equivalent, are all very real factors that make it unlikely that silver will ever play as major a role in the everyday life of the future as it has done in the past.

The following list of brief lives is merely a selection of some of the more prominent figures from the period covered by this book. To some extent arbitrary choices have been made, and for each goldsmith that has been chosen there are probably several with equal claim to inclusion. I have deliberately avoided discussing goldsmiths who, although distinguished, are known only by their mark, such as 'T Y L' from the early seventeenth century, and the 'hound sejant' maker from the mid century. In addition to specific sources mentioned at the bottom of individual entries, full acknowledgement is made to Arthur Grimwade's *London Goldsmiths 1697–1837, Their Marks and Lives* (1976) and Charles Oman's *Caroline Silver 1625– 1688* (1970).

ADAMAS, Robert (fl. *c.* 1490–1532)
Royal goldsmith to Henry VIII, he came from a family of goldsmiths and was presumably apprenticed to his father, from whom he inherited his working tools and 20 shillings in 1491. In 1503 he substantially improved his position by marrying the granddaughter and heiress of Sir Hugh Bryce, who had been one of the leading goldsmiths of his day. During the early part of Henry VIII's reign he received numerous orders for gold jewels to be sewn on to royal costumes, but in the 1520s the growth of international diplomacy and the custom of exchanging New Year's gifts at court accounted for lucrative business in more substantial plate. Other than the King, his most important client was Cardinal Wolsey. Although nothing survives that may be firmly attributed to Adamas, objects such as the Howard Grace Cup of 1525 or the Barber-Surgeons' instrument case of about 1518 give an idea of the kind of ornamental plate that he would have produced. He evidently ran a large workshop, employing a number of goldsmiths and apprentices among whom was Martin Bowes, who was apprenticed to him in 1513 and who, as Sir Martin Bowes, later presented the Bowes Cup to the Goldsmiths' Company. The key to success in Tudor England lay in patronage, and Adamas was no

exception in his appetite for appointments. On the occasion of the accession of the new King he was appointed Master of the Mint; from at least 1524 he was Master of the Jewels and in the same year he was Prime Warden of the Goldsmiths' Company. There is little doubt that he turned these positions to his own advantage and, in addition to his substantial money-lending activities, it was probably his role at the Mint that was chiefly responsible for the fact that he died reputedly the richest man in the City.

(See Philippa Glanville, 'Robert Adamas, Goldsmith', *Proceedings of the Silver Society,* 1984)

ARCHAMBO, Peter (d. 1767)

Huguenot goldsmith, apprenticed to Jacob Margas (q.v.) in 1710; entered his first mark in 1720. Like his master, he was free of the Butchers' Company rather than the Goldsmiths'. A leading, if not especially daring, exponent of the *Régence* and rococo styles, his most important patron was probably George, 2nd Earl of Warrington, for whom he made a wine fountain in 1728 (Goldsmiths' Company collection) and a wine cistern in the following year, which is still at Dunham Massey.

(See Judith Banister, 'Master of Elegant Silver', *Country Life,* 9 June 1983)

ASHBEE, Charles Robert (1863–1942)

Ashbee was not himself a working silversmith, but he was a leading figure in the Arts and Crafts movement of the turn of the century and in 1888 founded the Guild and School of Handicrafts at Toynbee Hall in the East End of London. The Guild rejected the contemporary dominance of the machine and set out to make small pieces of domestic plate by entirely hand-crafted means in a style that has certain affinities with art nouveau. The school closed in 1895 but the Guild continued until 1908, moving in 1902 to Chipping Campden in Gloucestershire. In 1909 Ashbee published *Modern English Silverwork,* but soon thereafter lost faith in handicrafts and his opposition to the machine wavered. After 1915 he gave up the arts altogether and became an academic.

BATEMAN, Hester (1708–94)

Widow of John Bateman, a gold chain maker who died in 1760, she registered her first mark in 1761. She was not trained in the craft herself, but was evidently a highly competent businesswoman and, in spite of being illiterate, expanded the

business into what was probably one of the largest in London. The workshop specialized in domestic wares of ordinary quality and made maximum use of mechanized methods at all stages of production. Her sons Peter and Jonathan took over the business, and the Bateman dynasty lasted well into the nineteenth century. (See David S. Shure, *Hester Bateman*, 1959)

BODENDICK, Jacob (fl. 1661–*c*. 1688)

Married in London and granted denization in 1661, Bodendick was described as a native of Limburg in Germany. Like Wolfgang Howzer (q.v.), he was protected by the King, who instructed the Goldsmiths' Company in 1664 to mark his plate. However, he was not granted the freedom of the company until 1673. Bodendick evidently played an important role in the introduction to England of certain techniques typical of north Germany, and is particularly associated with tankards with cast scroll handles of auricular design and cups with pierced and embossed cagework decoration. One of his most remarkable surviving pieces is a silver-gilt mounted carved walnut wood tankard of 1664 in the Boston Museum of Fine Arts.

BOULTON, Matthew (1728–1809) MB IF

Inherited his father's 'toy making' business in 1759 and moved to Soho, outside Birmingham, where he built a large and modern factory employing eventually more than 800 people. He formed a partnership with John Fothergill until the latter's death in 1782, and later with the engineer James Watt. Boulton produced a wide range of metalware, especially ormolu, silver and Sheffield plate. He lobbied intensively for the establishment of assay offices at Birmingham and Sheffield in 1771. His silver is ambitious in design and of fine quality and distinctive style, but was not a commercial success. His most important patron for silver was the society hostess Mrs Elizabeth Montagu, with whom he corresponded extensively and for whom he produced a dinner service in 1776. Production declined towards the end of the century, although the firm remained an important producer of Sheffield plate. (See Nicholas Goodison, *Ormolu: The Work of Matthew Boulton*, 1974)

BOWERS, George (fl. 1661–*c*. 1680)

An immigrant goldsmith who presumably came to England in the retinue of Charles II, since he was sworn 'embosser in ordinary' in 1661. He also benefited considerably from the protection of the King, who requested the Lord Mayor to grant him the freedom of the City of London after his denization in 1664. But such favouritism

was resented in the trade, and in 1663 he complained that his workshop had been broken into and goods seized by workmen belonging to the Goldsmiths' Company. Unlike the Mayor, the Goldsmiths' Company resisted the King's interference and he did not receive the freedom of the company until 1667. In spite of these personal details, little is known about Bowers's work. He is not known to have registered a mark, although the fact that Benjamin Pyne (q.v.) was apprenticed to him does suggest that he was fully conversant with all aspects of the craft, rather than being solely a chaser. The mark on an embossed tankard in the Toledo Museum, Ohio, a reversed monogram of G and B, has been attributed to him, as has an unmarked embossed toilet service in the Huntington Collection in California and a similar service at Woburn Abbey.

CAFE, John (c. 1716–57)
One of a number of London eighteenth-century goldsmiths whose workshop specialized in one particular branch of the trade. He was apprenticed in 1730 to James Gould, a fellow Somerset man and specialist candlestick maker, and entered his first mark in 1740. John Cafe and his younger brother William, who was apprenticed to him in 1742, produced candlesticks and candelabra almost exclusively and in particular had a virtual monopoly of one popular type on shaped square base modelled with shells. John Cafe left a substantial sum of money in his will, but his younger brother was evidently a less able businessman: production seems to have declined gradually during the 1760s, and in 1772 he was declared bankrupt. He died between 1802 and 1811, but had evidently retired many years earlier.
(See John P. Fallon, 'The Goulds and Cafes, Candlestick Makers', *Proceedings of the Silver Society*, 1974)

CHAWNER, Henry (1764–1851)
The most prominent member of a large family of goldsmiths, he was presumably apprenticed to his father and registered his first mark in 1786. His workshop produced neo-classical domestic plate, especially tea silver, of a consistently fine quality during the last part of the eighteenth century. In 1796 he entered into a partnership with John Emes.

COURTAULD, Augustine (c. 1685–1751)
A Huguenot goldsmith, brought to England as an infant and apprenticed in 1701 to Simon Pantin (q.v.), he entered his first mark in 1708. Most of his work is well made and well proportioned, but is essentially domestic and with restrained ornament. His most ambitious piece is the 1730 State Salt of the Swordbearer of

the City of London. His half-brother Peter, son Samuel and grandson Samuel were all goldsmiths. Samuel I's widow Louisa inherited her husband's business and formed a partnership with George Cowles in 1768.
(See J. F. Hayward, *The Courtauld Silver*, 1975)

CRESPIN, Paul (1694–1770)
Of French extraction, but born in London, Crespin entered his first marks in 1720 and 1721. He was described as being free of the Longbowstring Makers Company, but no record of his apprenticeship survives. He was one of the most outstanding goldsmiths of the second quarter of the eighteenth century. In 1724 he made a 'curious silver vessel for bathing' for the King of Portugal, weighing 6,030 ounces, and contributed in 1734 to a service for Catherine the Great of Russia. A deep basin of 1722 in the British Museum and a charger of 1727 in the Gilbert Collection, Los Angeles, illustrate his mastery of the *Régence* style. But his most original work dates from the 1740s, when he developed a highly sculptural approach to the rococo which suggests collaboration with Nicholas Sprimont (q.v.). The most remarkable of his surviving plate includes a soup tureen of 1740 in the Toledo Museum, Ohio, and the centrepiece made for Frederick, Prince of Wales in the royal collection. He retired in 1759 and died in Southampton.
(See A. G. Grimwade, 'Crespin or Sprimont?', *Apollo*, August 1969)

DE LAMERIE, Paul (1688–1751)
The most famous English goldsmith of the eighteenth century and head of one of the largest workshops in London. He was born of French Huguenot parents in 's Hertogenbosch in Holland, was brought to London in 1691 and apprenticed to Pierre Platel (q.v.) in 1703. He registered his first mark in 1713 and, presumably through connections formed under his old master, had a number of important aristocratic patrons from quite early in his career, for example the Duke of Sutherland, the Spencer family, Sir Robert Walpole and the Hon. George Treby. His early work is in both the plain Queen Anne and the more sophisticated *Régence* style, epitomized by the Sutherland wine cistern of 1719 (Minneapolis Museum) and the Treby toilet service of 1724 (Ashmolean Museum). From the 1730s he was arguably the leading exponent of the rococo style. Many of his most elaborate pieces suggest that he employed specialist craftsmen and designers whose individual characteristics can be recognized at different periods. In particular, from about 1739 to 1745 he evidently employed a talented but anonymous modeller who was largely responsible for the character of important commissions such as the plate made for Algernon, 6th Earl of Mountrath (Gilbert Collection, Los Angeles, etc.), and the ewer and basin of 1742 commissioned by the Goldsmiths' Company. He also made free and eclectic use of numerous different sources, such

as Dutch auricular silver and printed pattern books. Although occasionally in a highly embossed style, most of his more elaborate designs are in fact standard forms with applied cast decoration.

(See P. A. S. Phillips, *Paul de Lamerie*, London, 1935)

FARRELL, Edward Cornelius (*c.* 1780–after 1835)

No record exists of his apprenticeship, but he registered his first mark in 1815 and was from about 1815 to 1830 supplying plate to the flamboyant and innovative retailer Kensington Lewis. This association was one of the most important elements in the early nineteenth-century historicist movement and resulted in some of the most extraordinary silver of the period, particularly that produced for Lewis's leading patron, the Duke of York. The latter ordered huge quantities of plate through Lewis, perhaps the most splendid of which was a candelabrum of some 1,000 ounces, modelled in the form of Hercules slaying the Hydra. Farrell, however, described himself as a 'silversmith and chaser' and most of his work is embossed in high relief, mainly in seventeenth-century and rococo taste. He would also seem to have been one of the first goldsmiths habitually to 'improve' plain old plate by chasing it up in his characteristic style. It is impossible to tell whether he or Lewis was the dominant force in work bearing Farrell's mark, but it is clear that he had few opportunities to produce large-scale plate after the death of the Duke in 1827; most of his work thereafter is limited to novelties and tea services with heavily embossed decoration inspired by Dutch seventeenth-century genre painting.

(See John Culme, 'Kensington Lewis: A Nineteenth-Century Businessman', *The Connoiseur*, September 1975)

FOGELBERG, Andrew (*c.* 1732–1815)

Born in Sweden and probably to be identified with Andreas Fogelberg, who was apprenticed to Berent Halck of Halmsted. His first mark was entered in London around 1770, but no record of its exact date survives. From 1780 to 1793 he was in partnership with Stephen Gilbert, after which the premises were taken over by Paul Storr (q.v.). Whether produced before or during the partnership, Fogelberg's silver is invariably of fine quality, showing a sophisticated but restrained command of neo-classicism and illustrated by a silver-gilt teapot and stand of 1784 in the Victoria and Albert Museum. Many of his pieces are characterized by the use of silver medallions copied from James Tassie's castings of ancient cameos.

GARTHORNE, Francis (fl. *c.* 1680–1726)
One of the leading native English goldsmiths at the time of the Huguenot influx, and a signatory to the petitions of 1697 and 1711 against 'aliens and foreigners' and 'necessitous strangers'. No records of apprenticeship or the date of his first mark survive, although he is known to have been free of the Girdlers' company. From 1702 to 1723 he was one of the Subordinate Goldsmiths to Queen Anne and George I; he produced a fine ewer at Windsor Castle and a twelve-branch chandelier at Hampton Court. His later work shows an increasing assimilation of the Huguenot style.

HARACHE, Pierre (fl. *c.* 1682–*c.* 1700)
One of the first Huguenot goldsmiths to make a major impact on the craft in England. Thought to be a native of Rouen, his origins have yet to be established. His name appears on the denization lists of 1682 and he became free of the Goldsmiths' Company in the same year. His earliest known pieces date from 1683, although he was obviously a fully trained goldsmith before coming to England. There has in the past been confusion between the work of Harache and that of his son, also Pierre (1653–after 1717). Both goldsmiths produced work of the finest quality, distinguished by relatively squat proportions, remarkably heavy gauge metal and cast and cut-card ornament. Among Pierre I's finest works are a ewer and dish of 1697 in the British Museum and a wine cistern of 1699 made for the Barber-Surgeons' Company.

HEMING, Thomas (*c.* 1725–after 1795)
Apprenticed in 1738 to Peter Archambo (q.v.) and entered his first mark in 1745. In 1760 he was appointed Principal Goldsmith to the King and continued in that position until 1782, when the warrant was withdrawn, apparently on account of his excessive charges. His work is invariably of fine quality, in both a late rococo and early neo-classical style. Some of his most characteristic pieces among the former are a group of two-handled cups and covers with caryatid handles and applied vine ornament. His later silver uses ornament that is derived from classical architecture, but is of a curvilinear form that is in complete contrast to the Adam style. Among the most important of his works are a silver-gilt rococo toilet service of 1766 made for Queen Matilda of Denmark (Kunstindustrie Museum, Copenhagen), another made two years later for Sir Watkin Williams Wynn, a neo-classical bowl made in 1771 for the same patron (both National Museum of Wales) and the Brownlow wine cistern of 1770 at Belton.

HENNELL, David (1712–85)
Founder of a family of goldsmiths that continued in trade until the late nineteenth century and of a firm that is still in existence today. Apprenticed to Edward Wood, a salt-cellar maker, in 1728, he entered his first mark in 1736. Hennell and his descendants specialized in practical domestic silver, especially salt cellars. He retired in 1773 in order to become Deputy Warden of the Goldsmiths' Company (head of the Assay Office).

HOWZER, Wolfgang (fl. 1652–after 1688)
Like George Bowers and Jacob Bodendick (both q.v.), he was presumably a goldsmith in Charles II's service. He came from a family of goldsmiths in Zürich and was apprenticed to his father, becoming free of the guild in 1652. In 1664 he was furnished with a letter from the King instructing the Goldsmiths' Company to mark his plate. The company resented such pressures, but reluctantly agreed to comply, and the mark W H above a cherub has been attributed to him by Charles Oman. A silver-gilt mounted Chinese porcelain vase of about 1670 in the Victoria and Albert Museum bears this mark. His most important surviving pieces, however, predate this and were produced by him through the influence of Sir Robert Viner (q.v.) for Bishop Cozins of Durham's chapel at Bishop Auckland in 1660–61. Some of these pieces were evidently sponsored by Francis Leake (q.v.) and are struck with his mark.

JENKINS, Thomas (fl. c, 1665–1707)
This important goldsmith has long been known from his Britannia standard mark, registered in 1697, but it is only recently that his work prior to that date has been recognized. Jenkins was free of the Butchers' Company, of which he was a prominent member and served as Master in 1699. Over a hundred pieces with his mark have been recorded, the earliest dating from 1668, and they include a pair of tankards of 1671 at Dunham Massey and a large wine cistern of 1677 in the Victoria and Albert Museum. His most productive period was undoubtedly that prior to the introduction of the new standard, and although Jacob Margas (q.v.) was apprenticed to him in 1699, it has been suggested that by this time, like many successful goldsmiths, he was acting mainly in the capacity of a retailer or banker. (See A. G. Grimwade and J. Banister, 'Thomas Jenkins', *Proceedings of the Silver Society*, 1977)

KANDLER, Charles Frederick (fl. 1727– after 1773)
Almost complete mystery surrounds this important maker. He was clearly of German origin and was perhaps related to the Meissen porcelain modeller, J. J.

Kändler, but no record of his apprenticeship or freedom exists and it has proved impossible to establish any significant details about his life. The picture has been further confused by the fact that he would seem to have been known by his first name until 1735 and by his second thereafter. His first mark, C K, was registered in 1727, and his second, F K, in 1735, and it was until recently not unreasonably supposed that the marks were for two separate individuals, a supposition that is *prima facie* supported by the unusual length of his working career. A number of other marks were also registered, including a partnership mark for both sterling and Britannia standards with James Murray in 1727 and two different Britannia standard marks, one in 1751 and another undated and surmounted by a bishop's mitre. His work is of the finest quality and includes some of the earliest soup tureens in English silver, as well as a group of plate from the early 1730s with highly distinctive engraving. But his most important surviving work is undoubtedly the Jerningham wine cistern of 1735 in the Hermitage Museum, Leningrad, which was modelled by the sculptor Michael Rysbrach.

LEAKE, Francis (fl. 1655–after 1683)
Apprenticed to Henry Starkey and free of the Goldsmiths' Company in 1655. Together with his younger brother Ralph, his surviving work reflects most current tastes, especially that for embossed foliage, while the fact that a standing salt from the 1660 regalia in the Tower of London bears his mark indicates that he was among the most prominent goldsmiths of the period. There would also appear to be grounds for supposing that he was prepared to sponsor the work of certain foreign goldsmiths at the Assay Office (see Wolfgang Howzer).

LIGER, Isaac (d. 1730)
A Huguenot goldsmith whose name appears on the denization lists for 1700, he was made free of the Broderers' Company in 1704 and entered his first mark in the same year. Most of his work is domestic plate, usually plain but of excellent quality and heavy gauge, although the toilet service he supplied for the marriage of the 2nd Earl of Warrington's daughter is magnificent by any standards. The largest surviving corpus of his work is among the domestic and chapel plate at Dunham Massey, and his patronage by the Earl of Warrington lasted from 1708 until the end of his working life.

MANWARING, Arthur (fl. 1643–c. 1696)
Completed his apprenticeship under William Tyler in 1643 and was active for over fifty years, his last recorded work being hallmarked for 1696. Manwaring clearly ran a highly successful workshop and probably sponsored other makers' work,

since his work is relatively prolific and suggests command of a wide range of styles and techniques. Among his earliest known works is a porringer and stand of 1655 in the austere Commonwealth style, but the Feake Cup of ten years later in the Goldsmiths' Company Collection shows complete command of the embossed style, which is evident in much of his later work. From 1688, after the death of Sir Robert Viner (q.v.), he received a number of royal commissions.

MARGAS, Jacob (c. 1685–after 1730)

Son of a Huguenot goldsmith, Samuel Margas, who had been in London since at least 1687, Jacob was apprenticed to Thomas Jenkins (q.v.) in 1699 and made free of the Butchers' Company in 1706. He registered his first mark in the same year and apparently served as one of the Subordinate Goldsmiths to the King from 1723 to 1730, although he is recorded by Heal as bankrupt in 1725, and Grimwade has pointed out that the fact of several goldsmiths from one family working over the same period has led to some confusion between the different individuals. His known works span the period 1706–25 and are generally in the plain Queen Anne style, one of the best examples of which is a polygonal silver-gilt two-handled cup and cover of 1710 in the Huntington Collection in California. Margas's younger brother, Samuel, was apprenticed to him in 1708 and was free of the same company in 1714, registering his first mark in the following year. He is also recorded as having been Subordinate Goldsmith to the King from 1723–30 and 1732–3.

NELME, Anthony (c. 1660–1723)

Apprenticed to Richard Rowley in 1672 and later turned over to Isaac Deighton. He registered his first mark in c. 1680 and became one of the leading native English goldsmiths after the arrival of the Huguenots, signing the 1697 petition against 'aliens and foreigners'. He evidently ran a large workshop, and produced a striking range of silver from ordinary domestic wares to large-scale display and ceremonial pieces such as toilet services, maces and pilgrim bottles. Like most successful native makers, his work was of equal quality to that of the Huguenots and gradually assimilated many of the technical and stylistic aspects of the new style. Many pieces from his workshop survive, among the most impressive of which are a pair of large altar candlesticks of 1694 at St George's Chapel, Windsor, and a toilet service of 1691, now dispersed, applied with the monogram of Judith Bridgeman.

PANTIN, Simon (c. 1680–1728)

A native of Rouen, Pantin's name appears on the London denization lists of 1687. He was apprenticed to Pierre Harache (q.v.) and registered his first mark in 1701. The peacock included in his mark is a reference to the address of his first workshop, which was situated in Peacock Street, St Martin's Lane. Much of his work is of excellent quality but simple design, his most important surviving pieces being the Bowes kettle, stand and table of 1719 in the Untermyer Collection, New York, and a soup tureen of 1726 in the Hermitage Museum, Leningrad. Among the most beautiful of his works is a pair of silver-gilt salvers of 1713 in the *Régence* style, made for Sir Henry Featherstone. On his death the workshop was taken over by his son, Simon, who died in 1733 and was succeeded consecutively by Lewis Pantin I, II and III, the last named entering his mark as a goldworker in 1788.

PARTRIDGE, Affabel (fl. c. 1550–80)

Little is known of his early life other than his apprenticeship around 1535 to Richard Crompton, but he was evidently one of the leading goldsmiths of Queen Elizabeth's reign and rose to become Prime Warden of the Goldsmiths' Company. He is mentioned in 1560 and again in 1575/6, together with Robert Brandon, as 'one of her Ma[jest]ies goldsmiths'. The maker's mark here attributed to him is ascribed by Jackson to John Bird, but this can hardly be right, as Heal gives the latter's working dates as 1568–78, whereas the mark is found over the period 1554–78. It is invariably found on pieces of the finest quality, often of a character to suggest the use of continental pattern books or journeymen. That they were made by a goldsmith with connections at court is demonstrated by the Bacon Cups of 1573 (one in the British Museum), made for Sir Francis Bacon from the discarded matrices of the Great Seal of England. The royal associations of the so-called Queen Elizabeth Salt of 1572 (Tower of London), perhaps his most outstanding surviving work, however, are traditional only.

PILLEAU, Pezé (1696–1776)

The first native English member of a family of French goldsmiths dating back at least to 1612. Apprenticed to John Chartier in 1710, he married his master's daughter in 1724. His first mark was entered in, or a little before, 1724. He evidently retired from the trade by about 1755 and his surviving work is comparatively rare, although he would appear to have specialized in jugs with simple but technically sophisticated faceted sides. Like his father, Alexis Pilleau, he is also recorded as a maker of artificial teeth, and it is possible that this occupation formed the main part of his business.

PITTS, Thomas (c. 1723–93)
Apprenticed in 1737 to Charles Hatfield and turned over in 1742 to David Willaume II. Pitts is recorded as a 'goldsmith and chaser', and from his surviving work it is clear that he specialized in the production of epergnes and baskets, many of which were supplied to Parker and Wakelin (q.v.) for retail. His sons William, Thomas and Joseph were all apprenticed to him in 1769, 1767 and 1772 respectively. The first named of these eventually took over the business, entering his first mark in 1781 and forming a partnership from 1791 and 1799 with Joseph Preedy.

PLATEL, Pierre (c. 1664–1719)
Born in Lille and fled with his father and brother to Flanders after the revocation of the Edict of Nantes in 1685. He settled in England in 1688 and entered his first mark in 1699. Platel numbered leading supporters of William III, such as the Dukes of Devonshire and Portland, among his clients, and his most magnificent works include the gold ewer and basin of 1701 at Chatsworth and a silver-gilt toilet service at Welbeck Abbey. These epitomize the style developed by Platel, which often involved more fully worked surfaces and more sophisticated applied decoration and engraving than is found in the work of contemporaries such as David Willaume (q.v.) and Pierre Harache (q.v.). He clearly had a considerable influence over his most illustrious apprentice, Paul de Lamerie (q.v.), whose important early works are in precisely the same style as his master's.

PYNE, Benjamin (c. 1653–1732)
Apprenticed to George Bowers (q.v.) in 1667 and probably working alone from about 1680, when the first mark attributed to him (a crowned P) appears. He was one of the signatories to the petition against the newcomers in 1697, and by the time of the main Huguenot influx after 1685 was clearly well established. By the end of the century there can be no question that he, together with Anthony Nelme (q.v.), was the leading native English goldsmith in London. In 1714 he was appointed Subordinate Goldsmith to the King for the coronation of George I, and rose in 1725 to become Prime Warden of the Goldsmiths' Company. His long career, however, ended in relative poverty, and in 1727 he was obliged to apply for the position of Beadle of the Goldsmiths' Company. Much of Pyne's work shows a relative restraint which balances command of Huguenot techniques with an adherence to native English style. A significant part of his output consisted of church plate and municipal regalia, but among his most important surviving works are the thirty-two-piece silver-gilt toilet service of 1708 made for the Duke of Norfolk and the Earl of Kent's ewers and basin of 1699 (see p. 147).

ROLLOS, Philip (d. 1721)
A shadowy figure whose name appears on the denization lists for 1691, but of whose earlier history nothing is known. He was made free of the Goldsmiths' Company in 1697, but the maker's mark PR in an oblong punch which appears from around 1680 has been plausibly attributed to him. He clearly ran one of the most successful workshops in London and was appointed one of the Subordinate Goldsmiths to both William III and Queen Anne. A number of impressive pieces in the Huguenot style survive with his mark, including the wine-cistern of 1701 at Dunham Massey, another of 1699 in the Hermitage Museum, Leningrad, and a third in the Marlborough ambassadorial plate at Althorp. His son, also Philip, succeeded him in the post of Subordinate Goldsmith to the Crown.

RUNDELL, Philip (1743–1827)
One of the most remarkable entrepreneurs of the early nineteenth century, Rundell was not a practising goldsmith. He was apprenticed in 1760 to William Rogers of Bath, subsequently worked for Theed and Pickett in London, and was made a partner by the latter in 1772. By 1785 he was sole proprietor and by 1803 had brought in John Bridge and his nephew Edmund Rundell as partners of what was now styled Rundell, Bridge and Rundell. Bridge's fortuitous connection with the King is said to have accounted for the firm being awarded the royal warrant in 1797, which in turn led to an enormous increase in business. Rundell employed Paul Storr (q.v.) and other goldsmiths such as Benjamin and James Smith, Digby Scott and Philip Cornman to work exclusively for him and to produce plate exactly in accordance with the specifications drawn up by his design team. By around 1810 the firm was employing over 500 people and entirely dominated the market for extravagant display plate in the Regency style. It was not until his break with Storr in 1819 that Rundell registered his own mark. He would appear to have retired from active business around 1823, when John Bridge entered his mark. He left a fortune of £1$\frac{1}{4}$ million.

SCOFIELD, John (fl. 1776–96)
One of the leading makers of the last quarter of the eighteenth century, although no record survives of his apprenticeship. His first mark was entered in 1776 in partnership with Robert Jones, and his second alone two years later. His work concentrates on domestic silver, especially dinner services and candelabra. It is almost entirely in restrained Adam taste, but is distinguished by superb quality,

especially of chased detail. Among his finest plate are the candlesticks and cruet frame at Brodick Castle, made for William Beckford in 1781 and 1784.

SHARP, Robert (c. 1733–1803)
Apprenticed to Thomas Gladwin in 1747 and became free of the Goldsmiths' Company in 1757. In 1763 he entered his first mark in a partnership with Daniel Smith, which was maintained until 1788, except for a brief period between 1778 and 1780 when a third partner, Robert Carter, was introduced. Smith and Sharp were leading exponents of the Adam style and a number of pieces with their mark are made to designs in Robert Adam's hand, such as a cup of 1764, the design for which is in Sir John Soane's Museum. A magnificent silver-gilt toilet service of 1779 from the partnership is in the Kungl Livrustkammaren, Stockholm.

SHRUDER, James (fl. 1737–c. 1752)
Although he was responsible for some of the most remarkable rococo silver, little is known of this maker, who was presumably of German origin. His first mark was registered in 1737, but there is no record of his apprenticeship or freedom. He is stated by Heal to have been bankrupt in 1749, although a kettle of as late as 1752 with his mark is known. His work is distinguished by the use of spiky Germanic rococo cartouches, and perhaps his most remarkable pieces are a coffee pot and kettle of 1749, engraved with the arms of Okeover, the spouts of which are formed as putti astride dolphins.

SPRIMONT, Nicholas (1716–71)
Born at Liège and apprenticed there to his uncle, Sprimont arrived in London in 1742 and registered his mark in January of the following year, but he only worked as a silversmith for about five years. From about 1747 he became exclusively occupied with the management of the new Chelsea porcelain factory, after which no silver with his mark is known. Beyond these bare details, those of his marriage in 1742 to Ann Protin and the sale of his picture collection at Christie's after his death, little is known of this interesting but shadowy character. Sprimont's silver is extremely rare and its scarcity, together with its individuality of style, suggests that he ran a very small workshop. This small corpus of surviving plate is among the most interesting of all English rococo silver. The most important pieces are the Ashburnham centrepiece of 1747 in the Victoria and Albert Museum, a tea kettle of 1745 in the Hermitage Museum, Leningrad, and the lobster and crab salts

and shell-shaped sauceboats of 1742 and 1743 in the royal collection. In addition it has been suggested that the centrepiece of 1741–2 in the royal collection which is struck with Paul Crespin's mark may have been substantially his work. All these pieces are unusually sculptural and characterized by the use of marine motifs and fluid scrolls.

(See A. G. Grimwade, 'Crespin or Sprimont?', *Apollo*, August 1969)

STORR, Paul (1771–1844)

The most famous silversmith of the Regency period, apprenticed in 1785 to Andrew Fogelburg (q.v.) and free of the Goldsmiths' Company in 1792. His first mark was entered in partnership with William Frisbee in the same year and was followed in 1793 by his first mark alone. In 1807 he moved from his workshop in Air Street, Piccadilly, to Dean Street, Soho, and from then until 1819 worked – apparently exclusively – for Rundell, Bridge and Rundell (q.v.), producing grand, often gilt, display plate precisely to their specifications. Storr became a partner in the firm, but eventually broke away from Rundells and was again independent until forming a partnership with John Mortimer, which lasted from 1822 until Storr's retirement in 1838. Although work with his mark is almost invariably of excellent quality, the evidence suggests that he was not a particularly innovative designer. His early work, such as a pair of gilt baskets of 1798 and other plate made for William Beckford, is superbly executed, but of unexceptional neo-classical design. His finest work all dates from the period of the Rundells association, but is indistinguishable from that made for the same firm by Benjamin Smith, and his work after 1819 generally betrays a decline in design.

(See N. M. Penzer, *Paul Storr*, 1954)

VAN VIANEN, Christian (1598–1666 or later)

Born in Utrecht, Holland, van Vianen was son and nephew of two of the most distinguished seventeenth-century Dutch goldsmiths, Adam and Paul van Vianen. The latter are credited with the invention of the auricular style of ornament, which Christian popularized by the publication of his father's designs in 1650. The younger van Vianen became master of the guild of goldsmiths in Utrecht in 1628, and between 1630 and 1647 spent at least two extended periods in London in the service of Charles I. Nearly all his major works, such as a ewer and basin made for the King in 1635 and the service of altar plate for St George's Chapel, completed in 1637, have been lost, but an auricular two-handled bowl and cover made for the 10th Earl of Northumberland and a basin of 1635 survive from his English

period. He apparently never registered a maker's mark and the basin is signed 'C. V. Vianen fecit 1636'.

(See R. W. Lightbown, 'Christian van Vianen at the Court of Charles I', *Apollo*, June 1968)

VINER, Sir Robert (1631–88)

Although not a practising goldsmith, Sir Robert Viner was one of the most influential figures in the craft during the reign of Charles II. He was apprenticed to his uncle, Sir Thomas Viner, and in 1660 succeeded him as royal goldsmith. In this capacity he was responsible for the distribution of royal patronage and played a major part in the promotion of immigrant goldsmiths such as Bodendick, Bowers and Howzer (all q.v.). In a partially successful attempt to win his greater support for native craftsmen, the Goldsmiths' Company brought him on to the Court in 1666 and made him Prime Warden in the following year. It was in connection with the first of these events that he presented the company with a silver-gilt bell for which Paul de Lamerie's (q.v.) inkstand of 1741 was subsequently made. Viner was evidently an influential man in the City (his uncle had been Lord Mayor before him and in 1674 he too was elected Mayor); in 1665 he increased his already considerable wealth by £100,000 through his marriage to Mary, widow of Sir Thomas Hyde. Samuel Pepys visited him in that year and wrote that 'there lives no man in England in greater plenty'. But his massive and unrepaid loans to the Crown led to his downfall: by 1672 he had outstanding debts of £416,000 and in 1682 he was declared bankrupt. His portrait, with his wife and family, is in the National Portrait Gallery.

WAKELIN, Edward (c. 1716–84)

Apprenticed to John Le Sage in 1730 and already in partnership with George Wickes (q.v.) by 1747. He entered his first mark almost immediately afterwards and was free of the Goldsmiths' Company in the following year. From this date he apparently took virtual charge of the running of the silversmithing side of the business. In or after 1758, after Wickes's retirement, he went into partnership with John Parker. This was superseded in 1777 by that between Wakelin's son, John, and William Taylor. The younger Wakelin in turn formed a new partnership in 1792 with Robert Garrard, from which the present-day firm of Garrards is descended. Whether or not Edward Wakelin was a practising goldsmith, there can be no doubt as to his business acumen, and during the 1760s, to judge both from surviving plate and the firm's ledgers in the Victoria and Albert Museum, the Parker and Wakelin workshop was evidently one of the most fashionable in London.

(See Elaine Barr, *George Wickes, Royal Goldsmith*, 1980)

WICKES, George (1698–1761)

Apprenticed to Samuel Wastell in 1712 and registered his first mark in 1721. For much of his career Wickes worked as the sole proprietor of his workshop, but was in partnership between 1730 and 1735 with John Craig (probably a jeweller) and from 1747 until his retirement in 1760 with Edward Wakelin (q.v.). In 1735 he was appointed goldsmith to Frederick, Prince of Wales, a fact which did not in itself lead to very much lucrative royal patronage, but which was immensely prestigious and must have generated business from other clients. He celebrated the fact by incorporating into his mark a coronet in 1735 and the Prince of Wales's feathers in 1739. Wickes was by no means the greatest or most original silversmith of the period, but more is known about him than his contemporaries, thanks to the unique survival of his ledgers, which record the day-to-day details of his business, his patrons and sub-contractors. His work is invariably of excellent quality, but generally of conservative character. Among his most important pieces are an unmarked gold cup and cover made to designs by William Kent for Colonel Pelham in 1736, a large dinner service of 1745–7 made for the Duke of Leinster, and a ewer and basin of 1735 with applied rococo ornament.

(See Elaine Barr, *George Wickes, Royal Goldsmith*, 1980)

WILLAUME, David (1658–1741)

Born in Metz, the son of a goldsmith, and settled in London at least by 1687, when his denization is recorded. He married in 1690 Marie Mettayer, sister of the goldsmith Louis Mettayer. His first known mark was registered in 1697, although he had presumably registered one earlier, since he was free of the Goldsmiths' Company by 1694. Willaume was one of the most outstanding of the 'first generation' Huguenot goldsmiths and his work represents the new style at its best. His patrons included many of the most important nobility, including the Dukes of Devonshire, Portland and Buccleuch, and underscores the concern of those native English goldsmiths who were signatory to the petitions of 1697 and 1711 against immigrants. He probably retired in about 1728, the year in which his son, David II, registered his first mark.

Notes

CHAPTER 1

SILVER: THE METAL AND THE CRAFT

1. Although discovered as early as the seventeenth century, platinum's hardness makes it comparatively unsuitable for plate, and it was not used extensively, even for jewellery, until quite recently. A separate hallmark for platinum was not introduced until 1975.
2. Theophilus, *On Divers Arts*, translated by John G. Hawthorne and Cyril Stanley Smith, New York (1963).
3. I am grateful to Mr James R. Curtis, silversmith at Colonial Williamsburg, where eighteenth-century techniques are still used, for this information.
4. On the continent the idea of preserving family plate seems to have been accepted much earlier than in England. For example, in 1565 Duke Albrecht V of Bavaria listed a number of objects that were to be designated hereditary heirlooms of his family in perpetuity. See J. F. Hayward, *Virtuoso Goldsmiths* (1976), p. 32.
5. For a fuller account of the history of hallmarks in England, see *Touching Gold and Silver, 500 Years of Hallmarks* (exhibition catalogue), Goldsmiths' Hall (1978).
6. I am grateful to Mr David Beasley, Deputy Librarian of the Goldsmiths' Company, for this information.
7. See Chapter 6, p. 142.
8. Quoted from a document of 1577 by Robin D. Gwynn, *Huguenot Heritage* (1985), p. 61.

CHAPTER 2

THE EARLY TUDORS

1. Quoted by Ronald Lightbown, *Tudor Domestic Silver* (1970), p. 1.
2. See Chapter 3, p. 56.

3. Although the silver-gilt mounted Chinese porcelain ewer at Hardwick is contemporary with the house, there is no evidence of its presence at Hardwick before the mid nineteenth century (see Gervase Jackson-Stops (ed.), *The Treasure Houses of Britain* (exhibition catalogue) (1985), p. 105).

4. Illustrated by Gerald Taylor, *Silver Through the Ages* (1964), 2nd edition, pl. 1.

5. Joyce Youings, *Sixteenth-Century England* (1984), p. 128.

6. Illustrated by J. F. Hayward, *Virtuoso Goldsmiths* (1976), pl. 41.

7. See Ronald Lightbown, *Secular Goldsmiths' Work in Medieval France: A History* (1978), p. 40.

8. Illustrated by Joan Evans, *Art in Medieval France* (1948), pl. 150.

9. 'Inventory of Archbishop Parker's Goods & C.', *Archaeologia*, XXX, p. 25.

10. 'An Inventory of the Effects of Henry Howard KG, Earl of Northampton', *Archaeologia*, XLIII, pp. 352–3.

11. Quoted by Lightbown (1970), p. 4, from George Cavendish's biography of Cardinal Wolsey.

12. See Philippa Glanville, 'Tudor Drinking Vessels', *Burlington Magazine* (September 1985), pp. 19–22.

13. Illustrated by Michael Clayton, *Christie's Pictorial History of English and American Silver* (1985), pl. 1.

14. Illustrated in *Cambridge Plate* (exhibition catalogue) (1975), p. 23.

15. Illustrated in Carl Hernmarck, *The Art of the European Silversmith* (1977), pl. 71.

16. Illustrated in H. C. Moffatt, *Old Oxford Plate* (1906), pl. 31.

17. Illustrated in *Cambridge Plate*, p. 23.

18. Illustrated in Hernmarck (1977), pl. 294.

19. Illustrated by C. J. Jackson, *An Illustrated History of English Plate* (1911), opposite p. 146.

20. Illustrated by Moffatt (1906), pls. 43 and 33.

21. Illustrated by Moffatt (1906), pl. 65.

22. Illustrated by J. B. Carrington and G. R. Hughes, *The Plate of the Worshipful Company of Goldsmiths* (1926), pl. 14.

23. See A. J. Collins, *Jewels and Plate of Queen Elizabeth I, The Inventory of 1574* (1955), pp. 433, 541, 564, etc.

24. Quoted by Gerald Taylor, *Silver Through the Ages* (1964), 2nd edition, p. 127.

25. Illustrated by Moffatt (1906), pl. 66.

26. See Michael Clayton, *The Collector's Dictionary of the Silver and Gold of Great Britain and North America* (1985), 2nd edition, p. 180.

27. Illustrated by Claude Blair (ed.), *The History of Silver* (1987), p. 76.

28. See Hayward (1976), pls. 32–5. Although thought to have been published around 1540, at least some of its pages had probably been in circulation some years earlier, perhaps in looseleaf form.

29. This was essentially a plagiarism of Jacques Androuet du Cerceau's pattern

book, which was itself derived from one published in Paris in 1530 by Francesco Pelligrino.

30. See Hayward (1976), pls. 211–14.
31. Illustrated by Clayton, *Dictionary* (1985), pl. 425.
32. Illustrated by Charles Oman, *The English Silver in the Kremlin* (1961), pls. 42 and 43.
33. Illustrated by Moffatt (1906), pl. 69, and *Cambridge Plate*, p. 39.
34. Illustrated by Jackson (1911), p. 683, fig. 889.
35. Formerly in the Swaythling collection, sold at Christie's, 6 and 7 May 1924, lot 125, illustrated in the catalogue.
36. Quoted by John Hatcher and T. C. Barker, *A History of English Pewter* (1974), p. 66.
37. William Harrison, *A Description of England* [original title], reprinted *c.* 1921 (undated) by the Walter Scott Publishing Co., p. 147.
38. See Hatcher and Barker (1974), p. 61.
39. See Peter Hornsby, *Pewter, Copper and Brass* (1981), p. 50.
40. Illustrated in *The Worshipful Company of Pewterers of London, Supplementary Catalogue of Pewterware* (1979), p. 19 (S1/104).
41. Illustrated in Chapter 3, p. 80.
42. See Hatcher and Barker (1974), p. 161.
43. Quoted by Lightbown (1970), p. 7.
44. Illustrated in *Cambridge Plate*, p. 17.
45. Cited by Clayton, *Dictionary* (1985), p. 244.
46. Illustrated by Hugh Tait, *The Golden Age of Venetian Glass* (1979), pl. 11.
47. Illustrated by Moffatt (1906), pl. 34.
48. Illustrated by Lightbown (1978), pl. 54.
49. Illustrated by Robert Wark, *British Silver in the Huntington Collection* (1978), pp. 131 and 132.
50. See Norman Gask, *Old Silver Spoons of England* (1926), pp. 81–90.

CHAPTER 3

THE ELIZABETHAN AGE

1. See Christopher Hill, *Reformation to Industrial Revolution* (1967), p. 83.
2. Joyce Youings, in *Sixteenth-Century England* (1984), p. 16, suggests that the book may have been written as early as 1550.
3. William Harrison, *A Description of England* [original title], reprinted c. 1921 [undated], by the Walter Scott Publishing Co., p. 118.
4. See Hill, (1967), p. 26.
5. See Roy Strong, *Artists of the Tudor Court* (1983), p. 12.

6. A. J. Collins, *Jewels and Plate of Queen Elizabeth I, The Inventory of 1574* (1955), p. 569.

7. ibid, p. 577.

8. ibid., p. 563.

9. ibid., p. 579.

10. ibid., p. 589.

11. ibid., pp. 549–50.

12. See Robin D. Gwynn, *Huguenot Heritage* (1985), p. 72.

13. Quoted by Ronald Lightbown, *Tudor Domestic Plate* (1970), p. 3.

14. See J. F. Hayward, 'The Destruction of Nuremberg Plate by the Goldsmiths' Company', *Proceedings of the Silver Society*, vol. 2, pp. 195–201.

15. Illustrated by J. F. Hayward, *Virtuoso Goldsmiths* (1976), pl. 650.

16. Illustrated in ibid., pl. 671.

17. Illustrated by Lightbown (1970), pls. 22 and 23. This is the largest of all extant pre-seventeenth-century salts and weighs 58 oz.

18. Illustrated by Michael Clayton, *The Collector's Dictionary of the Silver and Gold of Great Britain and North America*, (1985), 2nd edition, colour pl. 52.

19. Sold at Christie's, 6 and 7 May 1924, lot 103, illustrated in the catalogue.

20. See Collins (1955), pp. 466–7.

21. John Hatcher and T. C. Barker, *A History of British Pewter* (1974), p. 166.

22. See Collins (1955). Compare pp. 358 f. with 416 f.

23. Illustrated by Claude Blair (ed.), *The History of Silver* (1987), p. 70.

24. 'Inventories made for Sir William and Sir Thomas Fairfax', *Archaeologia*, XLVIII, p. 153.

25. Sold at Christie's, 6 and 7 May 1924, lot 121, illustrated in the catalogue.

26. Harrison [1921], p. 89.

27. ibid., p. 90.

28. ibid., p. 90.

29. See Chapter 2, note 3.

30. *Inventory of Robert, Earl of Essex* (1588); quoted by Hatcher (1974), p. 107.

31. See Muriel St Clare Byrne (ed.), *The Lisle Letters*, Chicago (1981), vol. 6, Appendix E, pp. 189–91.

32. 'Inventory of Archbishop Parker's Goods & C.', *Archaeologia*, XXX, pp. 25–6.

33. 'Inventories made for Sir William and Sir Thomas Fairfax', *Archaeologia*, XLVIII, pp. 153–4.

34. Collins (1955), pp. 523–6.

35. ibid., pp. 515, 522, etc.

36. Harrison [1921], p. 147.

37. ibid.

38. *Inventory of Thomas Yeat, smith of Worcester* (1563); quoted by Hatcher and Barker (1974), p. 106.

39. Illustrated in *A Short History of the Worshipful Company of Pewterers of London and a Catalogue of Pewterware in Its Possession* (1968), p. 30.
40. See Lindsay Boynton (ed.), *The Hardwick Hall Inventories of 1601* (1971), p. 37.
41. Illustrated by H. Cotterell, *Old Pewter, its Makers and Marks* (1929), pl. XX.
42. Illustrated by Michael Clayton, *Christie's Pictorial History of English and American Silver* (1985), p. 44.
43. 'Cristine Burgh of Richmond, late Prioress of the late dissolved nunery of Nunkylbyng in the County of York (1566)', *Surtees Society*, vol. 26, p. 193.
44. See Charles Oman, *English Engraved Silver* (1978), pp. 47–8.

CHAPTER 4

THE EARLY SEVENTEENTH CENTURY

1. See Christopher Hill, *Reformation to Industrial Revolution* (1967), p. 148.
2. See J. F. Hayward, 'The Destruction of Nuremberg Plate by the Goldsmiths' Company', *Proceedings of the Silver Society*, vol. 2, p. 195.
3. ibid., p. 197.
4. For example, a salver illustrated by Charles Oman, *Caroline Silver* (1970), frontispiece.
5. See J. F. Hayward, *Virtuoso Goldsmiths* (1976), p. 195.
6. 'An Inventory of the Effects of Henry Howard KG, Earl of Northampton', *Archaeologia*, XLII, pp. 351–3.
7. See Ronald Lightbown, 'Christian van Vianen at the Court of Charles I', *Proceedings of the Silver Society*, vol. 2, p. 6.
8. 'An Inventory of Archbishop Parker's Goods & C.', *Archaeologia*, XXX, pp. 25–7.
9. For an illustrated example, see Oman (1970), pl. 7B.
10. Illustrated by Oman (1970), pl. 7A.
11. This is the conclusion reached by Oman (1970), p. 39n.
12. Illustrated by Ronald F. Michaelis, *Old Domestic Base-Metal Candlesticks* (1978), fig. 109.
13. Illustrated by Christopher Peal, *Pewter of Great Britain* (1983), p. 14.
14. Robert Latham and William Matthews (eds.), *The Diary of Samuel Pepys* (1972), vol. 7, p. 10.
15. 'An Inventory of Household Goods, 1612' (of Edward Catherall, a brewer and small farmer of Luton, Bedfordshire), *The Antiquary*, vol. 42, p. 28.

CHAPTER 5

THE RESTORATION

1. See Robert Latham and William Matthews (eds.), *The Diary of Samuel Pepys* (1970), vol. 2, p. 5n. Charles Oman, *Caroline Silver* (1970), p. 12, records that

about 7,000 ounces a year was required for the King's New Year's gifts to peers and senior officers of state.

2. Latham and Matthews (1970), vol. 2, p. 5.
3. See Oman (1970), p. 5n. for tables of the quantities of plate assayed between 1653 and 1662.
4. Illustrated by Charles Oman, *English Church Plate* (1957), pl. 113A.
5. See Oman (1970), pls. 93A and B.
6. See ibid., p. 8.
7. Illustrated ibid., pl. 3A.
8. Illustrated ibid., pl. 9B.
9. For a fuller account of these goldsmiths, see ibid., pp. 32–6.
10. Arthur Grimwade and Judith Banister, 'Thomas Jenkins: The Man and the Master Craftsman', *Proceedings of the Silver Society*, vol. 2, pp. 185–93 and 228.
11. Illustrated by Oman (1970), pl. 37B.
12. See Lindsay Boynton (ed.), *The Hardwick Hall Inventories of 1601* (1971), p. 25.
13. A. J. Collins, *Jewels and Plate of Queen Elizabeth I, The Inventory of 1574* (1955), p. 422.
14. See Oman (1970), pl. 94.
15. Illustrated by Robin Feddon (ed.), *Treasures of the National Trust* (1976), pl. 161.
16. Illustrated by Michael Clayton, *The Collector's Dictionary of the Silver and Gold of Great Britain and North America*, (1985), 2nd edition, colour pl. 64.
17. See Richard Garnier, *The Mostyn Tompion*, Christie's Review of the Season (1982), pp. 228–31. Athough the Chatsworth table was in fact made in Paris in about 1710, Gentot, described but not identified by Oman in *English Engraved silver*, was evidently working in England during the latter part of the seventeenth century.
18. Illustrated by Oman (1970), pl. 40B.
19. Sold at Sotheby's, 13 June 1983, lot 25.
20. For a fuller account of these cups, see Hugh Tait, 'The Advent of the Two-handled Cup', *Proceedings of the Silver Society*, vol. 2, pp. 202–10.
21. Illustrated by Feddon (1976), pl. 160.
22. Latham and Matthews (1972), vol. 6, p. 132.
23. ibid., vol. 1, p. 15.
24. ibid., vol. 9, p. 405.
25. Anthony Wood, Diary, quoted by Oman (1970), p. 45.
26. Latham and Matthews (1970), vol. 1, p. 253.

CHAPTER 6

THE HUGUENOT CONTRIBUTION

1. Robin Gwynn, *Huguenot Heritage* (1985), p. 23.

2. ibid., p. 36.

3. ibid., p. 72.

4. Quoted from J. F. Hayward, *Huguenot Silver* (1959), p. 17.

5. Quoted from *The Quiet Conquest* (exhibition catalogue), Museum of London (1985), no. 332, p. 232.

6. Quoted from Hayward (1959), pp. 20–21.

7. See Christopher Hill, *Reformation to Industrial Revolution*, (1967), p. 174.

8. Quoted from Hayward (1959), pp. 25–6.

9. For a fuller account of George Booth, 2nd Earl of Warrington, and his silver, see J. F. Hayward, 'The Earl of Warrington's Plate', *Apollo*, July 1978.

10. Illustrated by Charles Oman, *The English Silver in the Kremlin* (1961), pl. 11, and Frank Davis, *French Silver* (1970), pl. 18.

11. Now in the collection of the Goldsmiths' Company; illustrated in *The Quiet Conquest*, p. 233. See Chapter 7, note 2.

12. No record of the circumstances of their acquisition exists, although they are known to have been at Blenheim from an early date.

13. See *The Quiet Conquest*, no. 337, p. 234.

14. Quoted from Hayward (1959), p. 82.

15. Illustrated by Hayward (1959), pl. 38.

16. See Hill (1967), p. 237.

17. See Hayward (1959), p. 83.

CHAPTER 7

THE ROCOCO PERIOD

1. See Linda Colley, 'The English Rococo, Historical Background', in *Rococo, Art and Design in Hogarth's England* (exhibition catalogue), Victoria and Albert Museum (1984), p. 10.

2. See *Touching Gold and Silver* (exhibition catalogue), Goldsmiths' Hall (1978), p. 17.

3. See Philippa Glanville, 'Patrons and Craftsman' in *Rococo, Art and Design in Hogarth's England* (1984), p. 324, note 22.

4. In 1738 George Wickes charged £181 1s. for a set of twenty-four plates weighing 488 oz 5 dwt. These were presumably of fairly elaborate design, since the metal alone would have accounted for approximately £135 of the cost, leaving about £46 for the 'fashion'.

5. See Aileen Ribeiro, *Dress in Eighteenth-Century Europe 1715–1789*, New York, p. 202.

6. See *Rococo, Art and Design in Hogarth's England* (1984), p. 259.

7. See Elaine Barr, *George Wickes, Royal Goldsmith* (1980).

8. Arthur Grimwade, *Rococo Silver* (1974), p. 10.

9. Still in the collection of the Goldsmiths' Company; illustrated by Grimwade (1974), pl. 55.
10. Illustrated by Hannelore Muller, *The Thyssen-Bornemisza Collection, European Silver* (1986), p. 99.
11. For an example, see Grimwade (1974), pl. 5.
12. Illustrated in ibid., pls. 45 and 95.
13. Illustrated *Rococo, Art and Design in Hogarth's England* (1984), colour pl. IV.
14. Examples of this type include the centrepiece of 1741 in the royal collection, made for Frederick, Prince of Wales, by Paul Crespin (illustrated Grimwade (1974), pl. 48), and the Ashburnham centrepiece, by Nicholas Sprimont, 1747 (illustrated Grimwade (1974), pl. 50).
15. A full list of this service is given by Charles Oman, *Caroline Silver* (1970), pp. 64–5.
16. Now in the Al Tajir Collection; illustrated by Barr (1980), pp. 197–205.
17. Sold at Sotheby's, 22 November 1984, extensively illustrated in the catalogue.
18. Illustrated Robin Feddon (ed.), *Treasures of the National Trust* (1976), pl. 169.
19. Illustrated Feddon (1976), pl. 152.
20. Christopher Hill, *Reformation to Industrial Revolution*, (1967), p. 247.
21. See David Vaisey (ed.), *The Diary of Thomas Turner 1754–1765* (1985), p. 188.
22. The entire cargo was sold by Christie's, Amsterdam, 28 April–2 May 1986.
23. Both drawing and candlestick are illustrated in *Rococo, Art and Design in Hogarth's England* (1984), E13 and E14, p. 70.
24. The porcelain version of the model is illustrated by Yvonne Hackenbroch, *Chelsea and Other English Porcelain, Pottery and Enamel in the Irwin Untermyer Collection*, Cambridge, Massachusetts (1957), pl. 2.

CHAPTER 8

NEO-CLASSICISM AND INDUSTRIALIZATION

1. Quoted by Helena Hayward, 'English Rococo Designs for Silver', *Proceedings of the Silver Society*, vol. 2, p. 70.
2. Quoted by Robert Rowe, *Adam Silver* (1965), pp. 23–4.
3. ibid., p. 28.
4. Illustrated by Grimwade (1974), pl. 12.
5. For a fuller account of the early history of Sheffield plate, see Frederick Bradbury, *History of Sheffield Plate* (1912).
6. Quoted ibid., p. 30.
7. Robert Rowe (1965), p. 22.
8. Illustrated Bradbury (1912), pp. 398–424.
9. Quoted ibid., p. 2.
10. See *Brass Candlesticks*, privately printed for Rupert Gentle (1973). This facsimile

of a late eighteenth-century brassfounder's catalogue is marked with the price of each model, many of which were available in various sizes.

11. See *Touching Gold and Silver* (exhibition catalogue), Goldsmiths' Hall (1978), p. 17.
12. See Kenneth Quickenden, 'Boulton and Fothergill: Business Plans and Miscalculations', *Art History*, vol. 3, no. 3, p. 277.
13. See Michael Clayton, *The Collector's Dictionary of the Silver and Gold of Great Britain and North America* (1985), 2nd edition, p. 424.
14. The best and fullest account of Boulton's life is in Nicholas Goodison, *Ormolu: The Work of Matthew Boulton* (1974). A more specific account of his silver is contained in Eric Delieb and Michael Roberts, *The Great Silver Manufactory* (1971).
15. Letter to Lord Shelbourne, 1768, quoted by Quickenden, 'Boulton and Fothergill', p. 274.
16. Quoted from Goodison (1974), p. 14.
17. See ibid.
18. See Quickenden, 'Boulton and Fothergill', p. 279.
19. James Keir, *Memorandum of Matthew Boulton* (3 December 1809), p. 1 (Assay Office, Birmingham). Quoted from Goodison (1974), p. 12.
20. Quoted by Quickenden, 'Boulton and Fothergill', p. 280.
21. ibid., p. 281.
22. ibid., p. 282.
23. ibid., p. 281.
24. ibid., pp. 283–4.
25. ibid., p. 279.
26. In this he was far from alone; a set of tea vases by Louisa Courtauld and George Cowles, 1771, formerly at Kedleston and now in the Boston Museum of Fine Arts (p. 214), are exact copies of plates from d'Hancarville. In the following century extensive use was made of Piranesi's prints for copies of the Warwick vase and other classical models.
27. Quoted by Goodison (1974), p. 46.
28. John Culme, 'Beauty and the Beast', *Proceedings of the Silver Society*, vol. 2, pp. 158–64.

CHAPTER 9

THE EARLY NINETEENTH CENTURY

1. See John Culme, *Nineteenth-Century Silver* (1976), p. 33.
2. See J. F. Hayward, 'Royal Silversmiths of the Regency: Rundell, Bridge and Rundell', *Proceedings of the Silver Society*, vol. 2, p. 58.
3. See Culme (1974), p. 65.

4. ibid., p. 63.
5. See Michael Snodin, 'J. J. Boileau: A Forgotten Designer of Silver', *Connoisseur*, June 1978.
6. For a fuller account of the shield, see Shirley Bury and Michael Snodin, 'The Shield of Achilles by John Flaxman, R.A.', in *Art at Auction. The Year at Sotheby's 1983–84*, pp. 275–83.
7. See preface to Christie's sale catalogue, 29 May 1963, 'The Sale of Royal Plate, 1808'.
8. See J. F. Hayward, introduction to *Beckford and Hamilton Silver from Brodick Castle*, National Trust for Scotland (1980) (exhibition catalogue).
9. In 1823 Lewis caused something of a scandal by publicly announcing at the Fonthill sale that a mounted topaz cup, catalogued as the work of Benvenuto Cellini, was not topaz at all, but rock-crystal. For further information on Lewis, see John Culme, 'Kensington Lewis: A Nineteenth-Century Businessman', *Connoisseur*, September 1975.
10. See Michael Snodin and Malcolm Baker, 'William Beckford's Silver', *Burlington Magazine*, November 1980. For a fully illustrated catalogue of the Brodick Castle collection of Beckfordiana, see *Beckford and Hamilton Silver from Brodick Castle*.
11. See Hayward, introduction to *Beckford and Hamilton Silver from Brodick Castle* (1980).
12. See Culme, (1976) p. 13.

CHAPTER 10

THE VICTORIAN ERA: CRAFT AND INDUSTRY

1. Arthur Grimwade, 'A New List of English Gold Plate', *The Connoisseur*, October 1951.
2. See Chapter 2, p. 22.
3. Quoted by John Culme, *Nineteenth-Century Silver* (1976), p. 94.
4. Quoted by Patricia Wardle, *Victorian Silver and Silver-Plate* (1963), pp. 23–4.
5. This passage was also quoted by Patricia Wardle (1963), p. 19, as the preface to her book.
6. Quoted by Culme (1976), p. 216.
7. The quotations given below are taken from a typewritten transcript of the manuscript in the Goldsmiths' Hall library. I am grateful to the librarian, Miss Susan Hare, for making this available to me.
8. *The Journal of Beatrix Potter*, ed. Leslie Linder (1966), also quoted at greater length by Culme (1976), p. 53.
9. Quoted by Wardle (1963), p. 93.
10. Quoted by Culme (1976), p. 105.

11. Quoted by Wardle (1963), p. 94.
12. Culme, (1976), pp. 24–5.
13. Quoted ibid., p. 85.
14. Illustrated by Wardle, pl. 41.
15. Taken from a longer extract, quoted by Wardle (1963), p. 149.
16. Illustrated by Hayward, *Virtuoso Goldsmiths* (1976), pl. 70.
17. Sold at Christie's, 21 October 1981, lot 85.
18. See Culme (1976), p. 206.
19. C. R. Ashbee, *Craftsmanship in Competitive Industry* (1908), p. 5.

Suggested Further Reading

Banister, Judith: *An Introduction to Old English Silver*, London, 1965.

Barr, Elaine: *George Wickes Royal Goldsmith 1698–1761*, London, 1980.

Blair, Claude (ed.): *The History of Silver*, London, 1987.

Brett, Vanessa: *Sotheby's Directory of Silver*, London, 1985.

Clayton, Michael: *The Collector's Dictionary of the Silver and Gold of Great Britain and North America*, London, 1985 (2nd edition).

Clayton, Michael: *Christie's Pictorial History of English and American Silver*, London, 1985.

Culme, John: *Nineteenth-Century Silver*, London, 1976.

Drury, Elizabeth (ed.): *Antiques, Traditional Techniques of the Master Craftsmen*, 1986.

Glanville, Philippa: *Silver in England*, London, 1987.

Grimwade, Arthur: *Rococo Silver 1727–1765*, London, 1974.

Grimwade, Arthur: *London Goldsmiths 1697–1837, Their Marks and Lives*, London, 1976.

Hayward, J. F.: *Huguenot Silver in England 1688–1727*, London, 1959.

Hayward, J. F.: *Virtuoso Goldsmiths and the Triumph of Mannerism 1540–1620*, London, 1976.

Jackson, Sir Charles James: *English Goldsmiths and Their Marks*, London, 1921 (reprinted New York, 1964).

Oman, Charles: *Caroline Silver 1625–1688*, London, 1970.

Oman, Charles: *English Engraved Silver 1150–1900*, London, 1978.

Penzer, N. M.: *Paul Storr*, London, 1954.

Phillips, P. A. S.: *Paul de Lamerie*, London, 1935.

Rowe, Robert: *Adam Silver*, London, 1965.

Schroder, Timothy: *The Gilbert Collection of Gold and Silver*, Los Angeles, 1988.

Taylor, Gerald: *Silver Through the Ages*, London, 1964.

Glossary

ACANTHUS. Classical ornament in the form of stylized leaf decoration based on the scalloped leaves of the acanthus plant.

ALLOY. An amalgam formed of two or more metals.

ANDIRON. Metal objects, in pairs, with horizontal iron bar for supporting logs in the fireplace and decorative vertical element at the front, in iron, brass or silver. Popular in England until the eighteenth century, when coal generally replaced wood fires.

ANNEALING. Process for restoring the malleability of silver or other metals made brittle by hammering; the metal is heated until red hot and then plunged into cold water. Necessary at frequent intervals during raising.

ANTHEMION. From the Greek word for flower; bands of stylized palmettes and lotus motifs derived from classical architecture.

ARABESQUE. Surface decoration of scrolling and intertwining foliage, tendrils and scrolls. Thought to be of Saracenic origin, first found in northern Europe around the middle of the sixteenth·century and popular in English decorative arts during the second half of the century.

ARGYLL. Vessel resembling a small coffee pot and designed for keeping gravy warm while on the table. An inner chamber is filled with hot water which in turn keeps the surrounding gravy hot. First recorded around 1760; possibly originally made for the use of the 4th Duke of Argyll.

AURICULAR. Early seventeenth-century Dutch style characterized by curious lobe-like or cartilaginous forms; developed by Paul and Adam van Vianen of Utrecht. Found in English silver during the second quarter of the seventeenth century. Also known as the lobate style.

BALUSTER. Small vertical moulding of undulating profile and usually of circular section, commonly used for candlesticks and stems and finials of cups, etc.

BRASS. Golden coloured alloy composed of 70–90 per cent copper and 10–30 per cent zinc. Ductile, malleable and capable of taking a high polish. Produced in large

quantities in south Germany and Flanders during the fifteenth and sixteenth centuries; the industry was developed in England in the late seventeenth century.

BRITANNIA STANDARD. Silver alloy composed in the proportion of 95.84 per cent silver to 4.16 per cent of other metals, also expressed as 11 ounces 10 pennyweight of pure silver to 8 pennyweight per pound Troy. The standard enforced in English silver from 1697–1719 and optional thereafter.

BUFFET OF PLATE. The display of rows of precious vessels standard in the dining halls of princes, nobility and great ecclesiastics during the Middle Ages and the sixteenth century.

BULLET SHAPE. Spheroid form popular for teapots during the second quarter of the eighteenth century, with flush cover and tapering sides.

BURNISH. To polish metals by means of rubbing the surface with a hard, smooth object; in the eighteenth century materials such as dogs' teeth and agate were commonly used.

CANDELABRUM. A candlestick with arms and nozzles for two or more candles.

CARAT. Measure of the purity of gold. Pure gold is 24 carats; alloyed with 50 per cent of other metals it is 12 carats. Until the hallmarking act of 1798 all gold plate had to be 22 carat, although marked with the same marks as sterling silver. Legal standards of purity are now 9 ct, 14 ct, 18 ct and 22 ct.

CARTOUCHE. A decorative shield, normally engraved, embossed or cast, and generally containing an inscription or coat of arms.

CASTER. A box or container of variable form but with pierced cover, for sprinkling sugar, salt or ground pepper.

CASTING. A process for making metal objects, or their components, whereby molten metal is poured into a mould and then soldered to other parts. Stronger but more extravagant in metal than raising, it is frequently used in plate for components such as feet, stems, spouts and finials.

CAUDLE CUP. Popular two-handled vessel during the second half of the seventeenth century, alternatively known as a porringer or posset cup and supposedly used for drinking a warm spiced gruel.

CHAMBER CANDLESTICK. A small portable candlestick set on a plate-shaped base with a scroll or ring handle; often equipped with snuffers or extinguisher. Found from the late seventeenth century and throughout the eighteenth.

CHARGER. A large, shallow plate or dish on which meat was served. Some times made for purely decorative purposes and unusual after the early eighteenth century.

CHASING. The tooling or surface working of metal to create a relief pattern. Unlike engraving or carving, this involves the repositioning, rather than the removal, of metal.

CHINOISERIE. A frivolous and escapist Western style loosely inspired by Chinese art, usually applied to European forms. Especially popular in silver during the late seventeenth and mid eighteenth centuries.

COASTER. A small tray for circulating food or bottles around the dining table, especially a circular decanter stand with silver sides and turned wood base. A standard form from the third quarter of the eighteenth century.

COMMUNION CUP. The vessel which took the place of the chalice in Anglican communion services after the Reformation, generally with beaker-shaped bowl, knopped stem and circular foot.

CREST. Heraldic device surmounting a coat of arms. Originally worn on a medieval knight's helmet, it is usually displayed on a wreath. Used on silver to denote ownership and often found instead of a full coat of arms.

CRUET. Small bottles, usually with a stopper, used for oil and vinegar in domestic settings and for wine and water in the eucharist; usually of glass, with silver stopper from the eighteenth century.

CRUET FRAME. Silver stand, fitted for cruet bottles, often designed in the eighteenth century for several bottles or for two bottles and three casters.

CUT-CARD. A form of decoration probably introduced by Huguenot goldsmiths in the seventeenth century, whereby patterns cut from silver sheet are applied and soldered to the main surface of the object, thereby producing a sharply defined layered effect.

DIAPER WORK. Pattern of squares or lozenge shapes to create a trellis network of surface ornament. Especially popular during the early eighteenth century.

EGG AND DART. A repeating pattern of alternate egg shapes and arrow heads, derived from classical architecture and often stamped around the borders of late sixteenth- and early seventeenth-century silver.

ELECTROPLATE. Wares made of base metal, generally nickel, and plated with silver deposited by electrolysis; a process used commercially from the middle of the nineteenth century.

ELECTROTYPE. A process patented by Elkington and Co. about 1840 for exactly reproducing forms in electro-plate by means of moulds.

EMBOSSING. A generic term for chased or *repoussé* (q.v.) relief decoration in metal.

ENGRAVING. Surface decoration of metal made by cutting fine V-shaped grooves with a sharp tool. Most commonly used in silver for heraldic decoration.

EPERGNE. The English term, of uncertain origin, for a table centrepiece, usually of silver, composed of branches, baskets and dishes or candle branches. A popular form of plate during the second and third quarters of the eighteenth century.

FLAGON. A tall covered pouring vessel with a handle, usually of cylindrical or pear-shaped form.

FLAT-CHASING. A technique for the surface decoration of metal, resembling engraving, but produced with a hammer and punch and not involving the removal of metal.

FLATWARE. Generic term usually denoting spoons, forks and cutlery. Sometimes extended to other non- 'hollow wares', such as salvers.

FLUTING. Shallow rounded parallel grooves, used on the shafts of classical columns and frequently found on silver.

GADROONING. Convex curves or inverted fluting, often used for the decoration of borders.

HALLMARK. The official mark struck on a piece of gold or silver by an assay office or guild as a guarantee of its standard of purity.

HELMET EWER. A type of ewer reminiscent of an inverted Roman helmet, with ovoid body on low stem; particularly favoured by Huguenot goldsmiths.

HOLLOW WARE. Generic term denoting all vessel forms.

KNOP. A decorative bulbous moulding, usually placed at the mid-point of the stem of a cup.

LAMBREQUIN. A deeply scalloped stylized fringe-like ornament, common in late seventeenth-century French decorative arts and introduced to England by Daniel Marot.

LATTEN. A yellow, copper based alloy similar to brass.

MATTING. A matted texture produced by punching small dots or circles closely over the surface; commonly found contrasting with highly burnished surfaces on seventeenth-century English and German silver and silver-gilt.

MAZARINE. A flat or almost flat plate fitting into a large oval dish and pierced for the purpose of straining off excess water from fish, common in the mid and late eighteenth century and often decorated with elaborate engraving.

MONTEITH. A cooler for wine glasses, resembling a punch bowl, but with notched rim to suspend the glasses by their feet in the water. First found around 1680 and fashionable for about forty years.

MORESQUE. Linear decoration, popular during the mid sixteenth century, and composed of scrolling stylized foliage. Derived from Near Eastern art and similar to the Arabesque, but less tightly arranged.

MUFFINEER. A small, plain caster, found during the late seventeenth and early eighteenth centuries in silver and brass and often with a scroll handle to the side.

PARCEL-GILT. Silver gilded in selected areas.

PATINA. The effect produced either naturally or artificially by oxidization on the surface of the metal or, especially for bronze statuettes, by the deliberate application of a lacquer.

PENNYWEIGHT. A unit of weight for precious metals; one twentieth of a troy ounce.

PEWTER. An alloy consisting principally of tin and lead or bismuth. The Pewterer's Company required that an alloy of not less than 94 per cent tin and 6 per cent of other metals be used for the finest quality English pewter,

PLANISH. The first stage in finishing the surface of plate before polishing; the removal of hammer marks which occur during raising, by the use of a special flat-headed hammer.

PLATE. Generic term for wrought silver and gold, derived from the Spanish word *plata*, meaning silver. Not to be confused with Sheffield plate (q.v.).

PORRINGER. A small shallow circular vessel with one or two flat handles, in silver and pewter, found in pewter from the mid sixteenth century. Also a deeper vessel, often covered, with two scroll handles, occurring mainly in silver, but sometimes in base metal and pottery, from mid to late seventeenth century.

REEDING. Decorative moulding composed of narrow parallel convex threadlike forms; usually restricted to borders.

REPOUSSÉ. Relief decoration on metal produced by hammering from the reverse so that the decoration projects, then to be finished from the front by chasing.

SALVER. A tray or plate, sometimes footed, for serving food or drink; often with moulded border and decorated with an engraved coat of arms in the centre.

SCONCE. A wall-light consisting of a bracket candlestick with mirror or polished back-plate to reflect light; normally of brass in the sixteenth and early seventeenth centuries, popular in silver during the late seventeenth and early eighteenth.

SHAGREEN. (From the Turkish *saghri*.) The granulated grey-green skin of sharks and rays, used since the seventeenth century for covering small boxes or tea caddy cases.

SHEFFIELD PLATE. Wares made of copper fused between thin sheets of silver under rollers, used as a substitute for solid silver; first developed in Sheffield during the third quarter of the eighteenth century.

SILVER-GILT. Silver plated with a thin layer of gold.

SKILLET. English medieval term for a saucepan with round bowl, three feet and a long handle, found in bronze from the fifteenth century. Silver skillets survive from the mid seventeenth century.

SNUFFERS. An instrument of scissor form with a box at the end, for trimming candle wicks; a redundant form after the invention of the self-consuming wick at the end of the eighteenth century.

STANDISH. Early term for an inkstand, usually fitted with inkwell and sand box and, until the mid eighteenth century, often with a bell.

STERLING STANDARD. Silver alloy commonly used in England, composed in the proportion 92.5 per cent pure silver to 7.5 per cent of other metal (11 ounces 2 pennyweight to 18 pennyweight per pound Troy).

STRAPWORK. Form of decoration resembling cut and curling strips of leather, first used for the decoration of François I's palace at Fontainebleau and very popular in English silver and other decorative arts during the second half of the sixteenth century.

TANKARD. A mug with hinged cover, usually for beer.

VERMEIL. The French term for silver-gilt.

WARWICK CRUET FRAME. Design of cruet frame, usually consisting of three casters and four glass bottles on cinquefoil frame with central handle; popular during the second quarter of the eighteenth century.

General Index

Italics indicate illustrations

Index of Goldsmiths and Manufacturers

Index of Collections